JOHN MILTON

PARADISE LOST

Edited by Christopher Ricks

PENGUIN BOOKS

PENGUIN BOOKS

Published by the Penguin Group
Penguin Books Ltd, 27 Wrights Lane, London W8 5TZ, England
Penguin Putnam Inc., 375 Hudson Street, New York, New York 10014, USA
Penguin Books Australia Ltd, Ringwood, Victoria, Australia
Penguin Books Canada Ltd, 10 Alcorn Avenue, Toronto, Ontario, Canada M4V 3B2
Penguin Books (NZ) Ltd, Private Bag 102902, NSMC, Auckland, New Zealand

Penguin Books Ltd, Registered Offices: Harmondsworth, Middlesex, England

First published in the USA, as a Signet Classic edition,
by New American Library, New York 1968
Published simultaneously in Canada by The New American Library
of Canada Ltd, Scarborough, Ontario
First published in Great Britain in Penguin Classics 1989
10

Introduction and notes copyright © Christopher Ricks, 1968
Published by arrangement with NAL Inc., New York
All rights reserved

Printed in England by Clays Ltd, St Ives plc

Contents

PENGUIN ([penguin logo]) CLASSICS

PARADISE LOST WITHDRAWN

JOHN MILTON was born in 1608, the son of a prosper-
ous scrivener in Cheapside. He was educated at St Paul's
School and at Christ's College, Cambridge, where he
took a BA and an MA and began to write his first
serious verse. After leaving Cambridge he lived in
Hammersmith until 1635 and then spent five years on his
father's estate at Horton, Buckinghamshire, reading the
classics and preparing for a vocation as a poet. He then
travelled abroad for two years, mostly in Italy, where he
met Galileo. He hoped to visit Greece, but his journey
was cut short by the outbreak of the Episcopal War with
the Scots in 1639. This, together with the ensuing Civil
War, drastically changed Milton's career; he turned to
prose writing to defend his ideals of civil and religious
liberty and became heavily involved in the controversy
about Church government. He soon gained a reputation
as a brilliant pamphleteer, and one who continually
emphasized the need to bring the English Reformation to
glorious completion.

On his return from Italy Milton lodged near Fleet
Street and then settled in Aldersgate, London, and
became a tutor to his nephews and other young pupils. In
1642 he married Mary Powell; the union was unhappy
and prompted Milton to write a series of highly contro-
versial pamphlets on divorce. He was able to give up
teaching after his father's death in 1647 and in 1649 was
made Latin Secretary to the Council of State. He
retained this post until the Restoration, when he was
heavily fined and lost the greater part of his fortune.
During the same period his eyesight began to deteriorate
and by 1652 he was totally blind. His first wife died the

same year, leaving him three daughters and a son who died at fifteen months. In 1656 he married Katherine Woodcock, who died only two years later, and in 1663 Elizabeth Minshull, who survived him. After the loss of his eyesight he concentrated chiefly on his poetry, working on his two great epics. *Paradise Lost* is said to have been finished by 1665, but was published in 1667. *Paradise Regained* and *Samson Agonistes* appeared in 1671. Milton died of gout in 1674 and was buried like his father in St Giles's, Cripplegate.

CHRISTOPHER RICKS has held a permanent post at Boston University since 1986. He was formerly a Fellow of Worcester College, Oxford, and later a professor first at Bristol and then King Edward VII Professor of English at Cambridge University, where he was a Fellow of Christ's College. He is a Fellow of the British Academy, and of the American Academy of Arts and Sciences.

His publications include *Milton's Grand Style* (1963), *Tennyson* (1972), *Keats and Embarrassment* (1974), *The Force of Poetry* (1984), *T. S. Eliot and Prejudice* (1988), *Beckett's Dying Words* (1993) and *Essays in Appreciation* (1996). He has edited a collection of critical essays on A. E. Housman (1968), *The Poems of Tennyson* (1969, rev. 1987), *The New Oxford Book of Victorian Verse* (1987), Milton's *Paradise Lost* (Penguin Classics 1989) and *A. E. Housman: Collected Poems and Selected Prose* (Penguin Classics 1989). He was co-editor of *The State of the Language* (1980, and a new collection 1990). He is the general editor of the annotated Penguin English Poets and has also edited Volumes 2 and 3 in The Penguin History of Literature series, *English Poetry and Prose: 1540–1674* and *English Drama to 1710*.

Introduction

A controversial poet, Milton. Against Milton, there is Ezra Pound, despising "his asinine bigotry, his beastly hebraism, the coarseness of his mentality."[1] For Milton, there is Dr. Johnson:

> His great works were performed under discountenance and in blindness, but difficulties vanished at his touch; he was born for whatever is arduous; and his work is not the greatest of heroic poems, only because it is not the first.[2]

Yet Milton was a hard-hitting controversialist, and he would not have been shocked at "the Milton Controversy" of this century. But before reaching that controversy, let us trace through Milton's own words his journey toward *Paradise Lost* (1667).

At the age of nineteen, Milton took part in a vacation entertainment at his college in Cambridge. The poem which he wrote for this occasion in 1628 dedicated itself to the English language ("Hail native Language . . ."), in preference to the dead classicism which still thought it more grand to write in Latin. "At a Vacation Exercise" is, in fact, something of a manifesto, and it shows how huge were the ambitions of this young man:

> Yet I had rather if I were to choose,
> Thy service in some graver subject use,
> Such as may make thee search thy coffers round,
> Before thou clothe my fancy in fit sound:

[1] "Notes on Elizabethan Classicists" (1917) in *Literary Essays of Ezra Pound*, ed. T. S. Eliot (London: Faber & Faber, 1954), p. 238.
[2] "Milton" (1779) in *The Lives of the Poets*.

Such where the deep transported mind may soar
Above the wheeling poles, and at Heav'ns door
Look in, and see each blissful Deity
How he before the thunderous throne doth lie,
Listening to what unshorn Apollo sings
To th' touch of golden wires, while Hebe brings
Immortal Nectar to her Kingly Sire:
Then passing through the Spheres of watchful fire,
And misty Regions of wide air next under,
And hills of Snow and lofts of piled Thunder,
May tell at length how green-ey'd Neptune raves,
In Heav'ns defiance mustering all his waves;
Then sing of secret things that came to pass
When Beldam Nature in her cradle was;
And last of Kings and Queens and Heroes old,
Such as the wise Demodocus once told
In solemn Songs at King Alcinous' feast,
While sad Ulysses' soul and all the rest
Are held with his melodious harmony
In willing chains and sweet captivity.
But fie my wand'ring Muse how thou dost stray! . . .

That "fie" is mock-modest—Milton's thoughts were not
straying at all, they were right to the point. Except, of
course, for the reference to "each blissful Deity." For
Milton, there was only one Deity—and a truly great poem
would not deal in fairy tales.

In 1637 he made use of one such tale, that of the
winged horse Pegasus (he was to use it with great force
in the opening of Book VII of *Paradise Lost*), but his
reference to the Deity is heartfelt enough. He was writing
to his friend Charles Diodati, and he did not attempt to
conceal his ambitions:

Hearken, Theodotus, but let it be in your private ear,
lest I blush; and allow me for a little to use big lan-
guage with you. You ask what I am thinking of? So
may the good Deity help me, of immortality! And
what am I doing? Growing my wings and meditating
flight; but as yet our Pegasus raises himself on very
tender pinions. [Translation, Columbia edition of
Milton's *Works*]

Then in his Latin poem *Mansus* (1639), Milton mentioned his plans for an epic on King Arthur; and he returned to his projected poems again in 1640 in another Latin poem, *Epitaphium Damonis*. But it was not until 1642, in *The Reason of Church-Government,* that he developed his ripest account of his hopes and ambitions. It needs to be quoted at length, since it combines a large-scale eloquence with a specific literary program:

But much latelier in the private academies of Italy [in 1638–9], whither I was favoured to resort, perceiving that some trifles which I had in memory, composed at under twenty or thereabout (for the manner is that everyone must give some proof of his wit and reading there), met with acceptance above what was looked for, and other things which I had shifted in scarcity of books and conveniences to patch up amongst them were received with written encomiums, which the Italian is not forward to bestow on men of this side the Alps, I began thus far to assent both to them and divers of my friends here at home, and not less to an inward prompting which now grew daily upon me, that by labour and intent study (which I take to be my portion in this life) joined with the strong propensity of nature, I might perhaps leave something so written to aftertimes, as they should not willingly let it die. These thoughts at once possessed me, and these other: that if I were certain to write as men buy leases, for three lives and downward, there ought no regard be sooner had than to God's glory by the honour and instruction of my country. For which cause, and not only for that I knew it would be hard to arrive at the second rank among the Latins, I applied myself to that resolution which Ariosto followed against the persuasions of Bembo, to fix all the industry and art I could unite to the adorning of my native tongue; not to make verbal curiosities the end (that were a toilsome vanity), but to be an interpreter and relater of the best and sagest things among mine own citizens throughout this island, in the mother dialect. That what the greatest and choicest wits of Athens, Rome, or modern Italy, and those Hebrews of old, did for their country, I in my proportion with this over and above of being a Christian, might do for mine: not caring to be once named abroad, though perhaps I could attain to that, but content with these British Islands as my world, whose fortune hath hitherto been, that if the Athenians, as some say, made their small deeds great and renowned by their eloquent writers, England hath had her noble achievements made small by the unskilful handling of monks and mechanics.

Time serves not now, and perhaps I might seem too profuse to give any certain account of what the mind at home in the spacious circuits of her musing hath liberty to propose to herself, though of highest hope and hardest attempting: whether that epic form whereof the two poems of Homer and those other two of Virgil and Tasso are a diffuse, and the book of Job a brief model: or whether the rules of Aristotle herein are strictly to be kept, or nature to be followed, which in them that know art and use judgement is no transgression, but an enriching of art: and lastly what king or knight before the conquest might be chosen in whom to lay the pattern of a Christian hero. And as Tasso gave to a prince of Italy his choice whether he would command him to write of Godfrey's expedition against the infidels, or Belisarius against the Goths, or Charlemagne against the Lombards, if to the instinct of nature and the emboldening of art aught may be trusted, and that there be nothing adverse in our climate or the fate of this age, it haply would be no rashness from an equal diligence and inclination to present the like offer in our own ancient stories. Or whether those dramatic constitutions wherein Sophocles and Euripides reign shall be found more doctrinal and exemplary to a nation . . .

There, full-grown, is Milton's noble ambition, and there in embryo are the epic *Paradise Lost,* the "brief" epic *Paradise Regained,* and the "dramatic constitution" *Samson Agonistes.*

Milton's dedication to great poetry entailed a profound dedication of his own life:

> And long it was not after, when I was confirmed in
> this opinion, that he who would not be frustrate of
> his hope to write well hereafter in laudable things,
> ought himself to be a true poem, that is, a composi-
> tion and pattern of the best and honourablest things;
> not presuming to sing high praises of heroic men or
> famous cities unless he have in himself the experience
> and the practice of all that which is praiseworthy.
>
> (*An Apology for Smectymnuus*, 1642)

But the Civil War intervened. It was not until about 1655 that he put his mind firmly to the creation of *Paradise Lost;* he began writing it in 1658, and he finished his masterpiece in about 1663.

A masterpiece, but a controversial one. In our day, "the Milton Controversy" has been bitter and important. "The literati," Douglas Bush[3] has said, "have not for decades granted Milton a place in the canon of poets who minister to our needs." An overstatement, of course—Miltonists like Cleanth Brooks, William Empson, C. S. Lewis, and Northrop Frye are scarcely illiterati. But the exaggeration certainly illustrates how Milton all along has been the most argued-about poet in English.

Of the needs to which he ministers, one of the greatest is our need to commit ourselves in passionate argument about literature. Not as part of the academic industry, but because literature is a supreme controversy concerning "the best that has been thought and said in the world" (to adopt the words which Matthew Arnold applied to culture). By the energy and sincerity of his poetry, Milton stands—as no other poet quite does—in heartening and necessary opposition to all aestheticisms, old and new.

Poetry, said Dr. Johnson in his life of Milton, "is the art of uniting pleasure with truth, by calling imagination

[3] *John Milton* (New York: The Macmillan Company, 1964; London: Weidenfeld & Nicolson, 1965), p. 9.

to the help of reason." Truth must involve debate—William Empson[4] has rightly protested against the aestheticism of some Milton critics: "The idea that there actually couldn't be a moral debate in a literary work amounts to a collapse of the Western mind." But one must first try to hack a path through the objections made by those who cannot believe that taking *Paradise Lost* seriously must entail grappling with its central concerns and with Milton's God.

1. "Our concern is with the poem *as a poem*." Agreed —but the fact that a poem like *Paradise Lost* isn't *only* a moral debate doesn't mean that it isn't *at all* a moral debate. "Literature is not argument, whether moral or religious," we may say, sending such argument out of the room—nor is it history, biography, psychology, sociology. . . . But if each of these is sent out of the room, the "pure literature" which remains is a wispy ghostly thing. Literature is, among other things, the meeting of many human concerns, even though it shouldn't be *identified* with any of them.

2. "It is impossible to present God in a poem anyway, so there is not much point in discussing whether or not Milton succeeded." But there are degrees of failure. Abraham Cowley, in his poem *The Davideis* (1656), does not present God as powerfully as does Milton—and could it be that George Herbert in *The Temple* (1633) writes of God even more powerfully than Milton?

3. "The infinite God cannot be argued about by finite minds." But Milton thought that you had to do your best, otherwise you were reduced to helpless silence in the face of the many wicked and false religions in the world. His prose-treatise *De Doctrina Christiana* puts forward arguments for the justice of the Christian God.

4. "The goodness of God is a datum, a premise, a *donnée* of the poem." No—it is the *subject* of the poem.

5. "We all simply line up anyway, the Christians on one side, the non-Christians on the other." But this is not so. Christians like T. S. Eliot and Bernard Bergonzi have blamed Milton for travestying what they believe, and atheists like William Empson have applauded him.

---

[4] *Milton's God* (London: Chatto & Windus Ltd., 2nd edition, 1965), p. 262.

6. "We have no right to criticise Milton's presentation unless we could do better ourselves." Dr. Johnson answered this one.

> DEMPSTER: We have hardly a right to abuse this tragedy; for bad as it is, how vain should either of us be to write one not near so good.
>
> JOHNSON: Why no, Sir; this is not just reasoning. You *may* abuse a tragedy, though you cannot write one. You may scold a carpenter who has made you a bad table, though you cannot make a table. It is not your trade to make tables.[5]

But perhaps the clearest indication as to how we ought to engage with *Paradise Lost* is provided by Milton himself. In a magnificent passage in *The Reason of Church-Government* (1642), he praises poetic abilities—and he praises them with a Renaissance moral fervor which has none of the shriveled lifelessness which we associate with the word "didactic":

> These abilities, wheresoever they be found, are the inspired gift of God rarely bestowed, but yet to some (though most abuse) in every nation, and are of power beside the office of a pulpit to inbreed and cherish in a great people the seeds of virtue and public civility, to allay the perturbations of the mind and set the affections in right tune, to celebrate in glorious and lofty hymns the throne and equipage of God's almightiness and what He works and what He suffers to be wrought with high providence in His church, to sing the victorious agonies of martyrs and saints, the deeds and triumphs of just and pious nations doing valiantly through faith against the enemies of Christ, to deplore the general relapses of kingdoms and states from justice and God's true worship. Lastly, whatsoever in religion is holy and sublime, in virtue amiable or grave, whatsoever hath passion or admiration in all the changes of that which is called fortune from without or the wily subtleties and refluxes of man's

5 Boswell's *Life of Johnson* (ed. G. B. Hill, revised L. F. Powell; Oxford University Press, 1934–50), i. 409.

thoughts from within, all these things with a solid and treatable smoothness to paint out and describe, teaching over the whole book of sanctity and virtue through all the instances of example with such delight, to those especially of soft and delicious temper who will not so much as look upon Truth herself unless they see her elegantly dressed, that whereas the paths of honesty and good life appear now rugged and difficult, though they be indeed easy and pleasant, they would then appear to all men both easy and pleasant, though they were rugged and difficult indeed.

Milton's principles, like his practice, make him the great enemy of any pretty or petty aestheticism. Art for art's sake? Art for God's sake. Archibald MacLeish gave aestheticism a witty shape: "Poems should not mean but be." W. B. Yeats gave aestheticism a tragic tone: "Words alone are certain good." But words are not enough for Milton, though his are certainly good. His moral and intellectual commitment to literature as (among other things) argument, his anti-aestheticism, comes the more powerfully from one whose poetry lacks none of the subtlety, suppleness, and formality of patterning which aestheticism rightly relishes. So that we can push "our needs" back a stage—Milton ministers superbly to our need to comprehend how variously magnificent and strange the English language is, how finely it can communicate what we wish to say, how dextrously it can help us to discover what we wish to say. Milton's mastery of language fortifies not merely our sense of what is beautiful, but our sense of what is human.

Yet this, in some degree, must be true of all good poets. What is more immediately true of Milton is that he leaves his readers no choice but to commit themselves with their minds and hearts. To stand up and be counted—all the more important when so much poetry merely leaves us "stretched on the rack of a too easy chair." When Mr. Bush[6] says of *Lycidas,* "Milton is wrestling with Job's question: why should the just man suffer?", the word "wrestling" (which is altogether right for Milton) serves to

6 *John Milton,* p. 62.

remind us of our suspicion, on other occasions, that the wrestling is all fixed, that the antagonists are merely going through the motions. Not only in literature itself, but also in our tussle with it. Faked wrestling, shadowboxing. Lionel Trilling has wittily said about modern criticism: "Attributing to literature virtually angelic powers, it has passed the word to the readers of literature that the one thing you do not do when you meet an angel is wrestle with him."[7] But the over-polite word cannot be passed to readers of Milton—not even the most arid of Miltonists has been able to make Milton safe for pedagogocracy.

Milton engages, he even makes you give yourself away. This is why the criticism of him is so freshly infuriating. What in other contexts might be irrelevant autobiographical eruptions are the very stuff of the argument. Milton has the power to get under your skin. Listen to Ezra Pound: "Milton is the worst sort of poison. He is a thorough-going decadent in the worst sense of the term."[8] Mr. Pound does at least follow his beliefs wherever they lead him, even if they bring him to say, "If he had stopped after writing the short poems one might respect him." There are no passive readers of Milton—we are impelled by him. The impulse may be to attack him, or perhaps to attack modern man. Mr. Bush can snort that however well Milton might have presented his God, He "would still be antipathetic to an age that has changed 'sinful' to 'antisocial.' "[9] But the snort is to the point— the way we live now is something which cannot be kept out of the terms of discussion, and that is why Milton's greatness resembles that of another fiery and searching moralist: D. H. Lawrence. Moments of decision for the writer and the reader.

For Mr. Empson, Christianity is a "system of torture-worship." For Mr. Bush, it is an "all-embracing creed of liberty and discipline." It is *Paradise Lost* which can bring together, in a relevant poetic argument, two such views, and can do so without succumbing either to a rarefied

---

7 "The Two Environments" in *Beyond Culture* (London: Secker & Warburg, 1966), p. 231.
8 "The Renaissance" (1914) in *Literary Essays*, p. 216.
9 *John Milton*, p. 154.

aestheticism (beauty, not beliefs), or to a rarefied theol-
ogizing (beliefs, not beauty).

And not just the religious and moral issues, whose
formulation (whether you are a Christian or not) is im-
possible to ignore in *Paradise Lost* where they "rape the
mind and will not be unimagined." (The phrase is from
a poem by Empson.) Again like Lawrence, Milton makes
us give ourselves away on the most intimate and secretive
of matters. That is why one can even condone Professor
Jackson Cope,[10] who has said of Adam and Eve: "Their
sexuality is condoned in the bower scenes of Book IV."
Condoned!

> These lull'd by Nightingales embracing slept,
> And on their naked limbs the flow'ry roof
> Show'r'd Roses, which the Morn repair'd . . .
> (IV 771-3)

Milton, without blustering or blinking, has given us some
of the greatest and most mature erotic poetry in the lan-
guage, and the Professor grudgingly accepts it with the
word "condoned." Still, this is in a way a tribute to Milton
—it brings out how Milton searches you out and knows
you. And to return to "our needs," one of the most obvi-
ous is for an erotic poetry which will not sell short our
summer and autumn, marriage and maturity, in the inter-
ests of the spring, youthfulness, "the poor benefit of a
bewildering minute."

To claim that Milton is our greatest poet of married
love might excite the obvious retort of "How many others
are there?" Yet that scarcity must surely make Milton's
achievements not less but more valuable. We think of
Adam's words to himself when he hears of Eve's fall:

> How can I live without thee, how forgo
> Thy sweet Converse and Love so dearly join'd,
> To live again in these wild Woods forlorn? . . .
> (IX 908-10)

Or of Eve's touching plea for forgiveness:

[10] *The Metaphoric Structure of Paradise Lost* (Baltimore: The Johns
Hopkins Press, 1962), p. 82.

>   bereave me not,
> Whereon I live, thy gentle looks, thy aid,
> Thy counsel in this uttermost distress,
> My only strength and stay: forlorn of thee,
> Whither shall I betake me, where subsist?
>   (X 918–22)

The love poetry of John Donne is great and is not narrow, but nothing in it comes within light years of the particular gravity and maturity of the best of Milton's love poetry.

In the same way, Milton's determination not to permit any dichotomy between body and spirit has a meaning, an insight, and a humanity which go far beyond academic playthings like "the seventeenth-century world-picture." Body and spirit are both matter; there was sexual intercourse before the Fall; the body is not inherently degrading and was not the prime degrader: these may all seem to be battles long ago, victories that have been so assuredly won that we can now do without Milton. We cannot. The morbidly high-minded, the poor in spirit, we have always with us—and the decent sanity of Milton is still a vital force, the more vital because no one can accuse Milton of having sold out to godless materialism or carnality.

Likewise the devastating anti-heroics of *Paradise Lost*. A more telling exposé of the cruel falsities of a dictatorial heroism has never been written. As many critics have said, Satan's rally is a fascist rally.

>   He through the armed Files
> Darts his experienc't eye, and soon traverse
> The whole Battalion views; their order due,
> Their visages and stature as of Gods,
> Their number last he sums. And now his heart
> Distends with pride, and hard'ning in his strength
> Glories: . . .   (I 567–73)

But fascism will never be a thing of the past. We may for the moment have passed beyond Thomas Carlyle's dangerous credulity about "Heroes and Hero-worship." But the time will never come when it will be wise to dispense with Milton. So delicate in portraying true heroism, so rich in creating the glamour of Satanic heroism, and so lethal in judging it. The achievement is gigantic, and of all Milton's critics, only Dr. Johnson has himself had the capaciousness of mind and heart which can do justice to the size of *Paradise Lost*:

> The characteristic quality of his poem is sublimity. He sometimes descends to the elegant, but his element is the great. He can occasionally invest himself with grace; but his natural port is gigantic loftiness. He can please when pleasure is required; but it is his peculiar power to astonish.

Another of our "needs" may be approached through a fine but perilous formulation in Northrop Frye's *The Return of Eden*.[11] He distinguishes two creative temperaments: the conservative, and the radical-revolutionary. The distinction is delicately and memorably made:

> In listening to the *Kyrie* of the Bach B minor Mass we feel what amazing things the fugue can do; in listening to the finale of Beethoven's Opus 106, we feel what amazing things can be done with the fugue.

A neat and important distinction. But then to pigeonhole Milton along with the revolutionaries does him less than justice. He belongs with Shakespeare and Wordsworth precisely because his writing balances so transcendently both the conservative and the revolutionary. In one artistic lifetime, he was both historian and explorer. Of all our writers, he pays the most sincere respect to classical literature (how could he ever have written without Homer and Virgil?), and at the same time he makes it tauntingly new; the epic becomes the anti-epic.

Surely, to adapt Mr. Frye's words, in reading Milton we feel very powerfully both "what amazing things the English language can do," and "what amazing things can be done with the English language." What is at issue is something more than the height of Milton's pedestal, since the literature of our own day has tended to value the revolutionary at the expense of the conservative. The

11 University of Toronto Press, 1965, p. 91.

writer whom T. S. Eliot[12] called "outside the theatre, our greatest master of freedom within form" made no such mistake.

Yet it would be wrong to imply that Milton's genius is unassailable. In the criticism of Milton, there are still many trouble-spots which are (rightly) embattled. First, there is the style of *Paradise Lost*. Dr. Johnson thought that Milton "had formed his style by a perverse and pedantic principle." Dr. F. R. Leavis thinks that "cultivating so complete and systematic a callousness to the intrinsic nature of English, Milton forfeits all possibility of subtle or delicate life in his verse."[13] I for one have had my say in defense of Milton's style.[14] But no such issue can ever be "settled"—at every point in even a line-by-line commentary on the whole of Milton's poetry there would be legitimate objection and counter-argument.

The crucial questions are what they have always been. Is the grandeur of Milton's style oppressive and insensitive? Does he care too much for magniloquence of sound, and too little for subtlety of sense? Does he use Latinisms, and, if so, does he choose them for their pomposity or for their precision and suggestiveness? Does he lack the great talent of creating metaphors—or does his particular talent find itself in bringing back to life metaphors which had gone dead? Does he manhandle word-order, or does he keep it fluid and flexible so that it may suggest a great deal more than it explicitly states?

It would be lazy to pretend that in such arguments the truth is six of one and half-a-dozen of the other. Milton's attackers seem to me usually wrong. But there are enough instances when they are right, when his style is working only by rote, for the argument to be a real one. A central one, too, since it raises fundamental questions about the nature of poetic style and its relationship to the ordinary spoken language.

Second, there are the problems about the construction

12 "Milton II" (1947) in *On Poetry and Poets* (New York: Farrar, Straus & Giroux; London: Faber & Faber Ltd., 1957), p. 183.

13 "Milton's Verse" (1933) in *Revaluation* (London: Chatto & Windus Ltd., 1936), p. 53.

14 Christopher Ricks, *Milton's Grand Style* (New York and London: Oxford University Press, 1963).

of *Paradise Lost*. Take the sequence of events. Does the plunge into Hell make it seem that it is always Hell, and never Heaven, which makes the running? The Council in Hell (Book II) is meant to be, in a sense, a diabolical parody of the Council in Heaven (Book III)—but does it inadvertently work the other way round? Does the War in Heaven (Book VI) make sense, with its mingling of the very solid (armor and chariots) with the incorporeal angels? And if it doesn't make sense, is that somehow the point? Arnold Stein[15] has argued that the whole episode is *meant* to be ludicrously comic in order to belittle Satan and epic "heroism." Again, there is the problem of Books XI and XII; this vision of the future (which C. S. Lewis[16] called an "untransmuted lump of futurity") is clearly necessary to the scheme of the poem, but does it have poetic vitality? In 1712, Joseph Addison said of Book XII: "In some Places the Author has been so attentive to his Divinity, that he has neglected his Poetry."[17]

Third, there are the problems which cluster around Satan. Is his heroism put in its place, or does it run off with the poem? Helen Gardner has written of Milton's "creating the last great tragic figure in our literature and destroying the unity of his poem in doing so."[18] William Blake believed that "The reason Milton wrote in fetters when he wrote of Angels and God, and at liberty when of Devils and Hell, is because he was a true Poet and of the Devil's party without knowing it."[19] Again, if the poem does "place" Satan, is this done scrupulously or unscrupulously? A. J. A. Waldock[20] has argued that what is shown us is not (as it should be) the degeneration of Satan, self-rotted, but a "technique of degradation" by which Satan is often unjustly and cheaply vilified.

Fourth, there is Milton's presentation of the Fall. For the poet to succeed in his aspiration to "justify the ways

15 *Answerable Style* (Minneapolis: University of Minnesota Press, 1953).
16 *A Preface to Paradise Lost* (New York and London: Oxford University Press, 1942), p. 125.
17 *The Spectator*, No. 369, May 3, 1712.
18 "Milton's Satan and the Theme of Damnation in Elizabethan Tragedy" (1948) in *A Reading of Paradise Lost* (New York and London: Oxford University Press, 1965), p. 120.
19 "The Marriage of Heaven and Hell," 1793.
20 *"Paradise Lost" and Its Critics* (London: Cambridge University Press, 1947).

of God to men," the readers will have to condemn Adam when, in full consciousness, he falls. Yet to many people Adam's words to himself are one of the noblest moments in the poem—an expression not of "gregariousness" or "uxoriousness" (the timid words of critics), but of selfless love. So Waldock argues that

> The poem asks from us, at one and the same time, two incompatible responses. It requires us, not tentatively, not half-heartedly (for there can be no place really for half-heartedness here) but with the full weight of our minds to believe that Adam did right, and simultaneously requires us with the full weight of our minds to believe that he did wrong.[21]

Among the arguments brought against such a criticism, there is one which says that such readers as Waldock are not granting Milton's "premises" (but are there *moral* premises to be granted in advance?), and that, for Milton, God's claims are higher than Eve's. But in this essential argument about the counterclaims on Adam (his love for Eve versus "higher claims"), what needs to be shown is that these higher claims are truly embodied in the poem itself. It is all very well to claim that we must disapprove of Adam because we know that on certain occasions there are higher claims. What has to be shown is that here, in the poem itself, there is a convincing embodiment of those higher claims. Before we can weigh man's love in the scales with God's love, God's love will have to be as truly present—as it certainly is in the poetry of George Herbert.

Finally, last but not least, there are the problems of Milton's God. *Milton's God:* that is the title of Mr. Empson's remarkable book. The issues which it raises are of the greatest importance, whether or not Mr. Empson's own judgment of them is accepted. The traditional view of Milton's God has been that Milton failed, and inadvertently portrayed, not divinity, but a "school-divine":

> In Quibbles, Angel and Archangel join,
> And God the· Father turns a School-Divine.
> > (*The First Epistle of the Second Book
> > of Horace Imitated,* 1737)

21 *"Paradise Lost" and Its Critics*, p. 56.

Alexander Pope's word pinpointed the lordliness, aridity, and narrow cruelty which most readers find at times in Milton's God. Mr. Empson's query is piercingly simple: why be so sure that this was altogether inadvertent? Why is it out of the question that the poem might wish to show us these things about its God?

The reaction to this question has not been argument, but murmuring: *of course* Milton couldn't have intended any such thing. But matters of intention are not as simple as all that. There is no reason why the critic should not invoke the idea of an unconscious intention—which is after all no more than we do continually in ordinary life ("Some part of him really intended to say such a wounding thing, though he could honestly deny it"). Emily Dickinson could honestly have denied, might indeed have been appalled at, the suggestion that her poem "In winter in my room" is about a fear of sex, but her denial would not necessarily be enough to overturn such evidence as is contained within the poem itself.

"The reason why the poem is so good," says Mr. Empson, "is that it makes God so bad."[22] In other words, the critics have all been right in their description of what Milton's God feels like, but wrong in deducing that Milton had simply botched his job. From one point of view, Milton may be praised for having consciously cleared his mind of cant, for having understood that a belief in the story of the Fall implied many things about God which make the blood run cold. (It is a strange fact that you could just about date the decline of the story itself, as an essential vehicle for moral and religious truth, from Milton's great telling of it. Ever since Milton retold the story of the Fall, that story has gradually become less and less essential to the Christian faith. And ever since Milton wrote of the eternal punishments of Hell, that doctrine has become less essential to the Christian faith.[23])

Mr. Empson's praise here is for a certain bleakness or unsentimentality which doesn't gloss over the price that has to be paid for worshiping this God. On the other hand, he also claims the opposite: that the poem "is so startlingly innocent compared to the religion it claims to describe"[24]—that is, it reduces almost to insignificance the Crucifixion, and it does its best to eliminate as much as possible of the torture inherent in the system. In fact, the praise of the moral qualities of the poem, its generosity and breadth (moral qualities which in the greatest literature are inseparable from literary qualities), must face in two different directions: an honesty which presents as almost intolerably severe what other men varnish over, and a sensitivity which struggles to minimize or remove the characteristic vices of the religion. Such is Mr. Empson's view of the poem.

The magic word for making the whole argument vanish has been *"donnée"*—a word that has lately been used more and more unscrupulously or ingenuously in literary criticism. The things which are indeed "given" in a work of literature, and which the reader must accept if he is to get anything at all from the work, are not matters of meaning, conscience, and profound belief, but matters of situation, incident, and convention. Things have come to a strange pass when a critic like Chauncey B. Tinker can describe as one of the "given" conditions of *Samson Agonistes* the fact that the reader must delight in the destruction of the race of the Philistines, men and women:

> There is only one barbaric tradition left in Milton's drama, but it is a necessary one without which the plot could not move on to its conclusion. It is the will of Jehovah that the enemies of Israel should be wiped out, men, women, servants, and cattle. In their destruction the reader must feel nothing but satisfaction. This is the one concession which must be taken over from the ancient legend, like the mythical elements common in the plots of Greek tragedy. These are among the conditions "given," under which the author must work and which the reader must accept.[25]

But elements of a plot are different in kind from moral

24 *Milton's God*, p. 269.
25 *"Samson Agonistes"* in *Tragic Themes in Western Literature*, ed. Cleanth Brooks (New Haven: Yale University Press, 1955), pp. 64–65.

feelings. There are limits to what a *donnée* in great litera-
ture can be asked to encompass, and genocide is beyond
them. (Perhaps *Samson Agonistes* does indeed persuade
us that we are right to feel satisfaction—but that is differ-
ent from not even being under any obligation to persuade
us.)

Hence the inherent difficulties in postulating that *Para-
dise Lost* requires the initial *donnée* that "Everything
which God is said to have done is self-evidently good." In
any case, it is clear that Milton himself offers God's jus-
tice, not as the *donnée* of the poem, but as its subject.
His aspiration is to

> assert Eternal Providence,
> And justify the ways of God to men.
>
> (I 25–26)

If the justice of God's ways to men is smugly self-evident,
if it is out of the question for a true believer to cry out
because of the excruciating strain between his ultimate
belief in God's justice and the things which he is told of
his God, then why did the poem get written at all? Milton
himself plainly says, as the conclusion and climax of his
opening paragraph, that his hope is to "justify the ways
of God to men." What then can it mean to say that the
question of God's justice is not something that the poem
explores, but something postulated as a datum before the
poem can even start? The bland piety which invokes a
donnée simply removes from the poem its reason for
existing.

"Just are the ways of God," say the Chorus in *Samson
Agonistes*—but they do not leave it at that: "And justifi-
able to men." Dr. Johnson insisted that in *Paradise Lost*
Milton's "purpose was the most useful and the most
arduous . . . to show the reasonableness of religion."
Similarly, the *De Doctrina Christiana* is a work of heroic
energy and pertinacity in which Milton wrestles with the
problems which are at the heart of *Paradise Lost*. It asks
"What is truth?"—and stays grimly for an answer, instead
of murmuring sweetly that God moves in a mysterious
way. *Why* is it morally tolerable that God should punish
Adam's children for Adam's sin? And in that chapter

(XI), Milton uses human history and precedent to argue that God is not being—as he may seem—unjust in so doing. Which is very different from setting aside as beyond discussion the whole question of God's justice.

In *The Doctrine and Discipline of Divorce* (1643), Milton contrasts our duty as to providence ("we adore and search not") with our duty as to moral inquiry into God's "legal justice":

> Herein he appears to us as it were in human shape, enters into covenant with us, swears to keep it, binds himself like a just lawgiver to his own prescriptions, gives himself to be understood by men, judges and is judged, measures and is commensurate to right reason.

Milton is the last man to wish his profound exploration of the moral problems of God's justice to be patronizingly protected by a *donnée*.

Milton had asseverated: "I cannot praise a fugitive and cloistered virtue, unexercised and unbreathed, that never sallies out and sees her adversary, but slinks out of the race, where that immortal garland is to be run for, not without dust and heat" (*Areopagitica*, 1644). This man was, in Shelley's words, "a bold inquirer into morals and religion," and he despised those who feared inquiry. Moral inquiry, however, was for Milton no easy matter:

> Good and evil we know in the field of this world grow up together almost inseparably; and the knowledge of good is so involved and interwoven with the knowledge of evil, and in so many cunning resemblances hardly to be discerned, that those confused seeds which were imposed on Psyche as an incessant labour to cull out, and sort asunder, were not more intermixed. It was from out the rind of one apple tasted, that the knowledge of good and evil as two twins cleaving together leapt forth into the world.
> (*Areopagitica*)

Of course Milton is not the only believer to be under pressure, to face the strain. Gerard Manley Hopkins could affirm

> Thou art indeed just, Lord, if I contend
> With thee . . .

Yet Hopkins could persist too, insisting on a *but:*

>   but, sir, so what I plead is just.
> Why do sinners' ways prosper? and why must
> Disappointment all I endeavour end?

Anybody who thinks that Milton did not deeply care about Justice ought simply to look up the word in the magnificent index to the Columbia edition of his works. Milton in *The Doctrine and Discipline of Divorce* is superbly scornful of an opponent who

> would fain work himself aloof these rocks and quick-sands, and thinks it best to conclude that God certainly did dispense, but by some way to us unknown, and so to leave it. But to this I oppose, that a Christian by no means ought rest himself in such an ignorance . . .

Those are not the accents of a man afraid to argue about his God. The rocks and quicksands were for Milton the landscape of belief, and we do him no service by tidying them away.

Milton's poem is, from one aspect, a fierce argument about God's justice. And it could well be agreed (I should agree, but without thinking the evidence overwhelming) that the notorious narrative inconsistencies[26] (all of which damage God's standing unless they are explained away as mere technical blunderings) press coincidence too far, and manifest an unconscious hostility toward, and criticism of, Milton's God. The fact that the inconsistencies all pull the same way ought at least to make us uneasy about attributing them simply to technical mischance. But of course this is very different from arguing that Milton *consciously* doubted that God was just. Consciously, he wrestled with the problems; unconsciously, he may not

---

[26] The best discussions of the narrative problems and inconsistencies are in Waldock's *Paradise Lost and Its Critics*, and in John Peter's *A Critique of "Paradise Lost"* (London. Longmans, Green & Co., 1960).

have been altogether satisfied that they were explicable to the glory of God.

Consciously, Milton wrote as if man's reason, if it really made the effort, could steer between the rocks and quicksands. Unconsciously, he often writes as if the rocks and quicksands are inescapable (and then God is blamed by the poem, whatever Milton's other self might have preferred the poem to say). An early formulation by Mr. Empson is to the point:

> That his feelings were crying out against his appalling theology in favour of freedom, happiness and the pursuit of truth was I think not obvious to him. . . . The poem gets its great merit from presenting the real ambiguity of its theme with such dramatic and insinuating power.[27]

Is it out of the question that Milton could have had mixed feelings about the God whom he worshiped? Devout, he certainly was—but he was also restive under authority. In Dr. Johnson's harsh but truthful words:

> He hated monarchs in the state and prelates in the church; for he hated all whom he was required to obey. It is to be suspected that his predominant desire was to destroy rather than establish, and that he felt not so much the love of liberty as repugnance to authority.

Milton's God is not by any means the whole of *Paradise Lost,* but no reading of the poem which tries to sidestep the problems of Milton's God will be able to do justice to what Johnson called "that wonderful performance *Paradise Lost.*"

CHRISTOPHER RICKS
1968

---

[27] *The Structure of Complex Words* (London: Chatto & Windus, 1951), p. 104.

A Note on This Edition

The text of *Paradise Lost*, based on the first edition (1667), is partially modernized. Most of the changes in wording made in 1674 are incorporated, and the rest are recorded in the footnotes. The capitalization and punctuation—with a very few exceptions—have been preserved. Milton's capitalization is not likely to impede a modern reader, and it serves as a reminder that this is a seventeenth-century poem. His punctuation is a trickier matter, but the impulse to tidy it up has been resisted. Although it sometimes may be momentarily puzzling, it has great advantages. It is light and flexible, so that the verse keeps momentum even while it holds open many possibilities as to suggestive relationships among the words and phrases—relationships which a more rigorous punctuation would have sealed up and prevented.

Milton's spelling has been partially modernized. The gain in convenience of reading far outweighs any loss. But the more important of Milton's spellings (*Ammiral, sovran*, etc.) have been retained, together with his emphatic forms *mee, hee, shee*, and his various forms for the past participle (such as *abasht, seduc'd*). An editor is bound to have twinges of regret about any such changes, especially as Milton's spelling may sometimes indicate his pronunciation; but his use of language does already present problems to a modern reader, and the awkwardly unfamiliar spelling must on occasion have proved to be the last straw. Moreover, a partially modernized text is of most help metrically and rhythmically—a good text of Milton will make his words sound in your head or out loud.

The notes have concentrated especially on Milton's words and phrases. It is true that he is a profoundly allusive poet—the Bible and classical literature are continually called upon, and since Milton is a great poet the more we know of his allusions the richer and subtler his writing is seen to be. But it is also characteristic of him to build his allusions in, so that they become self-explanatory:

> hee who to be deem'd
> A God, leap'd fondly into Etna flames,
> Empedocles, and hee . . .   (III 469–71)

Which means that the first priority ought to be, not his allusions, but his words—those which no longer survive, those which have lost part of their seventeenth-century meaning, and those which survive but with a different meaning. The footnotes provide instances (instances only, since the language of *Paradise Lost* is unceasingly active) of his verbal nuances and puns. Nuances and puns are, of course, matters of critical opinion, not of fact—even though there is evidence within the *Oxford English Dictionary* to substantiate such puns.

PARADISE LOST

THE VERSE

The Measure is English Heroic Verse without Rhyme, as that of Homer in Greek, and of Virgil in Latin; Rhyme being no necessary Adjunct or true Ornament of Poem or good Verse, in longer Works especially, but the Invention of a barbarous Age, to set off wretched matter and lame Meter; grac't indeed since by the use of some famous modern Poets, carried away by Custom, but much to their own vexation, hindrance, and constraint to express many things otherwise, and for the most part worse than else they would have exprest them. Not without cause therefore some both Italian and Spanish Poets of prime note have rejected Rhyme both in longer and shorter Works, as have also long since our best English Tragedies, as a thing of itself, to all judicious ears, trivial and of no true musical delight; which consists only in apt Numbers, fit quantity of Syllables, and the sense variously drawn out from one Verse into another, not in the jingling sound of like endings, a fault avoided by the learned Ancients both in Poetry and all good Oratory. This neglect then of Rhyme so little is to be taken for a defect, though it may seem so perhaps to vulgar Readers, that it rather is to be esteem'd an example set, the first in English, of ancient liberty recover'd to Heroic Poem from the troublesome and modern bondage of Rhyming.   [added 1668]

BOOK I

THE ARGUMENT

This first Book proposes first in brief the whole Subject, Man's disobedience, and the loss thereupon of Paradise wherein he was plac't: Then touches the prime cause of his fall, the Serpent, or rather Satan in the Serpent; who revolting from God, and drawing to his side many Legions of Angels, was by the command of God driven out of Heaven with all his Crew into the great Deep. Which action past over, the Poem hastes into the midst of things, presenting Satan with his Angels now fallen into Hell, describ'd here, not in the Center (for Heaven and Earth may be suppos'd as yet not made, certainly not yet accurst) but in a place of utter darkness, fitliest call'd Chaos: Here Satan with his Angels lying on the burning Lake, thunder-struck and astonisht, after a certain space recovers, as from confusion, calls up him who next in Order and Dignity lay by him; they confer of their miserable fall. Satan awakens all his Legions, who lay till then in the same manner confounded; They rise, their Numbers, array of Battle, their chief Leaders nam'd, according to the Idols known afterwards in Canaan and the Countries adjoining. To these Satan directs his Speech, comforts them with hope yet of regaining Heaven, but tells them lastly of a new World and new kind of Creature to be created, according to an ancient Prophecy or report in Heaven; for that Angels were long before this visible Creation, was the opinion of many ancient Fathers. To find out the truth of this Prophecy, and what to determine thereon he refers to a full Council. What his Associates thence attempt. Pandemonium the Palace of Satan rises, suddenly built out of the Deep: The infernal Peers there sit in Council.   [added 1668]

      Of Man's First disobedience, and the Fruit°
Of that Forbidden Tree, whose mortal° taste
Brought Death into the World, and all our woe,
With loss of Eden, till one greater Man
Restore us, and regain the blissful Seat,   *5*
Sing Heav'nly Muse, that on the secret top
Of Oreb, or of Sinai, didst inspire
That Shepherd, who first taught the chosen Seed,°
In the Beginning how the Heav'ns and Earth
Rose out of Chaos: Or if Sion Hill   *10*
Delight thee more, and Siloa's Brook that flow'd
Fast by the Oracle of God;° I thence
Invoke thy aid to my advent'rous Song,
That with no middle flight intends to soar
Above th'Aonian Mount,° while it pursues   *15*
Things unattempted yet in Prose or Rhyme.
And chiefly Thou O Spirit, that dost prefer
Before all Temples th'upright heart and pure,
Instruct° me, for Thou know'st; Thou from the first
Wast present, and with mighty wings outspread   *20*
Dove-like sat'st brooding on the vast Abyss
And mad'st it pregnant: What in me is dark
Illumine, what is low raise and support;
That to the heighth of this great Argument°
I may assert° Eternal Providence,   *25*
And justify° the ways of God to men.
      Say first, for Heav'n hides nothing from thy
      view
Nor the deep Tract of Hell, say first what cause
Mov'd our Grand° Parents in that happy State,
Favour'd of Heav'n so highly, to fall off   *30*

---

1 **Fruit** including consequences, fruits.   2 **mortal** human and deadly.
7–8 **Of . . . Seed** Moses, who set down GENESIS, was visited by God
on Mount Horeb and Sinai.   11–12 **Siloa's . . . God** near the Temple
in Jerusalem; the brook is to parallel the one haunted by the classical
Muses.   15 **Mount** Helicon, sacred to the Muses.   19 **Instruct** Latin
instruere, to build, perfectly linking "Temples" and "heart."   24
Argument subject-matter and process of reasoning.   25 **assert** affirm.
26 **justify** bear witness to the justice of; both "justify to men" and
"ways of God to men."   29 **Grand** original and pre-eminent.

From their Creator, and transgress his Will
For° one restraint, Lords of the World besides?
Who first seduc'd them to that foul revolt?
Th'infernal Serpent; he it was, whose guile
35 Stirr'd up with Envy and Revenge, deceiv'd
The Mother of Mankind, what time his Pride
Had cast him out from Heav'n, with all his Host
Of Rebel Angels, by whose aid aspiring
To set himself in Glory above his Peers,
40 He trusted to have equall'd the most High,
If he oppos'd; and with ambitious aim
Against° the Throne and Monarchy of God
Rais'd impious War in Heav'n and Battle proud
With vain attempt. Him the Almighty Power
45 Hurl'd headlong flaming from th'Ethereal Sky
With hideous ruin° and combustion down
To bottomless perdition, there to dwell
In Adamantine° Chains and penal Fire,
Who durst defy th'Omnipotent to Arms.
50 Nine times the Space that measures Day and Night
To mortal men, he with his horrid crew
Lay vanquisht, rolling in the fiery Gulf
Confounded° though immortal: But his doom
Reserv'd him to more wrath; for now the thought
55 Both of lost happiness and lasting pain
Torments him; round he throws his baleful° eyes
That witness'd° huge affliction and dismay
Mixt with obdúrate pride and steadfast hate:
At once as far as Angel's ken° he views
60 The dismal Situation° waste and wild,
A Dungeon° horrible, on all sides round
As one great Furnace flam'd, yet from those flames
No light, but rather darkness visible
Serv'd only to discover sights of woe,
65 Regions of sorrow, doleful shades, where peace

32 **For** both "transgress because of one restraint," and "Lords. . . .
except for one restraint." 42 **Against** both "aim against" and "war
against." 46 **ruin** falling, Latin *ruina*. 48 **Adamantine** of the
hardest rocks or minerals. 53 **Confounded** overthrown. 56 **baleful** full both of woe and of evil. 57 **witness'd** showed his. 59 **Angel's ken** Milton's spelling "Angels kenn" leaves "kenn" as possibly
noun or verb. 60 **Situation** site and predicament. 61 **Dungeon**
from *domnionem*, "lord's tower," from Latin *dominus*, lord. See X
466.

And rest can never dwell, hope never comes
That comes to all; but torture without end
Still urges, and a fiery Deluge, fed
With ever-burning Sulphur unconsum'd:
Such place Eternal Justice had prepar'd   70
For those rebellious, here their Prison ordain'd
In utter° darkness, and their portion set
As far remov'd from God and light of Heav'n
As from the Center° thrice to th'utmost Pole.°
O how unlike the place from whence they fell!   75
There the companions of his fall, o'erwhelm'd
With Floods and Whirlwinds of tempestuous fire,
He soon discerns, and welt'ring by his side
One next himself in power, and next in crime,
Long after known in Palestine, and nam'd   80
Beëlzebub. To whom th'Arch-Enemy,°
And thence in Heav'n call'd Satan, with bold words
Breaking the horrid silence thus began.
          "If thou beest he; but O how fall'n! how
              chang'd
From him, who in the happy Realms of Light   85
Cloth'd with transcendent brightness didst outshine
Myriads though bright: If he whom mutual league,
United thoughts and counsels, equal hope,
And hazard in the Glorious Enterprise,
Join'd with me once, now misery hath join'd   90
In equal ruin: into what Pit thou seest
From what heighth fall'n, so much the stronger prov'd
He with his Thunder: and till then who knew
The force of those dire Arms? yet not for those
Nor what the Potent Victor in his rage   95
Can else inflict do I repent or change,
Though chang'd in outward lustre, that fixt mind
And high disdain, from sense of injur'd merit,
That with the mightiest rais'd me to contend,
And to the fierce contention brought along   100
Innumerable force of Spirits arm'd
That durst dislike his reign, and me preferring,
His utmost power with adverse° power oppos'd

72 **utter** outer and total.   74 **the Center** the earth.   74 **utmost Pole**
outermost point of the universe.   81 **Arch-Enemy** Hebrew ṣāṭān,
adversary.   103 **adverse** hostile, as in "adversary."

In dubious° Battle on the Plains of Heav'n,
105 And shook his throne. What though the field be lost?
All is not lost; the unconquerable Will,
And study of° revenge, immortal hate,
And courage never to submit or yield:
And what is else not to be overcome?°
110 That Glory never shall his wrath or might
Extort from me. To bow and sue for grace
With suppliant knee, and deify his power
Who from the terror of this Arm so late
Doubted° his Empire, that were low indeed,
115 That were an ignominy and shame beneath
This downfall; since by Fate the strength of Gods°
And this Empyreal substance° cannot fail,
Since through experience of this great event
In Arms not worse, in foresight much advanc't,
120 We may with more successful hope° resolve
To wage by force or guile eternal War
Irreconcilable, to our grand Foe,
Who now triúmphs, and in th'excess of joy
Sole reigning holds the Tyranny of Heav'n."
125   So spake th'Apostate Angel, though in pain,
Vaunting aloud, but rackt with deep despair:
And him thus answer'd soon his bold Compeer.
   "O Prince, O Chief of many Throned Powers,
That led th'imbattled Seraphim° to War
130 Under thy conduct, and in dreadful deeds
Fearless, endanger'd Heav'n's perpetual King;
And put to proof his high Supremacy,
Whether upheld by strength, or Chance, or Fate,
Too well I see and rue the dire event,
135 That with sad overthrow and foul defeat
Hath lost us Heav'n, and all this mighty Host
In horrible destruction laid thus low,
As far as Gods and Heav'nly Essences
Can Perish: for the mind and spirit remains

104 **dubious** of which the outcome was doubtful. 107 **study of** zeal for. 109 **And ... overcome** "In what else does 'not being overcome' consist?" 114 **Doubted** feared for. 116 **Gods** Both Satan and God apply the word to angels. 117 **Empyreal substance** fiery and heavenly essence (see line 138). 120 **successful hope** hope of success. 128–29 **Powers ... Seraphim** two of the nine orders of angels, the others being Cherubim, Thrones, Dominations, Virtues, Principalities, Archangels, Angels.

Invincible, and vigour soon returns,   *140*
Though all our Glory extinct,° and happy state
Here swallow'd up in endless misery.
But what if he our Conqueror, (whom I now
Of force° believe Almighty, since no less
Than such could have o'erpow'r'd such force as ours) *145*
Have left us this our spirit and strength entire
Strongly to suffer and support our pains,
That we may so suffice his vengeful ire,
Or do him mightier service as his thralls
By right of War, whate'er his business be,   *150*
Here in the heart of Hell to work in Fire,
Or do his Errands in the gloomy Deep;
What can it then avail though yet we feel
Strength undiminisht, or eternal being
To undergo eternal punishment?"   *155*
Whereto with speedy words th'Arch-fiend repli'd.
       "Fall'n Cherub, to be weak is miserable
Doing or Suffering: but of this be sure,
To do aught good never will be our task,
But ever to do ill our sole delight,   *160*
As being the contrary to his high will
Whom we resist. If then his Providence
Out of our evil seek to bring forth good,
Our labour must be to pervert that end,
And out of good still to find means of evil;   *165*
Which oft-times may succeed, so as perhaps
Shall grieve him, if I fail not, and disturb
His inmost counsels from their destin'd° aim.
But see the angry Victor hath recall'd
His Ministers of vengeance and pursuit   *170*
Back to the Gates of Heav'n: The Sulphurous Hail
Shot after us in storm, o'erblown hath laid
The fiery Surge, that from the Precipice
Of Heav'n receiv'd us falling, and the Thunder,
Wing'd with red Lightning and impetuous rage,   *175*
Perhaps hath spent his shafts, and ceases now
To bellow through the vast and boundless Deep.

---

141 **extinct** extinguished, "Glory" being both splendor and halo.
144 **Of force** both "necessarily" and "because of this force."   168
destin'd intended (but the sense of "destiny" undercuts Satan's
words).

Let us not slip° th'occasion, whether scorn,
Or satiate fury yield it from our Foe.
180 Seest thou yon dreary Plain, forlorn and wild,
The seat of desolation, void of light,
Save what the glimmering of these livid flames
Casts pale and dreadful? Thither let us tend
From off the tossing of these fiery waves,
185 There rest, if any rest can harbour there,
And reassembling our afflicted° Powers,°
Consult how we may henceforth most offend°
Our Enemy, our own loss how repair,
How overcome this dire Calamity,
190 What reinforcement we may gain from Hope,
If not what resolution from despair."
       Thus Satan talking to his nearest Mate
With Head uplift above the wave, and Eyes
That sparkling blaz'd, his other Parts besides
195 Prone on the Flood, extended long and large
Lay floating many a rood,° in bulk as huge
As whom the Fables name of monstrous size,
Titanian, or Earth-born, that warr'd on Jove,
Briareos or Typhon,° whom the Den
200 By ancient Tarsus held, or that Sea-beast
Leviathan,° which God of all his works
Created hugest that swim th'Oceän stream:
Him haply° slumb'ring on the Norway° foam
The Pilot of some small night-founder'd° Skiff,
205 Deeming some Island, oft, as Sea-men tell,
With fixed Anchor in his scaly rind
Moors by his side under the Lee, while Night
Invests° the Sea, and wished Morn delays:
So stretcht out huge in length the Arch-fiend lay
210 Chain'd on the burning Lake, nor ever thence

178 **slip** let slip.   186 **afflicted** struck down.   186 **Powers** armies,
with a suggestion of "faculties."   187 **offend** take the offensive
against.   196 **rood** a land-measure, 40 square poles.   198–99 Classi-
cal counterparts to Satan's rebellion, **Briareos** among the Titans,
Typhon among the "Earth-born" Giants.   201 **Leviathan** Biblical
sea-monster, here the whale. The tales of its being mistaken for an
island were used in the bestiaries as a type of Satan's deception of
man.   203 **haply** perchance.   203 **Norway** Satan traditionally asso-
ciated with the north (I 293, V 689).   204 **night-founder'd** sunk in
night, *not yet* literally sunk; see the ominous line 208.   208 **Invests**
enwraps.

Had ris'n or heav'd his head, but that the will
And high permission of all-ruling Heaven
Left him at large to his own dark designs,
That with reiterated crimes he might
Heap on himself damnation, while he sought   215
Evil to others, and enrag'd might see
How all his malice serv'd but to bring forth
Infinite goodness, grace and mercy shown
On Man by him seduc't, but on himself
Treble confusion, wrath and vengeance pour'd.   220
Forthwith upright he rears from off the Pool
His mighty Stature; on each hand the flames
Driv'n backward slope their pointing spires, and roll'd
In billows, leave i' th'midst a horrid Vale.°
Then with expanded wings he steers his flight   225
Aloft, incumbent on° the dusky Air
That felt unusual weight, till on dry Land
He 'lights, if it were Land that ever burn'd
With solid, as the Lake with liquid fire;
And such appear'd in hue, as when the force   230
Of subterranean wind transports a Hill
Torn from Pelorus,° or the shatter'd side
Of thund'ring Etna, whose combustible
And fuell'd entrails thence conceiving Fire,
Sublim'd with Mineral fury, aid the Winds,   235
And leave a singed bottom all involv'd°
With stench° and smoke: Such resting found the sole
Of unblest feet. Him follow'd his next Mate,
Both glorying to have 'scap't the Stygian° flood
As Gods, and by their own recover'd strength,   240
Not by the sufferance of supernal° Power.
        "Is this the Region, this the Soil, the Clime,"°
Said then the lost Arch Angel, "this the seat
That we must change for Heav'n, this mournful gloom

222–24 Douglas Bush points out that this suggests the Israelites'
miraculous passage through the Red Sea (I 306–10); Satan's doings
in the poem are often a grim parody of God's.   226 **incumbent on**
weighing upon (contrast I 20–21).   232 **Pelorus** near Etna.   236 **in-
volv'd** rolled around.   234–37 **entrails . . . stench** the volcanic land-
scape of Hell, seen as a disgusting body; so "Sublim'd" here has a
sardonic tone (*not* sublime in any other sense). See III 494.   239
Stygian Styx, river of Hell; here the lake.   241 **supernal** in the
heavens above.   242 **Clime** zone and temperature.

245 For that celestial light? Be it so, since hee
    Who now is Sovran° can dispose and bid
    What shall be right: farthest from him is best
    Whom reason hath equall'd, force hath made supreme
    Above his equals. Farewell happy Fields
250 Where Joy for ever dwells: Hail horrors, hail
    Infernal world, and thou profoundest Hell
    Receive thy new Possessor: One who brings
    A mind not to be chang'd by Place or Time.
    The mind is its own place, and in itself
255 Can make a Heav'n of Hell, a Hell of Heav'n.
    What matter where, if I be still the same,
    And what I should be, all but less than hee
    Whom Thunder hath made greater? Here at least
    We shall be free; th'Almighty hath not built
260 Here for his envy, will not drive us hence:
    Here we may reign secure, and in my choice
    To reign is worth ambition though in Hell:
    Better to reign in Hell, than serve in Heav'n.
    But wherefore let we then our faithful friends,
265 Th'associates and co-partners of our loss
    Lie thus astonisht° on th'oblivious° Pool,
    And call them not to share with us their part
    In this unhappy Mansion, or once more
    With rallied Arms to try what may be yet
270 Regain'd in Heav'n, or what more lost in Hell?"
         So Satan spake, and him Beëlzebub
    Thus answer'd. "Leader of those Armies bright,
    Which but th'Omnipotent none could have foil'd,
    If once they hear that voice, their liveliest pledge
275 Of hope in fears and dangers, heard so oft
    In worst extremes, and on the perilous edge°
    Of battle when it rag'd, in all assaults
    Their surest signal, they will soon resume
    New courage and revive, though now they lie
280 Grovelling and prostrate on yon Lake of Fire,
    As we erewhile, astounded and amaz'd,°
    No wonder, fall'n such a pernicious° heighth."

246 **Sovran** Milton's spelling follows the Italian *sovrano*.   266 **aston-isht** literally thunderstruck, connected with Latin *extonare*, as is "astounded," line 281.   266 **oblivious** causing oblivion, like the river Lethe.   276 **edge** front-line.   281 **amaz'd** overwhelmed.   282 **pernicious** destructive.

He scarce had ceas't when the superior Fiend
Was moving toward the shore; his ponderous shield°
Ethereal temper,° massy, large and round   285
Behind him cast; the broad circumference
Hung on his shoulders like the Moon, whose Orb
Through Optic Glass the Tuscan Artist views
At Ev'ning from the top of Fesole,
Or in Valdarno, to descry new Lands,°   290
Rivers or Mountains in her spotty Globe.
His Spear, to equal which the tallest Pine
Hewn on Norwegian hills, to be the Mast
Of some great Ammiral,° were but a wand,
He walkt with to support uneasy steps   295
Over the burning Marl,° not like those steps
On Heaven's Azure, and the torrid Clime
Smote on him sore besides, vaulted with Fire;
Nathless he so endur'd, till on the Beach
Of that inflamed Sea, he stood and call'd   300
His Legions, Angel Forms, who lay intranc't
Thick as Autumnal Leaves that strow the Brooks
In Vallombrosa,° where th'Etrurian shades
High overarch't embow'r;° or scatter'd sedge°
Afloat, when with fierce Winds Orion arm'd°   305
Hath vext the Red-Sea Coast, whose waves o'erthrew
Busiris and his Memphian Chivalry,°
While with perfidious hatred they pursu'd
The Sojourners of Goshen, who beheld
From the safe shore their floating Carcasses   310

284 **shield** Contrast the shield of Achilles; Satan is Milton's "hero,"
but such heroism is suspect. 285 **Ethereal temper** tempered in
Heaven. 288–90 **Through . . . Lands** The telescope of the skilled
Galileo, who lived at Fiesole above the river Arno; Milton visited
him in 1638–39. 294 **Ammiral** admiral's flagship; Milton uses
the spelling which gives the true etymology, from *emir* (associating
Satan, as elsewhere, with eastern tyrants), not from *admire*. 296
Marl soil. 303 **Vallombrosa** near Florence, "shady valley"—as in
some ways is Hell itself (the whole of the simile reverberates with
correspondences). 304 **embow'r** form a bower, the pastoral word
contrasting with the horrors of Hell. 304 **sedge** the Red Sea is "sea
of sedge" in Hebrew. 305 **Orion arm'd** The constellation Orion
(some of whose stars represent his weapons) ushers in the storms
which "vex" (buffet) the sea. 307 **Busiris . . . Chivalry** Milton takes
Busiris as the "perfidious" Pharaoh who hunted down the Israelites,
"the Sojourners of Goshen" in Egypt, with his Egyptian cavalry.
"Chivalry" is etymologically identical with "cavalry"; Milton chooses
it as part of his questioning of chivalric values; see IX 28–41.

And broken Chariot Wheels, so thick bestrown
Abject° and lost lay these, covering the Flood,
Under amazement of their hideous change.
He call'd so loud, that all the hollow Deep
315 Of Hell resounded. "Princes, Potentates,
Warriors, the Flow'r of Heav'n, once yours, now lost,
If such astonishment as this can seize
Eternal spirits; or have ye chos'n this place
After the toil of Battle to repose
320 Your wearied virtue, for the ease you find
To slumber here, as in the Vales of Heav'n?
Or in this abject posture have ye sworn
To adore the Conqueror? who now beholds
Cherub and Seraph rolling in the Flood
325 With scatter'd Arms and Ensigns, till anon
His swift pursuers from Heav'n Gates discern
Th'advantage, and descending tread us down
Thus drooping, or with linked Thunderbolts
Transfix us to the bottom of this Gulf.
330 Awake, arise, or be for ever fall'n."
                    They heard, and were abasht, and up they
                          sprung
Upon the wing, as when men wont to watch
On duty, sleeping found by whom they dread,
Rouse and bestir themselves ere well awake.
335 Nor did they not perceive the evil plight
In which they were, or the fierce pains not feel;
Yet to their General's Voice they soon obey'd
Innumerable. As when the potent Rod
Of Amram's Son in Egypt's evil day
340 Wav'd round the Coast, upcall'd a pitchy cloud°
Of Locusts, warping° on the Eastern Wind,
That o'er the Realm of impious Pharaoh hung
Like Night, and darken'd all the land of Nile:
So numberless were those bad Angels seen
345 Hovering on wing under the Cope of Hell
'Twixt upper, nether, and surrounding Fires;
Till, as a signal giv'n, th'uplifted Spear
Of their great Sultan waving to direct

312 **Abject** cast down, literal and metaphorical. 338–40 **As . . .
cloud** Contrasting Moses' rod (working God's will) with Satan's
spear. 341 **warping** twisting, writhing themselves forward.

Their course, in even balance down they 'light
On the firm brimstone, and fill all the Plain;   350
A multitude, like which the populous North
Pour'd never from her frozen loins,° to pass
Rhene or the Danaw,° when her barbarous Sons
Came like a Deluge on the South, and spread
Beneath Gibraltar to the Libyan sands.   355
Forthwith from every Squadron and each Band
The Heads and Leaders thither haste where stood
Their great Commander; Godlike shapes and forms
Excelling human, Princely Dignities,
And Powers that erst in Heaven sat on Thrones;   360
Though of their Names in heav'nly Records now
Be no memorial, blotted out and raz'd
By their Rebellion, from the Books of Life.
Nor had they yet among the sons of Eve
Got them new Names, till wand'ring o'er the Earth,   365
Through God's high sufferance for the trial of man,
By falsities and lies the greatest part
Of Mankind they corrupted to forsake
God their Creator, and th'invisible
Glory of him, that made them, to transform   370
Oft to the Image of a Brute, adorn'd
With gay Religions full of Pomp and Gold,
And Devils to adore for Deities:
Then were they known to men by various Names,
And various Idols through the Heathen World.   375
Say, Muse, their Names then known, who first, who
    last,
Rous'd from the slumber, on that fiery Couch,
At their great Emperor's call, as next in worth
Came singly where he stood on the bare strand,
While the promiscuous° crowd stood yet aloof?   380
The chief were those who from the Pit of Hell
Roaming to seek their prey on earth, durst fix
Their Seats long after next the Seat of God,
Their Altars by his Altar, Gods ador'd
Among the Nations round, and durst abide   385

351–52 A multitude . . . loins The invasions of the Goths, Huns and
Vandals, pouring forth—by an evil paradox—from "frozen loins"
(contrasted with "brimstone," burn-stone). 353 Rhene, Danaw
Rhine, Danube. 380 promiscuous mixed.

Jehovah thund'ring out of Sion, thron'd
Between the Cherubim; yea, often plac'd
Within his Sanctuary itself their Shrines,
Abominations; and with cursed things°
390 His holy Rites, and solemn Feasts profan'd,
And with their darkness durst affront° his light.
First Moloch, horrid King besmear'd with blood
Of human sacrifice, and parents' tears,
Though for the noise of Drums and Timbrels loud
395 Their children's cries unheard, that past through fire
To his grim Idol. Him the Ammonite
Worshipt in Rabba and her wat'ry Plain,
In Argob and in Basan, to the stream
Of utmost Arnon.° Nor content with such
400 Audacious neighbourhood,° the wisest heart
Of Solomon he led by fraud to build
His Temple right against the Temple of God
On that opprobrious Hill,° and made his Grove
The pleasant Valley of Hinnom, Tophet thence
405 And black Gehenna call'd, the Type of Hell.°
Next Chemos,° th'óbscene° dread of Moab's Sons,
From Aroer to Nebo, and the wild
Of Southmost Abarim; in Hesebon
And Horonaim, Seon's° Realm, beyond
410 The flow'ry Dale of Sibma clad with Vines,
And Elealé to th'Asphaltic Pool.°
Peor his other Name, when he entic'd
Israel in Sittim on their march from Nile
To do him wanton rites, which cost them woe.°
415 Yet thence his lustful Orgies he enlarg'd
Even to that Hill of scandal,° by the Grove
Of Moloch homicide, lust hard by hate;
Till good Josiah drove them thence to Hell.

384–89 **things** Altars to heathen gods inside the Temple itself, where
were the golden Cherubim.   391 **affront** confront and insult.   397–
99 East of Jordan.   400 **Audacious neighbourhood** daring to live so
near.   400–03 Solomon, seduced by his wives, built temples to
Moloch and others on the (shameful) Mount of Olives (I 416, 443).
404–05 The valley of Hinnom provided two of the names for Hell:
Tophet and Gehenna.   406 **Chemos** heathen deity.   406 **obscene**
abominable, originally a term of augury (ill-omened), so here appli-
cable to an idol.   409 **Seon** King Sihon.   411 **Asphaltic Pool** the
Dead Sea, suggesting the landscape of Hell.   414 **woe** the plague
spoken of in NUMBERS 25:1–9.   416 **scandal** Biblical term, cause
of offense, stumbling-block.

With these came they, who from the bord'ring flood
Of old Euphrates to the Brook that parts   *420*
Egypt from Syrian ground,° had general Names
Of Baälim and Ashtaroth,° those male,
These Feminine. For Spirit when they please
Can either Sex assume, or both; so soft
And uncompounded is their Essence pure,   *425*
Not ti'd or manacl'd with joint or limb,
Nor founded on the brittle strength of bones,
Like cumbrous flesh; but in what shape they choose
Dilated or condens't, bright or obscure,
Can execute their airy purposes,   *430*
And works of love or enmity fulfill.
For those the Race of Israel oft forsook
Their living strength, and unfrequented left
His righteous Altar, bowing lowly down
To bestial° Gods; for which their heads as low   *435*
Bow'd down in Battle, sunk before the Spear
Of despicable foes. With these in troop
Came Astoreth, whom the Phoenicians call'd
Astarte, Queen of Heav'n, with crescent Horns;
To whose bright Image nightly by the Moon   *440*
Sidonian° Virgins paid their Vows and Songs,
In Sion also not unsung, where stood
Her Temple on th'offensive Mountain, built
By that uxorious King,° whose heart though large,
Beguil'd by fair Idolatresses, fell   *445*
To Idols foul. Thammuz came next behind,
Whose annual wound in Lebanon allur'd
The Syrian Damsels to lament his fate
In amorous ditties all a Summer's day,
While smooth Adonis from his native Rock   *450*
Ran purple to the Sea, suppos'd with blood
Of Thammuz yearly wounded:° the Love-tale
Infected Sion's daughters with like heat,
Whose wanton passions in the sacred Porch

420–21 Besor, the boundary between Palestine and Egypt.   422 (Ba-
älim), Ashtaroth plural of the gods prefixed by Baal-, and of the
forms of the goddess Ashtoreth. 435 bestial (literal and moral).
441 Sidonian Sidon in Phoenicia. 444 uxorious King Solomon,
excessively devoted to his wives. 446–52 Milton's "Nativity Ode"
line 204: "In vain the Tyrian maids their wounded Thammuz mourn."
Thammuz is a counterpart of Adonis in his death and revival; the
river Adonis ran red at times.

455 Ezekiel saw, when by the Vision led
His eye survey'd the dark Idolatries
Of alienated Judah. Next came one
Who mourn'd in earnest, when the Captive Ark
Maim'd his brute Image, head and hands lopt off
460 In his own Temple, on the grunsel°-edge,
Where he fell flat, and sham'd his Worshippers:
Dagon his Name, Sea Monster, upward Man
And downward Fish: yet had his Temple high
Rear'd in Azotus, dreaded through the Coast
465 Of Palestine, in Gath and Ascalon,
And Accaron and Gaza's frontier bounds.
Him follow'd Rimmon,° whose delightful Seat
Was fair Damascus, on the fertile Banks
Of Abbana and Pharphar, lucid streams.
470 He also against the house of God was bold:
A Leper once he lost and gain'd a King,°
Ahaz his sottish Conqueror, whom he drew
God's Altar to disparage and displace
For one of Syrian mode, whereon to burn
475 His odious off'rings, and adore the Gods
Whom he had vanquisht. After these appear'd
A crew who under Names of old Renown,
Osiris, Isis, Orus and their Train
With monstrous shapes and sorceries abus'd°
480 Fanatic° Egypt and her Priests, to seek
Their wand'ring Gods disguis'd in brutish forms
Rather than human. Nor did Israel 'scape
Th'infection when their borrow'd Gold compos'd
The Calf in Oreb: and the Rebel King
485 Doubled that sin in Bethel and in Dan,°
Lik'ning his Maker to the Grazed Ox,
Jehovah, who in one Night when he pass'd
From Egypt marching, equall'd with one stroke
Both her first-born and all her bleating Gods.°
490 Belial came last, than whom a Spirit more lewd
Fell not from Heaven, or more gross to love

460 **grunsel** threshold.   467 **Rimmon** Syrian god.   471 The Syrian, Naaman, came to God after being cured of leprosy; but King Ahaz of Judah adopted the Syrian religion.   479 **abus'd** deceived.   480 **Fanatic** inspired with demonic frenzy, from Latin *fanum*, fane or temple.   484–85 The golden calf made by Aaron; Jeroboam made two calves of gold.   489 The 10th plague of Egypt.

Vice for itself: To him no Temple stood
Or Altar smok'd; yet who more oft than hee
In Temples and at Altars, when the Priest
Turns Atheist, as did Eli's Sons, who fill'd 495
With lust and violence the house of God.
In Courts and Palaces he also Reigns
And in luxurious° Cities, where the noise
Of riot° ascends above their loftiest Tow'rs,
And injury and outrage: And when Night 500
Darkens the Streets, then wander forth the Sons
Of Belial, flown° with insolence and wine.
Witness the streets of Sodom, and that night
In Gibeah, when the hospitable door
Expos'd a Matron, to avoid worse rape.° 505
These were the prime in order and in might;
The rest were long to tell, though far renown'd,
Th'Ionian Gods, of Javan's° Issue held
Gods, yet confest later than Heav'n and Earth°
Their boasted Parents; Titan° Heav'n's first-born 510
With his enormous brood, and birthright seiz'd
By younger Saturn, he from mightier Jove,
His own and Rhea's Son like measure found;
So Jove usurping reign'd: these first in Crete
And Ida° known, thence on the Snowy top 515
Of cold Olympus rul'd the middle Air
Their highest Heav'n; or on the Delphian Cliff,
Or in Dodona,° and through all the bounds
Of Doric Land;° or who with Saturn old
Fled over Adria to th'Hesperian Fields, 520
And o'er the Celtic roam'd the utmost Isles.°
All these and more came flocking; but with looks
Downcast and damp,° yet such wherein appear'd
Obscure some glimpse of joy, to have found their chief

498 **luxurious** lustful. 499 **riot** debauchery, as in riotous living.
502 **flown** flushed and welling. 504–05 **when . . . rape** *1674*; hospita-
ble Doors/Yielded their Matrons to prevent *1667*. The story of a
threatened sodomitical rape, in JUDGES 19:12–30. 508 **Javan** ances-
tor of the Ionians, Greeks. 509 **Heav'n and Earth** the deities
Uranus and Gaia. 510 **Titan** eldest son of Uranus (whom he de-
posed), and brother of Saturn; Saturn was in turn deposed by Jove.
515 **Ida** mountain in Crete where Jove was born. 517-18 Apollo's
oracle at Delphi, Jove's at Dodona. 519 **Doric Land** southern
Greece. 520-21 The fields of Italy and France, and the isles of
Britain. 523 **damp** as if smothered in smoke.

525 Not in despair, to have found themselves not lost
    In loss itself; which on his count'nance cast
    Like doubtful° hue: but he his wonted pride
    Soon recollecting,° with high words, that bore
    Semblance of worth, not substance, gently rais'd
530 Their fainting° courage, and dispell'd their fears.
    Then straight commands that at the warlike sound
    Of Trumpets loud and Clarions be uprear'd
    His mighty Standard; that proud honour claim'd
    Azazel as his right, a Cherub tall:
535 Who forthwith from the glittering Staff unfurl'd
    Th'Imperial Ensign, which full high advanc't
    Shone like a Meteor streaming to the Wind
    With Gems and Golden lustre rich imblaz'd,
    Seraphic arms and Trophies: all the while
540 Sonórous metal blowing Martial sounds:
    At which the universal Host upsent
    A shout that tore Hell's Concave, and beyond
    Frighted the Reign of Chaos and old Night.
    All in a moment through the gloom were seen
545 Ten thousand Banners rise into the Air
    With Orient° Colours waving: with them rose
    A Forest huge of Spears: and thronging Helms
    Appear'd, and serried Shields in thick array
    Of depth immeasurable: Anon they move
550 In perfect Phalanx° to the Dorian mood°
    Of Flutes and soft Recorders; such as rais'd
    To heighth of noblest temper Heroes old
    Arming to Battle, and instead of rage
    Deliberate valour breath'd, firm and unmov'd
555 With dread cf death to flight or foul retreat,
    Nor wanting power to mitigate and 'suage°
    With solemn touches, troubl'd thoughts, and chase
    Anguish and doubt and fear and sorrow and pain
    From mortal or immortal minds. Thus they
560 Breathing united force with fixed thought
    Mov'd on in silence to soft Pipes that charm'd

527 **doubtful** full of doubt.   528 **recollecting** remembering and pull-
ing together (re-collecting).   530 **fainting** *1674*; fainted *1667*.   546
Orient bright as from the east, from Latin *oriens*, rising (notice "rise"
and "rose" here).   550 **Phalanx** line of battle.   550 **Dorian mood** a
musical "mode" expressive of courage, Dorian being Spartan.   556
'suage assuage, sweeten.

Their painful steps o'er the burnt soil; and now
Advanc't in view they stand, a horrid° Front
Of dreadful length and dazzling Arms, in guise
Of Warriors old with order'd Spear and Shield,   565
Awaiting what command their mighty Chief
Had to impose: He through the armed Files
Darts his experienc't eye, and soon traverse°
The whole Battalion views; their order due,
Their visages and stature as of Gods,   570
Their number last he sums.° And now his heart
Distends with pride, and hard'ning in his strength
Glories: For never since created° man,
Met such imbodied force,° as nam'd with these
Could merit more than that small infantry   575
Warr'd on by Cranes:° though all the Giant brood
Of Phlegra° with th'Heroic Race were join'd
That fought at Thebes and Ilium,° on each side
Mixt with auxiliar° Gods; and what resounds
In Fable or Romance of Uther's Son°   580
Begirt with British and Armoric° Knights;
And all who since, Baptiz'd or Infidel
Jousted in Aspramont or Montalban,°
Damasco, or Morocco, or Trebisond,°
Or whom Biserta° sent from Afric shore   585
When Charlemagne with all his Peerage fell
By Fontarabbia. Thus far these beyond
Compare of mortal prowess,° yet observ'd°
Their dread Commander: he above the rest
In shape and gesture proudly eminent   590
Stood like a Tow'r; his form had yet not lost

563 **horrid** including bristling, Latin *horridus*.   568 **traverse** across.
571 **sums** reckons up.   573 **created** the creation of.   574 **imbodied
force** both power and forces (in a body of men).   574–76 In com-
parison, no army would come to more than the pigmy army, who
fought against the cranes; "infantry" suggests sardonically an army
of babies (infant and infantry have the same derivation).   577
Phlegra where the Giants fought the Gods.   578 **Thebes and
Ilium** scenes of Greek heroism.   579 **auxiliar** the classical gods
intervening helpfully in battle (but "auxiliar Gods" has a belittling
ring).   580 **Uther's Son** King Arthur.   581 **Armoric** from Brittany.
583 **Aspramont or Montalban** in Italy and France, associated with
Charlemagne.   584 **Trebisond** on the Black Sea.   585 **Biserta** port
in Tunisia.   588 **prowess** valor, but the word is cognate with
"proud"; the angels show a more than humàn pride (I 572, 590,
603).   588 **observ'd** watched and obeyed.

All her Original° brightness, nor appear'd
Less than Arch Angel ruin'd and th'excess
Of Glory° obscured: As when the Sun new-ris'n
595 Looks through the Horizontal° misty Air
Shorn of his Beams, or from behind the Moon
In dim Eclipse disastrous° twilight sheds
On half the Nations, and with fear of change
Perplexes Monarchs. Darken'd so, yet shone
600 Above them all th'Arch Angel: but his face
Deep scars of Thunder had intrencht, and care
Sat on his faded cheek, but under Brows
Of dauntless courage, and considerate° Pride
Waiting revenge: cruel his eye, but cast
605 Signs of remorse and passion to behold
The fellows of his crime, the followers rather
(Far other once beheld in bliss) condemn'd
For ever now to have their lot in pain,
Millions of Spirits for his fault amerc't°
610 Of Heav'n, and from Eternal Splendors flung
For his revolt, yet faithful how they stood,
Their Glory wither'd. As when Heaven's Fire
Hath scath'd the Forest Oaks, or Mountain Pines,
With singed top their stately growth though bare
615 Stands on the blasted Heath. He now prepar'd
To speak; whereat their doubl'd Ranks they bend
From Wing° to Wing, and half enclose him round
With all his Peers: attention held them mute.
Thrice he assay'd, and thrice in spite of scorn,
620 Tears such as Angels weep, burst forth: at last
Words interwove with sighs found out their way.

"O Myriads of immortal Spirits, O Powers
Matchless, but with th'Almighty, and that strife
Was not inglorious, though th'event° was dire,
625 As this place testifies, and this dire change
Hateful to utter: but what power of mind
Foreseeing or presaging, from the Depth
Of knowledge past or present, could have fear'd,

592 **Original** including "pertaining to its origin," i.e. God. 594
Glory including halo. 595 **Horizontal** of the horizon. 597 **disastrous** ill-starred, from Latin *astrum*, star. 603 **considerate** conscious. 609 **amerc't** paying the fine (but notice the derivation *amercié*, being at the mercy of). 617 **Wing** formation. 624 **event** outcome, eventuality.

How such united force of Gods, how such
As stood like these, could ever know repulse?   630
For who can yet believe, though after loss,
That all these puissant° Legions, whose exíle
Hath emptied Heav'n, shall fail to re-ascend
Self-rais'd, and repossess their native seat.
For me, be witness all the Host of Heav'n,   635
If counsels different, or danger shunn'd
By me, have lost our hopes. But he who reigns
Monarch in Heav'n, till then as one secure
Sat on his Throne, upheld by old repute,
Consent or custom, and his Regal State   640
Put forth at full, but still his strength conceal'd,
Which tempted our attempt, and wrought our fall.
Henceforth his might we know, and know our own
So as not either to provoke, or dread
New war, provok't; our better part° remains   645
To work in close design, by fraud or guile
What force effected not: that he no less
At length from us may find, who overcomes
By force, hath overcome but half his foe.
Space may produce new Worlds; whereof so rife   650
There went a fame° in Heav'n that he ere long
Intended to create, and therein plant
A generation, whom his choice regard
Should favour equal to the Sons of Heaven:
Thither, if but to pry, shall be perhaps   655
Our first eruption,° thither or elsewhere:
For this Infernal Pit shall never hold
Celestial Spirits in Bondage, nor th'Abyss
Long under darkness cover. But these thoughts
Full Counsel must mature: Peace is despair'd,   660
For who can think Submission? War then, War
Open or understood must be resolv'd."
          He spake: and to confirm his words, out-flew
Millions of flaming swords, drawn from the thighs
Of mighty Cherubim; the sudden blaze   665
Far round illumin'd hell: highly they rag'd
Against the Highest, and fierce with grasped arms

632 **puissant** powerful.   645 **part** to be acted (in both senses).   651
fame rumor.   656 **eruption** breaking out forcibly (suggesting too
the volcanoes of Hell).

Clash'd on their sounding shields the din of war,
Hurling defiance° toward the vault of Heav'n.
670   There stood a Hill not far whose grisly top
Belch'd fire and rolling smoke; the rest entire
Shone with a glossy scurf, undoubted sign
That in his womb° was hid metallic Ore,
The work of Sulphur. Thither wing'd with speed
675 A numerous Brígade hasten'd. As when bands
Of Pioneers° with Spade and Pickaxe arm'd
Forerun the Royal Camp, to trench a Field,
Or cast a Rampart. Mammon led them on,
Mammon, the least erected° Spirit that fell
680 From heav'n, for even in heav'n his looks and thoughts
Were always downward bent, admiring more
The riches of Heav'n's pavement, trodd'n gold,
Than aught divine or holy else enjoy'd
In vision beatific:° by him first
685 Men also, and by his suggestion° taught,
Ransack'd the Center, and with impious hands
Rifled the bowels of their mother Earth
For Treasures better hid. Soon had his crew
Op'n'd into the Hill a spacious wound
690 And digg'd out ribs of Gold. Let none admire°
That riches grow in Hell; that soil may best
Deserve the precious° bane.° And here let those
Who boast in mortal things, and wond'ring tell
Of Babel, and the works of Memphian° Kings,
695 Learn how their greatest Monuments of Fame,
And Strength and Art are easily outdone
By Spirits reprobate,° and in an hour
What in an age they with incessant toil
And hands innumerable scarce perform.
700 Nigh on the Plain in many cells prepar'd,

669 **defiance** including the older sense, "declaration of war," defiance
itself meaning the breaking of faith.   673 **his womb** the perverted
body-landscape of Hell.   676 **Pioneers** soldiers preparing camp.
679 **erected** elevated.   684 **vision beatific** the blessed experience of
seeing God.   685 **suggestion** including temptation.   690 **admire**
wonder.   692 **precious** including "for which a price is paid."   **bane**
originally murderer; the word survives in poisonous plants (rat's-
bane)—notice "soil."   694 **Memphian** Egyptian.   697 **reprobate** re-
jected by God, a Biblical term.

That underneath had veins of liquid fire
Sluic'd from the Lake, a second multitude
With wondrous Art founded° the massy Ore,
Severing each kind, and scumm'd the Bullion dross:°
A third as soon had form'd within the ground   705
A various mould, and from the boiling cells
By strange conveyance fill'd each hollow nook,
As in an Organ from one blast of wind
To many a row of Pipes the sound-board breathes.
Anon out of the earth a Fabric huge   710
Rose like an Exhalation, with the sound°
Of Dulcet Symphonies and voices sweet,
Built like a Temple, where Pilasters° round
Were set, and Doric pillars overlaid
With Golden Architrave;° nor did there want   715
Cornice or Frieze, with bossy° Sculptures grav'n,
The Roof was fretted Gold. Not Babylon,
Nor great Alcairo° such magnificence
Equall'd in all their glories, to enshrine
Belus or Serapis their Gods, or seat   720
Their Kings, when Egypt with Assyria strove
In wealth and luxury. Th'ascending pile
Stood fixt her stately heighth, and straight the doors
Op'ning their brazen° folds discover° wide
Within, her ample spaces, o'er the smooth   725
And level pavement: from the arched roof
Pendent by subtle Magic many a row
Of Starry Lamps and blazing Cressets° fed
With Naphtha and Asphaltus yielded light
As from a sky. The hasty multitude   730
Admiring enter'd, and the work some praise
And some the Architect: his hand was known
In Heav'n by many a Tow'red structure high,
Where Scepter'd Angels held their residence,
And sat as Princes, whom the súpreme King   735

703 **founded** *1667*; found out *1674*.   704 **scumm'd ... dross** skimmed
the dregs of the metal, "bullion" being from *bouillon,* to boil; see
line 706.   711 **sound** The music of Apollo and of Amphion built the
walls of Troy and Thebes.   713 **Pilasters** square columns.   715
Architrave main beam.   716 **bossy** embossed.   718 **Alcairo** Cairo.
724 **brazen** including the effrontery of mimicking Heaven.   724 **dis-
cover** reveal.   728 **Cressets** torches, made of "Asphaltus," and burn-
ing "Naphtha."

Exalted to such power, and gave to rule,
Each in his Hierarchy, the Orders bright.
Nor was his name unheard or unador'd
In ancient Greece; and in Ausonian land°
740 Men call'd him Mulciber;° and how he fell
From Heav'n, they fabl'd, thrown by angry Jove
Sheer o'er the Crystal Battlements: from Morn
To Noon he fell, from Noon to dewy Eve,
A Summer's day; and with the setting Sun
745 Dropt from the Zenith like a falling Star,
On Lemnos th'Aegaean Isle: thus they relate,
Erring; for he with this rebellious rout°
Fell long before; nor aught avail'd him now
To have built in Heav'n high Tow'rs; nor did he 'scape
750 By all his Engines,° but was headlong sent
With his industrious crew to build in Hell.
Meanwhile the winged Heralds by command
Of Sovran power, with awful Ceremony
And Trumpets' sound throughout the Host proclaim
755 A solemn Council forthwith to be held
At Pandemonium,° the high Capital
Of Satan and his Peers: their summons call'd
From every Band and squared Regiment
By place or choice the worthiest; they anon
760 With hundreds and with thousands trooping came
Attended: all access was throng'd, the Gates
And Porches wide, but chief the spacious Hall
(Though like a cover'd field, where Champions bold
Wont° ride in arm'd, and at the Soldan's° chair
765 Defi'd the best of Paynim° chivalry
To mortal combat or career° with Lance)
Thick swarm'd, both on the ground and in the air,
Brusht with the hiss of rustling wings. As Bees
In springtime, when the Sun with Taurus° rides,
770 Pour forth their populous youth about the Hive
In clusters; they among fresh dews and flowers
Fly to and fro, or on the smoothed Plank,
The suburb of their Straw-built Citadel,

739 **Ausonian land** Italy.   740 **Mulciber** "The Softener" (of metal),
known too as Vulcan.   747 **rout** company.   750 **Engines** contriv-
ances.   756 **Pandemonium** "Abode of all devils."   764 **Wont** were
wont to.   764 **Soldan** Sultan.   765 **Paynim** pagan.   766 **career** gal-
lop at full speed.   769 **with Taurus** in the sign of the Bull.

New rubb'd with Balm, expatiate° and confer
Their State-affairs. So thick the airy crowd   *775*
Swarm'd and were strait'n'd; till the Signal giv'n,
Behold a wonder! they but now who seem'd
In bigness to surpass Earth's Giant Sons
Now less than smallest Dwarfs, in narrow room
Throng numberless, like that Pygmean Race   *780*
Beyond the Indian Mount, or Faery Elves,
Whose midnight Revels, by a Forest side
Or Fountain some belated° Peasant sees,
Or dreams he sees, while overhead the Moon
Sits Arbitress,° and nearer to the Earth   *785*
Wheels her pale course, they on their mirth and dance
Intent, with jocund Music charm his ear;
At once with joy and fear his heart rebounds.
Thus incorporeal Spirits to smallest forms
Reduc'd their shapes immense, and were at large,   *790*
Though without number° still amidst the Hall
Of that infernal Court. But far within
And in their own dimensions like themselves
The great Seraphic Lords and Cherubim
In close recess and secret conclave° sat   *795*
A thousand Demi-Gods on golden seats,
Frequent° and full. After short silence then
And summons read, the great consult began.

BOOK II

THE ARGUMENT

The Consultation begun, Satan debates whether another
Battle be to be hazarded for the recovery of Heaven: some

---

774 **expatiate** walk at large; the more usual sense, "discourse at
length," leads into "confer" and "the great consult."   783 **belated**
out late.   785 **Arbitress** deciding destinies; this superstition is to be
contrasted with the truth, "Heav'n's high Arbitrator," II 359.
791 **without number** numberless.   795 **conclave** The religious sug-
gestion both hits at cardinals in their meetings, and suggests blas-
phemous parody by the fallen angels.   797 **Frequent** crowded.

advise it, others dissuade: A third proposal is preferr'd,
mention'd before by Satan, to search the truth of that
Prophecy or Tradition in Heaven concerning another
world, and another kind of creature equal or not much
inferior to themselves, about this time to be created:
Their doubt who shall be sent on this difficult search:
Satan their chief undertakes alone the voyage, is honour'd
and applauded. The Council thus ended, the rest betake
them several ways and to several employments, as their
inclinations lead them, to entertain the time till Satan
return. He passes on his Journey to Hell Gates, finds them
shut, and who sat there to guard them, by whom at length
they are open'd, and discover to him the great Gulf be-
tween Hell and Heaven; with what difficulty he passes
through, directed by Chaos, the Power of that place, to
the sight of this new World which he sought.

       High on a Throne of Royal State, which far
Outshone the wealth of Ormus° and of Ind,
Or where the gorgeous East with richest hand
Show'rs on her Kings Barbaric Pearl and Gold,
5 Satan exalted sat, by merit rais'd
To that bad eminence; and from despair
Thus high uplifted beyond hope, aspires
Beyond thus high, insatiate to pursue
Vain War with Heav'n, and by success° untaught
10 His proud imaginations thus display'd.
      "Powers and Dominions, Deities of Heav'n,
For since no deep within her gulf can hold
Immortal vigour, though opprest and fall'n,
I give not Heav'n for lost. From this descent
15 Celestial virtues° rising, will appear
More glorious and more dread than from no fall,
And trust themselves to fear no second fate:
Mee though just right,° and the fixt Laws of Heav'n

2 **Ormus** in the Persian gulf. 9 **success** originally "outcome,"
whether good or bad; but the modern sense existed and may add a
sardonic note. 15 **virtues** including this rank of angels. 18 **just
right** the rights of justice.

Did first create your Leader, next, free choice,
With what besides, in Council° or in Fight,   20
Hath been achiev'd of merit, yet this loss
Thus far at least recover'd, hath much more
Establisht in a safe unenvied Throne
Yielded with full consent. The happier state
In Heav'n, which follows dignity, might draw   25
Envy from each inferior; but who here
Will envy whom the highest place exposes
Foremost to stand against the Thunderer's aim
Your bulwark, and condemns to greatest share
Of endless pain? where there is then no good   30
For which to strive, no strife can grow up there
From Faction; for none sure will claim in hell
Precédence, none, whose portion is so small
Of present pain, that with ambitious mind
Will covet more. With this advantage then   35
To union, and firm Faith, and firm accord,
More than can be in Heav'n, we now return
To claim our just inheritance of old,
Surer to prosper than prosperity
Could have assur'd us; and by what best way,   40
Whether of open War or covert guile,
We now debate; who can advise, may speak."

      He ceas'd, and next him Moloch, Scepter'd
        King,
Stood up, the strongest and the fiercest Spirit
That fought in Heav'n; now fiercer by despair: 45
His trust was with th'Eternal to be deem'd
Equal in strength, and rather than be less
Car'd not to be at all; with that care lost
Went all his fear: of God, or Hell, or worse
He reck'd not, and these words thereafter spake.   50

    "My sentence is for open War: Of Wiles,
More unexpert,° I boast not: them let those
Contrive who need, or when they need, not now.
For while they sit contriving, shall the rest,
Millions that stand in Arms, and longing wait   55
The Signal to ascend, sit ling'ring here
Heav'n's fugitives, and for their dwelling place

20 **Council** advice and assembly (Milton's spelling "Counsel").   52
More unexpert less experienced.

Accept this dark opprobrious Den of shame,
The Prison of his Tyranny who Reigns
60 By our delay? No, let us rather choose
Arm'd with Hell flames and fury all at once
O'er Heav'n's high Tow'rs to force resistless° way,
Turning our Tortures into horrid Arms
Against the Torturer; when to meet the noise
65 Of his Almighty Engine° he shall hear
Infernal Thunder, and for Lightning see
Black fire and horror shot with equal rage
Among his Angels; and his Throne itself
Mixt with Tartarean° Sulphur, and strange fire,
70 His own invented Torments. But perhaps
The way seems difficult and steep to scale
With upright wing against a higher foe.
Let such bethink them, if the sleepy drench°
Of that forgetful° Lake benumb not still,
75 That in our proper° motion we ascend
Up to our native seat: descent and fall
To us is adverse. Who but felt of late
When the fierce Foe hung on our brok'n Rear
Insulting,° and pursu'd us through the Deep,
80 With what compulsion and laborious flight
We sunk thus low? Th'ascent is easy then;
Th'event° is fear'd; should we again provoke
Our stronger, some worse way his wrath may find
To our destruction: if there be in Hell
85 Fear to be worse destroy'd: what can be worse
Than to dwell here, driv'n out from bliss, condemn'd
In this abhorred deep to utter woe;
Where pain of unextinguishable fire
Must exercise° us without hope of end
90 The Vassals of his anger, when the Scourge
Inexorably,° and the torturing hour
Calls us to Penance? More destroy'd than thus
We should be quite abolisht and expire.
What fear we then? what doubt we to incense

62 **resistless** irresistible.   65 **Engine** machine of war.   69 **Tartarean**
Tartarus, the classical Hell.   73 **drench** potion.   74 **forgetful** caus-
ing oblivion.   75 **proper** own natural.   79 **Insulting** with a sugges-
tion of the Latin, "leaping upon."   82 **event** outcome.   89 **exercise**
work on.   91 **Inexorably** not to be moved even by prayer (Latin
orare)—notice "Penance."

His utmost ire? which to the heighth enrag'd,   95
Will either quite consume us, and reduce
To nothing this essential,° happier far
Than miserable to have eternal being:
Or if our substance be indeed Divine,
And cannot cease to be, we are at worst   100
On this side nothing;° and by proof we feel
Our power sufficient to disturb his Heav'n,
And with perpetual inroads to Alarm,
Though inaccessible, his fatal° Throne:
Which if not Victory is yet Revenge."   105

      He ended frowning, and his look denounc'd°
Desperate revenge, and Battle dangerous
To less than Gods. On th'other side up rose
Belial, in act more graceful and humane;
A fairer person lost not Heav'n; he seem'd   110
For dignity compos'd and high exploit:
But all was false and hollow; though his Tongue
Dropt Manna,° and could make the worse appear
The better reason, to perplex and dash
Maturest Counsels: for his thoughts were low;   115
To vice industrious, but to Nobler deeds
Timorous and slothful: yet he pleas'd the ear,
And with persuasive accent thus began.

     "I should be much for open War, O Peers,
As not behind in hate; if what was urg'd   120
Main reason to persuade immediate War,
Did not dissuade me most, and seem to cast
Ominous conjecture on the whole success:
When he who most excels in fact° of Arms,
In what he counsels and in what excels   125
Mistrustful, grounds his courage on despair
And utter dissolution, as the scope°
Of all his aim, after some dire revenge.
First, what Revenge? the Tow'rs of Heav'n are fill'd
With Armed watch, that render all access   130
Impregnable; oft on the bordering Deep
Encamp their Legions, or with óbscure wing

97 **essential** essence.   100–01 **at worst . . . nothing** already in the
worst plight short of annihilation.   104 **fatal** upheld by fate.   106
denounc'd proclaimed.   113 **Manna** sweetness (but to be contrasted
with the heavenly gift of miraculous food).   124 **fact** feat.   127
scope target.

Scout far and wide into the Realm of night,
Scorning surprise. Or could we break our way
135 By force, and at our heels all Hell should rise
With blackest Insurrection, to confound
Heav'n's purest Light, yet our great Enemy
All incorruptible would on his Throne
Sit unpolluted, and th'Ethereal mould
140 Incapable of stain would soon expel
Her mischief, and purge off the baser fire
Victorious. Thus repuls'd, our final hope
Is flat despair: we must exasperate
Th'Almighty Victor to spend all his rage,
145 And that must end us, that must be our cure,
To be no more; sad cure; for who would lose,
Though full of pain, this intellectual being,
Those thoughts that wander through Eternity,
To perish rather, swallow'd up and lost
150 In the wide womb of uncreated night,
Devoid of sense and motion? and who knows,
Let this be good, whether our angry Foe
Can give it, or will ever? how he can
Is doubtful; that he never will is sure.
155 Will he, so wise, let loose at once his ire,
Belike° through impotence,° or unaware,
To give his Enemies their wish, and end
Them in his anger, whom his anger saves
To punish endless? 'Wherefore cease we then?'
160 Say they who counsel War, 'we are decreed,
Reserv'd and destin'd to Eternal woe;
Whatever doing, what can we suffer more,
What can we suffer worse?' Is this then worst,
Thus sitting, thus consulting, thus in Arms?
165 What when we fled amain,° pursu'd and struck
With Heav'n's afflicting Thunder, and besought
The Deep to shelter us? this Hell then seem'd
A refuge from those wounds; or when we lay
Chain'd on the burning Lake? that sure was worse.
170 What if the breath that kindl'd those grim fires
Awak'd should blow them into sevenfold rage

156 **Belike** no doubt.   156 **impotence** lack of self-restraint (sardon-ically contrasted with God's omnipotence).   165 **amain** with all speed and force.

And plunge us in the Flames? or from above
Should intermitted vengeance Arm again
His red right hand to plague us? what if all
Her stores were op'n'd, and this Firmament   175
Of Hell should spout her Cataracts of Fire,
Impendent horrors, threat'ning hideous fall
One day upon our heads; while we perhaps
Designing or exhorting glorious War,
Caught in a fiery Tempest shall be hurl'd   180
Each on his rock transfixt, the sport and prey
Of racking° whirlwinds, or forever sunk
Under yon boiling Ocean, wrapt in Chains;
There to converse° with everlasting groans,
Unrespited, unpitied, unrepriev'd,   185
Ages of hopeless end; this would be worse.
War therefore, open or conceal'd, alike
My voice dissuades; for what can force or guile
With him, or who deceive his mind, whose eye
Views all things at one view? he from heav'n's heighth 190
All these our motions° vain, sees and derides;
Not more Almighty to resist our might
Than wise to frustrate all our plots and wiles.
Shall we then live thus vile, the race of Heav'n
Thus trampl'd, thus expell'd to suffer here   195
Chains and these Torments? better these than worse
By my advice; since fate inevitable
Subdues us, and Omnipotent Decree,
The Victor's will. To suffer, as to do,
Our strength is equal, nor the Law unjust   200
That so ordains: this was at first resolv'd,
If we were wise, against so great a foe
Contending, and so doubtful what might fall.
I laugh, when those who at the Spear are bold
And vent'rous, if that fail them, shrink and fear   205
What yet they know must follow, to endure
Exile, or ignominy, or bonds, or pain,
The sentence of their Conqueror: This is now
Our doom; which if we can sustain and bear,
Our Súpreme Foe in time may much remit   210
His anger, and perhaps thus far remov'd

182 **racking** both "torturing" and "driving impetuously." 184 **con-
verse** including the older sense "live." 191 **motions** proposals.

Not mind° us not offending, satisfi'd
With what is punish't; whence these raging fires
Will slack'n, if his breath stir not their flames.
215 Our purer essence then will overcome
Their noxious vapour, or inur'd not feel,
Or chang'd at length, and to the place conform'd
In temper and in nature, will receive
Familiar the fierce heat, and void of pain;
220 This horror will grow mild, this darkness light,°
Besides what hope the never-ending flight
Of future days may bring, what chance, what change
Worth waiting, since our present lot appears
For happy° though but ill, for ill not worst,
225 If we procure not to ourselves more woe."
          Thus Belial with words cloth'd in reason's garb
Counsell'd ignoble ease, and peaceful sloth,
Not peace: and after him thus Mammon spake.
          "Either to disenthrone the King of Heav'n
230 We war, if war be best, or to regain
Our own right lost: him to unthrone we then
May hope, when everlasting Fate shall yield
To fickle Chance, and Chaos judge the strife:
The former vain to hope argues as vain
235 The latter: for what place can be for us
Within Heav'n's bound, unless Heav'n's Lord supreme
We overpower? Suppose he should relent
And publish Grace to all, on promise made
Of new Subjection; with what eyes could we
240 Stand in his presence humble, and receive
Strict Laws impos'd, to celebrate his Throne
With warbl'd Hymns, and to his Godhead sing
Forc't° Halleluliahs; while he Lordly° sits
Our envied Sovran, and his Altar breathes
245 Ambrosial Odours and Ambrosial Flowers,
Our servile offerings. This must be our task
In Heav'n, this our delight; how wearisome
Eternity so spent in worship paid
To whom we hate. Let us not then pursue

212 **mind** call to mind   220 **light** both "illumination" and "lightly
borne" (parallel with "mild").   224 **For happy** as to happiness.
243 **Forc't** both extorted and strained.   243 **Lordly** including
haughty.

By force impossible, by leave obtain'd   250
Unácceptáble, though in Heav'n, our state
Of splendid vassalage, but rather seek
Our own good from ourselves, and from our own
Live to ourselves, though in this vast recess,
Free, and to none accountable, preferring   255
Hard liberty before the easy yoke
Of servile Pomp. Our greatness will appear
Then most conspicuous, when great things of small,
Useful of hurtful, prosperous of adverse
We can create, and in what place soe'er   260
Thrive under evil, and work ease out of pain
Through labour and endurance. This deep world
Of darkness do we dread? How oft amidst
Thick clouds and dark doth Heav'n's all-ruling Sire
Choose to reside, his Glory unobscur'd,   265
And with the Majesty of darkness round
Covers his Throne; from whence deep thunders roar
Must'ring their rage, and Heav'n resembles Hell?
As he our Darkness, cannot we his Light
Imitate when we please? This Desert soil   270
Wants° not her hidden lustre, Gems and Gold;
Nor want we skill or art, from whence to raise
Magnificence; and what can Heav'n show more?
Our torments also may in length of time
Become our Elements,° these piercing Fires   275
As soft as now severe, our temper chang'd
Into their temper; which must needs remove
The sensible° of pain. All things invite
To peaceful Counsels, and the settl'd State
Of order, how in safety best we may   280
Compose° our present evils, with regard
Of what we are and where,° dismissing quite
All thoughts of War: ye have what I advise."
          He scarce had finisht, when such murmur fill'd
Th'Assembly, as when hollow Rocks retain   285
The sound of blust'ring winds, which all night long
Had rous'd the Sea, now with hoarse cadence lull

---

271 **Wants** lacks.   275 **Elements** Demons traditionally dwelt in the
elements (fire, etc.).   278 **The sensible** that which feels sensations.
281 **Compose** calm, gain composure in the face of.   282 **where** 1667;
were 1674.

Sea-faring men o'erwatcht,° whose Bark by chance
Or Pinnace anchors in a craggy Bay
290 After the Tempest: Such applause was heard
As Mammon ended, and his Sentence pleas'd,
Advising peace: for such another Field°
They dreaded worse than Hell: so much the fear
Of Thunder and the Sword of Michaël
295 Wrought still within them; and no less desire
To found this nether Empire, which might rise
By policy,° and long procéss of time,
In emulation opposite° to Heav'n.
Which when Beëlzebub perceiv'd, than whom,
300 Satan except, none higher sat, with grave
Aspéct he rose, and in his rising seem'd
A Pillar of State; deep on his Front engraven
Deliberation sat and public care;
And Princely counsel in his face yet shone,
305 Majestic though in ruin: sage he stood
With Atlantean° shoulders fit to bear
The weight of mightiest Monarchies; his look
Drew audience and attention still as Night
Or Summer's Noon-tide air, while thus he spake.
      "Thrones and imperial Powers, offspring of
310   heav'n,
Ethereal Virtues; or these Titles now
Must we renounce, and changing style be call'd
Princes of Hell? for so the popular vote
Inclines, here to continue, and build up here
315 A growing Empire; doubtless; while we dream,
And know not that the King of Heav'n hath doom'd
This place our dungeon, not our safe retreat
Beyond his Potent arm, to live exempt
From Heav'n's high jurisdiction, in new League
320 Banded against his Throne, but to remain
In strictest bondage, though thus far remov'd,
Under th'inevitable° curb, reserv'd
His captive multitude: For he, be sure,
In heighth or depth, still first and last will Reign

288 **o'erwatcht** worn out with watching.   292 **Field** battlefield.
297 **policy** including the bad sense, political cunning.   298 **opposite**
both diametrically different and antagonistic.   306 **Atlantean** Atlas
carried the world.   322 **inevitable** inescapable.

Sole King, and of his Kingdom lose no part   325
By our revolt, but over Hell extend
His Empire, and with Iron Scepter rule
Us here, as with his Golden those in Heav'n.
What sit we then projecting Peace and War?
War hath determin'd us,° and foil'd with loss   330
Irreparable; terms of peace yet none
Vouchsaf't or sought; for what peace will be giv'n
To us enslav'd, but custody severe,
And stripes,° and arbitrary° punishment
Inflicted? and what peace can we return,   335
But to our power hostility and hate,
Untam'd reluctance,° and revenge though slow,
Yet ever plotting how the Conqueror least
May reap his conquest, and may least rejoice
In doing what we most in suffering feel?   340
Nor will occasion want, nor shall we need
With dangerous expedition to invade
Heav'n, whose high walls fear no assault or Siege,
Or ambush from the Deep. What if we find
Some easier enterprise? There is a place   345
(If ancient and prophetic fame in Heav'n
Err not) another World, the happy seat
Of some new Race call'd Man, about this time
To be created like to us, though less
In power and excellence, but favour'd more   350
Of him who rules above; so was his will
Pronounc'd among the Gods, and by an Oath,
That shook Heav'n's whole circumference, confirm'd.
Thither let us bend all our thoughts, to learn
What creatures there inhabit, of what mould,   355
Or substance, how endu'd, and what their Power,
And where their weakness, how attempted best,
By force or subtlety: Though Heav'n be shut,
And Heav'n's high Arbitrator sit secure
In his own strength, this place may lie expos'd   360
The utmost border of his Kingdom, left
To their defence who hold it: here perhaps

330 **determin'd us** brought us to this end (also suggesting "War has chosen us—it is no longer for *us* to choose *war*").   334 **stripes** whippings.   334 **arbitrary** at the will of the powerful, but the older sense —see line 359—undercuts Beelzebub: "at the discretion of an authorized arbitrator."   337 **reluctance** struggling.

Some advantageous act may be achiev'd
By sudden onset, either with Hell fire
365 To waste his whole Creation, or possess
All as our own, and drive as we were driven,
The puny° habitants, or if not drive,
Seduce them to our Party, that their God
May prove their foe, and with repenting hand
370 Abolish his own works. This would surpass
Common revenge, and interrupt his joy
In our Confusion, and our Joy upraise
In his disturbance; when his darling Sons
Hurl'd headlong to partake with us, shall curse
375 Their frail Originals,° and faded bliss,
Faded so soon. Advise if this be worth
Attempting, or to sit in darkness here
Hatching vain Empires." Thus Beëlzebub
Pleaded his devilish Counsel, first devis'd
380 By Satan, and in part propos'd: for whence,
But from the Author of all ill could spring
So deep a malice, to confound the race
Of mankind in one root,° and Earth with Hell
To mingle and involve, done all to spite
385 The great Creator? But their spite still serves
His glory to augment. The bold design
Pleas'd highly those infernal States,° and joy
Sparkl'd in all their eyes; with full assent
They vote: whereat his speech he thus renews.
390   "Well have ye judg'd, well ended long debate,
Synod° of Gods, and like to what ye are,
Great things resolv'd; which from the lowest deep
Will once more lift us up, in spite of Fate,
Nearer our ancient Seat; perhaps in view
Of those bright confines, whence with neighbouring
395   Arms
And opportune° excursion we may chance
Re-enter Heav'n; or else in some mild Zone

---

367 **puny** weak and "born since [us]," *puisné*.   375 **Originals** *1667*;
Original *1674*.   383 **one root** Adam, but the word foreshadows the
forbidden Tree, "root of all our woe," IX 645.   387 **States** the es-
tates of the realm, comprising the assembly.   391 **Synod** assembly,
usually of clergy.   396 **opportune** well-timed, originally of a wind
driving to port, *portus;* notice "excursion" and "Re-enter," and II
1041–7.

Dwell not unvisited of Heav'n's fair Light
Secure, and at the bright'ning Orient beam
Purge off this gloom; the soft delicious Air,   400
To heal the scar of these corrosive Fires
Shall breathe her balm. But first whom shall we send
In search of this new world, whom shall we find
Sufficient? who shall tempt° with wand'ring feet
The dark unbottom'd infinite Abyss   405
And through the palpable obscure find out
His uncouth° way, or spread his airy flight
Upborne with indefatigable wings
Over the vast abrupt, ere he arrive
The happy Isle; what strength, what art can then   410
Suffice, or what evasion bear him safe
Through the strict Senteries and Stations thick
Of Angels watching round? Here he had need
All circumspection, and we now no less
Choice° in our suffrage; for on whom we send,   415
The weight of all and our last hope relies."
          This said, he sat; and expectation held
His look suspense,° awaiting who appear'd
To second, or oppose, or undertake
The perilous attempt: but all sat mute,   420
Pondering the danger with deep thoughts; and each
In other's countenance read his own dismay
Astonisht: none among the choice and prime
Of those Heav'n-warring Champions could be found
So hardy as to proffer or accept   425
Alone the dreadful voyage; till at last
Satan, whom now transcendent glory rais'd
Above his fellows, with Monarchal° pride
Conscious of highest worth, unmov'd thus spake.
          "O Progeny of Heav'n, Empyreal Thrones,   430
With reason hath deep silence and demur
Seiz'd us, though undismay'd: long is the way
And hard, that out of Hell leads up to Light;
Our prison strong, this huge convéx of Fire,
Outrageous to devour, immures us round   435
Ninefold, and gates of burning Adamant

404 **tempt** attempt (though the evil suggestion is relevant). 407 **un-couth** unknown. 415 **Choice** careful choosing. 418 **suspense** suspended. 428 **Monarchal** literally "ruling alone."

Barr'd over us prohibit all egress.
These past, if any pass, the void profound
Of unessential° Night receives him next
440 Wide gaping, and with utter loss of being
Threatens him, plung'd in that abortive gulf.
If thence he 'scape into whatever world,
Or unknown Region, what remains him less
Than unknown dangers and as hard escape.
445 But I should ill become this Throne, O Peers,
And this Imperial Sov'ranty, adorn'd
With splendour, arm'd with power, if aught propos'd
And judg'd of public moment, in the shape
Of difficulty or danger could deter
450 Me from attempting. Wherefore do I assume
These Royalties, and not refuse to Reign,
Refusing to accept as great a share
Of hazard as of honour, due alike
To him who Reigns, and so much to him due
455 Of hazard more, as he above the rest
High honour'd sits? Go therefore mighty powers,
Terror of Heav'n, though fall'n; intend° at home,
While here shall be our home, what best may ease
The present misery, and render Hell
460 More tolerable; if there be cure or charm
To respite or deceive, or slack the pain
Of this ill Mansion: intermit no watch
Against a wakeful Foe, while I abroad
Through all the coasts of dark destruction seek
465 Deliverance for us all: this enterprise
None shall partake with me." Thus saying rose
The Monarch, and prevented° all reply,
Prudent, lest from his resolution° rais'd
Others among the chief might offer now
470 (Certain to be refus'd) what erst they fear'd;
And so refus'd might in opinion stand
His rivals, winning cheap the high repute
Which he through hazard huge must earn. But they
Dreaded not more th'adventure than his voice
475 Forbidding; and at once with him they rose;
Their rising all at once was as the sound

439 **unessential** having no being.   457 **intend** put your mind to.
467 **prevented** forestalled.   468 **resolution** resoluteness.

Of Thunder heard remote. Towards him they bend
With awful reverence prone; and as a God
Extol him equal to the highest in Heav'n:
Nor fail'd they to express how much they prais'd,   480
That for the general safety he despis'd
His own: for neither do the Spirits damn'd
Lose all their virtue; lest bad men should boast
Their specious deeds on earth, which glory excites,
Or close ambition varnisht o'er with zeal.   485
Thus they their doubtful consultations dark
Ended rejoicing in their matchless Chief:
As when from mountain tops the dusky clouds
Ascending, while the North wind sleeps, o'erspread
Heav'n's cheerful face, the louring° Element   490
Scowls o'er the dark'n'd landscape Snow, or show'r;
If chance the radiant Sun with farewell sweet
Extend his ev'ning beam, the fields revive,
The birds their notes renew, and bleating herds
Attest their joy, that hill and valley rings.   495
O shame to men! Devil with Devil damn'd
Firm concord holds, men only disagree
Of Creatures rational, though under hope
Of heavenly Grace: and God proclaiming peace,
Yet live in hatred, enmity, and strife   500
Among themselves, and levy cruel wars,
Wasting the Earth, each other to destroy:
As if (which might induce us to accord)
Man had not hellish foes enow besides,
That day and night for his destruction wait.   505
          The Stygian Council thus dissolv'd; and forth
In order came the grand infernal Peers,
Midst came their mighty Paramount, and seem'd
Alone th'Antagonist of Heav'n, nor less
Than Hell's dread Emperor with pomp Supreme,   510
And God-like imitated State; him round
A Globe of fiery Seraphim enclos'd
With bright imblazonry, and horrent° Arms.
Then of their Session ended they bid cry
With Trumpet's regal sound the great result: 515
Toward the four winds four speedy Cherubim

490 **louring** glowering.   513 **horrent** bristling.

Put to their mouths the sounding Alchemy°
By Herald's voice explain'd: the hollow Abyss
Heard far and wide, and all the host of Hell
520 With deaf'ning shout, return'd them loud acclaim.
Thence more at ease their minds and somewhat rais'd
By false presumptuous hope, the ranged powers
Disband, and wand'ring, each his several way
Pursues, as inclination or sad choice
525 Leads him perplext, where he may likeliest find
Truce to his restless thoughts, and entertain
The irksome hours, till his° great Chief return.
Part on the Plain, or in the Air sublime°
Upon the wing, or in swift race contend,
530 As at th'Olympian Games or Pythian fields;
Part curb their fiery Steeds, or shun the Goal°
With rapid wheels, or fronted Brígades form.
As when to warn° proud Cities war appears
Wag'd in the troubl'd Sky, and Armies rush
535 To Battle in the Clouds, before each Van°
Prick forth the Airy Knights, and couch their spears
Till thickest Legions close; with feats of Arms
From either end of Heav'n the welkin° burns.
Others with vast Typhoean° rage more fell
540 Rend up both Rocks and Hills, and ride the Air
In whirlwind; Hell scarce holds the wild uproar.
As when Alcides from Oechalia Crown'd
With conquest, felt th'envenom'd robe, and tore
Through pain up by the roots Thessalian Pines,
545 And Lichas from the top of Oeta threw
Into th'Euboic Sea.° Others more mild,
Retreated in a silent valley, sing
With notes Angelical to many a Harp
Their own Heroic deeds and hapless fall
550 By doom of Battle; and complain that Fate
Free Virtue should enthrall to Force or Chance.
Their song was partial,° but the harmony

517 **sounding Alchemy** trumpets of gold-like metal.   527 **his** *1667*;
this *1674*.   528 **sublime** aloft.   531 **shun the Goal** swing round the
marking-posts.   533 **to warn** as an omen.   535 **Van** vanguard.   538
welkin sky.   539 **Typhoean** For the monstrous Typhon, see I 199;
his name (as in "typhoon") means whirlwind—see line 541.   542–46
In his pain, Hercules threw into the sea his companion Lichas, who
had brought the poisoned shirt of Nessus which tortured Hercules.
552 **partial** favorable to themselves (suggesting, too, musical "parts").

(What could it less when Spirits immortal sing?)
Suspended° Hell, and took with ravishment
The thronging audience. In discourse more sweet   555
(For Eloquence the Soul, Song charms the Sense,)
Others apart sat on a Hill retir'd,
In thoughts more elevate, and reason'd high
Of Providence, Foreknowledge, Will, and Fate,
Fixt Fate, free will, foreknowledge absolute,   560
And found no end, in wand'ring mazes lost.
Of good and evil much they argu'd then,
Of happiness and final misery,
Passion and Apathy,° and glory and shame,
Vain wisdom all, and false Philosophy: 565
Yet with a pleasing sorcery could charm
Pain for a while or anguish, and excite
Fallacious hope, or arm th'obdured breast
With stubborn patience as with triple steel.
Another part in Squadrons and gross° Bands,   570
On bold adventure to discover wide
That dismal world, if any Clime perhaps
Might yield them easier habitation, bend
Four ways their flying March, along the Banks
Of four infernal Rivers that disgorge   575
Into the burning Lake their baleful streams;
Abhorred Styx the flood of deadly hate,
Sad Acheron of sorrow, black and deep;
Cocytus, nam'd of lamentation loud
Heard on the rueful stream; fierce Phlegethon   580
Whose waves of torrent fire inflame with rage.°
Far off from these a slow and silent stream,
Lethe the River of Oblivion rolls
Her wat'ry Labyrinth, whereof who drinks,
Forthwith his former state and being forgets,   585
Forgets both joy and grief, pleasure and pain.
Beyond this flood a frozen Continent
Lies dark and wild, beat with perpetual storms
Of Whirlwind and dire Hail, which on firm land
Thaws not, but gathers heap, and ruin seems   590

---

554 **Suspended** held rapt ("suspension," again, being a musical term
—meanwhile Milton's parenthesis itself suspends the sentence).
564 **Apathy** the Stoic ideal of imperviousness to suffering.   570 **gross**
massed.   577–81 Giving the derivations of the names of Hell's
rivers.

Of ancient pile;° all else deep snow and ice,
A gulf profound as that Serbonian Bog
Betwixt Damiata and mount Casius old,°
Where Armies whole have sunk: the parching Air
595 Burns frore,° and cold performs th'effect of Fire.
Thither by harpy-footed Furies hal'd,°
At certain revolutions all the damn'd
Are brought: and feel by turns the bitter change
Of fierce extremes, extremes by change more fierce,
600 From Beds of raging Fire to starve° in Ice
Their soft Ethereal warmth, and there to pine
Immovable, infixt, and frozen round,
Periods of time, thence hurried back to fire.
They ferry over this Lethean Sound°
605 Both to and fro, their sorrow to augment,
And wish and struggle, as they pass, to reach
The tempting stream, with one small drop to lose
In sweet forgetfulness all pain and woe,
All in one moment, and so near the brink;
610 But fate withstands, and to oppose th'attempt
Medusa° with Gorgonian terror guards
The Ford, and of itself the water flies
All taste of living wight,° as once it fled
The lip of Tantalus.° Thus roving on
615 In cónfus'd march forlorn, th'advent'rous Bands
With shudd'ring horror pale, and eyes aghast
View'd first their lamentable lot, and found
No rest: through many a dark and dreary Vale
They pass'd, and many a Region dolorous,
620 O'er many a Frozen, many a Fiery Alp,
Rocks, Caves, Lakes, Fens, Bogs, Dens, and shades
    of death,
A Universe of death, which God by curse
Created evil, for evil only good,
Where all life dies, death lives, and nature breeds,
625 Perverse, all monstrous, all prodigious° things,

---

591 **pile** building. 593 Near the mouth of the Nile. 595 **frore** frosty. 596 The monstrous Harpies had talons. 600 **starve** originally to die of cold, hunger, etc., to become rigid (notice the contrast with "Beds," "soft," and then "infixt"). 604 **Sound** channel. 611 **Medusa** the Gorgon who turned men to stone. 613 **wight** person. 614 **Tantalus** who was unable to reach the waters, "tantalized." 625 **prodigious** ominously extraordinary.

Abominable, inutterable, and worse
Than Fables yet have feign'd, or fear conceiv'd,
Gorgons° and Hydras,° and Chimeras° dire.
   Meanwhile the Adversary of God and Man,
Satan with thoughts inflam'd of highest design,   630
Puts on swift wings, and toward the Gates of Hell
Explores his solitary flight; sometimes
He scours the right-hand coast, sometimes the left,
Now shaves with level wing the Deep, then soars
Up to the fiery concave tow'ring high.   635
As when far off at Sea a Fleet descri'd
Hangs in the Clouds, by Equinoctial Winds°
Close sailing from Bengala, or the Isles
Of Ternate and Tidore,° whence Merchants bring
Their spicy Drugs: they on the trading Flood   640
Through the wide Ethiopian° to the Cape
Ply stemming° nightly toward the Pole. So seem'd
Far off the flying Fiend: at last appear
Hell-bounds high reaching to the horrid Roof,
And thrice threefold the Gates; three folds were Brass,   645
Three Iron, three of Adamantine Rock,
Impenetrable, impal'd° with circling fire,
Yet unconsum'd. Before the Gates there sat
On either side a formidable° shape;
The one seem'd Woman to the waist, and fair,   650
But ended foul in many a scaly fold
Voluminous° and vast, a Serpent arm'd
With mortal sting: about her middle round
A cry° of Hell Hounds never ceasing bark'd
With wide Cerberean° mouths full loud, and rung   655
A hideous Peal: yet, when they list, would creep,
If aught disturb'd their noise, into her womb,
And kennel there, yet there still bark'd and howl'd
Within unseen. Far less abhorr'd than these
Vex'd Scylla bathing in the Sea that parts   660
Calabria from the hoarse Trinacrian shore:°

628 **Gorgons** female monsters with snakes for hair.   628 **Hydra** the nine-headed serpent killed by Hercules.   628 **Chimeras** fire-breathing monsters.   637 **Equinoctial Winds** trade winds at the time of the equinoxes.   639 **Ternate, Tidore** Malayan islands.   641 **Ethiopian** Indian Ocean.   642 **stemming** heading.   647 impal'd fenced in. 649 **formidable** terrifying.   652 **Voluminous** in coils.   654 **cry** pack. 655 **Cerberean** Cerberus, the many-headed dog that guarded the classical Hell.   660–61 Scylla, bathing, was changed into a monster, and haunted a dangerous rock on the Italian coast opposite Sicily.

Nor uglier follow the Night-Hag,° when call'd
In secret, riding through the Air she comes
Lur'd with the smell of infant blood, to dance
665 With Lapland° Witches, while the labouring° Moon
Eclipses at their charms. The other shape,
If shape it might be call'd that shape had none
Distinguishable in member, joint, or limb,
Or substance might be call'd that shadow seem'd,
670 For each seem'd either; black it stood as Night,
Fierce as ten Furies, terrible as Hell,
And shook a dreadful Dart; what seem'd his head
The likeness of a Kingly Crown had on.
Satan was now at hand, and from his seat
675 The Monster moving onward came as fast,
With horrid strides, Hell trembled as he strode.
Th'undaunted Fiend what this might be admir'd,°
Admir'd, not fear'd; God and his Son except,
Created thing naught valu'd he nor shunn'd;
680 And with disdainful look thus first began.

          "Whence and what art thou, execrable° shape,
That dar'st, though grim and terrible, advance
Thy miscreated Front athwart my way
To yonder Gates? through them I mean to pass,
685 That be assur'd, without leave askt of thee:
Retire, or taste thy folly, and learn by proof,
Hell-born, not to contend with Spirits of Heav'n."

          To whom the Goblin° full of wrath repli'd,
"Art thou that Traitor Angel, art thou hee,
690 Who first broke peace in Heav'n and Faith, till then
Unbrok'n, and in proud rebellious Arms
Drew after him the third part of Heav'n's Sons
Conjur'd° against the highest, for which both Thou
And they outcast from God, are here condemn'd
695 To waste Eternal days in woe and pain?
And reck'n'st thou thyself with Spirits of Heav'n,
Hell-doom'd, and breath'st defiance here and scorn,
Where I reign King, and to enrage thee more,

---

662 **Night-Hag** Hecate, goddess of witchcraft. 665 **Lapland** in
northern Europe, and traditionally associated with witches. 665
labouring in eclipse (but with a suggestion of "ruling over childbirth,"
as the moon did; notice "womb," "infant"). 677 **admir'd** wondered
at. 681 **execrable** accursed. 688 **Goblin** evil spirit. 693 **Conjur'd**
sworn together.

Thy King and Lord? Back to thy punishment,
False fugitive, and to thy speed add wings, 700
Lest with a whip of Scorpions I pursue
Thy ling'ring, or with one stroke of this Dart
Strange horror seize thee, and pangs unfelt before."
    So spake the grisly terror, and in shape,
So speaking and so threat'ning, grew tenfold 705
More dreadful and deform: on th'other side
Incens't° with indignation Satan stood
Unterrifi'd, and like a Comet burn'd,
That fires the length of Ophiuchus° huge
In th'Arctic Sky, and from his horrid hair° 710
Shakes Pestilence and War. Each at the Head
Levell'd his deadly aim; their fatal hands
No second stroke intend, and such a frown
Each cast at th'other, as when two black Clouds
With Heav'n's Artillery fraught, come rattling on 715
Over the Caspian, then stand front to front°
Hov'ring a space, till Winds the signal blow
To join their dark Encounter in mid-air:
So frown'd the mighty Combatants, that Hell
Grew darker at their frown, so matcht they stood; 720
For never but once more was either like
To meet so great a foe: and now great deeds
Had been achiev'd, whereof all Hell had rung,
Had not the Snaky Sorceress that sat
Fast by Hell Gate, and kept the fatal Key, 725
Ris'n, and with hideous outcry rush'd between.
    "O Father, what intends thy hand," she cri'd,
"Against thy only Son? What fury O Son,
Possesses thee to bend that mortal Dart
Against thy Father's head? and know'st for whom; 730
For him who sits above and laughs the while
At thee ordain'd his drudge, to execute°
Whate'er his wrath, which he calls Justice, bids,
His wrath which one day will destroy ye both."
    She spake, and at her words the hellish Pest° 735

707 **Incens't** inflamed, from Latin *incendere* (notice "burn'd"). 709
Ophiuchus "Serpent-holder," a northern constellation. 710 **hair**
"Comet" is from the Greek for "long-haired," and is an evil omen.
714–16 The clouds resemble great ships ("fraught," stored, as in
"freight"). 732 **execute** carry out (but what Death executes is exe-
cution). 735 **Pest** originally a deadly plague.

Forbore, then these to her Satan return'd:
       "So strange thy outcry, and thy words so
              strange
Thou interposest, that my sudden hand
Prevented spares° to tell thee yet by deeds
740 What it intends; till first I know of thee,
What thing thou art, thus double-form'd, and why
In this infernal Vale first met thou call'st
Me Father, and that Phantasm call'st my Son?
I know thee not, nor ever saw till now
745 Sight more detestable than him and thee."
       T'whom thus the Portress of Hell Gate repli'd;
"Hast thou forgot me then, and do I seem
Now in thine eye so foul, once deem'd so fair
In Heav'n, when at th'Assembly, and in sight
750 Of all the Seraphim with thee combin'd
In bold conspiracy against Heav'n's King,
All on a sudden miserable pain
Surpris'd thee, dim thine eyes, and dizzy swum
In darkness, while thy head flames thick and fast
755 Threw forth, till on the left side op'ning wide,
Likest to thee in shape and count'nance bright,
Then shining heav'nly fair, a Goddess arm'd
Out of thy head I sprung:° amazement seiz'd
All th'Host of Heav'n; back they recoil'd afraid
760 At first, and call'd me Sin, and for a Sign
Portentous° held me; but familiar grown,
I pleas'd, and with attractive graces won
The most averse, thee chiefly, who full oft
Thyself in me thy perfect image viewing
765 Becam'st enamour'd, and such joy thou took'st
With me in secret, that my womb conceiv'd
A growing burden. Meanwhile War arose,
And fields were fought in Heav'n; wherein remain'd
(For what could else) to our Almighty Foe
770 Clear Victory, to our part loss and rout
Through all the Empyrean: down they fell
Driv'n headlong from the Pitch of Heaven, down

739 **Prevented spares** forestalled refrains from.   754–58 To be con-
trasted with the birth of Athene, goddess of wisdom, from Zeus's
head; "the left side" because it was ill-omened, literally "sinister."
761 **Portentous** ominous.

Into this Deep, and in the general fall
I also; at which time this powerful Key
Into my hand was giv'n, with charge to keep   775
These Gates for ever shut, which none can pass
Without my op'ning. Pensive here I sat
Alone, but long I sat not, till my womb
Pregnant by thee, and now excessive grown
Prodigious motion felt and rueful throes.   780
At last this odious offspring whom thou seest
Thine own begotten, breaking violent way
Tore through my entrails, that with fear and pain
Distorted, all my nether shape thus grew
Transform'd: but he my inbred enemy   785
Forth issu'd, brandishing his fatal Dart
Made to destroy: I fled, and cri'd out *Death;*
Hell trembl'd at the hideous Name, and sigh'd
From all her Caves, and back resounded *Death.*
I fled, but he pursu'd (though more, it seems,   790
Inflam'd with lust than rage) and swifter far,
Me overtook his mother all dismay'd,
And in embraces forcible and foul
Engend'ring with me, of that rape begot
These yelling Monsters that with ceaseless cry   795
Surround me, as thou saw'st, hourly conceiv'd
And hourly born, with sorrow infinite
To me, for when they list into the womb
That bred them they return, and howl and gnaw
My Bowels, their repast; then bursting forth   800
Afresh with conscious° terrors vex me round,
That rest or intermission none I find.
Before mine eyes in opposition sits
Grim Death my Son and foe, who sets them on,
And me his Parent would full soon devour   805
For want of other prey, but that he knows
His end with mine involv'd; and knows that I
Should prove a bitter Morsel, and his bane,
Whenever that shall be; so Fate pronounc'd.
But thou O Father, I forewarn thee, shun   810
His deadly arrow; neither vainly hope
To be invulnerable in those bright Arms,

---

801 conscious inwardly guilty.

Though temper'd heav'nly, for that mortal dint,
Save he who reigns above, none can resist."
815   She finish'd, and the subtle Fiend his lore°
Soon learn'd, now milder, and thus answer'd smooth.
"Dear Daughter, since thou claim'st me for thy Sire,
And my fair Son here show'st me, the dear pledge
Of dalliance had with thee in Heav'n, and joys
820 Then sweet, now sad to mention, through dire change
Befall'n us unforeseen, unthought-of, know
I come no enemy, but to set free
From out this dark and dismal house of pain,
Both him and thee, and all the heav'nly Host
825 Of Spirits that in our just pretenses° arm'd
Fell with us from on high: from them I go
This uncouth errand sole, and one for all
Myself expose, with lonely steps to tread
Th'unfounded° deep, and through the void immense
830 To search with wand'ring quest a place foretold
Should be, and, by concurring signs, ere now
Created vast and round, a place of bliss
In the Purlieus° of Heav'n, and therein plac't
A race of upstart Creatures, to supply
835 Perhaps our vacant room, though more remov'd,
Lest Heav'n surcharg'd° with potent multitude
Might hap to move new broils: Be this or aught
Than this more secret now design'd, I haste
To know, and this once known, shall soon return,
840 And bring ye to the place where Thou and Death
Shall dwell at ease, and up and down unseen
Wing silently the buxom° Air, embalm'd°
With odours; there ye shall be fed and fill'd
Immeasurably, all things shall be your prey."
845 He ceas'd, for both seem'd highly pleas'd, and Death
Grinn'd horrible a ghastly smile, to hear
His famine should be fill'd, and blest his maw°
Destin'd to that good hour: no less rejoic'd
His mother bad, and thus bespake her Sire.
850   "The key of this infernal Pit by due,

815 **lore** lesson.   825 **pretenses** claims.   829 **unfounded** bottomless.
833 **Purlieus** outer districts.   836 **surcharg'd** crowded.   842 **buxom**
yielding.   842 **embalm'd** balmy, but with the funereal associations
appropriate to Death.   847 **maw** stomach.

And by command of Heav'n's all-powerful King
I keep, by him forbidden to unlock
These Adamantine Gates; against all force
Death ready stands to interpose his dart,
Fearless to be o'ermatcht by living might.   855
But what owe I to his commands above
Who hates me, and hath hither thrust me down
Into this gloom of Tartarus profound,
To sit in hateful Office° here confin'd,
Inhabitant of Heav'n, and heav'nly-born,   860
Here in perpetual agony and pain,
With terrors and with clamours compast round
Of mine own brood, that on my bowels feed:
Thou art my Father, thou my Author, thou
My being gav'st me; whom should I obey   865
But thee, whom follow? thou wilt bring me soon
To that new world of light and bliss, among
The Gods who live at ease, where I shall Reign
At thy right hand voluptuous, as beseems
Thy daughter and thy darling, without end."   870
          Thus saying, from her side the fatal Key,
Sad instrument of all our woe, she took;
And towards the Gate rolling her bestial train,
Forthwith the huge Portcullis high updrew,
Which but herself not all the Stygian powers   875
Could once have mov'd; then in the key-hole turns
Th'intrícate wards, and every Bolt and Bar
Of massy Iron or solid Rock with ease
Unfast'ns: on a sudden op'n fly
With impetuous recoil and jarring sound   880
Th'infernal doors, and on their hinges grate
Harsh Thunder, that the lowest bottom shook
Of Erebus.° She op'n'd, but to shut
Excell'd her power; the Gates wide op'n stood,
That with extended wings° a Banner'd Host   885
Under spread Ensigns marching might pass through
With Horse and Chariots rankt in loose array;
So wide they stood, and like a Furnace mouth
Cast forth redounding° smoke and ruddy flame.
Before their eyes in sudden view appear   890

859 **Office** duty.   883 **Erebus** Hell.   885 **wings** flanking formations.
889 **redounding** overflowing.

The secrets of the hoary deep, a dark
Illimitable Ocean without bound,
Without dimension, where length, breadth, and
  heighth,
And time and place are lost; where eldest Night
895 And Chaos, Ancestors of Nature, hold
Eternal Anarchy, amidst the noise
Of endless wars, and by confusion stand.
For hot, cold, moist, and dry, four Champions fierce
Strive here for Mast'ry, and to Battle bring
900 Their embryon° Atoms; they around the flag
Of each his faction, in their several Clans,
Light-arm'd or heavy, sharp, smooth, swift or slow,
Swarm populous, unnumber'd as the Sands
Of Barca or Cyrene's torrid soil,°
905 Levied to side with warring Winds, and poise°
Their lighter wings. To whom these most adhere,
He rules a moment; Chaos Umpire sits,
And by decision more embroils the fray
By which he Reigns: next him high Arbiter
910 Chance governs all. Into this wild Abyss,
The Womb of nature and perhaps her Grave,
Of neither Sea, nor Shore, nor Air, nor Fire,
But all these in their pregnant causes mixt
Confus'dly, and which thus must ever fight,
915 Unless th'Almighty Maker them ordain
His dark materials to create more Worlds,
Into this wild Abyss the wary fiend
Stood on the brink of Hell and look'd a while,
Pondering his Voyage; for no narrow frith°
920 He had to cross. Nor was his ear less peal'd
With noises loud and ruinous (to compare
Great things with small) than when Bellona° storms,
With all her battering Engines bent to raze
Some Capital City, or less than if this frame
925 Of Heav'n were falling, and these Elements
In mutiny had from her Axle torn
The steadfast Earth. At last his Sail-broad Vans°
He spreads for flight, and in the surging smoke

900 **embryon** as yet unborn.   904 **torrid soil** In North Africa.   905
poise lend weight to.   919 **frith** estuary.   922 **Bellona** goddess of
war.   927 **Vans** wings.

Uplifted spurns the ground, thence many a League
As in a cloudy Chair ascending rides   930
Audacious, but that seat soon failing, meets
A vast vacuity: all unawares
Flutt'ring his pennons vain plumb-down he drops
Ten thousand fathom deep, and to this hour
Down had been falling, had not by ill chance   935
The strong rebuff of some tumultuous cloud
Instínct° with Fire and Nitre hurried him
As many miles aloft: that fury stay'd,
Quencht in a Boggy Syrtis,° neither Sea,
Nor good dry Land: nigh founder'd on he fares,   940
Treading the crude consistence, half on foot,
Half flying; behooves him now both Oar and Sail.
As when a Gryphon° through the Wilderness
With winged course o'er Hill or moory° Dale,
Pursues the Arimaspian,° who by stealth   945
Had from his wakeful custody purloin'd
The guarded Gold: So eagerly the fiend
O'er bog or steep, through strait, rough, dense, or
    rare,
With head, hands, wings, or feet pursues his way,
And swims or sinks, or wades, or creeps, or flies: 950
At length a universal hubbub wild
Of stunning sounds and voices all confus'd
Borne through the hollow dark assaults his ear
With loudest vehemence: thither he plies,
Undaunted to meet there whatever power   955
Or Spirit of the nethermost Abyss
Might in that noise reside, of whom to ask
Which way the nearest coast of darkness lies
Bordering on light; when straight behold the Throne
Of Chaos, and his dark Pavilion spread   960
Wide on the wasteful Deep; with him Enthron'd
Sat Sable-vested Night, eldest of things,
The consort of his Reign; and by them stood
Orcus and Ades, and the dreaded name
Of Demogorgon;° Rumour next and Chance,   965

937 **Instínct** charged.   939 **Syrtis** North African quicksand.   943
Gryphon a mythical monster.   944 **moory** marshy.   945 **Arimaspian** member of a European tribe.   964-65 Various names for the gods of Hell.

And Tumult and Confusion all embroil'd,
And Discord with a thousand various mouths.
   T'whom Satan turning boldly, thus. "Ye Powers
And Spirits of this nethermost Abyss,
970 Chaos and ancient Night, I come no spy,
With purpose to explore or to disturb
The secrets of your Realm, but by constraint
Wand'ring this darksome desert, as my way
Lies through your spacious Empire up to light,
975 Alone, and without guide, half lost, I seek
What readiest path leads where your gloomy bounds
Confine with° Heav'n; or if some other place
From your Dominion won, th'Ethereal King
Possesses lately, thither to arrive
980 I travel this profound, direct my course;
Directed, no mean recompense it brings
To your behoof,° if I that Region lost,
All usurpation thence expell'd, reduce
To her original darkness and your sway
985 (Which is my present journey) and once more
Erect the Standard there of ancient Night;
Yours be th'advantage all, mine the revenge."
   Thus Satan; and him thus the Anarch° old
With falt'ring speech and visage incompos'd°
990 Answer'd. "I know thee, stranger, who thou art,
That mighty leading Angel, who of late
Made head against Heav'n's King, though overthrown.
I saw and heard, for such a numerous host
Fled not in silence through the frighted deep
995 With ruin upon ruin, rout on rout,
Confusion worse confounded; and Heav'n Gates
Pour'd out by millions her victorious Bands
Pursuing. I upon my Frontiers here
Keep residence; if all I can will serve,
1000 That little which is left so to defend
Encroacht on still through our intestine° broils
Weak'ning the Scepter of old Night: first Hell

---

977 **Confine with** meet the confines of.   982 **behoof** advantage.
988 **Anarch** ruler of anarchy—which yet has no ruler.   989 **incompos'd** in discomposure and here applied to Chaos.   1001 **intestine** internal.

Your dungeon stretching far and wide beneath;
Now lately Heaven and Earth, another World
Hung o'er my Realm, link'd in a golden Chain   *1005*
To that side Heav'n from whence your Legions fell:
If that way be your walk, you have not far;
So much the nearer danger; go and speed;°
Havoc and spoil and ruin are my gain."

    He ceas'd; and Satan stay'd not to reply,   *1010*
But glad that now his Sea should find a shore,
With fresh alacrity and force renew'd
Springs upward like a Pyramid° of fire
Into the wild expanse, and through the shock
Of fighting Elements, on all sides round   *1015*
Environ'd wins his way; harder beset
And more endanger'd, than when Argo° pass'd
Through Bosporus betwixt the justling Rocks:
Or when Ulysses on the Larboard° shunn'd
Charybdis,° and by th'other whirlpool steer'd.   *1020*
So he with difficulty and labour hard
Mov'd on, with difficulty and labour hee;
But hee once past, soon after when man fell,
Strange alteration! Sin and Death amain
Following his track, such was the will of Heav'n,   *1025*
Pav'd after him a broad and beat'n way
Over the dark Abyss, whose boiling Gulf
Tamely endur'd a Bridge of wondrous length
From Hell continu'd reaching th'utmost Orb
Of this frail World; by which the Spirits perverse   *1030*
With easy intercourse pass to and fro
To tempt or punish mortals, except whom
God and good Angels guard by special grace.
But now at last the sacred influence
Of light appears, and from the walls of Heav'n   *1035*
Shoots far into the bosom of dim Night
A glimmering dawn; here Nature first begins
Her farthest verge, and Chaos to retire
As from her outmost works a brok'n foe
With tumult less and with less hostile din,   *1040*

1008 **speed** hurry and succeed.   1013 **Pyramid** The etymology is uncertain; it was held to be connected with "pyre," from the Greek for fire.   1017 **Argo** the ship of Jason and the Argonauts, seeking the Golden Fleece.   1019 **Larboard** left.   1020 **Charybdis** the whirlpool opposite the rock of Scylla in the Sicilian straits.

That Satan with less toil, and now with ease
Wafts on the calmer wave by dubious light
And like a weather-beaten Vessel holds°
Gladly the Port, though Shrouds and Tackle torn;
1045 Or in the emptier waste, resembling Air,
Weighs his spread wings, at leisure to behold
Far off th'Empyreal Heav'n, extended wide
In circuit, undetermin'd° square or round,
With Opal Tow'rs and Battlements adorn'd
1050 Of living° Sapphire, once his native Seat;
And fast by hanging in a golden Chain
This pendent° world, in bigness as a Star
Of smallest Magnitude close by the Moon.
Thither full fraught with mischievous revenge,
1055 Accurst, and in a cursed hour he hies.

BOOK III

THE ARGUMENT

God sitting on his Throne sees Satan flying towards this
world, then newly created; shows him to the Son who sat
at his right hand; foretells the success of Satan in per-
verting mankind; clears his own Justice and Wisdom from
all imputation, having created Man free and able enough
to have withstood his Tempter; yet declares his purpose
of grace towards him, in regard he fell not of his own
malice, as did Satan, but by him seduc't. The Son of God
renders praises to his Father for the manifestation of his
gracious purpose towards Man; but God again declares,
that Grace cannot be extended towards Man without the
satisfaction of divine Justice; Man hath offended the

1043 **holds** makes for.   1048 **undetermin'd** (to Satan's eye) not dis-
tinctly.   1050 **living** vivid.   1052 **pendent** hanging—but "Chain"
suggests that the universe is like a beautiful jewel or "pendent,"
liable to be stolen.

majesty of God by aspiring to Godhead, and therefore
with all his Progeny devoted to death must die, unless
someone can be found sufficient to answer for his offence,
and undergo his Punishment. The Son of God freely offers
himself a Ransom for Man: the Father accepts him,
ordains his incarnation, pronounces his exaltation above
all Names in Heaven and Earth; commands all the Angels
to adore him; they obey, and hymning to their Harps in
full Choir, celebrate the Father and the Son. Meanwhile
Satan alights upon the bare convex of this World's outer-
most Orb; where wand'ring he first finds a place since
call'd The Limbo of Vanity; what persons and things
fly up thither; thence comes to the Gate of Heaven,
describ'd ascending by stairs, and the waters above the
Firmament that flow about it: His passage thence to the
Orb of the Sun; he finds there Uriel the Regent of that
Orb, but first changes himself into the shape of a meaner
Angel; and pretending a zealous desire to behold the new
Creation and Man whom God had plac't here, inquires
of him the place of his habitation, and is directed; alights
first on Mount Niphates.

      Hail holy light, offspring of Heav'n first-born,
Or of th'Eternal Coeternal beam
May I express thee unblam'd?° since God is light,
And never but in unapproached light
Dwelt from Eternity, dwelt then in thee,   5
Bright effluence of bright essence increate.°
Or hear'st thou rather° pure Ethereal° stream,
Whose Fountain who shall tell? before the Sun,
Before the Heavens thou wert, and at the voice
Of God, as with a Mantle didst invest   10
The rising world of waters dark and deep,
Won from the void and formless infinite.
Thee I re-visit now with bolder wing,
Escap't the Stygian Pool, though long detain'd

2–3 "Or may I, without being censured, describe thee as co-eternal
with God?"   6 **increate** uncreated.   7 **hear'st thou rather** "dost thou
prefer to be called."   7 **Ethereal** airy and celestial.

15 In that obscure sojourn, while in my flight
    Through utter° and through middle darkness° borne
    With other notes than to th'Orphean° Lyre
    I sung of Chaos and Eternal Night,
    Taught by the heav'nly Muse to venture down
20 The dark descent, and up to reascend,
    Though hard and rare: thee I revisit safe,
    And feel thy sovran° vital Lamp; but thou
    Revisit'st not these eyes, that roll in vain
    To find thy piercing ray, and find no dawn;
25 So thick a drop serene hath quencht their Orbs,
    Or dim suffusion° veil'd. Yet not the more
    Cease I to wander where the Muses haunt°
    Clear Spring, or shady Grove, or Sunny Hill,°
    Smit with the love of sacred song; but chief
30 Thee Sion° and the flow'ry Brooks beneath
    That wash thy hallow'd feet, and warbling flow,
    Nightly I visit: nor sometimes° forget
    Those other two equall'd with me in Fate,
    So° were I equall'd with them in renown,
35 Blind Thamyris° and blind Maeonides,°
    And Tiresias° and Phineus° Prophets old.
    Then feed on thoughts, that voluntary° move°
    Harmonious numbers;° as the wakeful Bird
    Sings darkling, and in shadiest Covert hid
40 Tunes her nocturnal Note. Thus with the Year
    Seasons return, but not to me returns
    Day, or the sweet approach of Ev'n or Morn,
    Or sight of vernal bloom, or Summer's Rose,
    Or flocks, or herds, or human face divine;
45 But cloud instead, and ever-during dark

16 **utter** outer. **middle darkness** of Chaos. 17 **Orphean** of Orpheus,
who had visited Hell and to whom was attributed a Hymn to Night.
22 **sovran** supreme and (literally) "from above" (from Latin *super*);
it is too a medical term (notice "vital"), e.g. "sovereign in cases
where the eyelids are ulcerated," [1793]. 25–26 **drop . . . suffusion**
diseases of the eye. 26–27 "Yet my passion for classical poetry has
by no means been quenched." 28 Parnassus and Helicon. 30 **Sion**
evoking the Hebrew poetry of Scripture. 32 **sometimes** ever. 34
So if only. 35 **Thamyris** a Thracian poet. 35 **Maeonides** Homer.
36 **Tiresias** the blind sage of Thebes. 36 **Phineus** king of Thrace,
blinded by the gods. 37 **voluntary** freely, and with the musical
suggestions of a "voluntary," chosen by the performer. 37 **move** put
forth, utter (as in VII 207), and instigate. 38 **numbers** verses,
musical measures.

Surrounds me, from the cheerful ways of men
Cut off, and for the Book of knowledge fair
Presented with a Universal blank
Of Nature's works to mee expung'd and raz'd,
And wisdom at one entrance quite shut out.   50
So much the rather thou Celestial light
Shine inward, and the mind through all her powers
Irradiate, there plant eyes, all mist from thence
Purge and disperse, that I may see and tell
Of things invisible to mortal sight.   55
      Now had the Almighty Father from above,
From the pure Empyrean where he sits
High Thron'd above all heighth, bent down his eye,
His own works and their works at once to view:
About him all the Sanctities of Heaven   60
Stood thick as Stars, and from his sight° receiv'd
Beatitude past utterance; on his right
The radiant image of his Glory sat,
His only Son; On Earth he first beheld
Our two first Parents, yet the only two   65
Of mankind, in the happy Garden plac't,
Reaping immortal fruits of joy and love,
Uninterrupted joy, unrivall'd love
In blissful solitude; he then survey'd
Hell and the Gulf between, and Satan there   70
Coasting the wall of Heav'n on this side Night
In the dun Air sublime, and ready now
To stoop° with wearied wings, and willing feet
On the bare outside of this World,° that seem'd
Firm land imbosom'd without Firmament,   75
Uncertain which, in Ocean or in Air.
Him God beholding from his prospect high,
Wherein past, present, future he beholds,
Thus to his only Son foreseeing spake.
      "Only-begotten Son, seest thou what rage   80
Transports° our adversary, whom no bounds
Prescrib'd, no bars of Hell, nor all the chains
Heapt on him there, nor yet the main Abyss

---

61 **his sight** seeing him, the Beatific Vision.   73 **stoop** descend, with
"wings" suggesting the application "of a hawk or other bird of prey:
to descend swiftly on its prey"; see III 431–41.   74 **World** universe.
81 **Transports** literally and metaphorically.

Wide interrupt° can hold; so bent he seems
85   On desperate revenge, that shall redound
Upon his own rebellious head. And now
Through all restraint broke loose he wings his way
Not far off Heav'n, in the Precincts of light,
Directly towards the new created World,
90   And Man there plac't, with purpose to assay
If him by force he can destroy, or worse,
By some false guile pervert; and shall pervert;
For man will heark'n to his glozing° lies,
And easily transgress the sole Command,
95   Sole pledge of his obedience: So will fall
Hee and his faithless Progeny: whose fault?
Whose but his own? ingrate,° he had of mee
All he could have; I made him just and right,
Sufficient to have stood, though free to fall.
100 Such I created all th'Ethereal Powers
And Spirits, both them who stood and them who
    fail'd;
Freely they stood who stood, and fell who fell.
Not free, what proof could they have giv'n sincere
Of true allegiance, constant Faith or Love,
105 Where only what they needs must do, appear'd,
Not what they would? what praise could they receive?
What pleasure I from such obedience paid,
When Will and Reason (Reason also is choice)
Useless and vain, of freedom both despoil'd,
110 Made passive both, had serv'd necessity,
Not mee. They therefore as to right belong'd,
So were created, nor can justly accuse
Their maker, or their making, or their Fate;
As if Predestination over-rul'd
115 Their will, dispos'd by absolute Decree
Or high foreknowledge; they themselves decreed
Their own revolt, not I: if I foreknew,
Foreknowledge had no influence on their fault,
Which had no less prov'd certain unforeknown.
120 So without least impúlse° or shadow of Fate,
Or aught by me immutably foreseen,
    trespass, Authors to themselves in all

                    forming a wide gulf.   93 **glozing** flattering.   97
                    impúlse impelling.

Both what they judge and what they choose; for so
I form'd them free, and free they must remain,
Til they enthrall themselves: I else must change   129
Their nature, and revoke the high Decree
Unchangeable, Eternal, which ordain'd
Their freedom, they themselves ordain'd their fall.
The first sort° by their own suggestion° fell,
Self-tempted, self-deprav'd: Man falls deceiv'd   130
By the other first: Man therefore shall find grace,
The other none: in Mercy and Justice both,
Through Heav'n and Earth, so shall my glory excel,
But Mercy first and last shall brightest shine."

   Thus while God spake, ambrosial fragrance
    fill'd   135
All Heav'n, and in the blessed Spirits elect
Sense of new joy ineffable diffus'd:
Beyond compare the Son of God was seen
Most glorious, in him all his Father shone
Substantially° express'd, and in his face   140
Divine compassion visibly appear'd,
Love without end, and without measure Grace,
Which uttering thus he to his Father spake.

   "O Father, gracious was that word which
    clos'd
Thy sovran sentence, that Man should find grace;   145
For which both Heav'n and Earth shall high extol
Thy praises, with th'innumerable° sound
Of Hymns and sacred Songs, wherewith thy Throne
Encompass'd shall resound thee ever blest.
For should Man finally be lost, should Man   150
Thy creature late so lov'd, thy youngest Son
Fall circumvented° thus by fraud, though join'd
With his own folly? that be from thee far,
That far be from thee, Father, who art Judge
Of all things made, and judgest only right.   155
Or shall the Adversary thus obtain
His end, and frustrate thine, shall he fulfill
His malice, and thy goodness bring to naught,

---

129 **first sort** fallen angels. 129 **suggestion** temptation. 140 **Substantially** a theological term, as in "transubstantiation." 147 **innumerable** in 17th-century English, commonly used with a singular noun. 152 **circumvented** contrasted with "Encompass'd."

Or proud return though to his heavier doom,
160 Yet with revenge accomplish't and to Hell
Draw after him the whole Race of mankind,
By him corrupted? or wilt though thyself
Abolish thy Creation, and unmake,
For him, what for thy glory thou hast made?
165 So should thy goodness and thy greatness both
Be question'd and blasphem'd without defence."
　　　To whom the great Creator thus repli'd.
"O Son, in whom my Soul hath chief delight,
Son of my bosom, Son who art alone
170 My word, my wisdom, and effectual might,°
All hast thou spok'n as my thoughts are, all
As my Eternal purpose hath decreed:
Man shall not quite be lost, but sav'd who will,
Yet not of will in him, but grace in me
175 Freely vouchsaf't; once more I will renew
His lapsed powers, though forfeit and enthrall'd
By sin to foul exorbitant desires;
Upheld by me, yet once more he shall stand
On even ground against his mortal foe,
180 By me upheld, that he may know how frail
His fall'n condition is, and to me owe
All his deliv'rance, and to none but me.
Some I have chosen of peculiar grace
Elect above the rest; so is my will:
185 The rest shall hear me call, and oft be warn'd
Their sinful state, and to appease betimes
Th'incensed° Deity, while offer'd grace
Invites; for I will clear their senses dark,
What may suffice, and soft'n stony hearts
190 To pray, repent, and bring obedience due.
To prayer, repentance, and obedience due,
Though but endeavour'd with sincere intent,
Mine ear shall not be slow, mine eye not shut.
And I will place within them as a guide
195 My Umpire Conscience, whom if they will hear,
Light after light well us'd they shall attain,

170 **effectual might** through whom my might takes effect, "effectual"
having many theological applications, e.g. to prayers, grace. 187
incensed burning with wrath; "appease" suggests the need to offer
"incense" before God, as in "the incensed altar," [1611]. The root of
the words is the same, and see XI 17–20.

And to the end persisting, safe arrive.
This my long sufferance and my day of grace
They who neglect and scorn, shall never taste;
But hard be hard'n'd, blind be blinded more,   200
That they may stumble on, and deeper fall;
And none but such from mercy I exclude.
But yet all is not done; Man disobeying,
Disloyal breaks his fealty, and sins
Against the high Supremacy of Heav'n,   205
Affecting° Godhead, and so losing all,
To expiate his Treason hath naught left,
But to destruction sacred and devote,°
He with his whole posterity must die,
Die hee or Justice must; unless for him   210
Some other able, and as willing, pay
The rigid° satisfaction,° death for death.
Say Heav'nly Powers, where shall we find such love,
Which of ye will be mortal to redeem
Man's mortal crime, and just th'unjust to save,   215
Dwells in all Heaven charity so dear?"
          He ask'd, but all the Heav'nly Choir stood
            mute,
And silence was in Heav'n: on man's behalf
Patron° or Intercessor none appear'd,
Much less that durst upon his own head draw   220
The deadly forfeiture, and ransom set.
And now without redemption all mankind
Must have been lost, adjudg'd to Death and Hell
By doom severe, had not the Son of God,
In whom the fullness dwells of love divine,   225
His dearest mediation thus renew'd.
          "Father, thy word is past, man shall find grace;
And shall grace not find means, that finds her way,
The speediest of thy winged messengers,
To visit all thy creatures, and to all   230
Comes unprevented,° unimplor'd, unsought,
Happy for man, so coming; he her aid
Can never seek, once dead in sins and lost;

206 **Affecting** aiming at.   208 **devote** doomed by a vow.   212 **rigid**
strict, with deathly suggestions (see IX 685).   212 **satisfaction** atone-
ment, the theological term for Christ's sacrifice.   219 **Patron** de-
fender.   231 **unprevented** unforestalled, before being even asked
for.

Atonement for himself or offering meet,
235 Indebted and undone, hath none to bring:
Behold mee then, mee for him, life for life
I offer, on mee let thine anger fall;
Account mee man; I for his sake will leave
Thy bosom, and this glory next to thee
240 Freely put off, and for him lastly die
Well pleas'd, on me let Death wreak all his rage;
Under his gloomy power I shall not long
Lie vanquisht; thou hast giv'n me to possess
Life in myself forever, by thee I live,
245 Though now to Death I yield, and am his due
All that of me can die, yet that debt paid,
Thou wilt not leave me in the loathsome grave
His prey, nor suffer my unspotted Soul
Forever with corruption there to dwell;
250 But I shall rise Victorious, and subdue
My Vanquisher, spoil'd of his vaunted spoil;
Death his death's wound shall then receive, and stoop
Inglorious, of his mortal sting disarm'd.
I through the ample Air in Triumph high
255 Shall lead Hell Captive maugre° Hell, and show
The powers of darkness bound. Thou at the sight
Pleas'd, out of Heaven shalt look down and smile,
While by thee rais'd I ruin all my Foes,
Death last, and with his Carcass glut the Grave:
260 Then with the multitude of my redeem'd
Shall enter Heaven long absent, and return,
Father, to see thy face, wherein no cloud
Of anger shall remain, but peace assur'd,
And reconcilement; wrath shall be no more
265 Thenceforth, but in thy presence Joy entire."
            His words here ended, but his meek aspéct
Silent yet spake, and breath'd immortal love
To mortal men, above which only shone
Filial obedience: as a sacrifice
270 Glad to be offer'd, he attends the will
Of his great Father. Admiration seiz'd
All Heav'n, what this might mean, and whither tend
Wond'ring; but soon th'Almighty thus repli'd:
            "O thou in Heav'n and Earth the only peace

255 **maugre** despite.

Found out for mankind under wrath, O thou   *275*
My sole complacence!° well thou know'st how dear
To me are all my works, nor Man the least
Though last created, that for him I spare
Thee from my bosom and right hand, to save,
By losing thee a while, the whole Race lost.   *280*
Thou therefore whom thou only canst redeem,
Their Nature° also to thy Nature join;
And be thyself Man among men on Earth,
Made flesh, when time shall be, of Virgin seed,
By wondrous birth: Be thou in Adam's room   *285*
The Head of all mankind, though Adam's Son.
As in him perish all men, so in thee
As from a second root shall be restor'd,
As many as are restor'd, without thee none.
His crime makes guilty all his Sons, thy merit   *290*
Imputed° shall absolve them who renounce
Their own both righteous and unrighteous deeds,
And live in thee transplanted,° and from thee
Receive new life. So Man, as is most just,
Shall satisfy for Man, be judg'd and die,   *295*
And dying rise, and rising with him raise
His Brethren, ransom'd with his own dear life.
So Heav'nly love shall outdo Hellish hate,
Giving° to death, and dying to redeem,
So dearly to redeem what Hellish hate   *300*
So easily destroy'd, and still destroys
In those who, when they may, accept not grace.
Nor shalt thou by descending to assume
Man's Nature, less'n or degrade thine own.
Because thou hast, though Thron'd in highest bliss   *305*
Equal to God, and equally enjoying
Godlike fruition,° quitted all to save
A World from utter loss, and hast been found
By Merit more than Birthright Son of God,
Found worthiest to be so by being Good,   *310*
Far more than Great or High; because in thee
Love hath abounded more than Glory abounds,

276 **complacence** source of delight.   281–82 **whom . . . their Nature**
"the nature of them whom only thou canst redeem."   291 **Imputed**
the doctrine of imputed righteousness.   293 **transplanted** suggesting
a new and better kind of growth; see "root" above.   299 **Giving**
yielding.   307 **fruition** pleasure in possession.

Therefore thy Humiliation shall exalt
With thee thy Manhood also to this Throne;
315 Here shalt thou sit incarnate, here shalt Reign
Both God and Man, Son both of God and Man,
Anointed universal King; all Power
I give thee, reign forever, and assume
Thy Merits;° under thee as Head Supreme
320 Thrones, Princedoms, Powers, Dominions I reduce:
All knees to thee shall bow, of them that bide
In Heaven, or Earth, or under Earth in Hell;
When thou attended gloriously from Heav'n
Shalt in the Sky appear, and from thee send
325 The summoning Arch-Angels to proclaim
Thy dread Tribunal: forthwith from all Winds
The living, and forthwith the cited° dead
Of all past Ages to the general Doom
Shall hast'n, such a peal shall rouse their sleep.
330 Then all thy Saints assembl'd, thou shalt judge
Bad men and Angels, they arraign'd° shall sink
Beneath thy Sentence; Hell, her numbers full,
Thenceforth shall be forever shut. Meanwhile
The World shall burn, and from her ashes spring
335 New Heav'n and Earth, wherein the just shall dwell,
And after all their tribulations long
See golden days, fruitful of golden deeds,
With Joy and Love triúmphing, and fair Truth.
Then thou thy regal Scepter shalt lay by,
340 For regal Scepter then no more shall need,
God shall be All in All. But all ye Gods,
Adore him, who to compass all this dies,
Adore the Son, and honour him as mee."
        No sooner had th'Almighty ceas't, but all
345 The multitude of Angels with a shout
Loud as from numbers without number, sweet
As from blest voices, uttering joy, Heav'n rung
With Jubilee,° and loud Hosannas° fill'd
Th'eternal Regions: lowly reverent

318–19 **assume Thy merits** take up that to which your merits entitle
you, "merits" having the specific theological sense "good works
entitled to reward from God." 327 **cited** summoned (legal). 331
arraign'd accused. 348 **Jubilee** jubilation. 348 **Hosannas** cries of
praise, the literal meaning "Save now" or "Save, pray" being ap-
propriate to Christ's triumph.

Towards either Throne they bow, and to the ground   350
With solemn adoration down they cast
Their Crowns inwove with Amaranth and Gold,
Immortal Amaranth, a Flow'r which once
In Paradise, fast by the Tree of Life
Began to bloom, but soon for man's offence   355
To Heav'n remov'd where first it grew, there grows,
And flow'rs aloft shading the Fount of Life,
And where the river of Bliss through midst of Heav'n
Rolls o'er Elysian Flow'rs her Amber stream;
With these that never fade the Spirits Elect   360
Bind their resplendent locks inwreath'd with beams,
Now in loose Garlands thick thrown off, the bright
Pavement that like a Sea of Jasper shone
Impurpl'd with Celestial Roses smil'd.
Then Crown'd again their gold'n Harps they took,   365
Harps ever tun'd, that glittering by their side
Like Quivers hung, and with Preamble sweet
Of charming symphony they introduce
Their sacred Song, and waken raptures high;
No voice exempt, no voice but well could join   370
Melodious part, such concord is in Heav'n.
       Thee Father first they sung Omnipotent,
Immutable, Immortal, Infinite,
Eternal King; thee Author of all being,
Fountain of Light, thyself invisible   375
Amidst the glorious brightness where thou sitt'st
Thron'd inaccessible, but° when thou shad'st
The full blaze of thy beams, and through a cloud
Drawn round about thee like a radiant Shrine,
Dark with excessive bright thy skirts° appear,   380
Yet dazzle Heav'n, that brightest Seraphim
Approach not, but with both wings veil their eyes.
Thee next they sang of all Creation first,
Begotten Son, Divine Similitude,
In whose conspicuous count'nance, without cloud   385
Made visible, th'Almighty Father shines,
Whom else no Creature can behold; on thee
Imprest the effulgence° of his Glory abides,
Transfus'd on thee his ample Spirit rests.
Hee Heav'n of Heavens and all the Powers therein   390

377 but except.   380 skirts robes.   388 effulgence gleaming forth.

By thee created, and by thee threw down
Th'aspiring Dominations: thou that day
Thy Father's dreadful Thunder didst not spare,
Nor stop thy flaming Chariot-wheels, that shook
395 Heav'n's everlasting Frame, while o'er the necks
Thou drov'st of warring Angels disarray'd.
Back from pursuit thy Powers with loud acclaim
Thee only extoll'd, Son of thy Father's might,
To execute fierce vengeance on his foes,
400 Not so on Man; him through their malice fall'n,
Father of Mercy and Grace, thou didst not doom
So strictly, but much more to pity incline:
No sooner did thy dear and only Son
Perceive thee purpos'd not to doom frail Man
405 So strictly, but much more to pity inclin'd,
He to appease thy wrath, and end the strife
Of Mercy and Justice in thy face discern'd,
Regardless of the Bliss wherein hee sat
Second to thee, offer'd himself to die
410 For man's offence. O unexampl'd love,
Love nowhere to be found less than Divine!
Hail Son of God, Saviour of Men, thy Name
Shall be the copious matter of my Song
Henceforth, and never shall my Harp thy praise
415 Forget, nor from thy Father's praise disjoin.
          Thus they in Heav'n, above the starry Sphere,
Their happy hours in joy and hymning spent.
Meanwhile upon the firm opacous° Globe
Of this round World,° whose first convex° divides
420 The luminous inferior Orbs,° enclos'd
From Chaos and th'inroad of Darkness old,
Satan alighted walks: a Globe far off
It seem'd, now seems a boundless Continent
Dark, waste, and wild, under the frown of Night
425 Starless expos'd, and ever-threat'ning storms
Of Chaos blust'ring round, inclement sky;
Save on that side which from the wall of Heav'n
Though distant far some small reflection gains
Of glimmering air less vext with tempest loud:
430 Here walk'd the Fiend at large in spacious field.

418 **opacous** dark, opaque.   419 **World** universe.   419 **first convex**
outer shell.   420 **inferior Orbs** the "spheres" within.

As when a Vulture on Imaus° bred,
Whose snowy ridge the roving Tartar bounds,°
Dislodging° from a Region scarce of prey
To gorge the flesh of Lambs or yeanling° Kids
On Hills where Flocks are fed, flies toward the Springs   435
Of Ganges or Hydaspes, Indian streams;
But in his way 'lights on the barren plains
Of Sericana, where Chineses drive
With Sails and Wind their cany Waggons light:
So on this windy Sea of Land, the Fiend   440
Walk'd up and down alone bent on his prey,
Alone, for other Creature in this place
Living or liveless to be found was none,
None yet, but store° hereafter from the earth
Up hither like Aërial vapours flew   445
Of all things transitory and vain, when Sin
With vanity had fill'd the works of men:
Both all things vain, and all who in vain things
Built their fond hopes of Glory or lasting fame,
Or happiness in this or th'other life;   450
All who have their reward on Earth, the fruits
Of painful° Superstition and blind Zeal,
Naught seeking but the praise of men, here find
Fit retribution, empty as their deeds;
All th'unaccomplisht works of Nature's hand,   455
Abortive,° monstrous, or unkindly° mixt,
Dissolv'd on earth, fleet hither, and in vain,°
Till final dissolution, wander here,
Not in the neighbouring Moon, as some have dream'd;
Those argent Fields more likely habitants,   460
Translated° Saints, or middle Spirits hold
Betwixt th'Angelical and Human kind:
Hither of ill-join'd Sons and Daughters born
First from the ancient World those Giants came
With many a vain exploit, though then renown'd: 465
The builders next of Babel on the Plain

431 **Imaus** mountains of central Asia.   432 **Tartar bounds** "confines
the Tartar," the cruel race of central Asia (also suggesting Hell,
Tartarus, where the vulture Satan began his journey; see II 858 and
X 431).   433 **Dislodging** a hunting term.   434 **yeanling** newborn.
444 **store** plenty.   452 **painful** including laborious.   456 **Abortive**
untimely born.   456 **unkindly** unnaturally.   457 **in vain** idly.   461
Translated like Enoch and Elijah, "translated" to Heaven by mira-
cle.

Of Sennaär, and still with vain design°
New Babels, had they wherewithal, would build:
Others came single; hee who to be deem'd
470 A God, leap'd fondly° into Etna flames,
Empedocles, and hee who to enjoy
Plato's Elysium, leap'd into the Sea,
Cleombrotus, and many more too long,
Embryos and Idiots, Eremites° and Friars
475 White, Black and Grey, with all their trumpery.°
Here Pilgrims roam, that stray'd so far to seek
In Golgotha° him dead, who lives in Heav'n;
And they who to be sure of Paradise
Dying put on the weeds° of Dominic,
480 Or in Franciscan think to pass disguis'd;
They pass the Planets seven, and pass the fixt,°
And that Crystálline Sphere whose balance weighs
The Trepidation talkt,° and that first mov'd;°
And now Saint Peter at Heav'n's Wicket° seems
485 To wait them with his Keys, and now at foot
Of Heav'n's ascent they lift their Feet, when lo
A violent cross-wind from either Coast
Blows them transverse ten thousand Leagues awry
Into the devious° Air; then might ye see
490 Cowls, Hoods and Habits with their wearers tost
And flutter'd into Rags, then Relics, Beads,°
Indulgences, Dispenses,° Pardons, Bulls,°
The sport of Winds: all these upwhirl'd aloft
Fly o'er the backside° of the World far off
495 Into a Limbo° large and broad, since call'd
The Paradise of Fools, to few unknown
Long after, now unpeopl'd, and untrod;
All this dark Globe the Fiend found as he pass'd,
And long he wander'd, till at last a gleam
500 Of dawning light turn'd thitherward in haste

---

467 **design** sardonically both intention and architectural plan.   470
fondly foolishly.   474 **Eremites** hermits.   475 **trumpery** deceitful
trash.   477 **Golgotha** where Christ was crucified.   479 **weeds** robes.
481 **the fixt** the sphere of the stars.   482–83 **whose . . . talkt** "which
is responsible for the swaying which is spoken of."   483 **first mov'd**
the tenth sphere, the Primum Mobile.   484 **Wicket** gate.   489 **de-
vious** both distant and causing to stray.   491 **Beads** of the rosary.
492 **Dispenses** dispensations.   492 **Bulls** papal edicts.   494 **backside**
contemptuous after "Winds," recalling the landscape of Hell.   495
Limbo region on the border of Hell.

His travell'd° steps; far distant hee descries
Ascending by degrees magnificent
Up to the wall of Heaven a Structure high,
At top whereof, but far more rich appear'd
The work as of a Kingly Palace Gate   505
With Frontispiece° of Diamond and Gold
Embellisht, thick with sparkling orient Gems
The Portal shone, inimitable on Earth
By Model, or by shading Pencil drawn.
The Stairs were such as whereon Jacob saw   510
Angels ascending and descending, bands
Of Guardians bright, when he from Esau fled
To Padan-Aram in the field of Luz,
Dreaming by night under the open Sky,
And waking cri'd, "This is the Gate of Heav'n."   515
Each Stair mysteriously° was meant, nor stood
There always, but drawn up to Heav'n sometimes
Viewless,° and underneath a bright Sea flow'd
Of Jasper, or of liquid Pearl, whereon
Who after came from Earth, sailing arriv'd,   520
Wafted by Angels, or flew o'er the Lake
Rapt in a Chariot drawn by fiery Steeds.
The Stairs were then let down, whether to dare
The Fiend by easy ascent, or aggravate°
His sad exclusion from the doors of Bliss.   525
Direct against which op'n'd from beneath,
Just o'er the blissful seat of Paradise,
A passage down to th'Earth, a passage wide,
Wider by far than that of after-times
Over Mount Sion, and, though that were large,   530
Over the Promis'd Land to God so dear,
By which, to visit oft those happy Tribes,
On high behests his Angels to and fro
Pass'd frequent, and° his eye with choice regard°
From Paneas the fount of Jordan's flood   535
To Beërsaba, where the Holy Land
Borders on Egypt and the Arabian shore;

501 **travell'd** including travailed, weary.   506 **Frontispiece** panel or
pediment.   516 **mysteriously** allegorically, as in the Book of Revela-
tion.   518 **Viewless** not in sight.   524 **aggravate** make more burden-
some.   534 **and** and so did.   534 **choice regard** careful scrutiny, sug-
gesting too God's "regard" (esteem) for his Chosen People (see the
same phrase, I 653).

So wide the op'ning seem'd, where bounds were set
To darkness, such as bound the Ocean wave.
540 Satan from hence now on the lower stair
That scal'd by steps of Gold to Heav'n Gate
Looks down with wonder at the sudden view
Of all this World at once. As when a Scout°
Through dark and desert ways with peril gone
545 All night; at last by break of cheerful dawn
Obtains° the brow of some high-climbing Hill,
Which to his eye discovers° unaware
The goodly prospect of some foreign land
First-seen, or some renown'd Metropolis
550 With glistering Spires and Pinnacles adorn'd,
Which now the Rising Sun gilds with his beams.
Such wonder seiz'd, though after Heaven seen,
The Spirit malign, but much more envy seiz'd
At sight of all this World beheld so fair.
555 Round he surveys, and well might, where he stood
So high above the circling Canopy
Of Night's extended shade; from Eastern Point
Of Libra to the fleecy Star° that bears
Andromeda° far off Atlantic Seas
560 Beyond th'Horizon; then from Pole to Pole
He views in breadth, and without longer pause
Down right into the World's first Region° throws
His flight precipitant,° and winds with ease
Through the pure marble° Air his oblique way
565 Amongst innumerable Stars, that shone
Stars distant, but nigh-hand seem'd other Worlds,
Or other Worlds they seem'd, or happy Isles,
Like those Hesperian Gardens° fam'd of old,
Fortunate Fields, and Groves and flow'ry Vales,
570 Thrice happy Isles, but who dwelt happy there
He stay'd not to inquire: above them all
The golden Sun in splendour likest Heaven
Allur'd his eye: Thither his course he bends
Through the calm Firmament; but up or down

543 **Scout** The military hint is ominous; see VI 529.   546 **Obtains**
gains.   547 **discovers** reveals.   558 **Libra . . . Star** the Scales and
the Ram.   559 **Andromeda** a northern constellation.   562 **first Re-
gion** of the air.   563 **precipitant** headlong and speedy.   564 **marble**
lucid.   568 **Hesperian Gardens** a Paradise, yet its apples were stolen.

By center, or eccentric, hard to tell,   575
Or Longitude, where the great Luminary°
Aloof° the vulgar° Constellations thick,
That from his Lordly eye keep distance due,
Dispenses Light from far; they as they move
Their Starry dance in numbers° that compute   580
Days, months, and years, towards his all-cheering
   Lamp
Turn swift their various motions, or are turn'd
By his Magnetic beam, that gently warms
The Universe, and to each inward part
With gentle penetration, though unseen,   585
Shoots invisible virtue even to the deep:
So wondrously was set his Station bright.
There lands the Fiend, a spot like which perhaps
Astronomer in the Sun's lucent Orb
Through his glaz'd Optic Tube yet never saw.   590
The place he found beyond expression bright,
Compar'd with aught on Earth, Metal or Stone;
Not all parts like, but all alike inform'd°
With radiant light, as glowing Iron with fire;
If metal, part seem'd Gold, part Silver clear;   595
If stone, Carbuncle most or Chrysolite,
Ruby or Topaz, to the Twelve that shone
In Aaron's Breastplate, and a stone besides
Imagin'd rather oft than elsewhere seen,
That stone,° or like to that which here below   600
Philosophers in vain so long have sought,
In vain, though by their powerful Art they bind
Volatile Hermes,° and call up unbound
In various shapes old Proteus° from the Sea,
Drain'd through a Limbec° to his Native form.   605
What wonder then if fields and regions here°

574–76 Not choosing between Copernicus's theory (sun-centered) and
Ptolemy's (earth-centered).   576 **Luminary** source of light, includ-
ing the sense of a person (notice "Lordly")—the poet Skelton called
God a luminary.   577 **Aloof** away from.   577 **vulgar** The stars form
constellations just as the common people form a crowd, Latin
vulgus.   580 **numbers** musical measures.   593 **inform'd** imbued.
600 **stone** The "philosopher's stone" which would turn base metals
to gold.   602–03 **bind … Hermes** use mercury in their experiments,
it tending to evaporate.   604 **Proteus** sea-god who could continually
change his shape, much as substances do in experiments.   605
Limbec a still, or glass alembic.   606 **here** in the sun.

Breathe forth Elixir pure, and Rivers run
Potable° Gold, when with one virtuous° touch
Th'Arch-chemic° Sun so far from us remote
610 Produces with Terrestrial Humour mixt°
Here in the dark so many precious things
Of colour glorious and effect so rare?
Here matter new to gaze the Devil met
Undazzl'd, far and wide his eye commands,
615 For sight no obstacle found here, nor shade,
But all Sunshine, as when his Beams at Noon
Culminate from th'Equator,° as they now
Shot upward still direct, whence no way round
Shadow from body opaque can fall, and the Air,
620 Nowhere so clear, sharp'n'd his visual ray
To objects distant far, whereby he soon
Saw within ken a glorious Angel stand,
The same whom John saw also in the Sun:
His back was turn'd, but not his brightness hid;
625 Of beaming sunny Rays, a golden tiar°
Circl'd his Head, nor less his Locks behind
Illustrious° on his Shoulders fledge° with wings
Lay waving round; on some great charge employ'd
Hee seem'd, or fixt in cogitation deep.
630 Glad was the Spirit impure as now in hope
To find who might direct his wand'ring flight
To Paradise the happy seat of Man,
His journey's end and our beginning woe.
But first he casts° to change his proper shape,
635 Which else might work him danger or delay:
And now a stripling Cherub he appears,
Not of the prime,° yet such as in his face
Youth smil'd Celestial, and to every Limb
Suitable grace diffus'd, so well he feign'd;
640 Under a Coronet his flowing hair
In curls on either cheek play'd, wings he wore

---

608 Potable drinkable; such a preparation from gold was used as a medicine, and is here assimilated to the magical elixir.   **608 virtuous** powerful, energizing.   **609 Arch-chemic** greatest alchemist of all. **610 with . . . mixt** even though mixed with the earth's damp.   **616–17 as . . . Equator** the shadowless counterpart of the sun's "culmination," high noon at the equator.   **625 tiar** crown.   **627 Illustrious** with luster.   **627 fledge** feathered.   **634 casts** both "cunningly contrives," and "throws off (clothes, appearance)."   **637 prime** mature youth (?).

Of many a colour'd plume sprinkl'd with Gold,
His habit fit for speed succinct,° and held
Before his decent° steps a Silver wand.
He drew not nigh unheard, the Angel bright,   645
Ere he drew nigh, his radiant visage turn'd,
Admonisht by his ear, and straight was known
Th'Arch-Angel Uriel, one of the sev'n
Who in God's presence, nearest to his Throne
Stand ready at command, and are his Eyes   650
That run through all the Heav'ns, or down to th'Earth
Bear his swift errands over moist and dry,
O'er Sea and Land: him Satan thus accosts.
          "Uriel, for thou of those sev'n Spirits that stand
In sight of God's high Throne, gloriously bright,   655
The first art wont his great authentic° will
Interpreter through highest Heav'n to bring,
Where all his Sons thy Embassy attend;
And here art likeliest by supreme decree
Like honour to obtain, and as his Eye   660
To visit oft this new Creation round;
Unspeakable desire to see, and know
All these his wondrous works, but chiefly Man,
His chief delight and favour, him for whom
All these his works so wondrous he ordain'd,   665
Hath brought me from the Choirs of Cherubim
Alone thus wand'ring. Brightest Seraph tell
In which of all these shining Orbs hath Man
His fixed seat, or fixed seat hath none,
But all these shining Orbs his choice to dwell;   670
That I may find him, and with secret gaze,
Or open admiration him behold
On whom the great Creator hath bestow'd
Worlds, and on whom hath all these graces pour'd;
That both in him and all things, as is meet,   675
The Universal Maker we may praise;
Who justly hath driv'n out his Rebel Foes
To deepest Hell, and to repair that loss
Created this new happy Race of Men
To serve him better: wise are all his ways."   680
          So spake the false dissembler unperceiv'd;

643 **succinct** close-fitting.   644 **decent** seemly.   656 **authentic** of
first-hand authority.

For neither Man nor Angel can discern
Hypocrisy, the only evil that walks
Invisible, except to God alone,
685 By his permissive will, through Heav'n and Earth:
And oft though wisdom wake, suspicion sleeps
At wisdom's Gate, and to simplicity
Resigns her charge, while goodness thinks no ill
Where no ill seems: Which now for once beguil'd
690 Uriel, though Regent of the Sun, and held
The sharpest-sighted Spirit of all in Heav'n;
Who to the fraudulent Impostor foul
In his uprightness answer thus return'd.
"Fair Angel, thy desire which tends° to know
695 The works of God, thereby to glorify
The great Work-Master, leads to no excess
That reaches blame, but rather merits praise
The more it seems excess, that led thee hither
From thy Empyreal Mansion thus alone,
700 To witness with thine eyes what some perhaps
Contented with report hear only in Heav'n:
For wonderful indeed are all his works,
Pleasant to know, and worthiest to be all
Had in remembrance always with delight;
705 But what created mind can comprehend
Their number, or the wisdom infinite
That brought them forth, but hid their causes deep.
I saw when at his Word the formless Mass,
This world's material mould, came to a heap:
710 Confusion heard his voice, and wild uproar
Stood rul'd, stood vast infinitude confin'd;
Till at his second bidding darkness fled,
Light shone, and order from disorder sprung:
Swift to their several Quarters hasted then
715 The cumbrous° Elements, Earth, Flood, Air, Fire,
And this Ethereal quintessence of Heav'n
Flew upward, spirited° with various forms,
That roll'd orbicular,° and turn'd to Stars
Numberless, as thou seest, and how they move;

694 tends is drawn.   715 cumbrous in comparison with the heavenly
ether (like light), the "quintessence," fifth essence, of which the
heavenly bodies were composed.   717 spirited animated.   718 or-
bicular with circular motion.

Each had his place appointed, each his course, 720
The rest in circuit walls this Universe.
Look downward on that Globe whose hither side
With light from hence, though but reflected, shines;
That place is Earth the seat of Man, that light
His day, which else as th'other Hemisphere 725
Night would invade, but there the neighbouring Moon
(So call that opposite fair Star) her aid
Timely interposes, and her monthly round
Still ending, still renewing, through mid-Heav'n,
With borrow'd light her countenance triform° 730
Hence fills and empties to enlighten the Earth,
And in her pale dominion checks° the night.
That spot to which I point is Paradise,
Adam's abode, those lofty shades his Bow'r.
Thy way thou canst not miss, me mine requires." 735
       Thus said, he turn'd, and Satan bowing low,
As to superior Spirits is wont in Heav'n,
Where honour due and reverence none neglects,
Took leave, and toward the coast of Earth beneath,
Down from th'Ecliptic,° sped° with hop'd success, 740
Throws his steep flight in many an Airy wheel,
Nor stay'd, till on Niphates'° top he 'lights.

BOOK IV

THE ARGUMENT

Satan now in prospect of Eden, and nigh the place where
he must now attempt the bold enterprise which he under-
took alone against God and Man, falls into many doubts
with himself, and many passions, fear, envy, and despair;

730 **triform** having three forms, crescent, full, and waning (and sug-
gesting the three goddesses of the moon). 732 **checks** both "holds
in check, curbs," and "chequers, variegates with its rays" as in
Robert Greene: "checkt the night with the golden rays," (1590,
O.E.D.). 740 **Ecliptic** the apparent orbit of the sun around the
earth. 740 **sped** spurred on, with a suggestion of "prospered"
("hop'd success"). 742 **Niphates** mountain of Armenia.

but at length confirms himself in evil, journeys on to
Paradise, whose outward prospect and situation is de-
scribed, overleaps the bounds, sits in the shape of a Cor-
morant on the Tree of life, as highest in the Garden to
look about him. The Garden describ'd; Satan's first sight
of Adam and Eve; his wonder at their excellent form and
happy state, but with resolution to work their fall; over-
hears their discourse, thence gathers that the Tree of
knowledge was forbidden them to eat of, under penalty
of death; and thereon intends to found his temptation, by
seducing them to transgress: then leaves them a while,
to know further of their state by some other means.
Meanwhile Uriel descending on a Sunbeam warns Gabriel,
who had in charge the Gate of Paradise, that some evil
spirit had escap'd the Deep, and past at Noon by his
Sphere in the shape of a good Angel down to Paradise,
discovered after by his furious gestures in the Mount.
Gabriel promises to find him out ere morning. Night com-
ing on, Adam and Eve discourse of going to their rest:
their Bower describ'd; their Evening worship. Gabriel
drawing forth his Bands of Night-watch to walk the round
of Paradise, appoints two strong Angels to Adam's Bower,
lest the evil spirit should be there doing some harm to
Adam or Eve sleeping; there they find him at the ear of
Eve, tempting her in a dream, and bring him, though
unwilling, to Gabriel; by whom question'd, he scornfully
answers, prepares resistance, but hinder'd by a Sign from
Heaven, flies out of Paradise.

       O for that warning voice, which he who saw
Th'Apocalypse, heard cry in Heav'n aloud,°
Then when the Dragon, put to second rout,
Came furious down to be reveng'd on men,
5 *Woe to the inhabitants on Earth!* that now,
While time was, our first Parents had been warn'd
The coming of their secret foe, and 'scap'd
Haply so 'scap'd his mortal snare; for now
Satan, now first inflam'd with rage, came down,

1–2 O for . . . aloud St. John, REVELATION 12:3–12.

The Tempter ere th'Accuser of mankind,   10
To wreak on innocent frail Man his loss
Of that first Battle, and his flight to Hell:
Yet not rejoicing in his speed, though bold,
Far off and fearless, nor with cause to boast,
Begins his dire attempt, which nigh the birth   15
Now rolling, boils in his tumultuous breast,
And like a devilish Engine back recoils
Upon himself; horror and doubt distract°
His troubl'd thoughts, and from the bottom stir
The Hell within him, for within him Hell   20
He brings, and round about him, nor from Hell
One step no more than from himself can fly
By change of place: Now conscience wakes despair
That slumber'd, wakes the bitter memory
Of what he was, what is, and what must be   25
Worse; of worse deeds worse sufferings must ensue.
Sometimes towards Eden which now in his view
Lay pleasant,° his griev'd look he fixes sad,
Sometimes towards Heav'n and the full-blazing Sun,
Which now sat high in his Meridian Tow'r: 30
Then much revolving, thus in sighs began.

        "O thou that with surpassing Glory crown'd,
Look'st° from thy sole° Dominion like the God
Of this new World; at whose sight all the Stars
Hide their diminisht heads; to thee I call,   35
But with no friendly voice, and add thy name
O Sun, to tell thee how I hate thy beams
That bring to my remembrance from what state
I fell, how glorious once above thy Sphere;°
Till Pride and worse Ambition threw me down   40
Warring in Heav'n against Heav'n's matchless King:
Ah wherefore! he deserv'd no such return
From me, whom he created what I was
In that bright eminence, and with his good
Upbraided none; nor was his service hard.   45
What could be less than to afford him praise,
The easiest recompense, and pay him thanks,

18 **distract** draw apart, as into madness.   28 **pleasant** Eden is from
the Hebrew for "delight, pleasure."   33 **Look'st** both "seems to be"
and "surveys."   33 **sole** unique (suggesting *sol*, sun, as in "the Merid-
ian Sol," 1609).   39 **Sphere** astronomical and hierarchical.

How due! yet all his good prov'd ill in me,
And wrought but malice; lifted up so high
50 I 'sdain'd° subjection, and thought one step higher
Would set me highest, and in a moment quit°
The debt immense of endless gratitude,
So burdensome, still° paying, still to owe;
Forgetful what from him I still receiv'd,
55 And understood not that a grateful mind
By owing owes not, but still pays, at once
Indebted and discharg'd; what burden then?
O had his powerful Destiny ordain'd
Me some inferior Angel, I had stood
60 Then happy; no unbounded hope had rais'd
Ambition. Yet why not? some other Power
As great might have aspir'd, and me though mean
Drawn to his part; but other Powers as great
Fell not, but stand unshak'n, from within
65 Or from without, to all temptations arm'd.
Hadst thou the same free Will and Power to stand?
Thou hadst: whom hast thou then or what to accuse,
But Heav'n's free Love dealt equally to all?
Be then his Love accurst, since love or hate,
70 To me alike, it deals eternal woe.
Nay curs'd be thou; since against his thy will
Chose freely what it now so justly rues.
Me miserable! which way shall I fly
Infinite wrath, and infinite despair?
75 Which way I fly is Hell; myself am Hell;
And in the lowest deep a lower deep
Still threat'ning to devour me opens wide,
To which the Hell I suffer seems a Heav'n.
O then at last relent: is there no place
80 Left for Repentance, none for Pardon left?
None left but by submission; and that word°
Disdain forbids me, and my dread of shame
Among the Spirits beneath, whom I seduc'd
With other promises and other vaunts
85 Than to submit, boasting I could subdue
Th'Omnipotent. Ay me, they little know
How dearly I abide that boast so vain,

50 **'sdain'd** disdained.   51 **quit** requite.   53 **still** always.   81 **that word** "submission."

Under what torments inwardly I groan:
While they adore me on the Throne of Hell,
With Diadem and Scepter high advanc't   90
The lower still I fall, only supreme
In misery; such joy Ambition finds.
But say I could repent and could obtain
By Act of Grace my former state; how soon
Would heighth recall high thoughts, how soon unsay   95
What feign'd submission swore: ease would recant
Vows made in pain, as violent° and void.
For never can true reconcilement grow
Where wounds of deadly hate have pierc'd so deep:
Which would but lead me to a worse relapse,   100
And heavier fall: so should I purchase dear
Short intermission° bought with double smart.
This knows my punisher; therefore as far
From granting hee, as I from begging peace:
All hope excluded thus, behold instead   105
Of us out-cast, exil'd, his new delight,
Mankind created, and for him this World.
So farewell Hope, and with Hope farewell Fear,
Farewell Remorse: all Good to me is lost;
Evil be thou my Good; by thee at least   110
Divided Empire with Heav'n's King I hold
By thee, and more than half perhaps will reign;
As Man erelong, and this new World shall know."
          Thus while he spake, each passion dimm'd his
          face
Thrice chang'd with pale,° ire, envy and despair,   115
Which marr'd his borrow'd visage, and betray'd
Him counterfeit, if any eye beheld.
For heav'nly minds from such distempers° foul
Are ever clear. Whereof hee soon aware,
Each perturbation smooth'd with outward calm,   120
Artificer of fraud; and was the first
That practis'd falsehood under saintly show,
Deep malice to conceal, couch't° with revenge:
Yet not enough had practis'd to deceive
Uriel once warn'd; whose eye pursu'd him down   125

97 **violent** extorted by force.   102 **intermission** contrasted with en-
during "submission" (lines 81, 96).   115 **pale** pallor.   118 **distem-**
pers disorders, diseases.   123 **couch't** lying hidden.

The way he went, and on th'Assyrian mount
Saw him disfigur'd, more than could befall
Spirit of happy sort: his gestures fierce
He mark'd and mad demeanor, then alone,
130 As he suppos'd, all unobserv'd, unseen.
So on he fares, and to the border comes
Of Eden, where delicious Paradise,
Now nearer, Crowns with her enclosure green,
As with a rural mound the champaign head°
135 Of a steep wilderness, whose hairy sides
With thicket overgrown, grotesque° and wild,
Access deni'd; and overhead upgrew
Insuperable heighth of loftiest shade,
Cedar, and Pine, and Fir, and branching Palm,
140 A Sylvan Scene, and as the ranks ascend
Shade above shade, a woody Theatre
Of stateliest view.° Yet higher than their tops
The verdurous wall of Paradise up-sprung:
Which to our general Sire gave prospect large
145 Into his nether Empire neighbouring round.
And higher than that Wall a circling row
Of goodliest Trees loaden with fairest Fruit,
Blossoms and Fruits at once of golden hue
Appear'd, with gay enamell'd° colours mixt:
150 On which the Sun more glad impress'd his beams
Than in fair Evening Cloud, or humid Bow,°
When God hath show'r'd the earth; so lovely seem'd
That Landscape: And of° pure now purer air
Meets his approach, and to the heart inspires
155 Vernal delight and joy, able to drive
All sadness but despair: now gentle gales
Fanning their odoriferous° wings dispense
Native perfumes, and whisper whence they stole
Those balmy spoils. As when to them who sail
160 Beyond the Cape of Hope,° and now are past
Mozambique, off at Sea North-East winds blow
Sabean° Odours from the spicy shore

134 **champaign head** open plateau.   136 **grotesque** picturesquely ir-
regular (ultimately from grotto, cave).   141–42 **Theatre . . . view**
"theatre" from the Greek for "place for viewing."   149 **enamell'd**
brightly varied.   151 **humid Bow** rainbow.   153 **of** following on.
157 **odoriferous** scent-bearing.   160 **Hope** Good Hope (contrast
Satan's despair, line 156).   162 **Sabean** from Sheba.

Of Araby the blest,° with such delay
Well pleas'd they slack their course, and many a
    League
Cheer'd with the grateful° smell old Ocean smiles.   165
So entertain'd° those odorous sweets the Fiend
Who came their bane, though with them better-pleas'd
Than Asmodeus° with the fishy fume,
That drove him, though enamour'd, from the Spouse
Of Tobit's Son, and with a vengeance° sent   170
From Media post to Egypt, there fast° bound.
    Now to th'ascent of that steep savage° Hill
Satan had journey'd on, pensive and slow;
But further way found none, so thick entwin'd,
As one continu'd brake,° the undergrowth   175
Of shrubs and tangling bushes had perplext°
All path of Man or Beast that past that way:
One Gate there only was, and that look'd East
On th'other side: which when th'arch-felon saw
Due entrance he disdain'd, and in contempt,   180
At one slight bound high overleap'd all bound
Of Hill or highest Wall, and sheer within
'Lights on his feet. As when a prowling Wolf,
Whom hunger drives to seek new haunt for prey,
Watching where Shepherds pen their Flocks at eve   185
In hurdl'd Cotes° amid the field secure,°
Leaps o'er the fence with ease into the Fold:
Or as a Thief bent to unhoard the cash
Of some rich Burgher,° whose substantial doors,
Cross-barr'd and bolted fast, fear no assault,   190
In at the window climbs, or o'er the tiles;
So clomb this first grand Thief into God's Fold:
So since into his Church lewd° Hirelings climb.
Thence up he flew, and on the Tree of Life,
The middle Tree and highest there that grew,   195

163 **Araby the blest** Arabia Felix.   165 **grateful** pleasing.   166 **entertain'd** received as a guest (but "bane" means murderer—Satan violates such a welcome).   168 **Asmodeus** Tobias (Tobit's son) was to marry a maiden who was pestered by the evil spirit Asmodeus; Raphael instructed Tobias to drive away the spirit by burning fish. 170 **with a vengeance** both "with a curse" and "with all force." 171 **fast** speedily and tightly.   172 **savage** wild (from Latin *silva*, a wood).   175 **brake** thicket.   176 **perplext** made intricate. 186 **hurdl'd Cotes** sheep-pens of wattled bars.   186 **secure** overconfident in safety.   189 **Burgher** citizen.   193 **lewd** unprincipled.

Sat like a Cormorant; yet not true Life
Thereby regain'd, but sat devising Death
To them who liv'd; nor on the virtue thought
Of that life-giving Plant, but only us'd
200 For prospect, what well us'd had been the pledge
Of immortality. So little knows
Any, but God alone, to value right
The good before him, but perverts best things
To worst abuse, or to their meanest use.
205 Beneath him with new wonder now he views
To all delight of human sense expos'd
In narrow room Nature's whole wealth, yea more,
A Heaven on Earth: for blissful Paradise
Of God the Garden was, by him in the East
210 Of Eden planted; Eden stretch'd her Line
From Auran Eastward to the Royal Tow'rs
Of great Seleucia, built by Grecian Kings,
Or where the Sons of Eden long before
Dwelt in Telassar: in this pleasant soil
215 His far more pleasant Garden God ordain'd;
Out of the fertile ground he caus'd to grow
All Trees of noblest kind for sight, smell, taste;
And all amid them stood the Tree of Life,
High eminent, blooming Ambrosial Fruit
220 Of vegetable° Gold; and next to Life
Our Death the Tree of Knowledge grew fast by,
Knowledge of Good bought dear by knowing ill.
Southward through Eden went a River large,
Nor chang'd his course, but through the shaggy hill
225 Pass'd underneath ingulft, for God had thrown
That Mountain as his Garden-mould high rais'd
Upon the rapid current, which through veins
Of porous Earth with kindly° thirst updrawn
Rose a fresh Fountain, and with many a rill
230 Water'd the Garden; thence united fell
Down the steep glade, and met the nether Flood,
Which from his darksome passage now appears,
And now divided into four main Streams,
Runs diverse, wand'ring many a famous Realm
235 And Country whereof here needs no account,

220 **vegetable** vegetating, plant-like (contrasted with mineral).   228
kindly natural and beneficial.

But rather to tell how, if Art could tell,
How from that Sapphire° Fount the crisped° Brooks,
Rolling on Orient Pearl and sands of Gold,
With mazy error° under pendent shades
Ran Nectar, visiting each plant, and fed   240
Flow'rs worthy of Paradise which not nice° Art
In Beds and curious° Knots, but Nature boon°
Pour'd forth profuse on Hill and Dale and Plain,
Both where the morning Sun first warmly smote
The open field, and where the unpierc't shade   245
Embrown'd the noontide Bow'rs: Thus was this place,
A happy rural seat of various view;
Groves whose rich Trees wept odorous Gums and
    Balm,
Others whose fruit burnisht with Golden Rind
Hung amiable,° Hesperian Fables° true,   250
If true, here only,° and of delicious taste:
Betwixt them Lawns, or level Downs, and Flocks
Grazing the tender herb, were interpos'd,
Or palmy hillock, or the flow'ry lap
Of some irriguous° Valley spread her store,   255
Flow'rs of all hue, and without Thorn the Rose:
Another side, umbrageous° Grots and Caves
Of cool recess, o'er which the mantling° Vine
Lays forth her purple Grape, and gently creeps
Luxuriant; meanwhile murmuring waters fall   260
Down the slope hills, disperst, or in a Lake,
That to the fringed Bank with Myrtle crown'd,
Her crystal mirror holds, unite their streams.
The Birds their choir apply;° airs,° vernal airs,
Breathing the smell of field and grove, attune°   265
The trembling leaves, while Universal Pan°

237 **Sapphire** blue and precious.   237 **crisped** rippled.   239 **error** in
the innocent Latin sense, "wandering"—but already anticipating
guilty error (see lines 221–2).   241 **nice** fastidious.   242 **curious**
carefully wrought.   242 **boon** bounteous.   250 **amiable** lovely.   250
Hesperian Fables see III 568.   251 **If . . . only** If the fables are true,
they are so only in their application to Eden.   255 **irriguous** watered.
257 **umbrageous** shady.   258 **mantling** forming a mantle, covering.
264 **apply** both "join" and "bring to bear to create an effect" as in
Spenser: "Their pleasant tunes they sweetly thus applied."   264 **airs**
breezes, suggesting tunes ("attune").   265 **attune** bring into har-
mony.   266 **Universal Pan** god of all nature, his name from the
Greek for "all."

Knit with the Graces and the Hours° in dance
Led on th'Eternal Spring.° Not that fair field
Of Enna,° where Prosérpine gath'ring flow'rs,
270 Herself a fairer flow'r by gloomy Dis
Was gather'd, which cost Ceres all that pain
To seek her through the world; nor that sweet Grove
Of Daphne by° Orontes, and th'inspir'd
Castalian Spring° might with this Paradise
275 Of Eden strive; nor that Nyseian Isle
Girt with the River Triton, where old Cham,°
Whom Gentiles Ammon call and Libyan Jove,
Hid Amalthea and her Florid Son°
Young Bacchus from his Stepdame Rhea's° eye;
280 Nor where Abássin° Kings their issue° Guard,
Mount Amara, though this by some suppos'd
True Paradise under the Ethiop Line°
By Nilus' head,° enclos'd with shining Rock,
A whole day's journey high, but wide remote
285 From this Assyrian Garden, where the Fiend
Saw undelighted all delight, all kind
Of living Creatures new to sight and strange:
Two of far nobler shape erect and tall,
Godlike erect, with native Honour clad
290 In naked Majesty seem'd Lords of all,
And worthy seem'd, for in their looks Divine
The image of their glorious Maker shone,
Truth, Wisdom, Sanctitude severe and pure,
Severe, but in true filial freedom plac't;
295 Whence true authority in men;° though both
Not equal, as their sex not equal seem'd;
For contemplation hee and valour form'd,
For softness shee and sweet attractive Grace,

267 Graces . . . Hours the goddesses. 268 Eternal Spring only one
season in Eden. 269 Enna in Sicily, where Dis (Pluto) snatched
Prosérpine to the underworld; her mother Ceres sought her. (Antici-
pating Satan's seduction of Eve.) 273 Of Daphne by named
Daphne, near the river. 274 Castalian Spring Castalia, the spring
on Mount Parnassus, sacred to Apollo and the Muses. 276 Cham
son of Noah, held to be the god Ammon, Jove. 278 Florid Son
the beautiful and rosy god of wine. 279 Rhea Bacchus' stepmother,
Ammon's wife. 280 Abássin Abyssinian. 280 issue children. 282
Ethiop Line Equator. 283 Nilus' head Nile's source. 295 Whence
. . . men from the virtues of their Maker or Author (III 374, etc.), the
source of authority.

Hee for God only, shee for God in him:
His fair large Front° and Eye sublime declar'd   *300*
Absolute rule; and Hyacinthine° Locks
Round from his parted forelock manly hung
Clust'ring, but not beneath his shoulders broad:
Shee as a veil down to the slender waist
Her unadorned golden tresses wore   *305*
Dishevell'd, but in wanton° ringlets wav'd
As the Vine curls her tendrils, which impli'd
Subjection, but requir'd with gentle sway,
And by her yielded, by him best receiv'd,
Yielded with coy° submission, modest pride,   *310*
And sweet reluctant amorous delay.
Nor those mysterious° parts were then conceal'd,
Then was not guilty shame, dishonest° shame
Of nature's works, honour dishonourable,
Sin-bred, how have ye troubl'd all mankind   *315*
With shows instead, mere shows of seeming pure,
And banisht from man's life his happiest life,
Simplicity and spotless innocence.
So pass'd they naked on, nor shunn'd the sight
Of God or Angel, for they thought no ill: *320*
So hand in hand they pass'd, the loveliest pair
That ever since in love's embraces° met,
Adam the goodliest man of men since born
His Sons, the fairest of her Daughters Eve.°
Under a tuft of shade that on a green   *325*
Stood whispering soft, by a fresh Fountain-side
They sat them down, and after no more toil
Of their sweet Gard'ning labour than suffic'd
To recommend° cool Zephyr,° and make ease
More easy, wholesome thirst and appetite   *330*
More grateful, to their Supper Fruits they fell,

---

300 **Front** brow.   301 **Hyacinthine** colored like hyacinth.   306 **wanton** uncontrolled (here still innocent, but prophetic).   310 **coy** truly shy.   312 **mysterious** secret, sacramental, awe-inspiring; the paradox of life before the Fall, since a "mystery" (from the Greek, "to close lips or eyes") after the Fall is by definition "conceal'd."   313 **dishonest** unchaste.   322 **love's embraces** embraced both by each other's love, and by love, God's love.   323–24 This apparently illogical form of speech has both classical and English precedents; it works, too, to *include* Adam and Eve in their descendants—see IX 415–16.   329 **recommend** commend.   329 **Zephyr** mild west wind.

Nectarine° Fruits which the compliant° boughs
Yielded them, sidelong as they sat recline
On the soft downy Bank damaskt° with flow'rs:
335 The savoury pulp they chew, and in the rind
Still as they thirsted scoop the brimming stream;
Nor gentle purpose,° nor endearing smiles
Wanted, nor youthful dalliance as beseems
Fair couple, linkt in happy nuptial League,
340 Alone as they. About them frisking play'd
All Beasts of th'Earth, since wild, and of all chase°
In Wood or Wilderness, Forest or Den;
Sporting the Lion ramp'd, and in his paw
Dandl'd the Kid; Bears, Tigers, Ounces, Pards°
345 Gamboll'd before them, th'unwieldy Elephant
To make them mirth us'd all his might, and wreath'd
His Lithe Proboscis;° close the Serpent sly
Insinuating,° wove with Gordian° twine
His braided train, and of his fatal guile
350 Gave proof unheeded; others on the grass
Couch't, and now fill'd with pasture gazing sat,
Or Bedward ruminating:° for the Sun
Declin'd was hasting now with prone career°
To th'Ocean Isles,° and in th'ascending Scale
355 Of Heav'n the Stars that usher Evening rose:
When Satan still in gaze, as first he stood,
Scarce thus at length fail'd° speech recover'd sad.

        "O Hell! what do mine eyes with grief behold,
Into our room of bliss thus high advanc't
360 Creatures of other mould, earth-born perhaps,
Not Spirits, yet to heav'nly Spirits bright
Little inferior; whom my thoughts pursue
With wonder, and could love, so lively shines
In them Divine resemblance, and such grace

332 **Nectarine** peach-like (suggesting its divine source, nectar).   332
compliant pliant (innocent enough, but the other sense, "yielding to
desire," is ominous—see IX 994: "compliance bad").   334 **damaskt**
patterned, damask also being a rose.   337 **purpose** discourse.   341
chase unenclosed land.   344 **Ounces, Pards** lynxes, leopards.   347
Proboscis trunk.   348 **Insinuating** winding (ominously prophetic
too).   348 **Gordian** intricate like the Gordian knot.   352 **ruminating**
chewing the cud.   353 **career** gallop, linked with the word "car,"
chariot; here the horses of the sun, as in V 139–40.   354 **Ocean Isles**
in the west.   357 **fail'd** which had failed him.

The hand that form'd them on their shape hath pour'd.   365
Ah gentle pair, yee little think how nigh
Your change approaches, when all these delights
Will vanish and deliver ye to woe,
More woe, the more your taste is now of joy;
Happy, but for so happy ill secur'd   370
Long to continue, and this high seat your Heav'n
Ill fenc't for Heav'n to keep out such a foe
As now is enter'd; yet no purpos'd foe
To you whom I could pity thus forlorn°
Though I unpitied: League with you I seek,   375
And mutual amity so strait, so close,
That I with you must dwell, or you with me
Henceforth; my dwelling haply may not please
Like this fair Paradise, your sense, yet such
Accept your Maker's work; he gave it me,   380
Which I as freely give; Hell shall unfold,
To entertain° you two, her widest Gates,
And send forth all her Kings; there will be room,
Not like these narrow limits, to receive
Your numerous offspring; if no better place,   385
Thank him who puts me loath to this revenge
On you who wrong me not for him who wrong'd.
And should I at your harmless innocence
Melt, as I do, yet public reason just,
Honour and Empire with revenge enlarg'd,   390
By conquering this new World, compels me now
To do what else though damn'd I should abhor."
        So spake the Fiend, and with necessity,
The Tyrant's plea, excus'd his devilish deeds.
Then from his lofty stand on that high Tree   395
Down he alights among the sportful Herd
Of those four-footed kinds, himself now one,
Now other, as their shape serv'd best his end
Nearer to view his prey, and unespi'd
To mark what of their state he more might learn   400
By word or action markt: about them round
A Lion now he stalks with fiery glare,
Then as a Tiger, who by chance hath spi'd
In some Purlieu two gentle Fawns at play,
Straight couches close, then rising changes oft   405

374 **forlorn** lost, doomed.   382 **entertain** welcome formally.

His couchant watch, as one who chose his ground
Whence rushing he might surest seize them both
Gript in each paw: when Adam first of men
To first of women Eve thus moving speech,
410　Turn'd him all ear° to hear new utterance flow.
　　　　　"Sole partner and sole part of all these joys,
Dearer thyself than all; needs must the Power
That made us, and for us this ample World
Be infinitely good, and of his good
415　As liberal and free as infinite,
That rais'd us from the dust and plac't us here
In all this happiness, who at his hand
Have nothing merited, nor can perform
Aught whereof hee hath need, hee who requires
420　From us no other service than to keep
This one, this easy charge, of all the Trees
In Paradise that bear delicious fruit
So various, not to taste that only Tree
Of Knowledge, planted by the Tree of Life,
425　So near grows Death to Life, whate'er Death is,
Some dreadful thing no doubt; for well thou know'st
God hath pronounc't it death to taste that Tree,
The only sign of our obedience left
Among so many signs of power and rule
430　Conferr'd upon us, and Dominion giv'n
Over all other Creatures that possess
Earth, Air, and Sea. Then let us not think hard°
One easy prohibition, who enjoy
Free leave so large to all things else, and choice
435　Unlimited of manifold delights:
But let us ever praise him, and extol
His bounty, following our delightful task
To prune these growing Plants, and tend these Flow'rs,
Which were it toilsome, yet with thee were sweet."
440　　　　　To whom thus Eve repli'd. "O thou for whom
And from whom I was form'd flesh of thy flesh,
And without whom am to no end, my Guide
And Head, what thou hast said is just and right.
For wee to him indeed all praises owe,
445　And daily thanks, I chiefly who enjoy

410 **all ear** describing Eve.　432 **hard** harsh, but the sense "difficult
to keep"—contrasting with "easy"—is not auspicious.

So far the happier Lot, enjoying thee
Pre-eminent by so much odds,° while thou
Like consort to thyself canst nowhere find.
That day I oft remember, when from sleep
I first awak't and found myself repos'd   450
Under a shade on flow'rs, much wond'ring where
And what I was, whence thither brought, and how.
Not distant far from thence a murmuring sound
Of waters issu'd from a Cave and spread
Into a liquid Plain, then stood unmov'd   455
Pure as th'expanse of Heav'n; I thither went
With unexperienc't thought, and laid me down
On the green bank, to look into the clear
Smooth Lake, that to me seem'd another Sky.
As I bent down to look, just opposite,   460
A Shape within the wat'ry gleam appear'd
Bending to look on me, I started back,
It started back, but pleas'd I soon return'd,
Pleas'd it return'd as soon with answering looks°
Of sympathy and love, there I had fixt   465
Mine eyes till now, and pin'd with vain° desire,
Had not a voice thus warn'd me, 'What thou seest,
What there thou seest fair Creature is thyself,
With thee it came and goes: but follow me,
And I will bring thee where no shadow stays°   470
Thy coming, and thy soft embraces, hee
Whose image thou art, him thou shalt enjoy
Inseparably thine, to him shalt bear
Multitudes like thyself, and thence be call'd
Mother of human Race.' What could I do,   475
But follow straight, invisibly thus led?
Till I espi'd thee, fair indeed and tall,
Under a Platan,° yet methought less fair,
Less winning soft, less amiably mild,
Than that smooth wat'ry image; back I turn'd,   480
Thou following cried'st aloud, 'Return fair Eve,
Whom fli'st thou? whom thou fli'st, of him thou art,
His flesh, his bone; to give thee being I lent

447 **odds** inequality, difference.   460–64 **As . . . looks** Eve's be-
havior resembles that of Narcissus; she is still innocent, but in
danger.   466 **vain** futile (but ominously suggesting the "vanity" of
Narcissus and the fallen Eve).   470 **stays** awaits.   478 **Platan** plane
tree.

Out of my side to thee, nearest my heart
485 Substantial° Life, to have thee by my side
Henceforth an individual° solace dear;
Part of my Soul I seek thee, and thee claim
My other half.' With that thy gentle hand
Seiz'd mine, I yielded, and from that time see
490 How beauty is excell'd by manly grace
And wisdom, which alone is truly fair."

        So spake our general Mother, and with eyes
Of conjugal attraction unreprov'd,°
And meek surrender, half-embracing lean'd
495 On our first Father, half her swelling Breast
Naked met his under the flowing Gold
Of her loose tresses hid: he in delight
Both of her Beauty and submissive Charms
Smil'd with superior Love, as Jupiter
500 On Juno smiles, when he impregns° the Clouds
That shed May Flowers; and press'd her Matron lip
With kisses pure: aside the Devil turn'd
For envy, yet with jealous leer malign
Ey'd them askance, and to himself thus 'plain'd.

505   "Sight hateful, sight tormenting! thus these two
Imparadis't in one another's arms
The happier Eden, shall enjoy their fill
Of bliss on bliss, while I to Hell am thrust,
Where neither joy nor love, but fierce desire,
510 Among our other torments not the least,
Still unfulfill'd with pain of longing pines;°
Yet let me not forget what I have gain'd
From their own mouths;° all is not theirs it seems:
One fatal° Tree there stands of Knowledge call'd,
515 Forbidden them to taste: Knowledge forbidd'n?
Suspicious, reasonless. Why should their Lord
Envy them that? can it be sin to know,
Can it be death? and do they only stand
By Ignorance, is that their happy state,
520 The proof of their obedience and their faith?
O fair foundation laid whereon to build

485 **Substantial** in its essence; for the religious associations, see III
140.   486 **individual** indivisible, inseparable.   493 **unreprov'd** blame-
less.   500 **impregns** impregnates.   511 **pines** tortures.   513 **From
. . . mouths** a sardonic pun—see line 527.   514 **fatal** deadly, and
of fate.

Their ruin!° Hence I will excite their minds
With more desire to know, and to reject
Envious commands, invented with design
To keep them low whom knowledge might exalt   525
Equal with Gods; aspiring to be such,
They taste and die: what likelier can ensue?
But first with narrow search I must walk round
This Garden, and no corner leave unspi'd;
A chance but° chance may lead where I may meet   530
Some wand'ring Spirit of Heav'n, by Fountain-side,
Or in thick shade retir'd, from him to draw
What further would be learnt. Live while ye may,
Yet happy pair; enjoy, till I return,
Short pleasures, for long woes are to succeed."   535
          So saying, his proud step he scornful turn'd,
But with sly circumspection, and began
Through wood, through waste, o'er hill, o'er dale his
     roam.
Meanwhile in utmost Longitude,° where Heav'n
With Earth and Ocean meets, the setting Sun   540
Slowly descended, and with right aspéct°
Against the eastern Gate of Paradise
Levell'd his evening Rays: it was a Rock
Of Alabaster, pil'd up to the Clouds,
Conspicuous far, winding with one ascent   545
Accessible from Earth, one entrance high;
The rest was craggy cliff, that overhung
Still as it rose, impossible to climb.
Betwixt these rocky Pillars Gabriel sat
Chief of th'Angelic Guards, awaiting night;   550
About him exercis'd Heroic Games
Th'unarmed Youth of Heav'n, but nigh at hand
Celestial Armoury, Shields, Helms, and Spears
Hung high with Diamond flaming, and with Gold.
Thither came Uriel, gliding through the Even   555
On a Sunbeam, swift as a shooting Star

521–22 **O . . . ruin** "A cruel paradox; one doesn't, or at this date
didn't, build ruins. But there is also a pun-like effect using two
senses of *ruin*, not only what is left after the destructive act, but also
the fall itself" (Frank Kermode).   530 **A chance but** there is a faint
chance that.   539 **utmost Longitude** the far west.   541 **with right
aspéct** directly opposite.

In Autumn thwarts° the night, when vapours fir'd
Impress the Air, and shows the Mariner
From what point of his Compass to beware
560 Impetuous winds: he thus began in haste.
         "Gabriel, to thee thy course by Lot hath giv'n
Charge and strict watch that to this happy place
No evil thing approach or enter in;
This day at heighth of Noon came to my Sphere
565 A Spirit, zealous, as he seem'd, to know
More of th'Almighty's work, and chiefly Man
God's latest Image:° I describ'd° his way
Bent all on speed, and markt his Airy Gait;°
But in the Mount that lies from Eden North,
570 Where he first 'lighted, soon discern'd his looks
Alien from Heav'n, with passions foul obscur'd:
Mine eye pursu'd him still, but under shade
Lost sight of him; one of the banisht crew
I fear, hath ventur'd from the deep, to raise
575 New troubles;° him thy care must be to find."
         To whom the winged Warrior thus return'd:
"Uriel, no wonder if thy perfect sight,
Amid the Sun's bright circle where thou sitt'st,
See far and wide: in at this Gate none pass
580 The vigilance° here plac't, but such as come
Well known from Heav'n; and since Meridian hour
No Creature thence: if Spirit of other sort,
So minded, have o'erleapt these earthy bounds
On purpose, hard thou know'st it to exclude
585 Spiritual substance with corporeal bar.
But if within the circuit of these walks
In whatsoever shape he lurk, of whom
Thou tell'st, by morrow dawning I shall know."
         So promis'd hee, and Uriel to his charge
590 Return'd on that bright beam, whose point now rais'd
Bore him slope downward to the Sun now fall'n
Beneath th'Azores; whither the prime Orb,°
Incredible how swift, had thither roll'd
Diurnal,° or this less volúble° Earth

557 thwarts crosses.   567 latest Image the Son being His first image.
describ'd descried.   568 Gait manner (of flying).   575 troubles in-
cluding "wars, disturbances."   580 vigilance vigilant guards.   592
prime Orb sun.   594 Diurnal in a day.   594 volúble swift-rolling
(Milton's spelling here, "volubil").

By shorter flight to th'East, had left him there   595
Arraying with reflected Purple and Gold
The Clouds that on his Western Throne attend:
Now came still Ev'ning on, and Twilight grey
Had in her sober Livery all things clad;
Silence accompanied,° for Beast and Bird,   600
They to their grassy Couch, these to their Nests
Were slunk, all but the wakeful Nightingale;
She all night long her amorous descant° sung;
Silence was pleas'd: now glow'd the Firmament
With living Sapphires: Hesperus that led   605
The starry Host, rode brightest, till the Moon
Rising in clouded Majesty, at length
Apparent° Queen unveil'd her peerless light,
And o'er the dark her Silver Mantle threw.
   When Adam thus to Eve: "Fair Consort,
   th'hour   610
Of night, and all things now retir'd to rest
Mind° us of like repose, since God hath set
Labour and rest, as day and night to men
Successive, and the timely dew of sleep
Now falling with soft slumb'rous weight inclines   615
Our eyelids; other Creatures all day long
Rove idle unemploy'd, and less need rest;
Man hath his daily work of body or mind
Appointed, which declares his Dignity,
And the regard of Heav'n on all his ways;   620
While other Animals unactive range,
And of their doings God takes no account.
Tomorrow ere fresh Morning streak the East
With first approach of light, we must be ris'n,
And at our pleasant labour, to reform°   625
Yon flow'ry Arbours, yonder Alleys green,
Our walks at noon, with branches overgrown,
That mock our scant manuring,° and require
More hands than ours to lop their wanton growth:
Those Blossoms also, and those dropping Gums,   630

600 **accompanied** The musical suggestion of "accompaniment"
(which would make "Silence accompanied" a quiet paradox) leads
into lines 602–04.   603 **descant** melodious accompaniment to a sim-
ple theme.   608 **Apparent** plainly seen, manifest.   612 **Mind** remind.
625 **reform** trim.   628 **scant manuring** limited cultivation, from Old
French *manouvrer*, to work with the hands—see the next line.

That lie bestrewn unsightly and unsmooth,
Ask riddance,° if we mean to tread with ease;
Meanwhile, as Nature wills, Night bids us rest."
        To whom thus Eve with perfect beauty
        adorn'd.
635 "My Author° and Disposer, what thou bidd'st
Unargu'd I obey; so God ordains,
God is thy Law, thou mine: to know no more
Is woman's happiest knowledge and her praise.
With thee conversing I forget all time,
640 All seasons° and their change, all please alike.
Sweet is the breath of morn, her rising sweet,
With charm° of earliest Birds; pleasant the Sun
When first on this delightful Land he spreads
His orient Beams, on herb, tree, fruit, and flow'r,
645 Glist'ring with dew; fragrant the fertile earth
After soft showers; and sweet the coming-on
Of grateful Ev'ning mild, then silent Night
With this her solemn Bird and this fair Moon,
And these the Gems of Heav'n, her starry train:
650 But neither breath of Morn when she ascends
With charm of earliest Birds, nor rising Sun
On this delightful land, nor herb, fruit, flow'r,
Glist'ring with dew, nor fragrance after showers,
Nor grateful Evening mild, nor silent Night
655 With this her solemn Bird, nor walk by Moon,
Or glittering Starlight without thee is sweet.
But wherefore all night long shine these, for whom
This glorious sight, when sleep hath shut all eyes?"
        To whom our general Ancestor repli'd.
660 "Daughter of God and Man, accomplisht° Eve,
Those have their course to finish, round the Earth,
By morrow Ev'ning, and from Land to Land
In order, though to Nations yet unborn,
Minist'ring light prepar'd, they set and rise;
665 Lest total darkness should by Night regain
Her old possession, and extinguish life
In Nature and all things, which these soft fires

632 **Ask riddance** require to be cleared. 635 **Author** creator, and
having authority. 640 **seasons** times of day. 642 **charm** including
specifically the sense "song." 660 **accomplisht** complete, perfected
(leading into lines 661, 673).

Not only enlighten, but with kindly heat
Of various influence foment° and warm,
Temper or nourish, or in part shed down   *670*
Their stellar virtue on all kinds that grow
On Earth, made hereby apter to receive
Perfection from the Sun's more potent Ray.
These then, though unbeheld in deep of night,
Shine not in vain, nor think, though men were none,   *675*
That Heav'n would want spectators, God want praise;
Millions of spiritual Creatures walk the Earth
Unseen, both when we wake, and when we sleep:
All these with ceaseless praise his works behold
Both day and night: how often from the steep   *680*
Of echoing Hill or Thicket have we heard
Celestial voices to the midnight air,
Sole, or responsive each to other's note
Singing their great Creator: oft in bands°
While they keep watch, or nightly rounding° walk   *685*
With Heav'nly touch of instrumental sounds
In full harmonic number join'd, their songs
Divide° the night, and lift our thoughts to Heaven."
        Thus talking hand in hand alone they pass'd
On to their blissful Bower; it was a place   *690*
Chos'n by the sovran Planter, when he fram'd
All things to man's delightful use; the roof
Of thickest covert was inwoven shade
Laurel and Myrtle, and what higher grew
Of firm and fragrant leaf; on either side   *695*
Acanthus, and each odorous bushy shrub
Fenc'd up the verdant wall; each beauteous flow'r,
Iris all hues, Roses, and Jessamine
Rear'd high their flourisht° heads between, and
    wrought
Mosaic; underfoot the Violet,   *700*
Crocus, and Hyacinth with rich inlay
Broider'd the ground, more colour'd than with stone
Of costliest Emblem:° other Creature here
Beast, Bird, Insect, or Worm durst enter none;

669 **foment** bathe in heat.   684 **bands** armed bands (a faint musical
suggestion then taken up in lines 685–87).   685 **rounding** making
their rounds.   688 **Divide** into watches, like guards.   699 **flourisht**
adorned with flowers, "flourish" from Latin *flos*, flower.   703 **Emblem** inlaid work.

705 Such was their awe of man. In shadier Bower
      More sacred and sequester'd,° though but feign'd,°
      Pan or Sylvanus° never slept, nor Nymph,
      Nor Faunus haunted. Here in close recess
      With Flowers, Garlands, and sweet-smelling Herbs
710 Espoused Eve deckt first her Nuptial Bed,
      And heav'nly Choirs the Hymenean° sung,
      What day the genial° Angel to our Sire
      Brought her in naked beauty more adorn'd,
      More lovely than Pandora,° whom the Gods
715 Endow'd with all their gifts, and O too like
      In sad event,° when to the unwiser Son
      Of Japhet brought by Hermes, she ensnar'd
      Mankind with her fair looks, to be aveng'd
      On him who had stole Jove's authentic° fire.

720   Thus at their shady Lodge arriv'd, both stood,
      Both turn'd, and under op'n Sky ador'd
      The God that made both Sky, Air, Earth and Heav'n
      Which they beheld, the Moon's resplendent Globe
      And starry Pole: "Thou also mad'st the Night,
725 Maker Omnipotent, and thou the Day,
      Which we in our appointed work employ'd
      Have finisht happy in our mutual help
      And mutual love, the Crown of all our bliss
      Ordain'd by thee, and this delicious place
730 For us too large, where thy abundance wants°
      Partakers, and uncropt falls to the ground.
      But thou hast promis'd from us two a Race
      To fill the Earth, who shall with us extol
      Thy goodness infinite, both when we wake,
735 And when we seek, as now, thy gift of sleep."
                This said unanimous,° and other Rites
      Observing none, but adoration pure
      Which God likes best, into their inmost bower

---

706 **sequester'd** set apart.   706 **feign'd** imagined by pagan poets (un-
like the Biblical truth).   707 **Pan or Sylvanus** pastoral gods.   711
Hymenean marriage song.   712 **genial** ruling over nuptials.   714–19
Pandora Prometheus ("Fore-thought") stole Jove's fire to benefit
mankind; Jove, "to be aveng'd," sent Pandora ("All-gifts"), by his
messenger Hermes, to the "unwiser" Epimetheus ("After-thought"),
who married her, and loosed upon the world the evils from her box.
716 **event** outcome.   719 **authentic** original.   730 **wants** lacks.   736
unanimous with one mind.

Handed° they went; and eas'd the putting off°
These troublesome disguises which wee wear,   740
Straight side by side were laid, nor turn'd I ween
Adam from his fair Spouse, nor Eve the Rites
Mysterious° of connubial Love refus'd:
Whatever Hypocrites austerely talk
Of purity and place and innocence,   745
Defaming as impure what God declares
Pure, and commands to some, leaves free to all.
Our Maker bids increase, who bids abstain
But our Destroyer, foe to God and Man?
Hail wedded Love, mysterious Law, true source   750
Of human offspring, sole propriety,°
In Paradise of all things common else.
By thee adulterous lust was driv'n from men
Among the bestial herds to range, by thee
Founded in Reason, Loyal, Just, and Pure,   755
Relations° dear, and all the Charities
Of Father, Son, and Brother first were known.
Far be it, that I should write thee sin or blame,
Or think thee unbefitting holiest place,
Perpetual Fountain of Domestic sweets,   760
Whose Bed is undefil'd and chaste pronounc't,
Present, or past, as Saints and Patriarchs us'd.
Here Love° his golden shafts employs, here lights
His constant Lamp, and waves his purple° wings,
Reigns here and revels; not in the bought smile   765
Of Harlots, loveless, joyless, unendear'd,
Casual fruition, nor in Court Amours
Mixt Dance, or wanton Masque, or Midnight Ball,
Or Serenade, which the starv'd° Lover sings
To his proud fair, best quitted with disdain.   770
These lull'd by Nightingales embracing slept,
And on their naked limbs the flow'ry roof
Show'r'd Roses, which the Morn repair'd.° Sleep on,

739 **Handed** hand in hand, suggesting the dignity of the marriage ceremony; "If any two be but once handed in the Church . . ." (Milton, *Doctrine and Discipline of Divorce*).   739 **eas'd the putting off** having no need to remove.   743 **Mysterious** awe-inspiring.   751 **sole propriety** the one exclusive possession.   756 **Relations** relationships.   763 **Love** Cupid with his arrows of love.   764 **purple** brilliant.   769 **starv'd** suffering in the cold.   773 **repair'd** once more made up the sum of.

Blest pair; and O yet happiest if ye seek
775 No happier state, and know to know no more.
          Now had night measur'd with her shadowy
                        Cone
Halfway uphill this vast Sublunar° Vault,
And from their Ivory Port° the Cherubim
Forth issuing at th'accustom'd hour stood arm'd
780 To their night-watches in warlike Parade,
When Gabriel to his next in power thus spake.
          "Uzziel, half these draw off, and coast the
                        South
With strictest watch; these other wheel the North,
Our circuit meets full West." As flame they part
785 Half wheeling to the Shield, half to the Spear.°
From these, two strong and subtle Spirits he call'd
That near him stood, and gave them thus in charge.
          "Ithuriel and Zephon, with wing'd speed
Search through this Garden, leave unsearcht no nook,
790 But chiefly where those two fair Creatures Lodge,
Now laid perhaps asleep secure of° harm.
This Ev'ning from the Sun's decline arriv'd
Who° tells of some infernal Spirit seen
Hitherward bent (who could have thought?) escap'd
795 The bars of Hell, on errand bad no doubt:
Such where ye find, seize fast, and hither bring."
          So saying, on he led his radiant Files,
Dazzling the Moon; these to the Bower direct
In search of whom they sought: him there they found
800 Squat like a Toad, close at the ear of Eve;
Assaying by his Devilish art to reach
The Organs of her Fancy, and with them forge
Illusions as he list, Phantasms and Dreams,
Or if, inspiring venom, he might taint
805 Th'animal Spirits that from pure blood arise
Like gentle breaths from Rivers pure, thence raise
At least distemper'd, discontented thoughts,
Vain hopes, vain aims, inordinate desires
Blown up with high conceits engend'ring pride.°

777 **Sublunar** under the moon.   778 **Port** gate.   785 **Shield . . .
Spear** left, right.   791 **secure of** unsuspecting.   793 **Who** one who.
801–09 There are sexual implications throughout these lines (includ-
ing "conceits" as "things conceiv'd"); Eve's dream, caused here by
Satan and recounted later, has erotic force, and Satan's final con-
quest of her is presented as in many ways a seduction (e.g. IX 526).

Him thus intent Ithuriel with his Spear   810
Touch'd lightly; for no falsehood can endure
Touch of Celestial temper, but returns
Of force to its own likeness: up he starts
Discover'd° and surpris'd. As when a spark
'Lights° on a heap of nitrous Powder,° laid   815
Fit for the Tun° some Magazine° to store
Against a rumour'd War, the Smutty grain
With sudden blaze diffus'd, inflames the Air:
So started up in his own shape the Fiend.
Back stept those two fair Angels half amaz'd   820
So sudden to behold the grisly King;
Yet thus, unmov'd with fear, accost him soon.
        "Which of those rebel Spirits adjudg'd to Hell
Com'st thou, escap'd thy prison, and transform'd,
Why satt'st thou like an enemy in wait   825
Here watching at the head of these that sleep?"
        "Know ye not then" said Satan, fill'd with
                scorn,
"Know ye not me? ye knew me once no mate
For you, there sitting where ye durst not soar;
Not to know mee argues yourselves unknown,   830
The lowest of your throng; or if ye know,
Why ask ye, and superfluous begin
Your message, like to end as much in vain?"
To whom thus Zephon, answering scorn with scorn.
"Think not, revolted Spirit, thy shape the same,   835
Or undiminisht brightness, to be known
As when thou stood'st in Heav'n upright and pure;
That Glory then, when thou no more wast good,
Departed from thee, and thou resembl'st now
Thy sin and place of doom obscure and foul.   840
But come, for thou, be sure, shalt give account
To him who sent us, whose charge is to keep
This place inviolable, and these from harm."
        So spake the Cherub, and his grave rebuke
Severe in youthful beauty, added grace   845
Invincible: abasht the Devil stood,

---

814 **Discover'd** caught and uncovered.   815 **'Lights** alights, but sug-
gesting "kindles."   815 **nitrous Powder** gunpowder.   816 **Tun** bar-
rel. **Magazine** building for explosives.

And felt how awful goodness is, and saw
Virtue in her shape how lovely, saw, and pin'd
His loss; but chiefly to find here observ'd
850 His lustre visibly impair'd; yet seem'd
Undaunted. "If I must contend," said he,
"Best with the best, the Sender not the sent,
Or all at once; more glory will be won,
Or less be lost." "Thy fear," said Zephon bold,
855 "Will save us trial what the least can do
Single° against thee wicked, and thence weak."
      The Fiend repli'd not, overcome with rage;
But like a proud Steed rein'd, went haughty on,
Champing his iron curb: to strive or fly
860 He held it vain; awe from above had quell'd
His heart, not else dismay'd. Now drew they nigh
The western point, where those half-rounding guards
Just met, and closing stood in squadron join'd
Awaiting next command. To whom their Chief
865 Gabriel from the Front thus call'd aloud.
      "O friends, I hear the tread of nimble feet
Hasting this way, and now by glimpse discern
Ithuriel and Zephon through the shade,
And with them comes a third of Regal port,°
870 But faded splendour wan; who by his gait
And fierce demeanour seems the Prince of Hell,
Not likely to part hence without contést;
Stand firm, for in his look defiance lours."
      He scarce had ended, when those two ap-
           proach'd
875 And brief related whom they brought, where found,
How busied, in what form and posture coucht.
      To whom with stern regard thus Gabriel
        spake.
"Why hast thou, Satan, broke the bounds prescrib'd
To thy transgressions,° and disturb'd the charge°
880 Of others, who approve not to transgress
By thy example, but have power and right
To question thy bold entrance on this place;

856 **Single** both "alone" and "honestly upright" as in Shakespeare's
"a single heart."   869 **port** bearing.   879 **transgressions** a trans-
gression itself being something which breaks bounds (Latin *trans-
gredi*).   879 **charge** duty.

Employ'd it seems to violate sleep, and those
Whose dwelling God hath planted here in bliss?"

      To whom thus Satan with contemptuous brow.   *885*
"Gabriel, thou hadst in Heav'n th'esteem of° wise,
And such I held thee; but this question askt
Puts me in doubt. Lives there who loves his pain?
Who would not, finding way, break loose from Hell,
Though thither doom'd? Thou wouldst thyself, no
    doubt,   *890*
And boldly venture to whatever place
Farthest from pain, where thou mightst hope to
    change
Torment with ease, and soonest recompense
Dole with delight, which in this place I sought;
To thee no reason; who know'st only good,   *895*
But evil hast not tri'd: and wilt object°
His will who bound us? let him surer bar
His Iron Gates, if he intends our stay
In that dark durance:° thus much what was askt.
The rest is true, they found me where they say;   *900*
But that implies not violence or harm."

      Thus hee in scorn. The warlike Angel mov'd,
Disdainfully half smiling thus repli'd.
"O loss of one in Heav'n to judge of wise,°
Since Satan fell, whom folly overthrew,   *905*
And now returns him from his prison 'scap't,
Gravely in doubt whether to hold them wise
Or not, who ask what boldness brought him hither
Unlicens't from his bounds in Hell prescrib'd;
So wise he judges it to fly from pain   *910*
However,° and to 'scape his punishment.
So judge thou still, presumptuous, till the wrath,
Which thou incurr'st by flying, meet thy flight
Sev'nfold, and scourge that wisdom back to Hell,
Which taught thee yet no better, that no pain   *915*
Can equal anger infinite provok't.
But wherefore thou alone? wherefore with thee
Came not all Hell broke loose? is pain to them

886 **hadst . . . th'esteem of** wast esteemed.   896 **object** put forward
as an objection.   899 **durance** imprisonment (a sardonic pun, since
durance is by definition *staying*, from *durer*).   904 "What a loss to
Heaven of one who can so judge wisdom."   911 **However** howso-
ever.

Less pain, less to be fled, or thou than they
920 Less hardy to endure? courageous Chief,
The first in flight from pain, hadst thou alleg'd
To thy deserted host this cause of flight,
Thou surely hadst not come sole fugitive."
          To which the Fiend thus answer'd frowning
                    stern.
925 "Not that I less endure, or shrink from pain,
Insulting Angel, well thou know'st I stood°
Thy fiercest, when in Battle to thy aid
The blasting volley'd Thunder made all speed
And seconded thy else not dreaded Spear.
930 But still thy words at random,° as before,
Argue thy inexperience what behooves
From hard assays and ill successes past
A faithful Leader, not to hazard all
Through ways of danger by himself untri'd.
935 I therefore, I alone first undertook
To wing the desolate Abyss, and spy
This new-created World, whereof in Hell
Fame° is not silent, here in hope to find
Better abode, and my afflicted Powers°
940 To settle here on Earth, or in mid Air;
Though for possession put to try once more
What thou and thy gay Legions dare against;
Whose easier business were to serve their Lord
High up in Heav'n, with songs to hymn his Throne,
945 And practis'd distances° to cringe, not fight."
          To whom the warrior Angel soon repli'd.
"To say and straight unsay, pretending first
Wise to fly pain, professing next the Spy,
Argues no Leader, but a liar trac't,
950 Satan, and couldst thou 'faithful' add? O name,
O sacred name of faithfulness profan'd!
Faithful to whom? to thy rebellious crew?
Army of Fiends, fit body to fit head;

---

926 **stood** withstood.   930 **at random** both "haphazard" and—a military term—"at a range other than point-blank" (here, not hitting the target).   938 **Fame** report.   939 **afflicted Powers** armies struck down.   945 **practis'd distances** accustomed acts of deference—but played sardonically against "distance" as the interval between combatants; "He fights as you sing pricksong, keeps time, distance, and proportion" (*Romeo and Juliet*), where there is too the suggestion of "a musical interval."

Was this your discipline and faith engag'd,
Your military obedience, to dissolve   955
Allegiance to th'acknowledg'd Power supreme?
And thou sly hypocrite, who now wouldst seem
Patron of liberty, who more than thou
Once fawn'd, and cring'd, and servilely ador'd
Heav'ns awful Monarch? wherefore but in hope   960
To dispossess him, and thyself to reign?
But mark what I aread° thee now, avaunt;°
Fly thither whence thou fledd'st: if from this hour
Within these hallow'd limits thou appear,
Back to th'infernal pit I drag thee chain'd,   965
And Seal thee so, as henceforth not to scorn
The facile° gates of Hell too slightly barr'd."
          So threat'n'd hee, but Satan to no threats
Gave heed, but waxing more in rage repli'd.
          "Then when I am thy captive talk of chains,   970
Proud limitary° Cherub, but ere then
Far heavier load thyself expect to feel
From my prevailing arm, though Heaven's King
Ride on thy wings, and thou with thy Compeers,
Us'd to the yoke, draw'st his triumphant wheels   975
In progress° through the road of Heav'n Star-pav'd."
                    While thus he spake, th'Angelic Squadron
                    bright
Turn'd fiery red, sharp'ning in mooned horns
Their Phalanx,° and began to hem him round
With ported° Spears, as thick as when a field   980
Of Ceres° ripe for harvest waving bends
Her bearded Grove of ears, which way the wind
Sways them; the careful° Ploughman doubting° stands
Lest on the threshing-floor his hopeful sheaves
Prove chaff. On th'other side Satan alarm'd°   985
Collecting all his might dilated stood,
Like Tenerife° or Atlas unremov'd:°
His stature reacht the Sky, and on his Crest

962 **aread** advise. 962 **avaunt** begone. 967 **facile** easy. 971 **limitary** on guard duty at the boundary (taking up line 964); Satan's sarcasm includes the 17th-century sense "limited in powers." 976 **progress** state procession. 979 **Phalanx** line of battle. 980 **ported** held slanting ("port arms"). 981 **Ceres** goddess of agriculture. 983 **careful** anxious. 983 **doubting** fearing. 985 **alarm'd** called to arms. 987 **Tenerife** mountain in the Canary Isles. 987 **unremov'd** unremovable.

Sat horror° Plum'd; nor wanted in his grasp
What seem'd both Spear and Shield: now dreadful
990   deeds
Might have ensu'd, nor only Paradise
In this commotion, but the Starry Cope
Of Heav'n perhaps, or all the Elements
At least had gone to wrack, disturb'd and torn
995 With violence of this conflict, had not soon
Th'Eternal to prevent such horrid fray
Hung forth in Heav'n his golden Scales,° yet seen
Betwixt Astraea° and the Scorpion sign,
Wherein all things created first he weigh'd,
1000 The pendulous round Earth with balanc't Air
In counterpoise, now ponders° all events,
Battles and Realms: in these he put two weights
The sequel° each of parting and of fight;
The latter quick up flew, and kickt the beam;
1005 Which Gabriel spying, thus bespake the Fiend.
            "Satan, I know thy strength, and thou know'st
                mine,
Neither our own but giv'n; what folly then
To boast what Arms can do, since thine no more
Than Heav'n permits, nor mine, though doubl'd now
1010 To trample thee as mire: for proof look up,
And read thy Lot in yon celestial Sign
Where thou art weigh'd, and shown how light, how
    weak,
If thou resist." The Fiend lookt up and knew
His mounted scale aloft: nor more; but fled
1015 Murmuring, and with him fled the shades of night.

989 **horror** from Latin *horrere*, to stand on end (of hair).   997
Scales the constellation Libra.   998 **Astraea** Virgo.   1001 **ponders**
weighs.   1003 **sequel** consequence (to Satan).

BOOK V

THE ARGUMENT

Morning approach't, Eve relates to Adam her troublesome
dream; he likes it not, yet comforts her: They come forth
to their day labours: Their Morning Hymn at the Door
of their Bower. God to render Man inexcusable sends
Raphael to admonish him of his obedience, of his free
estate, of his enemy near at hand; who he is, and why his
enemy, and whatever else may avail Adam to know.
Raphael comes down to Paradise, his appearance de-
scrib'd, his coming discern'd by Adam afar off sitting at
the door of his Bower; he goes out to meet him, brings
him to his lodge, entertains him with the choicest fruits
of Paradise got together by Eve; their discourse at Table:
Raphael performs his message, minds Adam of his state
and of his enemy; relates at Adam's request who that
enemy is, and how he came to be so, beginning from his
first revolt in Heaven, and the occasion thereof; how he
drew his Legions after him to the parts of the North, and
there incited them to rebel with him, persuading all but
only Abdiel a Seraph, who in Argument dissuades and
opposes him, then forsakes him.

Now Morn her rosy steps in th'Eastern Clime°
Advancing, sow'd the Earth with Orient Pearl,
When Adam wak't, so custom'd, for his sleep
Was Airy light, from pure digestion bred,
And temperate vapours bland, which° th'only° sound   5
Of leaves and fuming rills, Aurora's° fan,

1 **Clime** region. 5 **which** (sleep). 5 **only** mere. 6 **Aurora** the
dawn.

Lightly dispers'd, and the shrill Matin Song
Of Birds on every bough; so much the more
His wonder was to find unwak'n'd Eve
10 With Tresses discompos'd, and glowing Cheek,
As through unquiet rest: he on his side
Leaning half-rais'd, with looks of cordial Love
Hung over her enamour'd, and beheld
Beauty, which whether waking or asleep,
15 Shot forth peculiar° Graces; then with voice
Mild, as when Zephyrus on Flora° breathes,
Her hand soft touching, whisper'd thus. "Awake
My fairest, my espous'd, my latest found,
Heav'n's last best gift, my ever-new delight,
20 Awake, the morning shines, and the fresh field
Calls us, we lose the prime,° to mark how spring
Our tended Plants, how blows° the Citron Grove,
What drops the Myrrh, and what the balmy Reed,
How Nature paints her colours, how the Bee
25 Sits on the Bloom extracting liquid sweet."
            Such whispering wak'd her, but with startl'd
            eye
On Adam, whom embracing, thus she spake.
            "O Sole in whom my thoughts find all repose,
My Glory, my Perfection, glad I see
30 Thy face, and Morn return'd, for I this Night,
Such night till this I never pass'd, have dream'd,
If dream'd, not as I oft am wont, of thee,
Works of day past, or morrow's next design,
But of offence and trouble, which my mind
35 Knew never till this irksome night; methought
Close at mine ear one call'd me forth to walk
With gentle voice, I thought it thine; it said,
'Why sleep'st thou Eve? now is the pleasant time,
The cool, the silent, save where silence yields
40 To the night-warbling Bird, that now awake
Tunes sweetest his love-labour'd° song; now reigns
Full-orb'd the Moon, and with more pleasing light
Shadowy sets off the face of things; in vain,

15 **peculiar** especial.   16 **Zephyrus on Flora** the west wind over
flowers (of which Flora was goddess).   21 **prime** early morning.
22 **blows** blooms.   41 **love-labour'd** wrought both by love and with
love.

If none regard; Heav'n wakes with all his eyes,
Whom to behold but thee, Nature's desire,   45
In whose sight all things joy, with ravishment
Attracted by thy beauty still° to gaze.'
I rose as at thy call, but found thee not;
To find thee I directed then my walk;
And on, methought, alone I pass'd through ways   50
That brought me on a sudden to the Tree
Of interdicted Knowledge: fair it seem'd,
Much fairer to my Fancy than by day:
And as I wond'ring lookt, beside it stood
One shap'd and wing'd like one of those from Heav'n   55
By us oft seen; his dewy locks distill'd
Ambrosia; on that Tree he also gaz'd;
And 'O fair Plant,' said he, 'with fruit surcharg'd,
Deigns none to ease thy load and taste thy sweet,
Nor God, nor Man; is Knowledge so despis'd?   60
Or envy, or what reserve° forbids to taste?
Forbid who will, none shall from me withhold
Longer thy offer'd good, why else set here?'
This said he paus'd not, but with vent'rous Arm
He pluckt, he tasted; mee damp horror chill'd   65
At such bold words voucht with° a deed so bold:
But he thus overjoy'd, 'O Fruit Divine,
Sweet of thyself, but much more sweet thus cropt,
Forbidd'n here, it seems, as only fit
For Gods, yet able to make Gods of Men: 70
And why not Gods of Men, since good, the more
Communicated,° more abundant grows,
The Author not impair'd, but honour'd more?
Here, happy Creature, fair Angelic Eve,
Partake thou also; happy though thou art,   75
Happier thou mayst be, worthier canst not be:
Taste this, and be henceforth among the Gods
Thyself a Goddess, not to Earth confin'd,
But sometimes in the Air, as wee, sometimes
Ascend to Heav'n, by merit thine, and see   80

47 still always.   **61 reserve** restriction.   **66 voucht with** backed by.
72 Communicated imparted; but with "tasted," "Divine," "Gods,"
etc., it suggests the sense "partake of or administer Holy Commun-
ion"—e.g. "He communicated the mysteries of the blessed body of
Christ" (1641).   The whole scene is a diabolical parody of Com-
munion; compare IX 755.

What life the Gods live there, and such live thou.'
So saying, he drew nigh, and to me held,
Even to my mouth of that same fruit held part
Which he had pluckt; the pleasant savoury smell
85 So quick'n'd appetite, that I, methought,
Could not but taste. Forthwith up to the Clouds
With him I flew, and underneath beheld
The Earth outstretcht immense, a prospect wide
And various: wond'ring at my flight and change
90 To this high exaltation; suddenly
My Guide was gone, and I, methought, sunk down,
And fell asleep; but O how glad I wak'd
To find this but a dream!" Thus Eve her Night
Related, and thus Adam answer'd sad.
95   "Best Image of myself and dearer half,
The trouble of thy thoughts this night in sleep
Affects me equally; nor can I like
This uncouth° dream, of evil sprung I fear;
Yet evil whence? in thee can harbour none,
100 Created pure. But know that in the Soul
Are many lesser Faculties that serve
Reason as chief; among these Fancy next
Her office holds; of all external things,
Which the five watchful Senses represent,
105 She forms Imaginations, Airy shapes,
Which Reason joining or disjoining, frames°
All what we affirm or what deny, and call
Our knowledge or opinion; then retires
Into her private Cell when Nature rests.
110 Oft in her absence mimic Fancy wakes
To imitate her; but misjoining shapes,
Wild work produces oft, and most in dreams,
Ill matching words and deeds long past or late.
Some such resemblances methinks I find
115 Of our last Ev'ning's talk, in this thy dream,
But with addition strange; yet be not sad.
Evil into the mind of God or Man
May come and go, so° unapprov'd, and leave
No spot or blame behind: Which gives me hope
120 That what in sleep thou didst abhor to dream,

98 **uncouth** unknown, strange.   106 **frames** shapes into.   118 **so** both "as in your case," and "provided that it be."

Waking thou never wilt consent to do.
Be not disheart'n'd, then, nor cloud those looks
That wont° to be more cheerful and serene
Than when fair Morning first smiles on the World,
And let us to our fresh employments rise   125
Among the Groves, the Fountains, and the Flow'rs
That open now their choicest bosom'd smells
Reserv'd from night, and kept for thee in store."
        So cheer'd he his fair Spouse, and she was
        cheer'd,
But silently a gentle tear let fall   130
From either eye, and wip'd them with her hair;
Two other precious drops that ready stood,
Each in their crystal sluice, hee ere they fell
Kiss'd as the gracious signs of sweet remorse
And pious awe, that fear'd to have offended.   135
        So all was clear'd° and to the Field they haste.
But first from under shady arborous roof,
Soon as they forth were come to open sight
Of day-spring, and the Sun, who scarce uprisen
With wheels yet hov'ring o'er the Ocean brim,   140
Shot parallel to the earth his dewy ray,
Discovering° in wide Landscape all the East
Of Paradise and Eden's happy Plains,
Lowly they bow'd adoring, and began
Their Orisons,° each Morning duly paid   145
In various style, for neither various style
Nor holy rapture wanted° they to praise
Their Maker, in fit strains pronounc't or sung
Unmeditated, such prompt eloquence
Flow'd from their lips, in Prose or numerous° Verse,   150
More tuneable than needed Lute or Harp
To add more sweetness, and they thus began.
        "These are thy glorious works, Parent of good,
Almighty, thine this universal Frame,
Thus wondrous fair; thyself how wondrous then!   155
Unspeakable,° who sitt'st above these Heavens
To us invisible or dimly seen
In these thy lowest works, yet these declare

---

123 **wont** are used.   136 **clear'd** made pure.   142 **Discovering** revealing.   145 **Orisons** prayers.   147 **wanted** lacked.   150 **numerous** melodious.   156 **Unspeakable** ineffable.

Thy goodness beyond thought, and Power Divine:
160 Speak yee who best can tell, ye Sons of light,
Angels, for yee behold him, and with songs
And choral symphonies, Day without Night,
Circle his Throne rejoicing, yee in Heav'n,
On Earth join all yee Creatures to extol
165 Him first, him last, him midst, and without end.
Fairest of Stars, last in the train of Night,
If better thou belong not to the dawn,°
Sure pledge of day, that crown'st the smiling Morn
With thy bright Circlet, praise him in thy Sphere
170 While day arises, that sweet hour of Prime.
Thou Sun, of this great World both Eye and Soul,
Acknowledge him thy Greater, sound his praise
In thy eternal course, both when thou climb'st,
And when high Noon hast gain'd, and when thou
    fall'st.
175 Moon, that now meet'st the orient Sun, now fli'st
With the fixt Stars, fixt in their Orb that flies,
And yee five other wand'ring Fires° that move
In mystic° Dance not without Song,° resound
His praise, who out of Darkness call'd up Light.
180 Air, and ye Elements the eldest birth
Of Nature's Womb, that in quaternion° run
Perpetual Circle, multiform; and mix
And nourish all things, let your ceaseless change
Vary to our great Maker still new praise.
185 Ye Mists and Exhalations that now rise
From Hill or steaming Lake, dusky or grey,
Till the Sun paint your fleecy skirts with Gold,
In honour to the World's great Author rise,
Whether to deck with Clouds the uncolour'd sky,
190 Or wet the thirsty Earth with falling showers,
Rising or falling still advance his praise.
His praise ye Winds, that from four Quarters blow,
Breathe soft or loud; and wave your tops, ye Pines,
With every Plant, in sign of Worship wave.
195 Fountains and yee, that warble, as ye flow,

166–67 The evening star, Hesperus, is the same as the morning star,
Venus.   177 five . . . Fires the planets Mars, Venus, Mercury, Jupi-
ter, Saturn.   178 mystic allegorical.   178 Song the music of the
spheres.   181 quaternion group of four.

Melodious murmurs, warbling tune his praise.
Join voices all ye living Souls, ye Birds,
That singing up to Heaven Gate ascend,
Bear on your wings and in your notes his praise;
Yee that in Waters glide, and yee that walk   200
The Earth, and stately tread, or lowly creep;
Witness if I be silent, Morn or Even,
To Hill, or Valley, Fountain, or fresh shade
Made vocal by my Song, and taught his praise.
Hail universal Lord, be bounteous still   205
To give us only good; and if the night
Have gathered aught of evil or conceal'd,
Disperse it, as now light dispels the dark."
        So pray'd they innocent, and to their thoughts
Firm peace recover'd soon and wonted calm.   210
On to their morning's rural work they haste
Among sweet dews and flow'rs; where any row
Of Fruit-trees overwoody reach'd too far
Their pamper'd boughs, and needed hands to check
Fruitless embraces: or they led the Vine   215
To wed her Elm; she spous'd about him twines
Her marriageable arms, and with her brings
Her dow'r th'adopted Clusters, to adorn
His barren leaves. Them thus employ'd beheld
With pity Heav'n's high King, and to him call'd   220
Raphaël, the sociable Spirit, that deign'd
To travel with Tobias, and secur'd
His marriage with the seven-times-wedded Maid.°
        "Raphaël," said hee, "thou hear'st what stir
            on Earth
Satan from Hell 'scapt through the darksome Gulf   225
Hath rais'd in Paradise, and how disturb'd
This night the human pair, how he designs
In them at once to ruin all mankind.
Go therefore, half this day as friend with friend
Converse with Adam, in what Bow'r or shade   230
Thou find'st him from the heat of Noon retir'd,
To respite his day-labour with repast,
Or with repose; and such discourse bring on,
As may advise him of his happy state,

221-23 See IV 167-71. The previous husbands of Sara had all been
murdered by the evil spirit Asmodeus.

235 Happiness in his power left free to will,
     Left to his own free Will, his Will though free,
     Yet mutable; whence warn him to beware
     He swerve not too secure:° tell him withal
     His danger, and from whom, what enemy
240 Late fall'n himself from Heav'n, is plotting now
     The fall of others from like state of bliss;
     By violence, no, for that shall be withstood,
     But by deceit and lies; this let him know,
     Lest wilfully transgressing he pretend°
245 Surprisal, unadmonisht, unforewarn'd."
            So spake th'Eternal Father, and fulfill'd
     All Justice: nor delay'd the winged Saint
     After his charge receiv'd; but from among
     Thousand Celestial Ardours,° where he stood
250 Veil'd with his gorgeous wings, up-springing light°
     Flew through the midst of Heav'n; th'angelic Choirs
     On each hand parting, to his speed gave way
     Through all th'Empyreal road; till at the Gate
     Of Heav'n arriv'd, the gate self-open'd wide
255 On golden Hinges turning, as by work
     Divine the sovran Architect had fram'd.
     From hence, no cloud, or, to obstruct his sight,
     Star interpos'd, however small he sees,
     Not unconform to other shining Globes,
260 Earth and the Gard'n of God, with Cedars crown'd
     Above all Hills. As when by night the Glass
     Of Galileo, less assur'd, observes
     Imagin'd Lands and Regions in the Moon:
     Or Pilot from amidst the Cyclades°
265 Delos or Samos first appearing kens
     A cloudy spot. Down thither prone in flight
     He speeds, and through the vast Ethereal Sky
     Sails between worlds and worlds, with steady wing
     Now on the polar winds, then with quick Fan
270 Winnows the buxom° Air; till within soar
     Of Tow'ring Eagles, to all the Fowls he seems
     A Phoenix, gaz'd by all, as that sole Bird
     When to enshrine his relics in the Sun's

238 **secure** overconfident of safety.   244 **pretend** claim.   249 **Ardours** bright angels.   250 **light** lightly (but notice "Ardours").   264 **Cyclades** Aegean islands.   270 **buxom** yielding.

Bright Temple, to Egyptian Thebes he flies.
At once on th'Eastern cliff of Paradise   275
He 'lights, and to his proper shape returns
A Seraph wing'd; six wings he wore, to shade
His lineaments Divine; the pair that clad
Each shoulder broad, came mantling o'er his breast
With regal Ornament; the middle pair   280
Girt like a Starry Zone° his waist, and round
Skirted his loins and thighs with downy Gold
And colours dipt in Heav'n; the third his feet
Shadow'd from either heel with feather'd mail
Sky-tinctur'd grain.° Like Maia's son° he stood,   285
And shook his Plumes, that Heav'nly fragrance fill'd
The circuit wide. Straight knew him all the Bands
Of Angels under watch; and to his state,°
And to his message high in honour rise;
For on some message high they guess'd him bound.   290
Their glittering Tents he pass'd, and now is come
Into the blissful field, through Groves of Myrrh,
And flow'ring Odours, Cassia, Nard, and Balm;
A Wilderness of sweets; for Nature here
Wanton'd as in her prime, and play'd at will   295
Her Virgin Fancies, pouring forth more sweet,
Wild above rule or Art; enormous° bliss.
Him through the spicy Forest onward come
Adam discern'd, as in the door he sat
Of his cool Bow'r, while now the mounted Sun   300
Shot down direct his fervid Rays to warm
Earth's inmost womb, more warmth than Adam
    needs;
And Eve within, due at her hour prepar'd
For dinner savoury fruits, of taste to please
True appetite, and not disrelish thirst   305
Of nectarous draughts between, from milky stream,
Berry or Grape: to whom thus Adam call'd.
        "Haste hither Eve, and worth thy sight behold

---

281 **Zone** belt. 285 **grain** dye. 285 **Maia's son** Mercury (Hermes),
messenger of the gods. 288 **state** stateliness and rank. 297 **enor-
mous** out of rule (Latin *norma*); the word is, as yet, innocent because
Eden has no need of rules—but it is ominous too, since the ordinary
sense was a bad one (as in "enormity"). There is the same combina-
tion of innocence and portent in lines 294–95, "Wilderness" and
"Wanton'd."

Eastward among those Trees, what glorious shape
310 Comes this way moving; seems another Morn
Ris'n on mid-noon; some great behest from Heav'n
To us perhaps he brings, and will vouchsafe
This day to be our Guest. But go with speed,
And what thy stores contain, bring forth and pour
315 Abundance, fit to honour and receive
Our Heav'nly stranger; well we may afford
Our givers their own gifts, and large bestow
From large bestow'd, where Nature multiplies
Her fertile growth, and by disburd'ning grows
320 More fruitful, which instructs us not to spare."
　　　　　To whom thus Eve. "Adam,° earth's hallow'd
　　　　　　　　mould,
Of God inspir'd,° small store will serve, where store,
All seasons, ripe for use hangs on the stalk;
Save what by frugal° storing firmness gains
325 To nourish, and superfluous moist consumes:
But I will haste and from each bough and brake,
Each Plant and juiciest Gourd° will pluck such
　　　　choice°
To entertain our Angel guest, as hee
Beholding shall confess that here on Earth
330 God hath dispenst his bounties as in Heav'n."
　　　　　So saying, with dispatchful looks in haste
She turns, on hóspitable thoughts intent
What choice to choose for delicacy best,
What order, so contriv'd as not to mix
335 Tastes, not well join'd, inelegant,° but bring
Taste after taste upheld with kindliest° change,
Bestirs her then, and from each tender stalk
Whatever Earth all-bearing Mother yields
In India° East or West, or middle shore°
340 In Pontus° or the Punic° Coast, or where
Alcinous° reign'd, fruit of all kinds, in coat,

---

321 **Adam** the name from "red earth."   322 **inspir'd** given the breath
of life.   324 **frugal** economical (and from Latin *fruges*, fruits).
327 **Gourd** fruit of the melon family.   327 **choice** excellence,
the "pick."   335 **inelegant** such as would not be delicate in taste
(the idea of "choosing," from Latin *eligere*, to select).   336 **kindliest**
most natural.   339 **India** Indies.   339 **middle shore** Mediterranean.
340 **Pontus** in Asia Minor.   340 **Punic** Carthaginian.   341 **Alcinous**
king of the Phaeacians, who entertained Odysseus and had fine gar-
dens.

Rough, or smooth rind, or bearded husk, or shell
She gathers, Tribute large, and on the board
Heaps with unsparing hand; for drink the Grape
She crushes, inoffensive must,° and meads   345
From many a berry, and from sweet kernels prest
She tempers dulcet creams, nor these to hold
Wants° her fit vessels pure, then strews the ground
With Rose and Odours from the shrub unfum'd.°
Meanwhile our Primitive° great Sire, to meet   350
His godlike Guest, walks forth, without more train
Accompani'd than with his own complete
Perfections, in himself was all his state,
More solemn than the tedious pomp that waits
On Princes, when their rich Retinue long   355
Of Horses led, and Grooms besmear'd with Gold
Dazzles the crowd, and sets them all agape.
Nearer his presence Adam though not aw'd,
Yet with submiss approach and reverence meek,
As to a superior Nature, bowing low,   360
Thus said. "Native of Heav'n, for other place
None can than Heav'n such glorious shape contain;
Since by descending from the Thrones above,
Those happy places thou hast deign'd awhile
To want, and honour these, vouchsafe with us   365
Two only, who yet by sovran gift possess
This spacious ground, in yonder shady Bow'r
To rest, and what the Garden choicest bears
To sit and taste, till this meridian heat
Be over, and the Sun more cool decline."   370
         Whom thus the Angelic Virtue answer'd mild.
"Adam, I therefore came, nor art thou such
Created, or such place hast here to dwell,
As may not oft invite, though Spirits of Heav'n
To visit thee; lead on then where thy Bow'r   375
O'ershades; for these mid-hours, till Ev'ning rise
I have at will." So to the Sylvan Lodge
They came, that like Pomona's° Arbour smil'd
With flow'rets deckt and fragrant smells; but Eve
Undeckt, save with herself more lovely fair   380

---

345 must unfermented wine.   348 Wants lacks.   349 unfum'd not
burned for incense, but naturally scented.   350 Primitive from the
first age.   378 Pomona goddess of fruit.

Than Wood-Nymph, or the fairest Goddess feign'd
Of three that in Mount Ida naked strove,°
Stood to entertain° her guest from Heav'n; no veil
Shee needed, Virtue-proof,° no thought infirm
385 Alter'd her cheek. On whom the Angel *Hail*
Bestow'd, the holy salutation us'd
Long after to blest Mary, second Eve.
      "Hail Mother of Mankind, whose fruitful
        Womb
Shall fill the World more numerous with thy Sons
390 Than with these various fruits the Trees of God
Have heap'd this Table." Rais'd of grassy turf
Their Table was, and mossy seats had round,
And on her ample Square from side to side
All Autumn pil'd, though Spring and Autumn here
395 Danc'd hand in hand. Awhile discourse they hold;
No fear lest Dinner cool; when thus began
Our Author. "Heav'nly stranger, please to taste
These bounties which our Nourisher, from whom
All perfect good unmeasur'd out, descends,
400 To us for food and for delight hath caus'd
The Earth to yield; unsavoury food perhaps
To spiritual Natures; only this I know,
That one Celestial Father gives to all."
      To whom the Angel. "Therefore what he gives
405 (Whose praise be ever sung) to man in part
Spiritual, may of purest Spirits be found
No ingrateful food: and food alike those pure
Intelligential° substances require
As doth your Rational; and both contain
410 Within them every lower faculty
Of sense, whereby they hear, see, smell, touch, taste,
Tasting concoct, digest, assimilate,
And corporeal to incorporeal turn.
For know, whatever was created, needs
415 To be sustain'd and fed; of Elements
The grosser feeds the purer, earth the sea,
Earth and the Sea feed Air, the Air those Fires
Ethereal, and as lowest first the Moon;

382 **Of three … strove** The judgment of Paris, who awarded the apple
to Aphrodite.   383 **entertain** formally welcome.   384 **-proof** arm-
ored in.   408 **Intelligential** An intelligence is a spirit, angel, as in
VIII 181.

Whence in her visage round those spots, unpurg'd
Vapours not yet into her substance turn'd.   420
Nor doth the Moon no nourishment exhale
From her moist Continent to higher Orbs.
The Sun that light imparts to all, receives
From all his alimental° recompense
In humid exhalations, and at Even   425
Sups with the Ocean: though in Heav'n the Trees
Of life ambrosial fruitage bear, and vines
Yield Nectar, though from off the boughs each Morn
We brush mellifluous° Dews, and find the ground
Cover'd with pearly grain: yet God hath here   430
Varied his bounty so with new delights,
As may compare with Heaven; and to taste
Think not I shall be nice."° So down they sat,
And to their viands fell, nor seemingly°
The Angel, nor in mist, the common gloss°   435
Of Theologians, but with keen dispatch
Of real hunger, and concoctive° heat
To transubstantiate;° what redounds,° transpires
Through Spirits with ease; nor wonder; if by fire
Of sooty coal th'Empiric° Alchemist   440
Can turn, or holds it possible to turn
Metals of drossiest° Ore to perfect Gold
As from the Mine. Meanwhile at Table Eve
Minister'd naked, and their flowing cups
With pleasant liquors crown'd: O innocence   445
Deserving Paradise! if ever, then,
Then had the Sons of God excuse to have been
Enamour'd at that sight; but in those hearts
Love unlibidinous reign'd, nor jealousy
Was understood, the injur'd Lover's Hell.   450
          Thus when with meats and drinks they had
               suffic'd,
Not burd'n'd Nature, sudden mind arose

424 **alimental** nourishing.   429 **mellifluous** flowing with honey, as in
Rowland: "The increase of bees is more in regard of . . . the plenty
of mellifluous dews" (1658).   433 **nice** fastidious.   434 **seemingly**
only seemed.   435 **gloss** explanation.   437 **concoctive** digestive.   438
transubstantiate change from one substance to another, with a sar-
donic pun against the "Theologians" because of the Roman Catholic
doctrine of "Transubstantiation"; "real" too is a theological term
from the Holy Communion.   438 **redounds** is superfluous.   440
Empiric quack-experimenter.   442 **drossiest** most full of dregs.

In Adam, not to let th'occasion pass
Given him by this great Conference to know
455 Of things above his World, and of their being
Who dwell in Heav'n, whose excellence he saw
Transcend his own so far, whose radiant forms
Divine effulgence, whose high Power so far
Exceeded human, and his wary speech
460 Thus to th'Empyreal Minister he fram'd.
          "Inhabitant with God, now know I well
Thy favour, in this honour done to man,
Under whose lowly roof thou hast vouchsaf't
To enter, and these earthly fruits to taste,
465 Food not of Angels, yet accepted so,
As that more willingly thou couldst not seem
At Heav'n's high feasts to have fed: yet what
     compare?"
          To whom the winged Hierarch° repli'd.
"O Adam, one Almighty is, from whom
470 All things proceed, and up to him return,
If not deprav'd from good, created all
Such to perfection, one first matter all,
Indu'd with various forms, various degrees
Of substance, and in things that live, of life;
475 But more refin'd, more spiritous, and pure,
As nearer to him plac't or nearer tending
Each in their several active Spheres assign'd,
Till body up to spirit work, in bounds
Proportion'd to each kind. So from the root
480 Springs lighter the green stalk, from thence the leaves
More airy, last the bright consummate° flow'r
Spirits odórous breathes: flow'rs and their fruit
Man's nourishment, by gradual scale sublim'd°
To vital Spirits° aspire, to animal,
485 To intellectual, give both life and sense,
Fancy and understanding, whence the soul
Reason receives, and reason is her being,
Discursive, or Intuitive;° discourse
Is oftest yours, the latter most is ours,

468 **Hierarch** sacred leader.   481 **consummate** perfected.   483 **sub-lim'd** refined.   484 **Spirits** "Spirits" (animal, vital, intellectual) were thought to permeate the body.   488 **Discursive, or Intuitive** Discourse is reasoning process; intuition, the immediate apprehension of truth.

Differing but in degree, of kind the same.   490
Wonder not then, what God for you saw good
If I refuse not, but convert, as you,
To proper° substance; time may come when men
With Angels may participate, and find
No inconvenient Diet, nor too light Fare: 495
And from these corporal nutriments perhaps
Your bodies may at last turn all to Spirit,
Improv'd by tract of time, and wing'd ascend
Ethereal, as wee, or may at choice
Here or in Heav'nly Paradises dwell;   500
If ye be found obedient, and retain
Unalterably firm his love entire°
Whose progeny you are. Meanwhile enjoy
Your fill what happiness this happy state
Can comprehend, incapable of more."   505
            To whom the Patriarch of mankind repli'd.
"O favourable spirit, propitious guest,
Well hast thou taught the way that might direct
Our knowledge, and the scale° of Nature set
From center to circumference, whereon   510
In contemplation° of created things
By steps we may ascend to God. But say,
What meant that caution join'd, *if ye be found
Obedient?* can wee want obedience then
To him, or possibly his love desert   515
Who form'd us from the dust, and plac'd us here
Full to the utmost measure of what bliss
Human desires can seek or apprehend?"
            To whom the Angel. "Son of Heav'n and Earth,
Attend: That thou art happy, owe to God,   520
That thou continu'st such, owe to thyself,
That is, to thy obedience; therein stand.
This was that caution giv'n thee; be advis'd.
God made thee perfect, not immutable;
And good he made thee, but to persevere   525
He left it in thy power, ordain'd thy will
By nature free, not overrul'd by Fate
Inextricable,° or strict necessity;

493 **proper** my own.   502 **entire** unblemished.   509 **scale** ladder.
511 **contemplation** from Latin *com + templum*, consecrated space
(temple); notice "steps," "God."   528 **Inextricable** inescapable.

Our voluntary service he requires,
530 Not our necessitated, such with him
Finds no acceptance, nor can find, for how
Can hearts, not free, be tri'd whether they serve
Willing or no, who will but what they must
By Destiny, and can no other choose?
535 Myself and all th'Angelic Host that stand
In sight of God enthron'd, our happy state
Hold, as you yours, while our obedience holds;
On other surety° none; freely we serve,
Because wee freely love, as in our will
540 To love or not; in this we stand or fall:
And some are fall'n, to disobedience fall'n,
And so from Heav'n to deepest Hell; O fall
From what high state of bliss into what woe!"
          To whom our great Progenitor. "Thy words
545 Attentive, and with more delighted ear
Divine instructor, I have heard, than when
Cherubic Songs by night from neighbouring Hills
Aereal Music send: nor knew I not
To be both will and deed created free;
550 Yet that we never shall forget to love
Our maker, and obey him whose command
Single,° is yet so just, my constant thoughts
Assur'd me and still assure: though what thou tell'st
Hath past in Heav'n, some doubt within me move,
555 But more desire to hear, if thou consent,
The full relation, which must needs be strange,
Worthy of Sacred silence to be heard;
And we have yet large day, for scarce the Sun
Hath finisht half his journey, and scarce begins
560 His other half in the great Zone of Heav'n."
          Thus Adam made request, and Raphaël
After short pause assenting, thus began.
          "High matter thou enjoin'st me, O prime of
                    men,
Sad task and hard, for how shall I relate
565 To human sense th'invisible exploits

---

538 **surety** ground of certainty (and with a hint at the specific appli-
cation to Christ as our "surety").   552 **Single** sole (command); also
absolute, as in Milton's *Comus* ("single darkness"), and openly up-
right (Shakespeare: "a single heart").

Of warring Spirits; how without remorse°
The ruin of so many glorious once
And perfect while they stood; how last unfold
The secrets of another world, perhaps
Not lawful to reveal? yet for thy good   570
This is dispens't,° and what surmounts the reach
Of human sense, I shall delineate so,
By lik'ning spiritual to corporal forms,
As may express them best, though what if Earth
Be but the shadow of Heav'n, and things therein   575
Each to other like, more than on earth is thought?
          As yet this world was not, and Chaos wild
Reign'd where these Heav'ns now roll, where Earth
    now rests
Upon her Center pois'd, when on a day
(For Time, though in Eternity, appli'd   580
To motion, measures all things durable
By present, past, and future) on such day
As Heav'n's great Year° brings forth, th'Empyreal
    Host
Of Angels by Imperial summons call'd,
Innumerable before th'Almighty's Throne   585
Forthwith from all the ends of Heav'n appear'd
Under their Hierarchs in orders bright
Ten thousand thousand Ensigns high advanc'd,
Standards, and Gonfalons° 'twixt Van and Rear
Stream in the Air, and for distinction serve   590
Of Hierarchies, of Orders, and Degrees;
Or in their glittering Tissues bear emblaz'd
Holy Memorials,° acts of Zeal and Love
Recorded eminent. Thus when in Orbs
Of circuit inexpressible they stood,   595
Orb within Orb, the Father infinite,
By whom in bliss imbosom'd sat the Son,
Amidst as from a flaming Mount, whose top
Brightness had made invisible, thus spake.
          'Hear all ye Angels, Progeny of Light,   600
Thrones, Dominations, Princedoms, Virtues, Powers,
Hear my Decree, which unrevok't shall stand.

566 **remorse** pity.   571 **dispens't** permitted (legal and ecclesiastical).
583 **great Year** the cycle of the years, borrowed from Plato.   589
Gonfalons banners.   593 **Memorials** commemorations.

This day I have begot whom I declare
My only Son, and on this holy Hill
605 Him have anointed,° whom ye now behold
At my right hand; your Head I him appoint;
And by my Self have sworn to him shall bow
All knees in Heav'n, and shall confess him Lord:
Under his great Vice-gerent° Reign abide
610 United as one individual° Soul
For ever happy; him who disobeys
Mee disobeys, breaks union, and that day
Cast out from God and blessed vision, falls
Into utter darkness, deep engulft, his place
615 Ordain'd without redemption, without end.'
          So spake th'Omnipotent, and with his words
All seem'd well pleas'd, all seem'd, but were not all.
That day, as other solemn days, they spent
In song and dance about the sacred Hill,
620 Mystical dance, which yonder starry Sphere
Of Planets and of fixt in all her Wheels
Resembles nearest, mazes intricate,
Eccentric,° intervolv'd, yet regular
Then most, when most irregular they seem:
625 And in their motions° harmony Divine
So smoothes her charming tones, that God's own ear
Listens delighted. Ev'ning now approach'd
(For we have also our Ev'ning and our Morn,
We ours for change delectable, not need)
630 Forthwith from dance to sweet repast they turn
Desirous, all in Circles as they stood,
Tables are set, and on a sudden pil'd
With Angels' Food, and rubied Nectar flows:
In Pearl, in Diamond, and massy Gold,
635 Fruit of delicious Vines, the growth of Heav'n.
On flow'rs repos'd, and with fresh flow'rets crown'd,
They eat, they drink, and in communion sweet
Quaff immortality and joy, secure
Of surfeit where full measure only bounds
640 Excess, before th'all-bounteous King, who show'r'd°

605 **anointed** the Hebrew meaning of "Messiah."   609 **Vice-gerent**
exercising deputed power.   610 **individual** indivisible.   623 **Eccen-**
tric in an orbit not precisely circular.   625 **motions** including a
musical suggestion, as in "movements."   637–40 **They eat . . .**
show'r'd *1674;* They eat, they drink, and with refection sweet/Are
fill'd, before th'all-bounteous King, who show'r'd *1667.*

With copious hand, rejoicing in their joy.
Now when ambrosial Night with Clouds exhal'd
From that high mount of God, whence light and shade
Spring both, the face of brightest Heav'n had chang'd
To grateful Twilight (for Night comes not there   645
In darker veil) and roseate Dews dispos'd
All but th'unsleeping eyes of God to rest,
Wide over all the Plain, and wider far
Then all this globous Earth in Plain outspread,
(Such are the Courts of God) Th'Angelic throng   650
Disperst in Bands and Files their Camp extend
By living Streams among the Trees of Life,
Pavilions numberless, and sudden rear'd,
Celestial Tabernacles, where they slept
Fann'd with cool Winds, save those who in their
    course   655
Melodious Hymns about the sovran Throne
Alternate° all night long: but not so wak'd
Satan, so call him now, his former name
Is heard no more in Heav'n; he of the first,
If not the first Arch-Angel, great in Power,   660
In favour and preeminence, yet fraught
With envy against the Son of God, that day
Honour'd by his great Father, and proclaim'd
Messiah King anointed, could not bear
Through pride that sight, and thought himself
    impair'd.   665
Deep malice thence conceiving and disdain,
Soon as midnight brought on the dusky hour
Friendliest to sleep and silence, he resolv'd
With all his Legions to dislodge, and leave
Unworshipt, unobey'd the Throne supreme   670
Contemptuous, and his next subordinate
Awak'ning, thus to him in secret spake.
        'Sleep'st thou Companion dear, what sleep can
            close
Thy eye-lids? and rememb'rest what Decree
Of yesterday, so late hath past the lips   675
Of Heav'n's Almighty. Thou to me thy thoughts

---

657 **Alternate** sing in alternation (specific musical application).

Wast wont, I mine to thee was wont to impart;
Both waking we were one; how then can now
Thy sleep dissent?° new Laws thou seest impos'd;
680 New Laws from him who reigns, new minds may raise
In us who serve, new Councils, to debate
What doubtful may ensue, more in this place
To utter is not safe. Assemble thou
Of all those Myriads which we lead the chief;
685 Tell them that by command, ere yet dim Night
Her shadowy Cloud withdraws, I am to haste,
And all who under me their Banners wave,
Homeward with flying march where we possess
The Quarters of the North,° there to prepare
690 Fit entertainment to receive our King
The great Messiah, and his new commands,
Who speedily through all the Hierarchies
Intends to pass triumphant, and give Laws.'
        So spake the false Arch-Angel, and infus'd
695 Bad influence into th'unwary breast
Of his Associate; hee together calls,
Or several° one by one, the Regent Powers,
Under him Regent, tells, as he was taught,
That the most High commanding, now ere Night,
700 Now ere dim Night had disencumber'd Heav'n,
The great Hierarchal Standard was to move;
Tells the suggested° cause, and casts between
Ambiguous° words and jealousies, to sound
Or taint integrity; but all obey'd
705 The wonted signal, and superior voice
Of their great Potentate; for great indeed
His name, and high was his degree in Heav'n;
His count'nance, as the Morning Star° that guides
The starry flock, allur'd them, and with lies
710 Drew after him the third part of Heav'n's Host:
Meanwhile th'Eternal eye, whose sight discerns
Abstrusest° thoughts, from forth his holy Mount
And from within the golden Lamps that burn
Nightly before him, saw without their light

679 dissent differ.   689 North traditionally associated with Satan
(ISAIAH 14:13).   697 several separate.   702 suggested both "insinu-
ated" and "falsely imputed."   703 Ambiguous equivocal (duplicity
contrasting with "integrity").   708 Morning Star Lucifer.   712 Ab-
strusest most hidden.

Rebellion rising, saw in whom, how spread   715
Among the sons of Morn, what multitudes
Were banded to oppose his high Decree;
And smiling to his only Son thus said.
      'Son, thou in whom my glory I behold
In full resplendence, Heir of all my might,   720
Nearly° it now concerns us to be sure
Of our Omnipotence, and with what Arms
We mean to hold what anciently we claim
Of Deity or Empire, such a foe
Is rising, who intends to erect his Throne   725
Equal to ours, throughout the spacious North;
Nor so content, hath in his thought to try
In battle, what our Power is, or our right.
Let us advise,° and to this hazard draw
With speed what force is left, and all employ   730
In our defence, lest unawares we lose
This our high place, our Sanctuary, our Hill.'
      To whom the Son with calm aspéct and clear
Light'ning Divine, ineffable, serene,
Made answer. 'Mighty Father, thou thy foes   735
Justly hast in derision, and secure
Laugh'st at their vain designs and tumults vain,
Matter to mee of Glory, whom their hate
Illústrates,° when they see all Regal Power
Giv'n me to quell their pride, and in event°   740
Know whether I be dextrous° to subdue
Thy Rebels, or be found the worst in Heav'n.'
      So spake the Son, but Satan with his Powers
Far was advanc't on winged speed, an Host
Innumerable as the Stars of Night,   745
Or Stars of Morning, Dew-drops, which the Sun
Impearls on every leaf and every flow'r.
Regions they pass'd, the mighty Regencies
Of Seraphim and Potentates and Thrones
In their triple Degrees, Regions to which   750
All thy Dominion, Adam, is no more
Than what this Garden is to all the Earth,

721 **Nearly** closely, particularly. 729 **advise** consult. 739 **Illústrates**
makes illustrious, gives luster to (following on "Light'ning" and
"Glory"). 740 **event** outcome. 741 **dextrous** Christ's powers de-
riving from his position on the right hand of God ("dextrous" in a
common 17th-century sense); see III 62–64.

And all the Sea, from one entire globose
Stretcht into Longitude; which having pass'd
755 At length into the limits of the North
They came, and Satan to his Royal seat
High on a Hill, far blazing, as a Mount
Rais'd on a Mount, with Pyramids and Tow'rs
From Diamond Quarries hewn, and Rocks of Gold,
760 The Palace of great Lucifer, (so call
That Structure in the Dialect of men
Interpreted) which not long after, hee
Affecting° all equality with God,
In imitation of that Mount whereon
765 Messiah was declar'd in sight of Heav'n,
The Mountain of the Congregation call'd;
For thither he assembl'd all his Train,
Pretending so commanded to consult
About the great reception of their King,
770 Thither to come, and with calumnious Art
Of counterfeited truth thus held their ears.
          'Thrones, Dominations, Princedoms, Virtues,
               Powers,
If these magnific Titles yet remain
Not merely titular, since by Decree
775 Another now hath to himself engross't°
All Power, and us eclipst under the name
Of King anointed, for whom all this haste
Of midnight march, and hurried meeting here,
This only to consult how we may best
780 With what may be devis'd of honours new
Receive him coming to receive from us
Knee-tribute yet unpaid, prostration vile,
Too much to one, but double how endur'd,
To one and to his image now proclaim'd?
785 But what if better counsels might erect
Our minds and teach us to cast off this Yoke?
Will ye submit your necks, and choose to bend
The supple° knee? ye will not, if I trust
To know ye right, or if ye know yourselves
790 Natives and Sons of Heav'n possest before
By none, and if not equal all, yet free,

763 **Affecting** aspiring to.   775 **engross't** monopolized.   788 **supple**
as in "suppliant."

Equally free; for Orders and Degrees
Jar not with liberty, but well consist.°
Who can in reason then or right assume
Monarchy over such as live by right   795
His equals, if in power and splendor less,
In freedom equal? or can introduce
Law and Edíct on us, who without law
Err not, much less for this to be our Lord,
And look for adoration to th'abuse   800
Of those Imperial Titles which assert
Our being ordain'd to govern, not to serve?'
          Thus far his bold discourse without control
Had audience, when among the Seraphim
Abdiel, than whom none with more zeal ador'd   805
The Deity, and divine commands obey'd,
Stood up, and in a flame of zeal severe
The current of his fury thus oppos'd.
          'O argument blasphémous, false and proud!
Words which no ear ever to hear in Heav'n   810
Expected, least of all from thee, ingrate
In place thyself so high above thy Peers.
Canst thou with impious obloquy condemn
The just Decree of God, pronounc't and sworn,
That to his only Son by right endu'd   815
With Regal Scepter, every Soul in Heav'n
Shall bend the knee, and in that honour due
Confess him rightful King? unjust thou say'st
Flatly unjust, to bind with Laws the free,
And equal over equals to let Reign,   820
One over all with unsucceeded° power.
Shalt thou give Law to God, shalt thou dispute
With him the points of liberty, who made
Thee what thou art, and form'd the Pow'rs of Heav'n
Such as he pleas'd, and circumscrib'd their being?   825
Yet by experience taught we know how good,
And of our good, and of our dignity
How provident he is, how far from thought
To make us less, bent rather to exalt
Our happy state under one Head more near   830
United. But to grant it thee unjust,

793 **consist** go together, harmonize.   821 **unsucceeded** without successor.

That equal over equals Monarch Reign:
Thyself though great and glorious dost thou count,
Or all Angelic Nature join'd in one,
835 Equal to him begotten Son, by whom
As by his Word the mighty Father made
All things, ev'n thee, and all the Spirits of Heav'n
By him created in their bright degrees,
Crown'd them with Glory, and to their Glory nam'd
840 Thrones, Dominations, Princedoms, Virtues, Powers,
Essential Powers, nor by his Reign obscur'd,
But more illustrious made, since he the Head
One of our number thus reduc't becomes,
His Laws our Laws, all honour to him done
845 Returns our own. Cease then this impious rage,
And tempt not these; but hast'n to appease
Th'incensed Father, and th'incensed Son,
While Pardon may be found in time besought.'
      So spake the fervent Angel, but his zeal
850 None seconded, as out of season judg'd,
Or singular and rash, whereat rejoic'd
Th'Apostate, and more haughty thus repli'd.
'That we were form'd then say'st thou? and the work
Of secondary hands, by task transferr'd
855 From Father to his Son? strange point and new!
Doctrine which we would know whence learnt: who
      saw
When this creation was? remember'st thou
Thy making, while the Maker gave thee being?
We know no time when we were not as now;
860 Know none before us, self-begot, self-rais'd
By our own quick'ning power, when fatal course
Had circl'd his full Orb, the birth mature
Of this our native Heav'n, Ethereal Sons.
Our puissance is our own, our own right hand
865 Shall teach us highest deeds, by proof to try
Who is our equal: then thou shalt behold
Whether by supplication we intend
Address,° and to begirt th'Almighty Throne
Beseeching or besieging. This report,
870 These tidings carry to th'anointed King;
And fly, ere evil intercept thy flight.'

868 **Address** dutiful approach, as in "pay one's addresses to."

He said, and as the sound of waters deep
Hoarse murmur echo'd to his words applause
Through the infinite Host, nor less for that
The flaming Seraph fearless, though alone   875
Encompass'd round with foes, thus answer'd bold.
　　　'O alienate from God, O spirit accurst,
Forsak'n of all good; I see thy fall
Determin'd, and thy hapless crew involv'd
In this perfidious fraud, contagion spread   880
Both of thy crime and punishment: henceforth
No more be troubl'd how to quit the yoke
Of God's Messiah; those indulgent Laws
Will not be now vouchsaf't, other Decrees
Against thee are gone forth without recall;   885
That Golden Scepter which thou didst reject
Is now an Iron Rod to bruise and break
Thy disobedience. Well thou didst advise,
Yet not for thy advise or threats I fly
These wicked Tents devoted,° lest the wrath   890
Impendent, raging into sudden flame
Distinguish not: for soon expect to feel
His Thunder on thy head, devouring fire.
Then who created thee lamenting learn,
When who can uncreate thee thou shalt know.'   895
　　　So spake the Seraph Abdiel faithful found,
Among the faithless, faithful only hee;
Among innumerable false, unmov'd,
Unshak'n, unseduc'd, unterrifi'd
His Loyalty he kept, his Love, his Zeal;   900
Nor number, nor example with him wrought
To swerve from truth, or change his constant mind
Though single. From amidst them forth he pass'd,
Long way through hostile scorn, which he sustain'd
Superior,° nor of violence fear'd aught;   905
And with retorted° scorn his back he turn'd
On those proud Tow'rs to swift destruction doom'd.

890 **devoted** doomed.   905 **Superior** too great to be overcome.   906
retorted flung back.

BOOK VI

THE ARGUMENT

Raphael continues to relate how Michael and Gabriel were
sent forth to Battle against Satan and his Angels. The first
Fight describ'd: Satan and his Powers retire under Night:
He calls a Council, invents devilish Engines, which in the
second day's Fight put Michael and his Angels to some
disorder; But they at length pulling up Mountains over-
whelm'd both the force and Machines of Satan: Yet the
Tumult not so ending, God on the third day sends Mes-
siah his Son, for whom he had reserv'd the glory of that
Victory: Hee in the Power of his Father coming to the
place, and causing all his Legions to stand still on either
side, with his Chariot and Thunder driving into the midst
of his Enemies, pursues them unable to resist towards
the wall of Heaven; which opening, they leap down with
horror and confusion into the place of punishment pre-
par'd for them in the Deep: Messiah returns with triumph
to his Father.

All night the dreadless Angel unpursu'd
Through Heav'n's wide Champaign° held his way, till
   Morn,
Wak't by the circling Hours, with rosy hand
Unbarr'd the gates of Light. There is a Cave
5   Within the Mount of God, fast by his Throne,
Where light and darkness in perpetual round
Lodge and dislodge by turns, which makes through
   Heav'n

2 **Champaign** plain.

Grateful vicissitude, like Day and Night;
Light issues forth, and at the other door
Obsequious° darkness enters, till her hour   10
To veil the Heav'n, though darkness there might well
Seem twilight here; and now went forth the Morn
Such as in highest Heav'n, array'd in Gold
Empyreal, from before her vanisht Night,
Shot through° with orient Beams: when all the Plain   15
Cover'd with thick embattled Squadrons bright,
Chariots and flaming Arms, and fiery Steeds
Reflecting blaze on blaze, first met his view:
War he perceiv'd, war in procinct,° and found
Already known what he for news had thought   20
To have reported: gladly then he mixt
Among those friendly Powers who him receiv'd
With joy and acclamations loud, that one
That of so many Myriads fall'n, yet one
Return'd not lost: On to the sacred hill   25
They led him high applauded, and present
Before the seat supreme; from whence a voice
From midst a Golden Cloud thus mild was heard.
          'Servant of God, well done, well hast thou
                fought
The better fight, who single hast maintain'd   30
Against revolted multitudes the Cause
Of Truth, in word mightier than they in Arms;
And for the testimony of Truth hast borne
Universal reproach, far worse to bear
Than violence: for this was all thy care   35
To stand approv'd in sight of God, though Worlds
Judg'd thee perverse: the easier conquest now
Remains thee, aided by this host of friends,
Back on thy foes more glorious to return
Than scorn'd thou didst depart, and to subdue   40
By force, who reason for their Law refuse,
Right reason for their Law, and for their King
Messiah, who by right of merit Reigns.
Go Michael of Celestial Armies Prince,
And thou in Military prowess next   45

10 **Obsequious** following dutifully.   15 **Shot through** The military
setting (so "pierced") plays against the visual beauty ("variegated
in colors").   19 **procinct** readiness.

Gabriel, lead forth to Battle these my Sons
Invincible, lead forth my armed Saints
By Thousands and by Millions rang'd for fight;
Equal in number to that Godless crew
50 Rebellious, them with Fire and hostile Arms
Fearless assault, and to the brow of Heav'n
Pursuing drive them out from God and bliss,
Into their place of punishment, the Gulf
Of Tartarus, which ready opens wide
55 His fiery Chaos to receive their fall.'
        So spake the Sovran voice, and Clouds began
To darken all the Hill, and smoke to roll
In dusky wreaths, reluctant° flames, the sign
Of wrath awak't: nor with less dread the loud
60 Ethereal Trumpet from on high 'gan blow:
At which command the Powers Militant,
That stood for Heav'n, in mighty Quadrate° join'd
Of Union irresistible, mov'd on
In silence their bright Legions, to the sound
65 Of instrumental Harmony that breath'd
Heroic Ardor to advent'rous deeds
Under their God-like Leaders, in the Cause
Of God and his Messiah. On they move
Indíssolúbly firm; nor obvious° Hill,
70 Nor strait'ning° Vale, nor Wood, nor Stream divides
Their perfect ranks; for high above the ground
Their march was, and the passive Air upbore
Their nimble tread; as when the total kind
Of Birds in orderly array on wing
75 Came summon'd over Eden to receive
Their names of thee; so over many a tract
Of Heav'n they march'd, and many a Province wide
Tenfold the length of this terrene:° at last
Far in th'Horizon to the North appear'd
80 From skirt to skirt a fiery Region, stretcht
In battailous aspéct, and nearer view
Bristl'd with upright beams innumerable
Of rigid Spears, and Helmets throng'd, and Shields
Various, with boastful Argument° portray'd,

58 **reluctant** struggling.   62 **Quadrate** square.   69 **obvious** in the way.   70 **strait'ning** hemming in.   78 **terrene** earth.   84 **Argument** heraldic slogans.

The banded Powers of Satan hasting on   85
With furious expedition; for they ween'd
That selfsame day by fight, or by surprise
To win the Mount of God, and on his Throne
To set the envier of his State, the proud
Aspirer, but their thoughts prov'd fond and vain   90
In the mid way: though strange to us it seem'd
At first, that Angel should with Angel war,
And in fierce hosting° meet, who wont to meet
So oft in Festivals of joy and love
Unanimous,° as sons of one great Sire   95
Hymning th'Eternal Father: but the shout
Of Battle now began, and rushing sound
Of onset ended soon each milder thought.
High in the midst exalted as a God
Th'Apostate in his Sun-bright Chariot sat   100
Idol of Majesty Divine, enclos'd
With Flaming Cherubim, and golden Shields;
Then 'lighted from his gorgeous Throne, for now
'Twixt Host and Host but narrow space was left,
A dreadful interval, and Front to Front   105
Presented stood in terrible array
Of hideous length: before the cloudy° Van,°
On the rough edge of battle ere it join'd,
Satan with vast and haughty strides advanc't,
Came tow'ring, armed in Adamant and Gold;   110
Abdiel that sight endur'd not, where he stood
Among the mightiest, bent on highest deeds,
And thus his own undaunted heart explores.
            'O Heav'n! that such resemblance of the
                    Highest
Should yet remain, where faith and realty°   115
Remain not; wherefore should not strength and might
There fail where Virtue fails, or weakest prove.
Where boldest; though to sight° unconquerable?
His puissance, trusting in th'Almighty's aid,
I mean to try, whose Reason I have tri'd   120
Unsound and false; nor is it aught but just,
That he who in debate of Truth hath won,

93 **hosting** encounter.   95 **Unanimous** of one mind.   107 **cloudy**
darkly foreboding.   107 **Van** vanguard.   115 **realty** honesty.   118
to sight to appearances.

Should win in Arms, in both disputes alike
Victor; though brutish that contést and foul,
125 When Reason hath to deal with force, yet so
Most reason is that Reason overcome.'
      So pondering, and from his armed Peers
Forth stepping opposite,° halfway he met
His daring foe, at this prevention° more
130 Incens't, and thus securely° him defi'd.
      'Proud, art thou met? thy hope was to have
        reacht
The heighth of thy aspiring unoppos'd,
The Throne of God unguarded, and his side
Abandon'd at the terror of thy Power
135 Or potent tongue; fool, not to think how vain
Against th'Omnipotent to rise in Arms;
Who out of smallest things could without end
Have rais'd incessant Armies to defeat
Thy folly; or with solitary hand
140 Reaching beyond all limit, at one blow
Unaided could have finisht thee, and whelm'd
Thy Legions under darkness; but thou seest
All are not of thy Train; there be who Faith
Prefer, and Piety to God, though then
145 To thee not visible, when I alone
Seem'd in thy World erroneous to dissent
From all: my Sect thou seest, now learn too late
How few sometimes may know, when thousands err.'
      Whom the grand foe with scornful eye askance
150 Thus answer'd. 'Ill for thee, but in wisht hour
Of my revenge, first sought for thou return'st
From flight, seditious Angel, to receive
Thy merited reward, the first assay
Of this right hand provok't, since first that tongue
155 Inspir'd with contradiction durst oppose
A third part of the Gods, in Synod° met
Their Deities to assert, who while they feel
Vigor Divine within them, can allow
Omnipotence to none. But well thou com'st
160 Before thy fellows, ambitious to win

---

128 **opposite** including "in opposition." 129 **prevention** forestalling.
130 **securely** confidently. 156 **Synod** assembly (usually of clergy).

From me some Plume, that thy success° may show
Destruction to the rest: this pause between
(Unanswer'd lest thou boast) to let thee know;
At first I thought that Liberty and Heav'n
To heav'nly Souls had been all one; but now   165
I see that most through sloth had rather serve,
Minist'ring Spirits, train'd up in Feast and Song;
Such hast thou arm'd, the Minstrelsy° of Heav'n,
Servility with freedom to contend,
As both their deeds compar'd this day shall prove.'   170
          To whom in brief thus Abdiel stern repli'd.
'Apostate, still thou err'st, nor end wilt find
Of erring, from the path of truth remote:
Unjustly thou deprav'st° it with the name
Of Servitude to serve whom God ordains,   175
Or Nature; God and Nature bid the same,
When he who rules is worthiest, and excels
Them whom he governs. This is servitude,
To serve th'unwise, or him who hath rebell'd
Against his worthier, as thine now serve thee,   180
Thyself not free, but to thyself enthrall'd;
Yet lewdly° dar'st our minist'ring upbraid.
Reign thou in Hell thy Kingdom, let mee serve
In Heav'n God ever blest, and his Divine
Behests obey, worthiest to be obey'd,   185
Yet Chains in Hell, not Realms expect: meanwhile
From mee return'd, as erst thou said'st, from flight,
This greeting on thy impious Crest receive.'
          So saying, a noble stroke he lifted high,
Which hung not, but so swift with tempest fell   190
On the proud Crest of Satan, that no sight,
Nor motion of swift thought, less could his Shield
Such ruin intercept: ten paces huge
He back recoil'd; the tenth on bended knee
His massy Spear upstay'd; as if on Earth   195
Winds under ground or waters forcing way
Sidelong, had push't a Mountain from his seat
Half sunk with all his Pines. Amazement seiz'd

---

161 **success** here "ill-fortune." 167–68 **Minist'ring . . . Minstrelsy**
The contemptuous jingle brings out the common origin, Latin *mi-
nisterialis*, an official. 174 **deprav'st** slanders. 182 **lewdly** vilely.

The Rebel Thrones, but greater rage to see
200 Thus foil'd their mightiest, ours joy fill'd, and shout,
Presage of Victory and fierce desire
Of Battle: whereat Michaël bid sound
Th'Arch-angel trumpet; through the vast of Heav'n
It sounded, and the faithful Armies rung
205 Hosanna to the Highest: nor stood at gaze
The adverse° Legions, nor less hideous join'd
The horrid shock: now storming fury rose,
And clamor such as heard in Heav'n till now
Was never, Arms on Armor clashing bray'd
210 Horrible discord, and the madding Wheels
Of brazen Chariots rag'd; dire was the noise
Of conflict; overhead the dismal hiss
Of fiery Darts in flaming volleys flew,
And flying vaulted either Host with fire.
215 So under fiery Cope together rush'd
Both Battles main,° with ruinous assault
And inextinguishable rage; all Heav'n
Resounded, and had Earth been then, all Earth
Had to her Center shook. What wonder? when
220 Millions of fierce encount'ring Angels fought
On either side, the least of whom could wield
These Elements, and arm him with the force
Of all their Regions: how much more of Power
Army against Army numberless to raise
225 Dreadful combustion° warring, and disturb,
Though not destroy, their happy Native seat;
Had not th'Eternal King Omnipotent
From his stronghold of Heav'n high overrul'd
And limited their might; though number'd such
230 As each divided Legion might have seem'd
A numerous Host,° in strength each armed hand
A Legion; led in fight, yet Leader seem'd
Each Warrior single as in Chief, expért
When to advance, or stand, or turn the sway
235 Of Battle, open when, and when to close
The ridges of grim War; no thought of flight,

206 **adverse** as in "adversary." 216 **Battles main** mighty armies, a "main battle" also being a pitched battle, contrasted with skirmishing. 225 **combustion** tumult, including the "fiery" sense of lines 213–15. 230–31 **Legion . . . Host** making use of the application "legion" to a vast multitude.

None of retreat, no unbecoming deed
That argu'd fear; each on himself reli'd,
As only in his arm the moment° lay
Of victory; deeds of eternal fame   240
Were done, but infinite: for wide was spread
That War and various; sometimes on firm ground
A standing fight, then soaring on main wing
Tormented° all the Air; all Air seem'd then
Conflicting Fire: long time in even scale   245
The Battle hung; till Satan, who that day
Prodigious power had shown, and met in Arms
No equal, ranging through the dire attack
Of fighting Seraphim confus'd, at length
Saw where the Sword of Michael smote, and fell'd   250
Squadrons at once, with huge two-handed sway
Brandisht aloft the horrid edge came down
Wide wasting; such destruction to withstand
He hasted, and oppos'd the rocky Orb
Of tenfold Adamant, his ample Shield   255
A vast circumference: At his approach
The great Arch-Angel from his warlike toil
Surceas'd,° and glad as hoping here to end
Intestine° War in Heav'n, the arch foe subdu'd
Or Captive dragg'd in Chains, with hostile frown   260
And visage all inflam'd first thus began.
        'Author of evil, unknown till thy revolt,
Unnam'd in Heav'n, now plenteous, as thou seest
These Acts of hateful strife, hateful to all,
Though heaviest by just measure on thyself   265
And thy adherents: how hast thou disturb'd
Heav'n's blessed peace, and into Nature brought
Misery, uncreated till the crime
Of thy Rebellion? how hast thou instill'd
Thy malice into thousands, once upright   270
And faithful, now prov'd false. But think not here
To trouble Holy Rest; Heav'n casts thee out
From all her Confines. Heav'n the seat of bliss
Brooks not the works of violence and War.
Hence then, and evil go with thee along   275

239 **moment** determining influence.   244 **Tormented** agitated (and
a "torment" was an engine of war which hurled stones or darts).
258 **Surceas'd** desisted.   259 **Intestine** internal, civil.

Thy offspring, to the place of evil, Hell,
Thou and thy wicked crew; there mingle broils,
Ere this avenging Sword begin thy doom,
Or some more sudden vengeance wing'd from God
280 Precipitate thee with augmented pain.'
         So spake the Prince of Angels; to whom thus
The Adversary. 'Nor think thou with wind
Of airy threats to awe whom yet with deeds
Thou canst not. Hast thou turn'd the least of these
285 To flight, or if to fall, but that they rise
Unvanquisht, easier to transact with mee
That thou shouldst hope, imperious, and with threats
To chase me hence? err not that so shall end
The strife which thou call'st evil, but wee style
290 The strife of Glory: which we mean to win,
Or turn this Heav'n itself into the Hell
Thou fablest, here however to dwell free,
If not to reign: meanwhile thy utmost force,
And join him nam'd Almighty to thy aid,
295 I fly not, but have sought thee far and nigh.'
         They ended parle,° and both addrest for fight
Unspeakable; for who, though with the tongue
Of Angels, can relate, or to what things
Liken on Earth conspicuous, that may lift
300 Human imagination to such heighth
Of Godlike Power: for likest Gods they seem'd,
Stood they or mov'd, in stature, motion, arms
Fit to decide the Empire of great Heav'n.
Now wav'd their fiery Swords, and in the Air
305 Made horrid Circles; two broad Suns their Shields
Blaz'd opposite, while expectation stood
In horror; from each hand with speed retir'd
Where erst was thickest fight, th'Angelic throng,
And left large field, unsafe within the wind
310 Of such commotion, such as to set forth
Great things by small, If Nature's concord broke,
Among the Constellations war were sprung,
Two Planets rushing from aspéct malign°
Of fiercest opposition in mid Sky,
315 Should combat, and their jarring Spheres confound.

296 **parle** parley.   313 **aspéct malign** astrological position, shedding
evil influence.

Together both with next to Almighty Arm,
Uplifted imminent° one stroke they aim'd
That might determine, and not need repeat,
As net of power, at once; nor odds appear'd
In might or swift prevention;° but the sword   320
Of Michael from the Armoury of God
Was giv'n him temper'd so, that neither keen
Nor solid might resist that edge: it met
The sword of Satan with steep force to smite
Descending, and in half cut sheer, nor stay'd,   325
But with swift wheel reverse, deep ent'ring shar'd°
All his right side; then Satan first knew pain,
And writh'd him to and fro convolv'd; so sore
The griding° sword with discontinuous° wound
Pass'd through him, but th'Ethereal substance clos'd 330
Not long divisible, and from the gash
A stream of Nectarous humour° issuing flow'd
Sanguine, such as Celestial Spirits may bleed,
And all his Armour stain'd erewhile so bright.
Forthwith on all sides to his aid was run   335
By Angels many and strong, who interpos'd
Defence, while others bore him on their Shields
Back to his Chariot; where it stood retir'd
From off the files of war; there they him laid
Gnashing for anguish and despite and shame   340
To find himself not matchless, and his pride
Humbl'd by such rebuke, so far beneath
His confidence to equal God in power.
Yet soon he heal'd; for Spirits that live throughout
Vital in every part, not as frail man   345
In Entrails, Heart or Head, Liver or Reins,°
Cannot but by annihilating die;
Nor in their liquid texture mortal wound
Receive, no more than can the fluid Air:
All Heart they live, all Head, all Eye, all Ear,   350
All Intellect, all Sense, and as they please,
They Limb themselves, and colour, shape or size
Assume, as likes them best, condense or rare.
          Meanwhile in other parts like deeds deserv'd

317 **imminent** overhanging. 320 **prevention** anticipation. 326 **shar'd**
sheared. 329 **griding** keenly cutting. 329 **discontinuous** gaping
(originally a medical term). 332 **humour** liquid. 346 **Reins** kid-
neys.

355 Memorial, where the might of Gabriel fought,
And with fierce Ensigns pierc'd the deep array
Of Moloch furious King, who him defi'd,
And at his Chariot-wheels to drag him bound
Threat'n'd, nor from the Holy One of Heav'n
360 Reffain'd° his tongue blasphémous; but anon
Down-clov'n to the waist, with shatter'd Arms
And uncouth° pain fled bellowing. On each wing
Uriel and Raphaël his vaunting foe,
Though huge, and in a Rock of Diamond Arm'd,
365 Vanquish'd Adramelec,° and Asmadai,°
Two potent Thrones, that to be less than Gods
Disdain'd, but meaner thoughts learn'd in their flight,
Mangl'd with ghastly wounds through Plate and Mail.
Nor stood unmindful Abdiel to annoy°
370 The Atheist crew, but with redoubl'd blow
Ariel and Arioc, and the violence
Of Ramiel scorcht and blasted overthrew.
I might relate of thousands, and their names
Eternise here on Earth; but those elect
375 Angels contented with their fame in Heav'n
Seek not the praise of men: the other sort
In might though wondrous and in Acts of War,
Nor of Renown less eager, yet by doom
Cancell'd from Heav'n and sacred memory,
380 Nameless in dark oblivion let them dwell.
For strength from Truth divided and from Just,
Illaudable, naught merits but dispraise
And ignominy, yet to glory aspires
Vainglorious, and through infamy seeks fame:
385 Therefore Eternal silence be their doom.
          And now their mightiest quell'd, the battle
              swerv'd,
With many an inroad gor'd; deformed rout
Enter'd, and foul disorder; all the ground
With shiver'd armor strewn, and on a heap
390 Chariot and Charioteer lay overturn'd
And fiery foaming Steeds; what stood, recoil'd
O'er-wearied, through the faint Satanic Host

360 **Refrain'd** curbed, from Latin *frenum*, a bridle, here following
line 358.   362 **uncouth** unknown hitherto.   365 **Adramelec** Samar-
ian god.   365 **Asmadai** see IV 168.   369 **annoy** injure.

Defensive scarce, or with pale fear surpris'd,
Then first with fear surpris'd and sense of pain
Fled ignominious, to such evil brought   395
By sin of disobedience, till that hour
Not liable to fear or flight or pain.
Far otherwise in th'inviolable Saints
In Cubic Phalanx firm advanc't entire,°
Invulnerable, impenetrably arm'd: 400
Such high advantages their innocence
Gave them above their foes, not to have sinn'd,
Not to have disobey'd; in fight they stood
Unwearied, unobnoxious° to be pain'd
By wound, though from their place by violence mov'd.   405
          Now Night her course began, and over Heav'n
Inducing darkness, grateful truce impos'd,
And silence on the odious din of War:
Under her Cloudy covert both retir'd,
Victor and Vanquisht: on the foughten field   410
Michaël and his Angels prevalent°
Encamping, plac'd in Guard their Watches round,
Cherubic waving fires: on th'other part
Satan with his rebellious disappear'd,
Far in the dark dislodg'd, and void of rest,   415
His Potentates to Council call'd by night;
And in the midst thus undismay'd began.
          'O now in danger tri'd, now known in Arms
Not to be overpower'd, Companions dear,
Found worthy not of Liberty alone,   420
Too mean pretense,° but what we more affect,°
Honour, Dominion, Glory, and renown,
Who have sustain'd one day in doubtful° fight,
(And if one day, why not Eternal days?)
What Heaven's Lord had powerfullest to send   425
Against us from about his Throne, and judg'd
Sufficient to subdue us to his will,
But proves not so: then fallible, it seems,
Of future we may deem him, though till now
Omniscient thought. True is, less firmly arm'd,   430
Some disadvantage we endur'd and pain,

399 **entire** unbroken (military).   404 **unobnoxious** not liable.   411
prevalent prevailing.   421 **pretense** a claim.   **affect** aim at.   423
doubtful undecided.

Till now not known, but known as soon contemn'd,
Since now we find this our Empyreal form
Incapable of mortal injury
435 Imperishable, and though pierc'd with wound,
Soon closing, and by native vigour heal'd.
Of evil then so small as easy think
The remedy; perhaps more valid° Arms,
Weapons more violent, when next we meet,
440 May serve to better us, and worse our foes,
Or equal what between us made the odds,
In Nature none: if other hidden cause
Left them Superior, while we can preserve
Unhurt our minds, and understanding sound,
445 Due search and consultation will disclose.'
          He sat; and in th'assembly next upstood
Nisroc,° of Principalities the prime;
As one he stood escap't from cruel fight,
Sore toil'd, his riv'n Arms to havoc hewn,
450 And cloudy in aspéct thus answering spake.
'Deliverer from new Lords, leader to free
Enjoyment of our right as Gods; yet hard
For Gods, and too unequal work we find
Against unequal arms to fight in pain,
455 Against unpain'd, impassive; from which evil
Ruin must needs ensue; for what avails
Valour° or strength, though matchless, quell'd with
     pain
Which all subdues, and makes remiss° the hands
Of Mightiest. Sense of pleasure we may well
460 Spare out of life perhaps, and not repine,
But live content, which is the calmest life:
But pain is perfect misery, the worst
Of evils, and excessive, overturns
All patience. He who therefore can invent
465 With what more forcible we may offend°
Our yet unwounded Enemies, or arm
Ourselves with like defence, to mee deserves
No less than for deliverance what we owe.'

438 valid powerful.   447 Nisroc Assyrian god.   456–57 avails Val-
our The two words are from the same root (Latin *valere*, to be strong
or worth), so the question sharply implies that valor ceases to be
itself when . . .   458 remiss forceless.   465 offend assail, as in "the
offensive."

    Whereto with look compos'd Satan repli'd.
'Not uninvented that, which thou aright   470
Believ'st so main to our success, I bring;
Which of us who beholds the bright surfáce
Of this Ethereous mould whereon we stand,
This continent of spacious Heav'n, adorn'd
With Plant, Fruit, Flow'r Ambrosial, Gems and Gold,   475
Whose Eye so superficially surveys
These things, as not to mind° from whence they grow
Deep under ground, materials dark and crude,
Of spiritous and fiery spume,° till toucht°
With Heav'n's ray, and temper'd they shoot forth   480
So beauteous, op'ning to the ambient light.
These in their dark Nativity° the Deep°
Shall yield us, pregnant with infernal flame,
Which into hollow Engines long and round
Thick-ramm'd, at th'other bore with touch of fire   485
Dilated and infuriate shall send forth
From far with thund'ring noise among our foes
Such implements of mischief as shall dash
To pieces, and o'erwhelm whatever stands
Adverse, that they shall fear we have disarm'd   490
The Thunderer of his only° dreaded bolt.
Nor long shall be our labour, yet ere dawn,
Effect shall end our wish. Meanwhile revive;
Abandon fear; to strength and counsel join'd
Think nothing hard, much less to be despair'd.'   495
He ended, and his words their drooping cheer°
Enlight'n'd, and their languisht hope reviv'd.
Th'invention all admir'd,° and each, how hee
To be th'inventor miss'd, so easy it seem'd
Once found, which yet unfound most would have
    thought   500
Impossible: yet haply of thy Race
In future days, if Malice should abound,
Someone intent on mischief, or inspir'd
With dev'lish machination° might devise

477 **mind** call to mind.   479 **spume** foam (a technical term in metal-
lurgy).   479 **toucht** including the suggestion "kindled"; see lines 485,
520.   482 **Nativity** native state.   482 **Deep** depths of the earth.   491
only unique   496 **cheer** mood.   498 **admir'd** wondered at.   504
machination plotting, leading into "instrument" since machination
had also been defined in 1613 as "warlike weapon."

505 Like instrument to plague the Sons of men
For sin, on war and mutual slaughter bent.
Forthwith from Council to the work they flew,
None arguing stood, innumerable hands
Were ready, in a moment up they turn'd
510 Wide the Celestial soil, and saw beneath
Th'originals° of Nature in their crude
Conception; Sulphurous and Nitrous Foam
They found, they mingl'd, and with subtle Art,
Concocted and adusted° they reduc'd
515 To blackest grain, and into store convey'd:
Part hidd'n veins digg'd up (nor hath this Earth
Entrails unlike) of Mineral and Stone,
Whereof to found their Engines and their Balls
Of missive° ruin; part incentive° reed
520 Provide, pernicious° with one touch to fire.
So all ere day-spring, under conscious° Night
Secret they finish'd, and in order set,
With silent circumspection unespi'd.
Now when fair Morn Orient in Heav'n appear'd
525 Up rose the Victor Angels, and to Arms
The matin Trumpet Sung: in Arms they stood
Of Golden Panoply, refulgent Host,
Soon banded; others from the dawning Hills
Look'd round, and Scouts each Coast light-armed
  scour,
530 Each quarter, to descry the distant foe,
Where lodg'd, or whither fled, or if for fight,
In motion or in halt: him soon they met
Under spread Ensigns moving nigh, in slow
But firm Battalion; back with speediest Sail
535 Zophiel, of Cherubim the swiftest wing,
Came flying, and in mid Air aloud thus cri'd.
      'Arm, Warriors, Arm for fight, the foe at hand,
Whom fled we thought, will save us long pursuit
This day, fear not his flight; so thick a Cloud
540 He comes, and settl'd in his face I see

---

511 **originals** a geological term.   514 **Concocted and adusted** ma-
tured by heat and scorched (geological).   519 **missive** missile.   519
incentive kindling.   520 **pernicious** both "rapid" (Latin *pernix*) and
"destructive" (Latin *perniciosus*).   521 **conscious** witnessing, with
suggestions of sharing a guilty secret.

Sad° resolution and secure:° let each
His Adamantine coat gird well, and each
Fit well his Helm, grip fast his orbed Shield,
Borne ev'n or high, for this day will pour down,
If I conjecture aught, no drizzling show'r,   *545*
But rattling storm of Arrows barb'd with fire.'
So warn'd he them aware themselves, and soon
In order, quit of all impediment;°
Instant without disturb they took Alarm,°
And onward move Embattl'd; when behold   *550*
Not distant far with heavy pace the Foe
Approaching gross and huge; in hollow Cube
Training° his devilish Enginry, impal'd°
On every side with shadowing° Squadrons Deep,
To hide the fraud. At interview° both stood   *555*
Awhile, but suddenly at head appear'd
Satan: And thus was heard Commanding loud.
     'Vanguard, to Right and Left the Front unfold;°
That all may see who hate us, how we seek
Peace and composure,° and with open breast   *560*
Stand ready to receive them, if they like
Our overture,° and turn not back perverse;
But that I doubt,° however witness Heaven,
Heav'n witness thou anon, while we discharge°
Freely our part:° yee who appointed° stand   *565*
Do as you have in charge,° and briefly touch°
What we propound,° and loud that all may hear.'
     So scoffing in ambiguous words, he scarce
Had ended; when to Right and Left the Front
Divided, and to either Flank retir'd.   *570*
Which to our eyes discover'd new and strange,

541 **Sad** steadfast. **secure** confident. 548 **impediment** military baggage. 549 **took Alarm** stood to arms. 553 **Training** hauling. 553 **impal'd** surrounded for defense. 554 **shadowing** screening (military). 555 **At interview** in mutual view. 558 **unfold** military: "unfolding his troops." 560 **composure** composition, truce, and also "compounded mixture" (gunpowder) as in line 613. 562 **overture** overtures of peace; opening of the proceedings; and aperture or orifice (line 577), as in Milton: "break in at this so great an overture." 563 **doubt** fear. 564 **discharge** fulfill and fire off. 565 **part** share and (a 17th-century sense) "conflict between two parties." 565 **appointed** agreed and equipped. 566 **in charge** entrusted and loaded (weapons). 566 **touch** touch upon and ignite. 567 **propound** punning on "put forward."

A triple-mounted row of Pillars laid
On Wheels (for like to Pillars most they seem'd
Or hollow'd bodies made of Oak or Fir
575 With branches lopt, in Wood or Mountain fell'd)
Brass, Iron, Stony mould, had not their mouths
With hideous orifice gap't on us wide,
Portending hollow truce; at each behind
A Seraph stood, and in his hand a Reed
580 Stood waving tipt with fire; while we suspense,
Collected stood within our thoughts amus'd,°
Not long, for sudden all at once their Reeds
Put forth, and to a narrow vent appli'd
With nicest touch. Immediate in a flame,
585 But soon obscur'd with smoke, all Heav'n appear'd,
From those deep-throated Engines belcht, whose roar
Embowel'd with outrageous noise the Air,
And all her entrails tore, disgorging foul
Their devilish glut,° chain'd° Thunderbolts and Hail
590 Of Iron Globes, which on the Victor Host
Levell'd,° with such impetuous fury smote,
That whom they hit, none on their feet might stand,
Though standing else as Rocks, but down they fell
By thousands, Angel on Arch-Angel roll'd;
595 The sooner for their Arms, unarm'd they might
Have easily as Spirits evaded swift
By quick contraction or remove; but now
Foul dissipation° follow'd and forc't rout;
Nor serv'd it to relax their serried files.
600 What should they do? if on they rusht, repulse
Repeated, and indecent° overthrow
Doubl'd, would render them yet more despis'd,°
And to their foes a laughter; for in view
Stood rankt of Seraphim another row
605 In posture to displode° their second tire°
Of Thunder: back defeated to return
They worse abhorr'd. Satan beheld their plight,
And to his Mates thus in derision call'd.

581 **amus'd** bewildered (also military, of tactics which deceive the enemy).   586–89 **deep-throated . . . glut** Compare the body-landscape of Hell.   589 **chain'd** chain-shot, cannonballs linked.   591 **Levell'd** military, to lay a gun.   598 **dissipation** dispersal.   601 **indecent** graceless.   602 **despis'd** looked down upon (Latin *despicere*); following "overthrow."   605 **displode** explode.   605 **tire** volley.

      'O Friends, why come not on these Victors
        proud?
Erewhile they fierce were coming, and when wee,   *610*
To entertain° them fair with open Front°
And Breast, (what could we more?) propounded terms
Of composition, straight they chang'd their minds,
Flew off, and into strange vagaries fell,
As they would dance, yet for a dance they seem'd   *615*
Somewhat extravagant and wild, perhaps
For joy of offer'd peace: but I suppose
If our proposals once again were heard
We should compel them to a quick result.'°
      To whom thus Belial in like gamesome mood.   *620*
'Leader, the terms we sent were terms of weight,
Of hard contents, and full of force urg'd home,
Such as we might perceive amus'd° them all,
And stumbl'd many, who receives them right,
Had need from head to foot well understand;°   *625*
Not understood, this gift they have besides,
They show us when our foes walk not upright.'
      So they among themselves in pleasant vein
Stood scoffing, height'n'd in their thoughts beyond
All doubt of Victory, eternal might   *630*
To match with their inventions they presum'd
So easy, and of his Thunder made a scorn,
And all his Host derided, while they stood
Awhile in trouble; but they stood not long,
Rage prompted them at length, and found them arms   *635*
Against such hellish mischief fit to oppose.
Forthwith (behold the excellence, the power
Which God hath in his mighty Angels plac'd)
Their Arms away they threw, and to the Hills
(For Earth hath this variety from Heav'n   *640*
Of pleasure situate in Hill and Dale)
Light as the Lightning glimpse they ran, they flew,
From their foundations loos'ning to and fro
They pluckt the seated° Hills with all their load,
Rocks, Waters, Woods, and by the shaggy tops   *645*

611 **entertain** receive. 611 **Front** brow and front-line. 619 **result** decision or resolution, with a pun on the etymology, Latin *resultare*, to leap back. 623 **amus'd** see line 581. 625 **understand** both "comprehend" and "be supported" (a common 17th-century sense). 644 **seated** firm-set.

Uplifting bore them in their hands: Amaze,
Be sure, and terror seiz'd the rebel Host,
When coming towards them so dread they saw
The bottom of the Mountains upward turn'd;
650 Till on those cursed Engines triple-row
They saw them whelm'd, and all their confidence°
Under the weight of Mountains buried deep,
Themselves invaded next, and on their heads
Main Promontories flung, which in the Air
655 Came shadowing, and opprest whole Legions arm'd,
Their armour help'd their harm, crush't in and bruis'd
Into their substance pent, which wrought them pain
Implacable, and many a dolorous groan,
Long struggling underneath, ere they could wind
660 Out of such prison, though Spirits of purest light,
Purest at first, now gross by sinning grown.
The rest in imitation to like Arms
Betook them, and the neighbouring Hills uptore;
So Hills amid the Air encounter'd Hills
665 Hurl'd to and fro with jaculation° dire,
That under ground they fought in dismal shade;
Infernal noise; War seem'd a civil° Game
To this uproar; horrid confusion heapt
Upon confusion rose: and now all Heav'n
670 Had gone to wrack, with ruin overspread,
Had not th'Almighty Father where he sits
Shrin'd in his Sanctuary of Heav'n secure,
Consulting° on the sum of things, foreseen
This tumult, and permitted all, advis'd:°
675 That his great purpose he might so fulfill,
To honour his Anointed Son aveng'd
Upon his enemies, and to declare°
All power on him transferr'd: whence to his Son
Th'Assessor° of his Throne he thus began.
680   'Effulgence of my Glory, Son belov'd,
Son in whose face invisible is beheld
Visibly, what by Deity I am,

---

651 **confidence** "that which gives confidence, boldness, or security"
(Johnson), as in PROVERBS 3:26, "For the Lord shall be thy confi-
dence."   665 **jaculation** throwing.   667 **civil** civilized, orderly (con-
trasting "civil war").   673 **Consulting** deliberating.   674 **advis'd**
having considered, as in "advisedly."   677 **declare** make manifest.
679 **Assessor** one who sits beside.

And in whose hand what by Decree I do,
Second Omnipotence, two days are past,
Two days, as we compute the days of Heav'n,   685
Since Michael and his Powers went forth to tame
These disobedient; sore hath been their fight,
As likeliest was, when two such Foes met arm'd;
For to themselves I left them, and thou know'st,
Equal in their Creation they were form'd,   690
Save what sin hath impair'd, which yet hath wrought
Insensibly,° for I suspend their doom;
Whence in perpetual fight they needs must last
Endless, and no solution° will be found:
War wearied hath perform'd what War can do,   695
And to disorder'd rage let loose the reins,
With Mountains as with Weapons arm'd, which makes
Wild work in Heav'n, and dangerous to the main.°
Two days are therefore past, the third is thine;
For thee I have ordain'd it, and thus far   700
Have suffer'd,° that the Glory may be thine
Of ending this great War, since none but Thou
Can end it. Into thee such Virtue and Grace
Immense I have transfus'd, that all may know
In Heav'n and Hell thy Power above compare,   705
And this perverse Commotion govern'd thus,
To manifest thee worthiest to be Heir
Of all things, to be Heir and to be King
By Sacred Unction,° thy deserved right.
Go then thou Mightiest in thy Father's might,   710
Ascend my Chariot, guide the rapid Wheels
That shake Heav'n's basis, bring forth all my War,
My Bow and Thunder, my Almighty Arms
Gird on, and Sword upon thy puissant Thigh;
Pursue these sons of Darkness, drive them out   715
From all Heav'n's bounds into the utter Deep:
There let them learn, as likes them, to despise
God and Messiah his anointed King.'
          He said, and on his Son with Rays direct
Shone full, he all his Father full exprest   720
Ineffably into his face receiv'd,
And thus the filial Godhead answering spake.

692 **Insensibly** imperceptibly.   694 **solution** termination.   698 **main**
land.   701 **suffer'd** permitted.   709 **Unction** anointing.

   'O Father, O Supreme of heav'nly Thrones,
  First, Highest, Holiest, Best, thou always seek'st
725 To glorify thy Son, I always thee,
  As is most just; this I my Glory account,
  My exaltation, and my whole delight,
  That thou in me well-pleas'd, declar'st thy will
  Fulfill'd, which to fufill is all my bliss.
730 Scepter and Power, thy giving, I assume,
  And gladlier shall resign, when in the end
  Thou shalt be All in All, and I in thee
  For ever, and in mee all whom thou lov'st:
  But whom thou hat'st, I hate, and can put on
735 Thy terrors, as I put thy mildness on,
  Image of thee in all things; and shall soon,
  Arm'd with thy might, rid Heav'n of these rebell'd,
  To their prepar'd ill Mansion driven down
  To chains of Darkness, and th'undying Worm,
740 That from thy just obedience could revolt,
  Whom to obey is happiness entire.
  Then shall thy Saints unmixt, and from th'impure
  Far separate, circling thy holy Mount
  Unfeigned Halleluiahs to thee sing,
745 Hymns of high praise, and I among them chief.'
  So said, he o'er his Scepter bowing, rose
  From the right hand of Glory where he sat,
  And the third sacred Morn began to shine
  Dawning through Heav'n: forth rush'd with whirlwind
   sound
750 The Chariot of Paternal Deity,
  Flashing thick flames, Wheel within Wheel undrawn,
  Itself instínct with Spirit, but convóy'd
  By four Cherubic shapes, four Faces each
  Had wondrous, as with Stars their bodies all
755 And Wings were set with Eyes, with Eyes the Wheels
  Of Beryl, and careering Fires between;
  Over their heads a crystal Firmament,
  Whereon a Sapphire Throne, inlaid with pure
  Amber, and colours of the show'ry Arch.
760 Hee in Celestial Panoply all arm'd
  Of radiant Urim,° work divinely wrought,
  Ascended, at his right hand Victory

761 Urim oraculous gems.

Sat Eagle-wing'd, beside him hung his Bow
And Quiver with three-bolted Thunder stor'd,
And from about him fierce Effusion° roll'd   765
Of smoke and bickering° flame, and sparkles dire;
Attended with ten thousand thousand Saints,
He onward came, far off his coming shone,
And twenty thousand (I their number heard)
Chariots of God, half on each hand were seen: 770
Hee on the wings of Cherub rode sublime
On the Crystálline Sky, in Sapphire Thron'd.
Illustrious° far and wide, but by his own
First seen, them unexpected joy surpris'd,
When the great Ensign of Messiah blaz'd   775
Aloft by Angels borne, his Sign in Heav'n:
Under whose Conduct Michael soon reduc'd°
His Army, circumfus'd on either Wing,
Under their Head imbodied° all in one.
Before him Power Divine his way prepar'd;   780
At his command the uprooted Hills retir'd
Each to his place, they heard his voice and went
Obsequious,° Heav'n his wonted face renew'd,
And with fresh Flow'rets Hill and Valley smil'd.
This saw his hapless Foes, but stood obdur'd,   785
And to rebellious fight rallied their Powers
Insensate, hope conceiving from despair.
In heav'nly Spirits could such perverseness dwell?
But to convince the proud what Signs avail,
Or Wonders move th'obdúrate to relent?   790
They hard'n'd more by what might most reclaim,
Grieving to see his Glory, at the sight
Took envy, and aspiring to his heighth,
Stood re-embattl'd fierce, by force or fraud
Weening to prosper, and at length prevail   795
Against God and Messiah, or to fall
In universal ruin last, and now
To final Battle drew, disdaining flight,
Or faint retreat; when the great Son of God
To all his Host on either hand thus spake.   800

765 **fierce Effusion** to be contrasted with the usual theological appli-
cation of "Effusion" to Christ and the Holy Ghost, pouring forth
grace.   766 **bickering** flashing.   773 **Illustrious** full of luster.   777
reduc'd brought back.   779 **imbodied** organized in a military body.
783 **Obsequious** obedient.

'Stand still in bright array ye Saints, here stand
Ye Angels arm'd, this day from Battle rest;
Faithful hath been your Warfare, and of God
Accepted, fearless in his righteous Cause,
805 And as ye have receiv'd, so have ye done
Invincibly; but of this cursed crew
The punishment to other hand belongs,
Vengeance is his, or whose he sole appoints;
Number to this day's work is not ordain'd
810 Nor multitude, stand only and behold
God's indignation on these Godless pour'd
By mee; not you but mee they have despis'd,
Yet envied; against mee is all their rage,
Because the Father, t'whom in Heav'n supreme
815 Kingdom and Power and Glory appertains,
Hath honour'd me according to his will.
Therefore to mee their doom he hath assign'd;
That they may have their wish, to try with mee
In Battle which the stronger proves, they all,
820 Or I alone against them, since by strength
They measure all, of other excellence
Not emulous, nor care who them excels;
Nor other strife with them do I vouchsafe.'
          So spake the Son, and into terror chang'd
825 His count'nance too severe to be beheld
And full of wrath bent on his Enemies.
At once the Four spread out their Starry wings
With dreadful shade contiguous, and the Orbs
Of his fierce Chariot roll'd, as with the sound
830 Of torrent Floods, or of a numerous Host.
Hee on his impious Foes right onward drove,
Gloomy as Night; under his burning Wheels
The steadfast Empyrean shook throughout,
All but the Throne itself of God. Full soon
835 Among them he arriv'd; in his right hand
Grasping ten thousand Thunders, which he sent
Before him, such as in their Souls infix'd
Plagues;° they astonisht° all resistance lost,
All courage; down their idle weapons dropp'd;
840 O'er Shields and Helms, and helmed heads he rode

838 **Plagues** the scourges of God, including the original sense
"wound."   838 **astonisht** thunderstruck.

Of Thrones and mighty Seraphim prostráte,
That wish'd the Mountains now might be again
Thrown on them as a shelter from his ire.
Nor less on either side tempestuous fell
His arrows, from the fourfold-visag'd Four,   845
Distinct° with eyes, and from the living Wheels,
Distinct alike with multitude of eyes.
One Spirit in them rul'd, and every eye
Glar'd lightning, and shot forth pernicious fire
Among th'accurst, that wither'd all their strength,   850
And of their wonted vigour left them drain'd,
Exhausted, spiritless, afflicted, fall'n.
Yet half his strength he put not forth, but check'd
His Thunder in mid Volley, for he meant
Not to destroy, but root them out of Heav'n: 855
The overthrown he rais'd, and as a Herd
Of Goats or timorous flock together throng'd
Drove them before him Thunder-struck, pursu'd
With terrors and with furies to the bounds
And Crystal wall of Heav'n, which op'ning wide,   860
Roll'd inward, and a spacious Gap disclos'd
Into the wasteful Deep; the monstrous sight
Struck them with horror backward, but far worse
Urg'd them behind; headlong themselves they threw
Down from the verge of Heav'n, Eternal wrath   865
Burnt after them to the bottomless pit.
        Hell heard th'unsufferable noise, Hell saw
Heav'n ruining from Heav'n and would have fled
Affrighted; but strict Fate had cast too deep
Her dark foundations, and too fast had bound.   870
Nine days they fell; confounded Chaos roar'd,
And felt tenfold confusion in their fall
Through his wild Anarchy, so huge a rout
Encumber'd him with ruin: Hell at last
Yawning receiv'd them whole, and on them clos'd,   875
Hell their fit habitation fraught with fire
Unquenchable, the house of woe and pain.
Disburd'n'd Heav'n rejoic'd, and soon repair'd
Her mural breach, returning whence it roll'd.
Sole Victor from th'expulsion of his Foes   880
Messiah his triumphal Chariot turn'd:

846 **Distinct** adorned.

To meet him all his Saints, who silent stood
Eye-witnesses of his Almighty Acts,
With Jubilee advanc'd; and as they went,
885 Shaded with branching palm, each order bright,
Sung Triumph, and him sung Victorious King,
Son, Heir, and Lord, to him Dominion giv'n,
Worthiest to Reign: he celebrated rode
Triumphant through mid Heav'n, into the Courts
890 And Temple of his mighty Father Thron'd
On high; who into Glory him receiv'd,
Where now he sits at the right hand of bliss.
          Thus measuring things in Heav'n by things on
               Earth
At thy request, and that thou mayst beware
895 By what is past, to thee I have reveal'd
What might have else to human Race been hid;
The discord which befell, and War in Heav'n
Among th'Angelic Powers, and the deep fall
Of those too high aspiring, who rebell'd
900 With Satan, hee who envies now thy state,
Who now is plotting how he may seduce
Thee also from obedience, that with him
Bereav'd of happiness thou mayst partake
His punishment, Eternal misery;
905 Which would be all his solace and revenge,
As a despite done against the most High,
Thee once to gain Companion of his woe.
But list'n not to his Temptations, warn
Thy weaker; let it profit thee to have heard
910 By terrible Example the reward
Of disobedience; firm they might have stood,
Yet fell; remember, and fear to transgress."

BOOK VII

THE ARGUMENT

Raphael at the request of Adam relates how and where-
fore this world was first created; that God, after the ex-
pelling of Satan and his Angels out of Heaven, declar'd
his pleasure to create another World and other Creatures
to dwell therein; sends his Son with Glory and attendance
of Angels to perform the work of Creation in six days:
the Angels celebrate with Hymns the performance thereof,
and his reascension into Heaven.

Descend from Heav'n Urania, by that name
If rightly thou art call'd, whose Voice divine
Following, above th'Olympian Hill° I soar,
Above the flight of Pegasean wing.°
The meaning,° not the Name I call: for thou   5
Nor of the Muses nine, nor on the top
Of old Olympus dwell'st, but Heav'nly born,
Before the Hills appear'd, or Fountain flow'd,
Thou with Eternal wisdom didst converse,°
Wisdom thy Sister, and with her didst play   10
In presence of th'Almighty Father, pleas'd
With thy Celestial Song. Up led by thee
Into the Heav'n of Heav'ns I have presum'd,
An Earthly Guest, and drawn Empyreal Air,
Thy temp'ring;° with like safety guided down   15

3 **Olympian Hill** Olympus, resort of the Muses.   4 **Pegasean wing**
Pegasus, the winged horse associated with the Muses and Bellerophon
(line 18).   5 **meaning** Urania, "Heavenly One"; Milton calls on
more than the "Name" of the classical Muse.   9 **converse** keep com-
pany.   15 **Thy temp'ring** the air tempered (made suitable) by thee.

Return me to my Native Element:
Lest from this flying Steed unrein'd, (as once
Bellerophon, though from a lower Clime)
Dismounted, on th'Aleian° Field I fall
20 Erroneous,° there to wander and forlorn.
Half yet remains unsung, but narrower bound
Within the visible Diurnal° Sphere;
Standing on Earth, not rapt above the Pole,
More safe I Sing with mortal voice, unchang'd
25 To hoarse or mute, though fall'n on evil days,
On evil days though fall'n, and evil tongues;
In darkness, and with dangers compast round,
And solitude; yet not alone, while thou
Visit'st my slumbers Nightly, or when Morn
30 Purples the East: still govern thou my Song,
Urania, and fit audience find, though few.
But drive far off the barbarous dissonance
Of Bacchus° and his Revellers, the Race
Of that wild Rout that tore the Thracian Bard°
35 In Rhodope, where Woods and Rocks had Ears
To rapture,° till the savage clamour drown'd
Both Harp and Voice; nor could the Muse defend
Her Son. So fail not thou, who thee implores:
For thou art Heav'nly, shee an empty dream.
40   Say Goddess, what ensu'd when Raphaël,
The affable° Arch-angel, had forewarn'd
Adam by dire example to beware
Apostasy, by what befell in Heaven
To those Apostates, lest the like befall
45 In Paradise to Adam or his Race,
Charg'd not to touch the interdicted Tree,
If they transgress, and slight that sole command,
So easily obey'd amid the choice
Of all tastes else to please their appetite,
50 Though wand'ring. He with his consorted Eve
The story heard attentive, and was fill'd
With admiration, and deep Muse to hear
Of things so high and strange, things to their thought

19 **Aleian** meaning "Land of Wandering." 20 **Erroneous** straying.
22 **Diurnal** daily (in its astronomical movement). 33 **Bacchus** god
of wine. 34 **Bard** the poet-seer Orpheus, murdered by the Bac-
chantes. 36 **rapture** be raptured. 41 **affable** easy to speak with
(Raphael's role in the poem).

So unimaginable as hate in Heav'n,
And War so near the Peace of God in bliss   55
With such confusion: but the evil soon
Driv'n back redounded as a flood on those
From whom it sprung, impossible to mix
With Blessedness. Whence Adam soon repeal'd°
The doubts that in his heart arose: and now   60
Led on, yet sinless, with desire to know
What nearer might concern him, how this World
Of Heav'n and Earth conspicuous° first began,
When, and whereof created, for what cause,
What within Eden or without was done   65
Before his memory, as one whose drouth
Yet scarce allay'd still eyes the current stream,
Whose liquid murmur heard new thirst excites,
Proceeded thus to ask his Heav'nly Guest.

          "Great things, and full of wonder in our ears,   70
Far differing from this World, thou hast reveal'd
Divine Interpreter,° by favour sent
Down from the Empyrean to forewarn
Us timely of what might else have been our loss,
Unknown, which human knowledge could not reach: 75
For which to the infinitely Good we owe
Immortal thanks, and his admonishment
Receive with solemn purpose to observe
Immutably his sovran will, the end
Of what we are. But since thou hast vouchsaf't   80
Gently for our instruction to impart
Things above Earthly thought, which yet concern'd
Our knowing, as to highest wisdom seem'd,
Deign to descend now lower, and relate
What may no less perhaps avail us known,   85
How first began this Heav'n which we behold
Distant so high, with moving Fires adorn'd
Innumerable, and this which yields or fills
All space, the ambient Air wide interfus'd
Embracing round this florid° Earth, what cause   90
Mov'd the Creator in his holy Rest
Through all Eternity so late to build

59 **repeal'd** retracted. 63 **conspicuous** visibly present. 72 **Interpreter** one who makes known the will of another, a title of Mercury as messenger of the gods. 90 **florid** flowery.

In Chaos, and the work begun, how soon
Absolv'd,° if unforbid thou may'st unfold
95   What wee, not to explore the secrets ask
Of his Eternal Empire, but the more
To magnify his works, the more we know.
And the great Light of Day yet wants to run
Much of his Race though steep, suspense in Heav'n
100 Held by thy voice, thy potent voice he hears,
And longer will delay to hear thee tell
His Generation,° and the rising Birth
Of Nature from the unapparent° Deep:
Or if the Star of Ev'ning and the Moon
105 Haste to thy audience, Night with her will bring
Silence, and Sleep list'ning to thee will watch,
Or we can bid his absence, till thy Song
End, and dismiss thee ere the Morning shine."
        Thus Adam his illustrious Guest besought:
110 And thus the Godlike Angel answer'd mild.
"This also thy request with caution askt
Obtain: though to recount Almighty works
What words or tongue of Seraph can suffice,
Or heart of man suffice to comprehend?
115 Yet what thou canst attain, which best may serve
To glorify the Maker, and infer°
Thee also happier, shall not be withheld
Thy hearing, such Commission from above
I have receiv'd, to answer thy desire
120 Of knowledge within bounds; beyond abstain
To ask, nor let thine own inventions° hope
Things not reveal'd, which th'invisible King,
Only Omniscient, hath supprest in Night,
To none communicable in Earth or Heaven:
125 Enough is left besides to search and know.
But Knowledge is as food, and needs no less
Her Temperance over Appetite, to know
In measure what the mind may well contain,
Oppresses else with Surfeit, and soon turns
130 Wisdom to Folly, as Nourishment to Wind.
        Know then, that after Lucifer from Heav'n
(So call him, brighter once amidst the Host

94 **Absolv'd** accomplished.   102 **Generation** creation.   103 **unapparent** invisible.   116 **infer** render.   121 **inventions** devisings.

Of Angels, than that Star the Stars among)
Fell with his flaming Legions through the Deep
Into his place, and the great Son return'd   135
Victorious with his Saints, th'Omnipotent
Eternal Father from his Throne beheld
Their multitude, and to his Son thus spake.
      'At least our envious Foe hath fail'd, who
          thought
All like himself rebellious, by whose aid   140
This inaccessible high strength, the seat
Of Deity supreme, us dispossest,
He trusted to have seiz'd, and into fraud
Drew many, whom their place knows here no more;
Yet far the greater part have kept, I see,   145
Their station, Heav'n yet populous retains
Number sufficient to possess her Realms
Though wide, and this high Temple to frequent
With Ministeries due and solemn Rites:
But lest his heart exalt him in the harm   150
Already done, to have dispeopl'd Heav'n,
My damage fondly deem'd, I can repair
That detriment, if such it be to lose
Self-lost, and in a moment will create
Another World, out of one man a Race   155
Of men innumerable, there to dwell,
Not here, till by degrees of merit rais'd
They open to themselves at length the way
Up hither, under long obedience tri'd,
And Earth be chang'd to Heav'n, and Heav'n to
    Earth,   160
One Kingdom, Joy and Union without end.
Meanwhile inhabit lax,° ye Powers of Heav'n,
And thou my Word, begotten Son, by thee
This I perform, speak thou, and be it done:
My overshadowing Spirit and might with thee   165
I send along, ride forth, and bid the Deep
Within appointed bounds be Heav'n and Earth,
Boundless the Deep, because I am who fill
Infinitude, nor vacuous the space.
Though I uncircumscrib'd myself retire,   170
And put not forth my goodness, which is free

162 **inhabit lax** dwell with ample room.

To act or not, Necessity and Chance
Approach not mee, and what I will is Fate.'
         So spake th'Almighty, and to what he spake
175 His Word, the Filial Godhead, gave effect.
Immediate are the Acts of God, more swift
Than time or motion, but to human ears
Cannot without procéss of speech be told,
So told as earthly notion° can receive.
180 Great triumph and rejoicing was in Heav'n
When such was heard declar'd the Almighty's will;
Glory they sung to the most High, good will
To future men, and in their dwellings peace:
Glory to him whose just avenging ire
185 Had driven out th'ungodly from his sight
And th'habitations of the just; to him
Glory and praise, whose wisdom had ordain'd
Good out of evil to create, instead
Of Spirits malign a better Race to bring
190 Into their vacant room, and thence diffuse
His good to Worlds and Ages infinite.
So sang the Hierarchies: Meanwhile the Son
On his great Expedition now appear'd,
Girt with Omnipotence, with Radiance crown'd
195 Of Majesty Divine, Sapience and Love
Immense, and all his Father in him shone.
About his Chariot numberless were pour'd
Cherub and Seraph, Potentates and Thrones,
And Virtues, winged Spirits, and Chariots wing'd,
200 From the Armoury of God, where stand of old
Myriads between two brazen Mountains lodg'd
Against a solemn day, harnest at hand,
Celestial Equipage; and now came forth
Spontaneous, for within them Spirit liv'd,
205 Attendant on their Lord: Heav'n op'n'd wide
Her ever-during Gates, Harmonious sound
On golden Hinges moving,° to let forth
The King of Glory in his powerful Word
And Spirit coming to create new Worlds.
210 On heav'nly ground they stood, and from the shore
They view'd the vast immeasurable Abyss

179 **notion** intellect.   207 **moving** including "putting forth, uttering
(the 'sound')," as in III 37.

Outrageous as a Sea, dark, wasteful, wild,
Up from the bottom turn'd by furious winds
And surging waves, as Mountains to assault
Heav'n's heighth, and with the Center mix the Pole.   215
            'Silence, ye troubl'd waves, and thou Deep,
                  peace,'
Said then th'Omnific° Word, 'your discord end':
            Nor stay'd, but on the Wings of Cherubim
Uplifted, in Paternal Glory rode
Far into Chaos, and the World unborn;   220
For Chaos heard his voice: him all his Train
Follow'd in bright procession to behold
Creation, and the wonders of his might.
Then stay'd the fervid Wheels, and in his hand
He took the golden Compasses, prepar'd   225
In God's Eternal store, to circumscribe
This Universe, and all created things:
One foot he center'd, and the other turn'd
Round through the vast profundity obscure,
And said, 'thus far extend, thus far thy bounds,   230
This be thy just Circumference, O World.'
Thus God the Heav'n created, thus the Earth,
Matter unform'd and void: Darkness profound
Cover'd th'Abyss: but on the wat'ry calm
His brooding wings the Spirit of God outspread,   235
And vital virtue infus'd, and vital warmth
Throughout the fluid Mass, but downward purg'd
The black tartareous° cold infernal dregs
Adverse to life: then founded,° then conglob'd°
Like things to like, the rest to several place   240
Disparted, and between spun out the Air,
And Earth self-ballanc't on her Center hung.
            'Let there be Light,' said God, and forthwith
                  Light
Ethereal, first of things, quintessence pure
Sprung from the Deep, and from her Native East   245
To journey through the airy gloom began,
Spher'd in a radiant Cloud, for yet the Sun
Was not; shee in a cloudy Tabernacle

217 **Omnific** all-making.   238 **tartareous** having gritty deposits (geo-
logical), and suggesting Tartarus, Hell.   239 **founded** made firm,
and cast like metal.   239 **conglob'd** compacted.

Sojourn'd° the while. God saw the Light was good;
250 And light from darkness by the Hemisphere
Divided: Light the Day, and Darkness Night
He nam'd. Thus was the first Day Ev'n and Morn:
Nor past uncelebrated, nor unsung
By the Celestial Choirs, when Orient Light
255 Exhaling first from Darkness they beheld;
Birth-day of Heav'n and Earth; with joy and shout
The hollow Universal Orb they fill'd,
And touch't their Golden Harps, and hymning prais'd
God and his works, Creator him they sung,
260 Both when first Ev'ning was, and when first Morn.
　　　　　Again, God said 'let there be Firmament
Amid the Waters, and let it divide
The Waters from the Waters': and God made
The Firmament, expanse of liquid, pure,
265 Transparent, Elemental Air, diffus'd
In circuit to the uttermost convéx
Of this great Round: partition firm and sure,
The Waters underneath from those above
Dividing: for as Earth, so hee the World
270 Built on circumfluous Waters calm, in wide
Crystálline Ocean, and the loud misrule
Of Chaos far remov'd, lest fierce extremes
Contiguous might distemper the whole frame:
And Heav'n he nam'd the Firmament: So Ev'n
275 And Morning Chorus sung the second Day.
　　　　　The Earth was form'd, but in the Womb as yet
Of Waters, Embryon immature involv'd,
Appear'd not: over all the face of Earth
Main Ocean flow'd, not idle, but with warm
280 Prolific humour soft'ning all her Globe,
Fermented the great Mother to conceive,
Satiate with genial° moisture, when God said
'Be gather'd now ye Waters under Heav'n
Into one place, and let dry Land appear.'
285 Immediately the Mountains huge appear
Emergent, and their broad bare backs upheave
Into the Clouds, their tops ascend the Sky:
So high as heav'd the tumid Hills, so low

---

249 **Sojourn'd** The following lines possibly recall that etymologically
"sojourn" is to spend the day.　　282 **genial** generative.

Down sunk a hollow bottom broad and deep,
Capacious bed of Waters: thither they   290
Hasted with glad precipitance, uproll'd
As drops on dust conglobing from the dry;
Part rise in crystal Wall, or ridge direct,
For haste; such flight the great command impress'd
On the swift floods: as Armies at the call   295
Of Trumpet (for of Armies thou hast heard)
Troop to their Standard, so the wat'ry throng,
Wave rolling after Wave, where way they found,
If steep, with torrent rapture,° if through Plain,
Soft-ebbing; nor withstood them Rock or Hill,   300
But they, or under ground, or circuit wide
With Serpent error° wand'ring, found their way,
And on the washy Ooze deep Channels wore;
Easy, ere God had bid the ground be dry,
All but within those banks, where Rivers now   305
Stream, and perpetual draw their humid train.
The dry Land, Earth, and the great receptacle°
Of congregated° Waters he call'd Seas:
And saw that it was good, and said, 'Let th'Earth
Put forth the verdant Grass, Herb yielding Seed,   310
And Fruit Tree yielding Fruit after her kind;
Whose Seed is in herself upon the Earth.'
He scarce had said, when the bare Earth, till then
Desert and bare, unsightly, unadorn'd,
Brought forth the tender Grass, whose verdure clad   315
Her Universal Face with pleasant green,
Then Herbs of every leaf, that sudden flow'r'd
Op'ning their various colours, and made gay
Her bosom smelling sweet: and these scarce blown,
Forth flourish't thick the clust'ring Vine, forth crept 320
The swelling° Gourd, up stood the corny Reed
Embattl'd in her field: add the humble Shrub,°
And Bush with frizzl'd hair implicit:° last

299 **rapture** momentum, suggesting delight too (line 291: "glad precipitance").   302 **error** meandering; this is consciously still innocent, but "Serpent" too is ominous.   307 **receptacle** a dignified word then, as in the 16th-century theologian, Richard Hooker (O.E.D.): "The soul of man is the receptacle of Christ's presence."   308 **congregated** assembled.   321 **swelling** conjecture by the 18th-century editor Richard Bentley; "smelling" in *1667–74*.   322 **humble Shrub** including the horticultural "low-growing"; "the humble shrub" contrasted with trees.   323 **implicit** entwined.

Rose as in Dance the stately Trees, and spread
325 Their branches hung with copious Fruit; or gemm'd°
Their Blossoms: with high Woods the Hills were
    crown'd,
With tufts the vallies and each fountain-side,
With borders long the Rivers. That Earth now
Seem'd like to Heav'n, a seat where Gods might dwell,
330 Or wander with delight, and love to haunt
Her sacred shades: though God had yet not rain'd
Upon the Earth, and man to till the ground
None was, but from the Earth a dewy Mist
Went up and water'd all the ground, and each
335 Plant of the field, which ere it was in the Earth
God made, and every Herb, before it grew
On the green stem; God saw that it was good:
So Ev'n and Morn recorded the Third Day.
         Again th'Almighty spake: 'Let there be Lights
340 High in th'expanse of Heaven to divide
The Day from Night; and let them be for Signs,
For Seasons, and for Days, and circling Years,
And let them be for Lights as I ordain
Their Office in the Firmament of Heav'n
345 To give Light on the Earth'; and it was so.
And God made two great Lights, great for their use
To Man, the greater to have rule by Day,
The less by Night alterne: and made the Stars,
And set them in the Firmament of Heav'n
350 To illuminate the Earth, and rule the Day
In their vicissitude, and rule the Night,
And Light from Darkness to divide. God saw,
Surveying his great Work, that it was good:
For of Celestial Bodies first the Sun
355 A mighty Sphere he fram'd, unlightsome first,
Though of Ethereal Mould: then form'd the Moon
Globose, and every magnitude of Stars,
And sow'd with Stars the Heav'n thick as a field:
Of Light by far the greater part he took,
360 Transplanted from her cloudy Shrine, and plac'd
In the Sun's Orb, made porous to receive

325 **gemm'd** budded, an English as well as Latin usage; it suggests a
contrast of Nature and Art (e.g. the arts which built Pandemonium,
I 710–17).

And drink the liquid Light, firm to retain
Her gather'd beams, great Palace now of Light.
Hither as to their Fountain other Stars
Repairing, in their gold'n Urns draw Light,   365
And hence the Morning Planet gilds her° horns;
By tincture of reflection they augment
Their small peculiar,° though from human sight
So far remote, with diminution seen.
First in his East the glorious Lamp was seen,   370
Regent of Day, and all th'Horizon round
Invested with bright Rays, jocund to run
His Longitude through Heav'n's high road: the gray
Dawn, and the Pleiades° before him danc'd
Shedding sweet influence: less bright the Moon,   375
But·opposite in levell'd° West was set
His mirror, with full face borrowing her Light
From him, for other light she needed none
In that aspéct,° and still that distance keeps
Till night, then in the East her turn she shines,   380
Revolv'd on Heav'n's great Axle, and her Reign
With thousand lesser Lights dividual° holds,
With thousand thousand Stars, that then appear'd
Spangling the Hemisphere: then first adorn'd
With their bright Luminaries that Set and Rose,   385
Glad Ev'ning and glad Morn crown'd the fourth day.
        And God said 'let the Waters generate
Reptile with Spawn abundant, living Soul:
And let Fowl fly above the Earth, with wings
Display'd on the op'n Firmament of Heav'n.'   390
And God created the great Whales, and each
Soul living, each that crept, which plenteously
The waters generated by their kinds,
And every Bird of wing after his kind;
And saw that it was good, and bless'd them, saying,   395
Be fruitful, multiply, and in the Seas
And Lakes and running Streams the waters fill;
And let the Fowl be multipli'd on the Earth.
Forthwith the Sounds and Seas, each Creek and Bay
With Fry innumerable swarm, and Shoals   400

---

366 **her** *1674;* his *1667.* 368 **peculiar** own possession. 374 **Pleiades**
a group of stars. 376 **levell'd** directly opposite. 379 **aspéct** astro-
logical position. 382 **dividual** distributed.

  Of Fish that with their Fins and shining Scales
  Glide under the green Wave, in Sculls° that oft
  Bank° the mid Sea: part single or with mate
  Graze the Sea-weed their pasture, and through Groves
405 Of Coral stray, or sporting with quick glance
  Show to the Sun their wav'd coats dropt with Gold,
  Or in their Pearly shells at ease, attend°
  Moist nutriment, or under Rocks their food
  In jointed Armour watch: on smooth the Seal,
410 And bended Dolphins play: part huge of bulk
  Wallowing unwieldy, enormous in their Gait
  Tempest the Ocean: there Leviathan°
  Hugest of living Creatures, on the Deep
  Stretcht like a Promontory sleeps or swims,
415 And seems a moving Land, and at his Gills
  Draws in, and at his Trunk spouts out a Sea.
  Meanwhile the tepid Caves, and Fens and shores
  Their Brood as numerous hatch, from the Egg that
   soon
  Bursting with kindly° rupture forth disclos'd
420 Their callow young, but feather'd soon and fledge
  They summ'd their Pens,° and soaring th'air sublime
  With clang despis'd the ground, under a cloud
  In prospect;° there the Eagle and the Stork
  On Cliffs and Cedar tops their Eyries build:
425 Part loosely wing the Region, part more wise
  In common, rang'd in figure wedge° their way,
  Intelligent° of seasons, and set forth
  Their Airy Caravan high over Seas
  Flying, and over Lands with mutual wing
430 Easing their flight; so steers the prudent Crane
  Her annual Voyage, borne on Winds; the Air
  Floats, as they pass, fann'd with unnumber'd plumes:
  From Branch to Branch the smaller Birds with song
  Solac'd the Woods, and spread their painted wings
435 Till Ev'n, nor then the solemn Nightingale

402 **Sculls** schools, shoals. 403 **Bank** form a bank (Daniel Defoe, 1719: "The banks, so they call the place where they catch the fish"). 407 **attend** watch for. 412 **Leviathan** the innocent contrast to the Satanic Leviathan, I 200–09. 419 **kindly** natural. 420–21 **fledge . . . Pens** fledged, they completed their total of feathers. 423 **In prospect** from their viewpoint. 426 **wedge** fly in a tapering formation. 427 **Intelligent** cognizant.

Ceas'd warbling, but all night tun'd her soft lays:
Others on Silver Lakes and Rivers Bath'd
Their downy Breast; the Swan with Arched neck
Between her white wings mantling proudly, Rows
Her state with Oary feet: yet oft they quit   *440*
The Dank,° and rising on stiff Pennons, tow'r
The mid Aereal Sky: Others on ground
Walk'd firm; the crested Cock whose clarion sounds
The silent hours, and th'other whose gay Train
Adorns him, colour'd with the Florid hue   *445*
Of Rainbows and Starry Eyes. The Waters thus
With Fish replenisht, and the Air with Fowl,
Ev'ning and Morn solémniz'd the Fifth day.
    The Sixth, and of Creation last arose
With Ev'ning Harps and Matin, when God said,   *450*
'Let th'Earth bring forth Soul° living in her kind,
Cattle and Creeping things, and Beast of th'Earth,
Each in their kind.' The Earth obey'd, and straight
Op'ning her fertile Womb teem'd at a Birth
Innumerous living Creatures, perfect forms,   *455*
Limb'd and full grown: out of the ground uprose
As from his Lair the wild Beast where he wons°
In Forest wild, in Thicket, Brake, or Den;
Among the Trees in Pairs they rose, they walk'd:
The Cattle in the Fields and Meadows green: *460*
Those rare and solitary, these in flocks
Pasturing at once, and in broad Herds upsprung.
The grassy Clods now Calv'd, now half appear'd
The Tawny Lion, pawing to get free
His hinder parts, then springs as broke from Bonds, *465*
And Rampant shakes his Brinded main; the Ounce,°
The Libbard,° and the Tiger, as the Mole
Rising, the crumbl'd Earth above them threw
In Hillocks; the swift Stag from under ground
Bore up his branching head: scarce from his mould   *470*
Behemoth° biggest born of Earth upheav'd
His vastness: Fleec't the Flocks and bleating rose,
As Plants: ambiguous° between Sea and Land

---

441 **Dank** water (without disagreeable associations). 451 **Soul** Bentley's conjecture; Fowle *1667*; Foul *1674*. 457 **wons** dwells. 466 **Ounce** lynx. 467 **Libbard** leopard. 471 **Behemoth** huge Biblical beast, here perhaps the elephant. 473 **ambiguous** amphibious.

The River Horse° and scaly Crocodile.
475 At once came forth whatever creeps the ground,
Insect or Worm; those wav'd their limber fans
For wings, and smallest Lineaments exact
In all the Liveries deckt of Summer's pride
With spots of Gold and Purple, azure and green:
480 These as a line their long dimension drew,
Streaking the ground with sinuous trace; not all
Minims of Nature;° some of Serpent kind
Wondrous in length and corpulence° involv'd
Their Snaky folds, and added wings. First crept
485 The Parsimonious Emmet,° provident
Of future, in small room large heart enclos'd,
Pattern of just equality perhaps
Hereafter, join'd in her popular Tribes
Of Commonalty: swarming next appear'd
490 The Female Bee that feeds her Husband Drone
Deliciously, and builds her waxen Cells
With Honey stor'd: the rest are numberless,
And thou their Natures know'st, and gav'st them
         Names,
Needless to thee repeated; nor unknown
495 The Serpent subtl'st Beast of all the field,
Of huge extent sometimes, with brazen Eyes
And hairy Main terrific, though to thee
Not noxious, but obedient at thy call.
Now Heav'n in all her Glory shone, and roll'd
500 Her motions, as the great first-Mover's hand
First wheel'd their course; Earth in her rich attire
Consummate° lovely smil'd; Air, Water, Earth,
By Fowl, Fish, Beast, was flown, was swum, was
         walkt
Frequent;° and of the Sixth day yet remain'd:
505 There wanted yet the Master work, the end
Of all yet done; a Creature who not prone
And Brute as other Creatures, but endu'd
With Sanctity of Reason, might erect
His Stature, and upright with Front° serene
510 Govern the rest, self-knowing, and from thence

474 **River Horse** hippopotamus.   482 **Minims of Nature** smallest
forms of animal life.   483 **corpulence** bulk.   485 **Emmet** ant.   502
Consummate perfected.   504 **Frequent** in throngs.   509 **Front** brow.

Magnanimous to correspond with° Heav'n,
But grateful to acknowledge whence his good
Descends, thither with heart and voice and eyes
Directed in Devotion, to adore
And worship God Supreme, who made him chief   515
Of all his works: therefore the Omnipotent
Eternal Father (For where is not hee
Present) thus to his Son audibly spake.
          'Let us make now Man in our image, Man
In our similitude, and let them rule   520
Over the Fish and Fowl of Sea and Air,
Beast of the Field, and over all the Earth,
And every creeping thing that creeps the ground.'
This said, he form'd thee, Adam, thee O Man
Dust of the ground, and in thy nostrils breath'd 525
The breath of Life; in his own Image hee
Created thee, in the Image of God
Express,° and thou becam'st a living Soul.
Male he created thee, but thy consort
Female for Race; then bless'd Mankind, and said, 530
'Be fruitful, multiply, and fill the Earth,
Subdue it, and throughout Dominion hold
Over Fish of the Sea, and Fowl of the Air,
And every living thing that moves on the Earth.'
Wherever thus created, for no place   535
Is yet distinct by name, thence, as thou know'st
He brought thee into this delicious Grove,
This Garden, planted with the Trees of God,
Delectable both to behold and taste;
And freely all their pleasant fruit for food   540
Gave thee, all sorts are here that all th'Earth yields,
Variety without end; but of the Tree
Which tasted works knowledge of Good and Evil,
Thou may'st not; in the day thou eat'st, thou di'st;
Death is the penalty impos'd, beware,   545
And govern well thy appetite, lest sin
Surprise thee, and her black attendant Death.
Here finish'd hee, and all that he had made
View'd, and behold all was entirely good;
So Ev'n and Morn accomplish'd the Sixth day: 550

511 **correspond with** "answer to," in all senses.   528 **Express** exact
in likeness.

Yet not till the Creator from his work
Desisting, though unwearied, up return'd
Up to the Heav'n of Heav'ns his high abode,
Thence to behold this new created World
555 Th'addition of his Empire, how it show'd
In prospect from his Throne, how good, how fair,
Answering his great Idea.° Up he rode
Follow'd with acclamation and the sound
Symphonious of ten thousand Harps that tun'd
560 Angelic harmonies: the Earth, the Air
Resounded, (thou remember'st, for thou heard'st)
The Heav'ns and all the Constellations rung,
The Planets in their station° list'ning stood,
While the bright Pomp ascended jubilant.
565 'Open, ye everlasting Gates,' they sung,
'Open, ye Heav'ns, your living doors; let in
The great Creator from his work return'd
Magnificent, his Six days' work, a World;
Open, and henceforth oft; for God will deign
570 To visit oft the dwellings of just Men
Delighted, and with frequent intercourse
Thither will send his winged Messengers
On errands of supernal Grace.' So sung
The glorious Train ascending: He through Heav'n,
575 That open'd wide her blazing Portals, led
To God's Eternal house direct the way,
A broad and ample road, whose dust is Gold
And pavement Stars, as Stars to thee appear,
Seen in the Galaxy, that Milky way
580 Which nightly as a circling Zone thou seest
Powder'd with Stars. And now on Earth the Seventh
Ev'ning arose in Eden, for the Sun
Was set, and twilight from the East came on,
Forerunning Night; when at the holy mount
585 Of Heav'n's high-seated top, th'Imperial Throne
Of Godhead, fixt for ever firm and sure,
The Filial Power arriv'd, and sat him down
With his great Father, for he also went
Invisible, yet stay'd (such privilege
590 Hath Omnipresence) and the work ordain'd,
Author and end of all things, and from work

557 **Idea** ideal conception.   563 **station** *1674*; stations *1667*.

Now resting, bless'd and hallow'd the Sev'nth day,
As resting on that day from all his work,
But not in silence holy kept; the Harp
Had work and rested not, the solemn Pipe,   595
And Dulcimer, all Organs of sweet stop,
All sounds on Fret° by String or Golden Wire
Temper'd soft Tunings, intermixt with Voice
Choral or Unison: of incense Clouds
Fuming from Golden Censers hid the Mount.   600
Creation and the Six days' acts they sung,
'Great are thy works, Jehovah, infinite
Thy power; what thought can measure thee or tongue
Relate thee; greater now in thy return
Than from the Giant Angels; thee that day   605
Thy Thunders magnifi'd; but to create
Is greater than created to destroy.
Who can impair thee, mighty King, or bound
Thy Empire? easily the proud attempt
Of Spirits apostate and their Counsels vain   610
Thou hast repell'd, while impiously they thought
Thee to diminish, and from thee withdraw
The number of thy worshippers. Who seeks
To lessen thee, against his purpose serves
To manifest the more thy might: his evil   615
Thou usest, and from thence creat'st more good.
Witness this new-made World, another Heav'n
From Heaven Gate not far, founded in view
On the clear Hyaline,° the Glassy Sea;
Of amplitude almost immense,° with Stars   620
Numerous, and every Star perhaps a World
Of destin'd habitation; but thou know'st
Their seasons: among these the seat of men,
Earth with her nether Ocean circumfus'd,
Their pleasant dwelling place. Thrice happy men,   625
And sons of men, whom God hath thus advanc't,
Created in his Image, there to dwell
And worship him, and in reward to rule
Over his Works, on Earth, in Sea, or Air,
And multiply a Race of Worshippers   630

597 **Fret** the bar which regulates the fingering. 619 **Hyaline** the "sea
of glass, like unto crystal" in REVELATION 4:6. 620 **immense** im-
measurable.

Holy and just: thrice happy if they know
Their happiness, and persevere upright.'
      So sung they, and the Empyrean rung,
With Halleluiahs: Thus was Sabbath kept.
635 And thy request think now fulfill'd, that ask'd
How first this World and face of things began,
And what before thy memory was done
From the beginning, that posterity
Inform'd by thee might know; if else thou seek'st
640 Aught, not surpassing human measure, say."

BOOK VIII

THE ARGUMENT

Adam inquires concerning celestial Motions, is doubtfully answer'd, and exhorted to search rather things more worthy of knowledge: Adam assents, and still desirous to detain Raphael, relates to him what he remember'd since his own Creation, his placing in Paradise, his talk with God concerning solitude and fit society, his first meeting and Nuptials with Eve, his discourse with the Angel thereupon; who after admonitions repeated departs.

The Angel ended, and in Adam's Ear
So Charming left his voice, that he awhile
Thought him still speaking, still stood fixt to hear;
Then as new wak't thus gratefully repli'd.°
"What thanks sufficient, or what recompense   5
Equal have I to render thee, Divine
Historian, who thus largely hast allay'd
The thirst I had of knowledge, and vouchsaf't
This friendly condescension° to relate
Things else by me unsearchable, now heard   10
With wonder, but delight, and, as is due,
With glory áttribúted to the high
Creator; something yet of doubt remains,
Which only thy solution can resolve.
When I behold this goodly Frame, this World   15
Of Heav'n and Earth consisting, and compute

1–4 Added in *1674*, when Book VII was divided in two at line 640. *1667* reads: "To whom thus Adam gratefully repli'd." **9 condescension** courteous disregard of rank.

175

Their magnitudes, this Earth a spot, a grain,
An Atom, with the Firmament compar'd
And all her number'd Stars, that seem to roll
20 Spaces incomprehensible (for such
Their distance argues and their swift return
Diurnal) merely to officiate° light
Round this opacous Earth, this punctual° spot,
One day and night; in all their vast survéy
25 Useless besides, reasoning I oft admire,°
How Nature wise and frugal could commit
Such disproportions, with superfluous hand
So many nobler Bodies to create,
Greater so manifold to this one use,
30 For aught appears, and on their Orbs impose
Such restless revolution day by day
Repeated, while the sedentary° Earth,
That better might with far less compass move,
Serv'd by more noble than herself, attains
35 Her end without least motion, and receives,
As Tribute such a sumless° journey brought
Of incorporeal speed, her warmth and light;
Speed, to describe whose swiftness Number fails."
        So spake our Sire, and by his count'nance
                seem'd
40 Ent'ring on studious thoughts abstruse, which Eve
Perceiving where she sat retir'd in sight,
With lowliness Majestic from her seat,
And Grace that won who saw to wish her stay,
Rose, and went forth among her Fruits and Flow'rs,
45 To visit how they prosper'd, bud and bloom,
Her Nursery;° they at her coming sprung
And toucht° by her fair tendance gladlier grew.
Yet went she not, as not with such discourse
Delighted, or not capable her ear
50 Of what was high: such pleasure she reserv'd,°

22 **officiate** supply, and with a strong religious suggestion, since an
original meaning was "perform divine service."   23 **punctual** tiny
like a point, and the suggestion of exact timing is relevant too.   25
admire wonder (at).   32 **sedentary** motionless.   36 **sumless** incal-
culable.   46 **Nursery** both the spot (nursery-garden), and the activity
(her tending or fostering).   47 **toucht** both literal (her gardening)
and metaphorical (moved to tender feeling, "gladlier grew").   50
reserv'd postponed.

Adam relating, she sole Auditress;
Her Husband the Relater° she preferr'd
Before the Angel, and of him to ask
Chose rather; hee, she knew would intermix
Grateful digressions, and solve high dispute   55
With conjugal Caresses, from his Lip
Not Words alone pleas'd her. O when meet now
Such pairs, in Love and mutual Honour join'd?
With Goddess-like demeanour forth she went;
Not unattended, for on her as Queen   60
A pomp° of winning Graces waited still,°
And from about her shot Darts of desire
Into all Eyes to wish her still in sight.
And Raphaël now to Adam's doubt propos'd
Benevolent and facile° thus repli'd.   65
        "To ask or search I blame thee not, for Heav'n
Is as the Book of God before thee set,
Wherein to read his wondrous Works, and learn
His Seasons, Hours, or Days, or Months, or Years:
This to attain, whether Heav'n move or Earth,   70
Imports not, if thou reck'n right, the rest
From Man or Angel the great Architect
Did wisely to conceal, and not divulge
His secrets to be scann'd by them who ought
Rather admire; or if they list to try   75
Conjecture, he his Fabric of the Heav'ns
Hath left to their disputes, perhaps to move
His laughter at their quaint Opinions wide°
Hereafter, when they come to model Heav'n
And calculate the Stars, how they will wield   80
The mighty frame, how build, unbuild, contrive
To save appearances,° how gird the Sphere
With Centric and Eccentric° scribbl'd o'er,
Cycle and Epicycle,° Orb in Orb:
Already by thy reasoning this I guess,   85

---

52 **Relater** narrator, but following "Husband" it suggests, too, "relative"—Eve preferred the man to whom she was related to relate.
61 **pomp** pageant. 61 **still** always. 65 **facile** equable. 78 **wide** astray.
82 **save appearances** explain away difficulties (in the Ptolemaic theory). 83 **Centric and Eccentric** with orbits centered or not centered on the earth. 84 **Epicycle** small cycle (Ptolemaic term).

Who art to lead thy offspring, and supposest
That Bodies bright and greater should not serve
The less not bright, nor Heav'n such journeys run,
Earth sitting still, when she alone receives
90   The benefit: consider first, that Great
Or Bright infers not Excellence: the Earth
Though, in comparison of Heav'n, so small,
Nor glistering, may of solid good contain
More plenty than the Sun that barren shines,
95   Whose virtue on itself works no effect,
But in the fruitful Earth; there first receiv'd
His beams, unactive else, their vigour find.
Yet not to Earth are those bright Luminaries
Officious,° but to thee Earth's habitant.
100 And for the Heav'n's wide Circuit, let it speak
The Maker's high magnificence, who built
So spacious, and his Line stretcht out so far;
That Man may know he dwells not in his own;
An Edifice too large for him to fill,
105 Lodg'd in a small partition, and the rest
Ordain'd for uses to his Lord best known.
The swiftness of those Circles áttribúte,
Though numberless, to his Omnipotence,
That to corporeal substances could add
110 Speed almost Spiritual; mee thou think'st not slow,
Who since the Morning hour set out from Heav'n
Where God resides, and ere mid-day arriv'd
In Eden, distance inexpressible
By Numbers that have name. But this I urge,
115 Admitting Motion in the Heav'ns, to show
Invalid that which thee to doubt it mov'd;
Not that I so affirm, though so it seem
To thee who hast thy dwelling here on Earth.
God to remove his ways from human sense,
120 Plac'd Heav'n from Earth so far, that earthly sight,
If it presume, might err in things too high,
And no advantage° gain. What if the Sun
Be Center to the World, and other Stars

99 **Officious** dutiful.   122 **advantage** including the common 17th-
century sense, "point of vantage."

By his attractive virtue° and their own
Incited, dance about him various rounds?   125
Their wand'ring course now high, now low, then hid,
Progressive, retrograde, or standing still,
In six thou seest, and what if sev'nth to these
The Planet Earth, so steadfast though she seem,
Insensibly three° different Motions move?   130
Which else to several Spheres thou must ascribe,
Mov'd contrary with thwart obliquities,
Or save the Sun his labour, and that swift
Nocturnal and Diurnal rhomb° suppos'd,
Invisible else above all Stars, the Wheel   135
Of Day and Night; which needs not thy belief,
If Earth industrious of herself fetch Day
Travelling East, and with her part averse
From the Sun's beam meet Night, her other part
Still luminous by his ray. What if that light   140
Sent from her through the wide transpicuous air,
To the terrestrial Moon be as a Star
Enlight'ning her by Day, as she by Night
This Earth? reciprocal, if Land be there,
Fields and Inhabitants: Her spots thou seest   145
As Clouds, and Clouds may rain, and Rain produce
Fruits in her soft'n'd Soil, for some to eat
Allotted there; and other Suns perhaps
With their attendant Moons thou wilt descry
Communicating Male and Female Light,   150
Which two great Sexes animate the World,
Stor'd in each Orb perhaps with some that live.
For such vast room in Nature unpossest
By living Soul, desért and desolate,
Only to shine, yet scarce to cóntribute   155
Each Orb a glimpse of Light, convey'd so far
Down to this habitable, which returns
Light back to them, is obvious° to dispute.
But whether thus these things, or whether not,

---

124 **attractive virtue** power of attraction.   130 **three** daily, yearly,
and on its own axis.   134 **rhomb** the supposed wheel of the Primum
Mobile, the first-moved sphere.   158 **obvious** open.

160 Whether the Sun predominant in Heav'n
    Rise on the Earth, or Earth rise on the Sun,
    Hee from the East his flaming road begin,
    Or Shee from West her silent course advance
    With inoffensive° pace that spinning sleeps
165 On her soft Axle, while she paces Ev'n,
    And bears thee soft with the smooth Air along,
    Solicit° not thy thoughts with matters hid,
    Leave them to God above, him serve and fear;
    Of other Creatures, as him pleases best,
170 Wherever plac't, let him dispose: joy thou
    In what he gives to thee, this Paradise
    And thy fair Eve; Heav'n is for thee too high
    To know what passes there; be lowly wise:
    Think only what concerns thee and thy being;
175 Dream not of other Worlds, what Creatures there
    Live, in what state, condition or degree,
    Contented that thus far hath been reveal'd
    Not of Earth only but of highest Heav'n."
               To whom thus Adam clear'd of doubt, repli'd.
180 "How fully hast thou satisfi'd mee, pure
    Intelligence° of Heav'n, Angel serene,
    And freed from intricacies, taught to live,
    The easiest way, nor with perplexing thoughts
    To interrupt the sweet of Life, from which
185 God hath bid dwell far off all anxious cares,
    And not molest us, unless we ourselves
    Seek them with wand'ring thoughts, and notions vain.
    But apt the Mind or Fancy is to rove
    Uncheckt, and of her roving is no end;
190 Till warn'd, or by experience taught, she learn,
    That not to know at large of things remote
    From use, obscure and subtle, but to know
    That which before us lies in daily life,
    Is the prime Wisdom, what is more, is fume,
195 Or emptiness, or fond impertinence,°

164 **inoffensive** unstumbling.   167 **Solicit** disturb (from the Latin for
"to put in motion"; Raphael remembers the context in which he
speaks).   181 **Intelligence** divine spirit.   195 **fond impertinence**
foolish irrelevance.

And renders us in things that most concern
Unpractis'd, unprepar'd, and still to seek.
Therefore from this high pitch let us descend
A lower flight, and speak of things at hand
Useful, whence haply mention may arise   *200*
Of something not unseasonable to ask
By sufferance, and thy wonted favour deign'd.
Thee I have heard relating what was done
Ere my remembrance: now hear mee relate
My Story, which perhaps thou hast not heard;   *205*
And Day is yet not spent; till then thou seest
How subtly to detain thee I devise,
Inviting thee to hear while I relate,
Fond, were it not in hope of thy reply:
For while I sit with thee, I seem in Heav'n,   *210*
And sweeter thy discourse is to my ear
Than Fruits of Palm-tree pleasantest to thirst
And hunger both, from labour, at the hour
Of sweet repast; they satiate, and soon fill,
Though pleasant, but thy words with Grace Divine *215*
Imbu'd, bring to their sweetness no satiety."
          To whom thus Raphaël answer'd heav'nly
          meek.
"Nor are thy lips ungraceful, Sire of men,
Nor tongue ineloquent; for God on thee
Abundantly his gifts hath also pour'd   *220*
Inward and outward both, his image fair:
Speaking or mute all comeliness and grace
Attends thee, and each word, each motion forms.
Nor less think wee in Heav'n of thee on Earth
Than of our fellow servant, and inquire   *225*
Gladly into the ways of God with Man:
For God we see hath honour'd thee, and set
On Man his equal Love: say therefore on;
For I that Day was absent, as befell,
Bound on a voyage uncouth and obscure,   *230*
Far on excursion toward the Gates of Hell;
Squar'd in full Legion (such command we had)
To see that none thence issu'd forth a spy,
Or enemy, while God was in his work,
Lest hee incens't at such eruption bold,   *235*

Destruction with Creation might have mixt.
Not that they durst without his leave attempt,
But us he sends upon his high behests
For state, as Sovran King, and to inure
240 Our prompt obedience. Fast we found, fast shut
The dismal Gates, and barricado'd strong;
But long ere our approaching heard within
Noise, other than the sound of Dance or Song,
Torment, and loud lament, and furious rage.
245 Glad we return'd up to the coasts of Light
Ere Sabbath Ev'ning: so we had in charge.
But thy relation now; for I attend,
Pleas'd with thy words no less than thou with mine."
      So spake the Godlike Power, and thus our
      Sire.
250 "For Man to tell how human Life began
Is hard; for who himself beginning knew?
Desire with thee still longer to converse
Induc'd me. As new wak't from soundest sleep
Soft on the flow'ry herb I found me laid
255 In Balmy Sweat, which with his Beams the Sun
Soon dri'd, and on the reeking° moisture fed.
Straight toward Heav'n my wond'ring Eyes I turn'd,
And gaz'd awhile the ample Sky, till rais'd
By quick instinctive motion up I sprung,
260 As thitherward endeavouring, and upright
Stood on my feet; about me round I saw
Hill, Dale, and shady Woods, and sunny Plains,
And liquid Lapse° of murmuring Streams; by these,
Creatures that liv'd, and mov'd, and walk'd, or flew,
265 Birds on the branches warbling; all things smil'd,
With fragrance and with joy my heart o'erflow'd.
Myself I then perus'd, and Limb by Limb
Survey'd, and sometimes went, and sometimes ran
With supple joints, as lively vigour led:
270 But who I was, or where, or from what cause,
Knew not; to speak I tri'd, and forthwith spake,

256 **reeking** rising in vapor (without disagreeable associations).   263
Lapse fall (consciously literal, since Paradise is as yet innocent; but
"the Lapse of Man" was a 17th-century phrase for the Fall).

My Tongue obey'd and readily could name
Whate'er I saw. 'Thou Sun,' said I, 'fair Light,
And thou enlight'n'd Earth, so fresh and gay,
Ye Hills and Dales, ye Rivers, Woods, and Plains,   275
And ye that live and move, fair Creatures, tell,
Tell, if ye saw, how came I thus, how here?
Not of myself; by some great Maker then,
In goodness and in power preeminent;
Tell me, how may I know him, how adore,   280
From whom I have that thus I move and live,
And feel that I am happier than I know.'
While thus I call'd, and stray'd I knew not whither,
From where I first drew Air, and first beheld
This happy Light, when answer none return'd,   285
On a green shady Bank profuse of Flow'rs
Pensive I sat me down; there gentle sleep
First found me, and with soft oppression seiz'd
My drowsed sense, untroubl'd, though I thought
I then was passing to my former state   290
Insensible, and forthwith to dissolve:
When suddenly stood at my Head a dream,
Whose inward apparition° gently mov'd
My Fancy to believe I yet had being,
And liv'd: One came, methought, of shape Divine,   295
And said, 'thy Mansion wants thee, Adam, rise,
First Man, of Men innumerable ordain'd
First Father, call'd by thee I come thy Guide
To the Garden of bliss, thy seat prepar'd.'
So saying, by the hand he took me rais'd,   300
And over Fields and Waters, as in Air
Smooth sliding without step, last led me up
A woody Mountain; whose high top was plain,
A Circuit wide, enclos'd, with goodliest Trees
Planted, with Walks, and Bowers, that what I saw   305
Of Earth before scarce pleasant seem'd. Each Tree
Load'n with fairest Fruit, that hung to the Eye
Tempting, stirr'd in me sudden appetite
To pluck and eat; whereat I wak'd, and found
Before mine Eyes all real, as the dream   310
Had lively shadow'd: Here had new begun
My wand'ring, had not hee who was my Guide

293 apparition appearing.

Up hither, from among the Trees appear'd,
Presence Divine. Rejoicing, but with awe
315 In adoration at his feet I fell
Submiss: he rear'd me, and 'Whom thou sought'st I
am,'
Said mildly, 'Author of all this thou seest
Above, or round about thee or beneath.
This Paradise I give thee, count it thine
320 To Till and keep, and of the Fruit to eat:
Of every Tree that in the Garden grows
Eat freely with glad heart; fear here no dearth:
But of the Tree whose operation brings
Knowledge of good and ill, which I have set
325 The Pledge of thy Obedience and thy Faith,
Amid the Garden by the Tree of Life,
Remember what I warn thee, shun to taste,
And shun the bitter consequence: for know,
The day thou eat'st thereof, my sole command
330 Transgrest, inevitably thou shalt die;
From that day mortal, and this happy State
Shalt lose, expell'd from hence into a World
Of woe and sorrow.' Sternly he pronounc'd
The rigid interdiction, which resounds
335 Yet dreadful in mine ear, though in my choice
Not to incur; but soon his clear aspéct
Return'd and gracious purpose° thus renew'd.
'Not only these fair bounds, but all the Earth
To thee and to thy Race I give; as Lords
340 Possess it, and all things that therein live,
Or live in Sea, or Air, Beast, Fish, and Fowl.
In sign whereof each Bird and Beast behold
After their kinds; I bring them to receive
From thee their Names, and pay thee fealty
345 With low subjection; understand the same
Of Fish within their wat'ry residence,
Not hither summon'd, since they cannot change
Their Element to draw the thinner Air.'
As thus he spake, each Bird and Beast behold
350 Approaching two and two, These cow'ring low
With blandishment, each Bird stoop'd on his wing.
I nam'd them, as they pass'd, and understood

337 **purpose** discourse.

Their Nature, with such knowledge God endu'd
My sudden apprehension: but in these
I found not what methought I wanted still;   355
And to the Heav'nly vision thus presum'd.

    'O by what Name, for thou above all these,
Above mankind, or aught than mankind higher,
Surpassest far my naming, how may I
Adore thee, Author of this Universe,   360
And all this good to man, for whose well-being
So amply, and with hands so liberal
Thou hast provided all things: but with mee
I see not who partakes. In solitude
What happiness, who can enjoy alone,   365
Or all enjoying, what contentment find?'
Thus I presumptuous; and the vision bright,
As with a smile more bright'n'd, thus repli'd.

    'What call'st thou solitude, is not the Earth
With various living creatures, and the Air   370
Replenisht, and all these at thy command
To come and play before thee, know'st thou not
Their language and their ways, they also know,
And reason not contemptibly; with these
Find pastime, and bear rule; thy Realm is large.'   375
So spake the Universal Lord, and seem'd
So ordering. I with leave of speech implor'd,
And humble deprecation thus repli'd.

    'Let not my words offend thee, Heav'nly
      Power,
My Maker, be propitious while I speak.   380
Hast thou not made me here thy substitute,°
And these inferior far beneath me set?
Among unequals what society
Can sort, what harmony or true delight?
Which must be mutual, in proportion due   385
Giv'n and receiv'd; but in disparity
The one intense, the other still remiss°
Cannot well suit with either, but soon prove
Tedious alike: Of fellowship I speak
Such as I seek, fit to participate   390
All rational delight, wherein the brute

381 **substitute** deputy.   387 **intense ... remiss** taut and slack, taking
up the metaphor of "harmony."

Cannot be human consort; they rejoice
Each with their kind, Lion with Lioness;
So fitly them in pairs thou hast combin'd;
395 Much less can Bird with Beast, or Fish with Fowl
So well converse,° nor with the Ox the Ape;
Worse then can Man with Beast, and least of all.'
      Whereto th'Almighty answer'd, not displeas'd.
'A nice° and subtle happiness I see
400 Thou to thyself proposest, in the choice
Of thy Associates, Adam, and wilt taste
No pleasure, thou in pleasure, solitary.
What think'st thou then of mee, and this my State,
Seem I to thee sufficiently possest
405 Of happiness, or not? who am alone
From all Eternity, for none I know
Second to mee or like, equal much less.
How have I then with whom to hold converse
Save with the Creatures which I made, and those
410 To me inferior, infinite descents
Beneath what other Creatures are to thee?'
      He ceas'd, I lowly answer'd. 'To attain
The heighth and depth of thy Eternal ways
All human thoughts come short, Supreme of things;
415 Thou in thyself art perfect, and in thee
Is no deficience found; not so is Man,
But in degree, the cause of his desire
By conversation with his like to help,
Or solace his defects. No need that thou
420 Shouldst propagate, already infinite;
And through all numbers absolute, though One;
But Man by number is to manifest
His single imperfection,° and beget
Like of his like, his Image multipli'd,
425 In unity° defective, which requires
Collateral love, and dearest amity.
Thou in thy secrecy although alone,
Best with thyself accompanied, seek'st not
Social communication, yet so pleas'd,
430 Canst raise thy Creature to what heighth thou wilt
Of Union or Communion, deifi'd;

396 **converse** associate.   399 **nice** fastidious.   423 **single imperfec-
tion** imperfection in being single.   425 **unity** oneness.

I by conversing cannot these erect
From prone, nor in their ways complacence° find.'
Thus I embold'n'd spake, and freedom us'd
Permissive, and acceptance found, which gain'd   435
This answer from the gracious voice Divine.

      'Thus far to try thee, Adam, I was pleas'd,
And find thee knowing not of Beasts alone,
Which thou hast rightly nam'd, but of thyself,
Expressing well the spirit within thee free,   440
My Image, not imparted to the Brute,
Whose fellowship therefore unmeet for thee
Good reason was thou freely shouldst dislike,
And be so minded still; I, ere thou spak'st,
Knew it not good for Man to be alone,   445
And no such company as then thou saw'st
Intended thee, for trial only brought,
To see how thou could'st judge of fit and meet:
What next I bring shall please thee, be assur'd,
Thy likeness, thy fit help, thy other self,   450
Thy wish, exactly to thy heart's desire.'

      Hee ended, or I heard no more, for now
My earthly by his Heav'nly overpower'd,
Which it had long stood under, strain'd to the heighth
In that celestial Colloquy sublime,   455
As with an object that excels° the sense,
Dazzl'd and spent, sunk down, and sought repair
Of sleep, which instantly fell on me, call'd
By Nature as in aid, and clos'd mine eyes.
Mine eyes he clos'd, but op'n left the Cell   460
Of Fancy my internal sight, by which
Abstráct° as in a trance methought I saw,
Though sleeping, where I lay, and saw the shape
Still glorious before whom awake I stood;
Who stooping op'n'd my left side, and took   465
From thence a Rib, with cordial spirits° warm,
And Life-blood streaming fresh; wide was the wound,
But suddenly with flesh fill'd up and heal'd:
The Rib he form'd and fashion'd with his hands;
Under his forming hands a Creature grew,   470

433 **complacence** satisfaction.   456 **excels** literally, rises above (the
context suggests gazing into the sky).   462 **Abstráct** withdrawn.
466 **cordial spirits** the heart's vital spirits.

Manlike, but different sex, so lovely fair,
That what seem'd fair in all the World, seem'd now
Mean, or in her summ'd up, in her contain'd
And in her looks, which from that time infus'd
475 Sweetness into my heart, unfelt before,
And into all things from her Air inspir'd
The spirit of love and amorous delight.
She disappear'd, and left me dark, I wak'd
To find her, or for ever to deplore
480 Her loss, and other pleasures all abjure:
When out of hope, behold her, not far off,
Such as I saw her in my dream, adorn'd
With what all Earth or Heaven could bestow
To make her amiable: On she came,
485 Led by her Heav'nly Maker, though unseen,
And guided by his voice, nor uninform'd
Of nuptial Sanctity and marriage Rites:
Grace was in all her steps, Heav'n in her Eye,
In every gesture dignity and love.
490 I overjoy'd could not forbear aloud.
            'This turn hath made amends; thou hast
                fulfill'd
Thy words, Creator bounteous and benign,
Giver of all things fair, but fairest this
Of all thy gifts, nor enviest. I now see
495 Bone of my Bone, Flesh of my Flesh, my Self
Before me; Woman is her Name, of Man
Extracted; for this cause he shall forgo
Father and Mother, and to his Wife adhere;
And they shall be one Flesh, one Heart, one Soul.'
            She heard me thus, and though divinely
500   brought,
Yet Innocence and Virgin Modesty,
Her virtue and the conscience° of her worth,
That would be woo'd, and not unsought be won,
Not obvious,° not obtrusive, but retir'd,
505 The more desirable, or to say all,
Nature herself, though pure of sinful thought,
Wrought in her so, that seeing me, she turn'd;
I follow'd her, she what was Honour knew,

502 conscience consciousness.   504 obvious "forward."

And with obsequious° Majesty approv'd
My pleaded reason. To the Nuptial Bow'r   *510*
I led her blushing like the Morn: all Heav'n,
And happy Constellations on that hour
Shed their selectest influence; the Earth
Gave sign of gratulation, and each Hill;
Joyous the Birds; fresh Gales and gentle Airs   *515*
Whisper'd it to the Woods, and from their wings
Flung Rose, flung Odours from the spicy Shrub,
Disporting, till the amorous Bird of Night
Sung Spousal, and bid haste the Ev'ning Star
On his Hill top, to light the bridal Lamp.   *520*
Thus I have told thee all my State, and brought
My Story to the sum of earthly bliss
Which I enjoy, and must confess to find
In all things else delight indeed, but such
As us'd or not, works in the mind no change,   *525*
Nor vehement° desire, these delicacies
I mean of Taste, Sight, Smell, Herbs, Fruits, and
    Flow'rs,
Walks, and the melody of Birds; but here
Far otherwise, transported I behold,
Transported touch; here passion first I felt,   *530*
Commotion strange, in all enjoyments else
Superior and unmov'd, here only weak
Against the charm of Beauty's powerful glance.
Or Nature fail'd in mee, and left some part
Not proof° enough such Object to sustain,   *535*
Or from my side subducting, took perhaps
More than enough; at least on her bestow'd
Too much of Ornament, in outward show
Elaborate,° of inward less exact.°
For well I understand in the prime end   *540*
Of Nature her th'inferior, in the mind
And inward Faculties, which most excel,
In outward also her resembling less
His Image who made both, and less expressing
The character of that Dominion giv'n   *545*

509 obsequious obedient (gently paradoxical in combination with
"Majesty").   526 vehement from "deprived of the mind" (Latin
mens), following line 525.   535 proof armored.   539 Elaborate
highly worked.   539 exact brought to perfection.

O'er other Creatures; yet when I approach
Her loveliness, so absolute° she seems
And in herself complete, so well to know
Her own, that what she wills to do or say,
550 Seems wisest, virtuousest, discreetest,° best;
All higher knowledge in her presence falls
Degraded, Wisdom in discourse with her
Loses discount'nanc't, and like folly shows;
Authority and Reason on her wait,
555 As one intended first, not after made
Occasionally;° and to consúmmate all,
Greatness of mind and nobleness their seat
Build in her loveliest, and create an awe
About her, as a guard Angelic plac't."
560 To whom the Angel with contracted brow.

    "Accuse not Nature, she hath done her part;
Do thou but thine, and be not diffident°
Of Wisdom, she deserts thee not, if thou
Dismiss not her, when most thou need'st her nigh,
565 By áttribúting overmuch to things
Less excellent, as thou thyself perceiv'st.
For what admir'st thou, what transports thee so,
An outside? fair no doubt, and worthy well
Thy cherishing, thy honouring, and thy love,
570 Not thy subjection: weigh with her thyself;
Then value: Oft times nothing profits more
Than self-esteem, grounded on just and right
Well manag'd; of that skill the more thou know'st,
The more she will acknowledge thee her Head,
575 And to realities yield all her shows;
Made so adorn for thy delight the more,
So awful, that with honour thou may'st love
Thy mate, who sees when thou art seen least wise.
But if the sense of touch whereby mankind
580 Is propagated seem such dear delight
Beyond all other, think the same vouchsaf't
To Cattle and each Beast; which would not be
To them made common and divulg'd, if aught
Therein enjoy'd were worthy to subdue

---

547 **absolute** perfect, with a suggestion of complete power.   550 **dis-
creetest** most discerning.   556 **Occasionally** for a particular occa-
sion.   562 **diffident** distrustful.

The Soul of Man, or passion in him move.   585
What higher in her society thou find'st
Attractive, human, rational, love still;
In loving thou dost well, in passion not,
Wherein true Love consists not; love refines
The thoughts, and heart enlarges, hath his seat   590
In Reason, and is judicious, is the scale
By which to heav'nly Love thou may'st ascend,
Not sunk in carnal pleasure, for which cause
Among the Beasts no Mate for thee was found."
          To whom thus half-abash't Adam repli'd.   595
"Neither her outside form'd so fair, nor aught
In procreation common to all kinds
(Though higher of the genial° Bed by far,
And with mysterious reverence I deem)
So much delights me, as those graceful acts,   600
Those thousand decencies that daily flow
From all her words and actions, mixt with Love
And sweet compliance, which declare unfeign'd
Union of Mind, or in us both one Soul;
Harmony to behold in wedded pair   605
More grateful than harmonious sound to the ear.
Yet these subject not;° I to thee disclose
What inward thence I feel, not therefore foil'd,
Who meet with various objects, from the sense
Variously representing; yet still free   610
Approve the best, and follow what I approve.
To love thou blam'st me not, for love thou say'st
Leads up to Heav'n, is both the way and guide;
Bear with me then, if lawful what I ask;
Love not the heav'nly Spirits, and how their Love   615
Express they, by looks only, or do they mix
Irradiance, virtual° or immediate touch?"
          To whom the Angel with a smile that glow'd
Celestial rosy red, Love's proper hue,
Answer'd. "Let it suffice thee that thou know'st   620
Us happy, and without Love no happiness.
Whatever pure thou in the body enjoy'st
(And pure thou wert created) we enjoy
In eminence, and obstacle find none

598 **genial** generative.   607 **subject not** do not bring into subjection.
617 **virtual** in essence.

625 Of membrane, joint, or limb, exclusive° bars:
    Easier than Air with Air, if Spirits embrace,
    Total they mix, Union of Pure with Pure
    Desiring; nor restrain'd conveyance° need
    As Flesh to mix with Flesh, or Soul with Soul.
630 But I can now no more; the parting Sun
    Beyond the Earth's green Cape° and verdant Isles
    Hesperean sets, my Signal to depart.
    Be strong, live happy, and love, but first of all
    Him whom to love is to obey, and keep
635 His great command; take heed lest Passion sway
    Thy Judgement to do aught, which else free Will
    Would not admit; thine and of all thy Sons
    The weal or woe in thee is plac't; beware.
    I in thy persevering shall rejoice,
640 And all the Blest: stand fast; to stand or fall
    Free in thine own Arbitrement it lies.
    Perfect within, no outward aid require;
    And all temptation to transgress repel."
            So saying, he arose; whom Adam thus
645 Follow'd with benediction. "Since to part,
    Go heav'nly Guest, Ethereal Messenger,
    Sent from whose sovran goodness I adore.
    Gentle to me and affable hath been
    Thy condescension, and shall be honour'd ever
650 With grateful Memory: thou to mankind
    Be good and friendly still, and oft return."
            So parted they, the Angel up to Heav'n
    From the thick shade, and Adam to his Bow'r.

625 **exclusive** having the power to exclude.   628 **restrain'd convey-ance** restricted conveying.   631 **green Cape** Cape Verde islands.

BOOK IX

THE ARGUMENT

Satan having compast the Earth, with meditated guile
returns as a mist by Night into Paradise, enters into the
Serpent sleeping. Adam and Eve in the Morning go forth
to their labours, which Eve proposes to divide in several
places, each labouring apart: Adam consents not, alleging
the danger, lest that Enemy, of whom they were fore-
warn'd, should attempt her found alone: Eve loath to
be thought not circumspect or firm enough, urges her
going apart, the rather desirous to make trial of her
strength; Adam at last yields: The Serpent finds her alone;
his subtle approach, first gazing, then speaking, with much
flattery extolling Eve above all other Creatures. Eve
wond'ring to hear the Serpent speak, asks how he attain'd
both human speech and such understanding not till now;
the Serpent answers, that by tasting of a certain Tree in
the Garden he attain'd to Speech and Reason, till then
void of both: Eve requires him to bring her to that Tree,
and finds it to be the Tree of Knowledge forbidden: The
Serpent now grown bolder, with many wiles and argu-
ments induces her at length to eat; she pleas'd with the
taste deliberates awhile whether to impart thereof to
Adam or not, at last brings him of the Fruit, relates what
persuaded her to eat thereof: Adam at first amaz'd, but
perceiving her lost, resolves through vehemence of love
to perish with her; and extenuating the trespass, eats also
of the Fruit: The effects thereof in them both; they seek
to cover their nakedness; then fall to variance and ac-
cusation of one another.

No more of talk where God or Angel Guest
With Man, as with his Friend, familiar° us'd
To sit indulgent, and with him partake
Rural repast, permitting him the while
5   Venial° discourse unblam'd: I now must change
Those Notes to Tragic; foul distrust, and breach
Disloyal on the part of Man, revolt,
And disobedience: On the part of Heav'n
Now alienated, distance and distaste,
10   Anger and just rebuke, and judgement giv'n,
That brought into this World a world of woe,
Sin and her shadow Death, and Misery
Death's Harbinger: Sad task, yet argument°
Not less but more Heroic than the wrath
15   Of stern Achilles° on his Foe pursu'd
Thrice Fugitive about Troy Wall; or rage
Of Turnus for Lavinia° disespous'd,
Or Neptune's ire or Juno's, that so long
Perplex'd the Greek° and Cytherea's Son;°
20   If answerable° style I can obtain
Of my Celestial Patroness, who deigns
Her nightly visitation° unimplor'd,
And dictates to me slumb'ring, or inspires
Easy my unpremeditated Verse:
25   Since first this Subject for Heroic Song
Pleas'd me long choosing, and beginning late;
Not sedulous by Nature to indite
Wars, hitherto the only Argument
Heroic deem'd, chief mast'ry to dissect°
30   With long and tedious havoc fabl'd Knights

2 **familiar** affable, habitual, and as if within a family.   5 **Venial** al-
lowable.   13 **argument** story.   15 **Achilles** in the *Iliad*.   17 **Lavinia**
whose betrothal was broken in the *Aeneid*.   19 **Greek** Odysseus,
persecuted by Neptune.   19 **Son** Aeneas, son of Venus, persecuted
by Juno.   20 **answerable** fitting.   22 **visitation** with the previous line,
the religious gravity hints at the Visitation of Our Lady, the Virgin
Mary.   29 **dissect** cut in pieces, and analyze.

In Battles feign'd; the better fortitude
Of Patience and Heroic Martyrdom
Unsung; or to describe Races and Games,
Or tilting Furniture,° emblazon'd Shields,
Impresses° quaint, Caparisons and Steeds;   35
Bases° and tinsel Trappings, gorgeous Knights
At Joust and Tournament; then marshall'd Feast
Serv'd up in Hall with Sewers,° and Seneshals;°
The skill of Artifice or Office mean,
Not that which justly gives Heroic name   40
To Person or to Poem. Mee of these
Nor skill'd nor studious, higher Argument
Remains, sufficient of itself to raise
That name, unless an age too late, or cold
Climate, or Years damp my intended° wing   45
Deprest,° and much they may, if all be mine,
Not Hers who brings it nightly to my Ear.

          The Sun was sunk, and after him the Star
Of Hesperus, whose Office is to bring
Twilight upon the Earth, short Arbiter   50
'Twixt Day and Night, and now from end to end
Night's Hemisphere had veil'd the Horizon round:
When Satan who late fled before the threats
Of Gabriel out of Eden, now improv'd°
In meditated fraud and malice, bent   55
On man's destruction, maugre° what might hap
Of heavier on himself, fearless return'd.
By Night he fled, and at Midnight return'd
From compassing the Earth, cautious of day,
Since Uriel Regent of the Sun descri'd   60
His entrance, and forewarn'd the Cherubim
That kept their watch; thence full of anguish driv'n,
The space of seven continu'd Nights he rode
With darkness, thrice the Equinoctial Line°

---

34 **tilting Furniture** equipment for jousting. 35 **Impresses** heraldic
devices. 36 **Bases** accouterments for horses. 38 **Sewers** stewards.
38 **Seneshals** ceremonial servants. 45 **intended** including the literal
"outstretched" (as in "extended"). 46 **Deprest** including the literal
"pressed down." 54 **improv'd** increased (in evil). 56 **maugre** de-
spite. 64 **Equinoctial Line** path of the sun.

65 He circl'd, four times cross'd the Car of Night
     From Pole to Pole, traversing each Colure;°
     On the eighth return'd, and on the Coast averse
     From entrance or Cherubic Watch, by stealth
     Found unsuspected way. There was a place,
70 Now not, though Sin, not Time, first wrought the
     change,
     Where Tigris at the foot of Paradise
     Into a Gulf shot under ground, till part
     Rose up a Fountain by the Tree of Life;
     In with the River sunk, and with it rose
75 Satan involv'd in rising Mist, then sought
     Where to lie hid; Sea he had searcht and Land
     From Eden over Pontus, and the Pool
     Mæotis, up beyond the River Ob;°
     Downward as far Antarctic; and in length
80 West from Orontes to the Ocean barr'd
     At Darien,° thence to the Land where flows
     Ganges and Indus: thus the Orb he roam'd
     With narrow search; and with inspection deep
     Consider'd every Creature, which of all
85 Most opportune might serve his Wiles, and found
     The Serpent subtlest Beast of all the Field.
     Him after long debate, irresolute
     Of thoughts revolv'd, his final sentence chose
     Fit Vessel, fittest Imp° of fraud, in whom
90 To enter, and his dark suggestions° hide
     From sharpest sight: for in the wily Snake,
     Whatever sleights none would suspicious mark,
     As from his wit and native subtlety
     Proceeding, which in other Beasts observ'd
95 Doubt might beget of Diabolic pow'r
     Active within beyond the sense of brute.
     Thus he resolv'd, but first from inward grief
     His bursting passion into plaints thus pour'd:
         "O Earth, how like to Heav'n, if not preferr'd
100 More justly, Seat worthier of Gods, as built

66 **Colure** circle from the poles.   78 **Ob** in Siberia.   81 **Darien**
Panama.   89 **Imp** offspring (of the devil).   90 **suggestions** tempta-
tions.

With second thoughts, reforming what was old!
For what God after better worse would build?
Terrestrial Heav'n, danc't round by other Heav'ns
That shine, yet bear their bright officious Lamps,
Light above Light, for thee alone, as seems,   105
In thee concentring all their precious beams
Of sacred influence: As God in Heav'n
Is Center, yet extends to all, so thou
Cent'ring receiv'st from all those Orbs; in thee,
Not in themselves, all their known virtue appears   110
Productive in Herb, Plant, and nobler birth
Of Creatures animate with gradual° life
Of Growth, Sense, Reason, all summ'd up in Man.
With what delight could I have walkt thee round
If I could joy in aught, sweet interchange   115
Of Hill and Valley, Rivers, Woods and Plains,
Now Land, now Sea, and Shores with Forest crown'd,
Rocks, Dens, and Caves; but I in none of these
Find place or refuge; and the more I see
Pleasures about me, so much more I feel   120
Torment within me, as from the hateful siege
Of contraries; all good to me becomes
Bane, and in Heav'n much worse would be my state.
But neither here seek I, no nor in Heav'n
To dwell, unless by mast'ring Heav'n's Supreme;   125
Nor hope to be myself less miserable
By what I seek, but others to make such
As I, though thereby worse to me redound:
For only in destroying I find ease
To my relentless thoughts; and him destroy'd,   130
Or won to what may work his utter loss,
For whom all this was made, all this will soon
Follow, as to him linkt in weal or woe,
In woe then; that destruction wide may range:
To mee shall be the glory sole among   135
The infernal Powers, in one day to have marr'd
What he *Almighty* styl'd, six Nights and Days
Continu'd making, and who knows how long

112 **gradual** in stages.

Before had been contriving, though perhaps
140 Not longer than since I in one Night freed
From servitude inglorious wellnigh half
Th'Angelic Name, and thinner left the throng
Of his adorers: hee to be aveng'd,
And to repair his numbers thus impair'd,
145 Whether such virtue spent of old now fail'd
More Angels to Create, if they at least
Are his Created or to spite us more,
Determin'd to advance into our room
A Creature form'd of Earth, and him endow,
150 Exalted from so base original,
With Heav'nly spoils, our spoils: What he decreed
He effected; Man he made, and for him built
Magnificent this World, and Earth his seat,
Him Lord pronounc'd, and, O indignity!
155 Subjected to his service Angel wings,
And flaming Ministers to watch and tend
Their earthy Charge: Of these the vigilance
I dread, and to elude, thus wrapt in mist
Of midnight vapour glide obscure, and pry
160 In every Bush and Brake, where hap may find
The Serpent sleeping, in whose mazy folds
To hide me, and the dark intent I bring.
O foul descent! that I who erst contended
With Gods to sit the highest, am now constrain'd
165 Into a Beast, and mixt with bestial slime,
This essence to incarnate° and imbrute,
That to the height of Deity aspir'd;
But what will not Ambition and Revenge
Descend to? who aspires must down as low
170 As high he soar'd, obnoxious° first or last
To basest things. Revenge, at first though sweet,
Bitter erelong back on itself recoils;
Let it; I reck not, so it 'light well aim'd,
Since higher I fall short, on him who next
175 Provokes my envy, this new Favorite
Of Heav'n, this Man of Clay, Son of despite,

166 **incarnate** the Satanic counterpart of the Incarnation.   170 **ob-
noxious** exposed.

Whom us the more to spite his Maker rais'd
From dust: spite then with spite is best repaid."
      So saying, through each Thicket Dank or Dry,
Like a black mist low creeping, he held on   *180*
His midnight search, where soonest he might find
The Serpent: him fast sleeping soon he found
In Labyrinth° of many a round self-roll'd,
His head the midst, well stor'd with subtle wiles:
Not yet in horrid Shade or dismal Den,   *185*
Nor° nocent° yet, but on the grassy Herb
Fearless unfear'd he slept: in at his Mouth
The Devil enter'd, and his brutal sense,
In heart or head, possessing soon inspir'd
With act intelligential; but his sleep   *190*
Disturb'd not, waiting close th'approach of Morn.
Now when as sacred Light began to dawn
In Eden on the humid Flow'rs, that breath'd
Their morning Incense, when all things that breathe,
From th'Earth's great Altar send up silent praise   *195*
To the Creator, and his Nostrils fill
With grateful° Smell, forth came the human pair
And join'd their vocal Worship to the Choir
Of Creatures wanting voice, that done, partake
The season, prime for sweetest Scents and Airs: *200*
Then cómmune how that day they best may ply
Their growing work: for much their work outgrew
The hands' dispatch of two Gard'ning so wide.
And Eve first to her Husband thus began.
      "Adam, well may we labour still to dress   *205*
This Garden, still to tend Plant, Herb and Flow'r,
Our pleasant task enjoin'd, but till more hands
Aid us, the work under our labour grows,
Luxurious by restraint; what we by day
Lop overgrown, or prune, or prop, or bind,   *210*
One night or two with wanton growth derides
Tending to wild. Thou therefore now advise

---

183 **Labyrinth** with a suggestion of the dangerous monster (the Minotaur). 186 **Nor** *1674;* Not *1667.* 186 **nocent** harmful (the opposite of "innocent"). 197 **grateful** pleasing, and expressing gratitude.

Or hear what to my mind first thoughts present,
Let us divide our labours, thou where choice
215 Leads thee, or where most needs, whether to wind
The Woodbine round this Arbour, or direct
The clasping Ivy where to climb, while I
In yonder Spring of Roses intermixt
With Myrtle, find what to redress till Noon:
220 For while so near each other thus all day
Our task we choose, what wonder if so near
Looks intervene and smiles, or object new
Casual discourse draw on, which intermits
Our day's work brought to little, though begun
225 Early, and th'hour of Supper comes unearn'd."
       To whom mild answer Adam thus return'd.
"Sole Eve, Associate sole, to me beyond
Compare above all living Creatures dear,
Well hast thou motion'd, well thy thoughts employ'd
230 How we might best fulfill the work which here
God hath assign'd us, nor of me shalt pass
Unprais'd: for nothing lovelier can be found
In woman, than to study household good,
And good works in her Husband to promote.
235 Yet not so strictly hath our Lord impos'd
Labour, as to debar us when we need
Refreshment, whether food, or talk between,
Food of the mind, or this sweet intercourse
Of looks and smiles, for smiles from Reason flow,
240 To brute deni'd, and are of Love the food,
Love not the lowest end of human life.
For not to irksome toil, but to delight
He made us, and delight to Reason join'd.
These paths and Bow'rs doubt not but our joint hands
245 Will keep from Wilderness with ease, as wide
As we need walk, till younger hands erelong
Assist us: But if much convérse perhaps
Thee satiate, to short absence I could yield.
For solitude sometimes is best society,
250 And short retirement urges sweet return.
But other doubt possesses me, lest harm
Befall thee sever'd from me; for thou know'st
What hath been warn'd us, what malicious Foe

Envying our happiness, and of his own
Despairing, seeks to work us woe and shame   255
By sly assault; and somewhere nigh at hand
Watches, no doubt, with greedy hope to find
His wish and best advantage, us asunder,
Hopeless to circumvent us join'd, where each
To other speedy aid might lend at need;   260
Whether his first design be to withdraw
Our fealty from God, or to disturb
Conjugal Love, than which perhaps no bliss
Enjoy'd by us excites his envy more;
Or this, or worse, leave not the faithful side   265
That gave thee being, still shades thee and protects.
The Wife, where danger or dishonour lurks,
Safest and seemliest by her Husband stays,
Who guards her, or with her the worst endures."
            To whom the Virgin Majesty of Eve,   270
As one who loves, and some unkindness meets,
With sweet austere composure thus repli'd.
        "Offspring of Heav'n and Earth, and all
            Earth's Lord,
That such an Enemy we have, who seeks
Our ruin, both by thee inform'd I learn,   275
And from the parting Angel overheard
As in a shady nook I stood behind,
Just then return'd at shut of Evening Flow'rs.
But that thou shouldst my firmness therefore doubt
To God or thee, because we have a foe   280
May tempt it, I expected not to hear.
His violence thou fear'st not, being such,
As wee, not capable of death or pain,
Can either not receive, or can repel.
His fraud is then thy fear, which plain infers   285
Thy equal fear that my firm Faith and Love
Can by his fraud be shak'n or seduc't;
Thoughts, which how found they harbour in thy
    breast,
Adam, misthought of her to thee so dear?"
            To whom with healing words Adam repli'd.   290
"Daughter of God and Man, immortal Eve,
For such thou art, from sin and blame entire:

Not ˈdiffident° of thee do I dissuade
Thy absence from my sight, but to avoid
295   Th'attempt itself, intended by our Foe.
For hee who tempts, though in vain, at least asperses
The tempted with dishonour foul, suppos'd
Not incorruptible of Faith, not proof
Against temptation: thou thyself with scorn
300   And anger wouldst resent the offer'd wrong,
Though ineffectual found: misdeem not then,
If such affront I labour to avert
From thee alone, which on us both at once
The Enemy, though bold, will hardly dare,
305   Or daring, first on mee th'assault shall 'light.
Nor thou his malice and false guile contemn;
Subtle he needs must be, who could seduce
Angels, nor think superfluous others' aid.
I from the influence of thy looks receive
310   Access° in every Virtue, in thy sight
More wise, more watchful, stronger, if need were
Of outward strength; while shame, thou looking on,
Shame to be overcome or over-reacht
Would utmost vigour raise, and rais'd unite.
315   Why shouldst not thou like sense within thee feel
When I am present, and thy trial choose
With me, best witness of thy Virtue tri'd."
          So spake domestic Adam in his care
And Matrimonial Love, but Eve, who thought
320   Less áttribúted to her Faith sincere,
Thus her reply with accent sweet renew'd.
          "If this be our condition, thus to dwell
In narrow circuit strait'n'd by a Foe,
Subtle or violent, we not endu'd
325   Single with like defence, wherever met,
How are we happy, still° in fear of harm?
But harm precedes not sin: only our Foe
Tempting affronts us with his foul esteem
Of our integrity: his foul esteem
330   Sticks no dishonour on our Front, but turns

---

293 **diffident** distrustful.   310 **Access** accession.   326 **still** always.

Foul on himself; then wherefore shunn'd or fear'd
By us? who rather double honour gain
From his surmise prov'd false, find peace within,
Favour from Heav'n, our witness from th'event.°
And what is Faith, Love, Virtue unassay'd   335
Alone, without exterior help sustain'd?
Let us not then suspect our happy State
Left so imperfect by the Maker wise,
As not secure to single or combin'd.
Frail is our happiness, if this be so,   340
And Eden were no Eden thus expos'd."
          To whom thus Adam fervently repli'd.
"O Woman, best are all things as the will
Of God ordain'd them, his creating hand
Nothing imperfect or deficient left   345
Of all that he Created, much less Man,
Or aught that might his happy State secure,
Secure from outward force; within himself
The danger lies, yet lies within his power:
Against his will he can receive no harm.   350
But God left free the Will, for what obeys
Reason, is free, and Reason he made right,
But bid her well beware, and still erect,°
Lest by some fair appearing good surpris'd
She dictate false, and misinform the Will   355
To do what God expressly hath forbid.
Not then mistrust, but tender love enjoins,
That I should mind° thee oft, and mind thou me.
Firm we subsist, yet possible to swerve,
Since Reason not impossibly may meet   360
Some specious object by the Foe suborn'd,
And fall into deception unaware,
Not keeping strictest watch, as she was warn'd.
Seek not temptation then; which to avoid
Were better, and most likely if from mee   365
Thou sever not: Trial will come unsought.
Wouldst thou approve thy constancy, approve
First thy obedience; th'other who can know,

<hr>

334 **event** outcome.   353 **still erect** always alert (and with "God-like
erect" contrasted with the Fall).   358 **mind** remind.

Not seeing thee attempted, who attest?
370 But if thou think, trial unsought may find
Us both securer° than thus warn'd thou seem'st,
Go; for thy stay, not free, absents thee more;
Go in thy native innocence, rely
On what thou hast of virtue, summon all,
375 For God towards thee hath done his part, do thine."
        So spake the Patriarch of Mankind, but Eve
Persisted, yet submiss, though last, repli'd.
        "With thy permission then, and thus fore-
            warn'd
Chiefly by what thy own last reasoning words
380 Touch'd only, that our trial, when least sought,
May find us both perhaps far less prepar'd,
The willinger I go, nor much expect
A Foe so proud will first the weaker seek;
So bent, the more shall shame him his repulse."
385 Thus saying, from her Husband's hand her hand
Soft she withdrew, and like a Wood-Nymph light
Oread or Dryad,° or of Delia's° Train,
Betook her to the Groves, but Delia's self
In gait surpass'd and Goddess-like deport,
390 Though not as shee with Bow and Quiver arm'd,
But with such Gard'ning Tools as Art yet rude,
Guiltless of° fire had form'd, or Angels brought.
To Pales,° or Pomona,° thus adorn'd,
Likest she seem'd, Pomona when she fled
395 Vertumnus,° or to Ceres° in her Prime,
Yet Virgin of Proserpina from Jove.
Her long with ardent look his Eye pursu'd
Delighted, but desiring more her stay.
Oft he to her his charge of quick return
400 Repeated, shee to him as oft engag'd
To be return'd by Noon amid the Bow'r,

371 **securer** too confident.   387 **Oread or Dryad** wood- or mountain-
nymph.   387 **Delia** Diana, goddess of hunting.   392 **Guiltless of**
without experience of (but fire is associated with guilt in the story of
Prometheus—see IV 715–19 —and "Guiltless" is prophetic here).
393 **Pales** goddess of pastures.   **Pomona** goddess of fruit.   395 **Ver-
tumnus** god of the seasons and of gardens.   395 **Ceres** goddess of
agriculture; see IV 268–72.

And all things in best order to invite
Noontide repast, or Afternoon's repose.
O much deceiv'd, much failing, hapless Eve,
Of thy presum'd return! event perverse!   405
Thou never from that hour in Paradise
Found'st either sweet repast, or sound repose;
Such ambush hid among sweet Flow'rs and Shades
Waited with hellish rancour imminent
To intercept thy way, or send thee back   410
Despoil'd of Innocence, of Faith, of Bliss.
For now, and since first break of dawn the Fiend,
Mere Serpent in appearance, forth was come,
And on his Quest, where likeliest he might find
The only two of Mankind, but in them   415
The whole included Race, his purpos'd prey.
In Bow'r and Field he sought, where any tuft
Of Grove or Garden-Plot more pleasant lay,
Their tendance or Plantation for delight,
By Fountain or by shady Rivulet   420
He sought them both, but wish'd his hap might find
Eve separate, he wish'd, but not with hope
Of what so seldom chanc'd, when to his wish,
Beyond his hope, Eve separate he spies,
Veil'd in a Cloud of Fragrance, where she stood,   425
Half spi'd, so thick the Roses bushing round
About her glow'd, oft stooping to support
Each Flow'r of slender stalk, whose head though gay
Carnation, Purple, Azure, or speckt with Gold,
Hung drooping unsustain'd, them she upstays   430
Gently with Myrtle band, mindless the while,
Herself, though fairest unsupported Flow'r,
From her best prop so far, and storm so nigh.
Nearer he drew, and many a walk travers'd
Of stateliest Covert, Cedar, Pine, or Palm,   435
Then voluble° and bold, now hid, now seen
Among thick-wov'n Arborets° and Flow'rs
Imborder'd on each Bank, the hand of Eve:

436 **voluble** rolling; the suggestion of fluent speech darkly antici-
pates Satan's skill—contrast the pronunciation (and Milton's spelling
"volubil") in IV 594.   437 **Arborets** shrubs.

Spot more delicious than those Gardens feign'd
440 Or of reviv'd Adonis,° or renown'd
Alcinous, host of old Laertes' Son,°
Or that, not Mystic,° where the Sapient King°
Held dalliance with his fair Egyptian Spouse.°
Much hee the Place admir'd, the Person more.
445 As one who long in populous City pent,
Where Houses thick and Sewers annoy° the Air,
Forth issuing on a Summer's Morn to breathe
Among the pleasant Villages and Farms
Adjoin'd, from each thing met conceives delight,
450 The smell of Grain, or tedded° Grass, or Kine,
Or Dairy, each rural sight, each rural sound;
If chance with Nymphlike step fair Virgin pass,
What pleasing seem'd, for her now pleases more,
She most, and in her look sums all Delight.
455 Such Pleasure took the Serpent to behold
This Flow'ry Plat, the sweet recess of Eve
Thus early, thus alone; her Heav'nly form
Angelic, but more soft, and Feminine,
Her graceful Innocence, her every Air
460 Of gesture or least action overaw'd
His Malice, and with rapine sweet bereav'd
His fierceness of the fierce intent it brought:
That space the Evil one abstracted stood
From his own evil, and for the time remain'd
465 Stupidly° good, of enmity disarm'd,
Of guile, of hate, of envy, of revenge;
But the hot Hell that always in him burns,
Though in mid Heav'n, soon ended his delight,
And tortures him now more, the more he sees
470 Of pleasure not for him ordain'd: then soon
Fierce hate he recollects,° and all his thoughts
Of mischief, gratulating, thus excites.
            "Thoughts, whither have ye led me, with what
                sweet
Compulsion thus transported to forget

440 **Adonis** in the myth, restored to life for half of each year.   441
Laertes' Son Odysseus.   442 **Mystic** allegorical; possibly also mythi-
cal.   442 **Sapient King** Solomon.   443 **Egyptian Spouse** Pharaoh's
daughter.   446 **annoy** make noisome.   450 **tedded** spread out to
dry.   465 **Stupidly** in a stupor.   471 **recollects** remembers and
recollects.

What hither brought us, hate, not love, nor hope   *475*
Of Paradise for Hell, hope here to taste
Of pleasure, but all pleasure to destroy,
Save what is in destroying, other joy
To me is lost. Then let me not let pass
Occasion which now smiles, behold alone   *480*
The Woman, opportune to all attempts,
Her Husband, for I view far round, not nigh,
Whose higher intellectual more I shun,
And strength, of courage haughty, and of limb
Heroic built, though of terrestrial mould,   *485*
Foe not informidable, exempt from wound,
I not; so much hath Hell debas'd, and pain
Enfeebl'd me, to what I was in Heav'n.
Shee fair, divinely fair, fit Love for Gods,
Not terrible, though terror be in Love   *490*
And beauty, not approach't by stronger hate,
Hate stronger, under show of Love well-feign'd,
The way which to her ruin now I tend."
          So spake the Enemy of Mankind, enclos'd
In Serpent, Inmate bad, and toward Eve   *495*
Address'd his way, not with indented wave,
Prone on the ground, as since, but on his rear,
Circular base of rising folds, that tow'r'd
Fold above fold a surging Maze, his Head
Crested aloft, and Carbuncle° his Eyes;   *500*
With burnisht Neck of verdant Gold, erect
Amidst his circling Spires,° that on the grass
Floated redundant:° pleasing was his shape,
And lovely, never since of Serpent kind
Lovelier, not those that in Illyria chang'd   *505*
Hermione and Cadmus, or the God
In Epidaurus; nor to which transform'd
Ammonian Jove, or Capitoline was seen,
Hee with Olympias, this with her who bore
Scipio the height of Rome.° With tract oblique   *510*

500 **Carbuncle** a fiery jewel. 502 **Spires** spirals. 503 **redundant** wave-like. 505–10 Cadmus and Harmonia were changed to serpents; Aesculapius, god of medicine, came from his temple at Epidaurus in the form of a serpent; the same form was taken by Jupiter Ammon, who was the father of Alexander the Great (the mother being Olympias), and by Jupiter Capitoline, father of Scipio who defeated Hannibal.

At first, as one who sought accéss, but fear'd
To interrupt, side-long he works his way.
As when a Ship by skilful Steersman wrought
Nigh River's mouth or Foreland, where the Wind
515 Veers oft, as oft so steers, and shifts her Sail;
So varied hee, and of his tortuous Train
Curl'd many a wanton wreath in sight of Eve,
To lure her Eye; shee busied heard the sound
Of rustling Leaves, but minded not, as us'd
520 To such disport before her through the Field,
From every Beast, more duteous at her call,
Then at Circean° call the Herd disguis'd.
Hee bolder now, uncall'd before her stood;
But as in gaze admiring: Oft he bow'd
525 His turret Crest, and sleek enamell'd Neck,
Fawning, and lick'd the ground whereon she trod.
His gentle dumb expression turn'd at length
The Eye of Eve to mark his play; he glad
Of her attention gain'd, with Serpent Tongue
530 Organic,° or impulse of vocal Air,
His fraudulent temptation thus began.
         "Wonder not, sovran Mistress, if perhaps
Thou canst, who art sole Wonder, much less arm
Thy looks, the Heav'n of mildness, with disdain,
535 Displeas'd that I approach thee thus, and gaze
Insatiate, I thus single, nor have fear'd
Thy awful brow, more awful thus retir'd.
Fairest resemblance of thy Maker fair,
Thee all things living gaze on, all things thine
540 By gift, and thy Celestial Beauty adore
With ravishment beheld, there best beheld
Where universally admir'd; but here
In this enclosure wild, these Beasts among,
Beholders rude, and shallow to discern
545 Half what in thee is fair, one man except,
Who sees thee? (and what is one?) who shouldst be
     seen
A Goddess among Gods, ador'd and serv'd
By Angels numberless, thy daily Train."

522 **Circean** Circe, the sorceress in the *Odyssey* who turned men to
beasts.   530 **Organic** as its organ.

So gloz'd° the Tempter, and his Proem° tun'd;
Into the Heart of Eve his words made way,   550
Though at the voice much marvelling; at length
Not unamaz'd she thus in answer spake.
"What may this mean? Language of Man pronounc't
By Tongue of Brute, and human sense exprest?
The first at least of these I thought deni'd   555
To Beasts, whom God on their Creation-Day
Created mute to all articulate sound;
The latter I demur,° for in their looks
Much reason, and in their actions oft appears.
Thee, Serpent, subtlest beast of all the field   560
I knew, but not with human voice endu'd;
Redouble then this miracle, and say,
How cam'st thou speakable of mute, and how
To me so friendly grown above the rest
Of brutal kind, that daily are in sight?   565
Say, for such wonder claims attention due."
        To whom the guileful Tempter thus repli'd.
"Empress of this fair World, resplendent Eve,
Easy to mee it is to tell thee all
What thou command'st, and right thou shouldst be
    obey'd: 570
I was at first as other Beasts that graze
The trodden Herb, of abject thoughts and low,
As was my food, nor aught but food discern'd
Or Sex, and apprehended nothing high:
Till on a day roving the field, I chanc'd   575
A goodly Tree far distant to behold
Loaden with fruit of fairest colours mixt,
Ruddy and Gold: I nearer drew to gaze;
When from the boughs a savoury odour blown,
Grateful to appetite, more pleas'd my sense   580
Than smell of sweetest Fennel, or the Teats
Of Ewe or Goat dropping with Milk at Ev'n,
Unsuckt of Lamb or Kid, that tend their play.
To satisfy the sharp desire I had
Of tasting those fair Apples, I resolv'd   585
Not to defer; hunger and thirst at once,
Powerful persuaders, quick'n'd at the scent

549 **gloz'd** flattered.   549 **Proem** prelude.   558 **demur** hesitate about.

Of that alluring fruit, urg'd me so keen.
About the Mossy Trunk I wound me soon,
590 For high from ground the branches would require
Thy utmost reach or Adam's: Round the Tree
All other Beasts that saw, with like desire
Longing and envying stood, but could not reach.
Amid the Tree now got, where plenty hung
595 Tempting so nigh, to pluck and eat my fill
I spar'd not, for such pleasure till that hour
At Feed or Fountain never had I found.
Sated at length, erelong I might perceive
Strange alteration in me, to degree
600 Of Reason in my inward Powers, and Speech
Wanted° not long, though to this shape retain'd.
Thenceforth to Speculations high or deep
I turn'd my thoughts, and with capacious mind
Consider'd all things visible in Heav'n,
605 Or Earth, or Middle,° all things fair and good;
But all that fair and good in thy Divine
Semblance, and in thy Beauty's heav'nly Ray
United I beheld; no Fair to thine
Equivalent or second, which compell'd
610 Mee thus, though importúne perhaps, to come
And gaze, and worship thee of right declar'd
Sovran of Creatures, universal Dame."°
          So talk'd the spirited° sly Snake; and Eve
Yet more amaz'd unwary thus repli'd.
615   "Serpent, thy overpraising leaves in doubt
The virtue of that Fruit, in thee first prov'd:
But say, where grows the Tree, from hence how far?
For many are the Trees of God that grow
In Paradise, and various, yet unknown
620 To us, in such abundance lies our choice,
As leaves a greater store of Fruit untoucht,
Still hanging incorruptible, till men
Grow up to their provision,° and more hands
Help to disburden Nature of her Bearth."°
625   To whom the wily Adder, blithe and glad.

---

601 **Wanted** lacked.   605 **Middle** air.   612 **universal Dame** mistress
of the universe.   613 **spirited** including "possessed by a spirit."   623
their provision what they provide.   624 **her Bearth** what she bears.

"Empress. the way is ready, and not long,
Beyond a row of Myrtles, on a Flat,
Fast by a Fountain, one small Thicket past
Of blowing° Myrrh and Balm; if thou accept
My conduct, I can bring thee thither soon."   630
          "Lead then," said Eve. Hee leading swiftly
     roll'd
In tangles, and made intricate seem straight,
To mischief swift. Hope elevates, and joy
Bright'ns his Crest, as when a wand'ring Fire
Compáct° of unctuous vapour, which the Night   635
Condenses, and the cold environs round,
Kindl'd through agitation to a Flame,
Which oft, they say, some evil Spirit attends,
Hovering and blazing with delusive Light,
Misleads th'amaz'd Night-wanderer from his way   640
To Bogs and Mires, and oft through Pond or Pool,
There swallow'd up and lost, from succour far.
So glister'd the dire Snake, and into fraud
Led Eve our credulous° Mother, to the Tree
Of prohibition, root of all our woe;   645
Which when she saw, thus to her guide she spake.
          "Serpent, we might have spar'd our coming
                hither,
Fruitless to me, though Fruit be here to excess,
The credit of whose virtue rest with thee,
Wondrous indeed, if cause of such effects.   650
But of this Tree we may not taste nor touch;
God so commanded, and left that Command
Sole Daughter of his voice; the rest, we live
Law to ourselves, our Reason is our Law."
          To whom the Tempter guilefully repli'd.   655
"Indeed? hath God then said that of the Fruit
Of all these Garden Trees ye shall not eat,
Yet Lords declar'd of all in Earth or Air?"
          To whom thus Eve yet sinless. "Of the Fruit
Of each Tree in the Garden we may eat,   660
But of the Fruit of this fair Tree amidst

629 **blowing** blossoming.   635 **Compáct** compacted; like "unctuous"
(oily), a scientific term for vapors.   644 **credulous** over-ready to be-
lieve (sadly contrasted with the original sense of the word, "faithful,"
as in "a credulous and plain heart is accepted with God," [1605]).

The Garden, God hath said, Ye shall not eat
Thereof, nor shall ye touch it, lest ye die."
      She scarce had said, though brief, when now
      more bold

665 The Tempter, but with show of Zeal and Love
To Man, and indignation at his wrong,
New part puts on, and as to passion mov'd,
Fluctuates° disturb'd, yet comely, and in act
Rais'd, as of some great matter to begin.

670 As when of old some Orator renown'd
In Athens or free Rome, where Eloquence
Flourish'd, since mute, to some great cause addrest,
Stood in himself collected, while each part,
Motion, each act won audience ere the tongue,

675 Sometimes in heighth began, as no delay
Of Preface brooking through his Zeal of Right.
So standing, moving, or to heighth upgrown
The Tempter all impassion'd thus began.
      "O Sacred, Wise, and Wisdom-giving Plant,

680 Mother of Science,° Now I feel thy Power
Within me clear, not only to discern
Things in their Causes, but to trace the ways
Of highest Agents, deem'd however wise.
Queen of this Universe, do not believe

685 Those rigid threats of Death; ye shall not Die:
How should ye? by the Fruit? it gives you Life
To Knowledge: By the Threat'ner? look on mee,
Mee who have touch'd and tasted, yet both live,
And life more perfect have attain'd than Fate

690 Meant mee, by vent'ring higher than my Lot.
Shall that be shut to Man, which to the Beast
Is open? or will God incense his ire
For such a petty Trespass, and not praise
Rather your dauntless virtue, whom the pain

695 Of Death denounc't,° whatever thing Death be,
Deterr'd not from achieving what might lead
To happier life, knowledge of Good and Evil;
Of good, how just? of evil, if what is evil
Be real, why not known, since easier shunn'd?

700 God therefore cannot hurt ye, and be just;

668 **Fluctuates** moves like a wave.   680 **Science** knowledge.   695
denounc't threatened.

Not just, not God; not fear'd then, nor obey'd:
Your fear itself of Death removes the fear.
Why then was this forbid? Why but to awe,
Why but to keep ye low and ignorant,
His worshippers; he knows that in the day   705
Ye Eat thereof, your Eyes that seem so clear,
Yet are but dim, shall perfectly be then
Op'n'd and clear'd, and ye shall be as Gods,
Knowing both Good and Evil as they know.
That ye should be as Gods, since I as Man,   710
Internal Man, is but proportion meet,
I of brute human, yee of human Gods.
So ye shall die perhaps, by putting off
Human, to put on Gods, death to be wisht,
Though threat'n'd, which no worse than this can bring.   715
And what are Gods that Man may not become
As they, participating God-like food?
The Gods are first, and that advantage use
On our belief, that all from them proceeds;
I question it, for this fair Earth I see,   720
Warm'd by the Sun, producing every kind,
Them nothing: If they all things, who enclos'd
Knowledge of Good and Evil in this Tree,
That whoso eats thereof, forthwith attains
Wisdom without their leave? and wherein lies   725
Th'offence, that Man should thus attain to know?
What can your knowledge hurt him, or this Tree
Impart against his will if all be his?
Or is it envy, and can envy dwell
In heav'nly breasts? these, these and many more   730
Causes import your need of this fair Fruit.
Goddess humane,° reach then, and freely taste."
          He ended, and his words replete with guile
Into her heart too easy entrance won:
Fixt on the Fruit she gaz'd, which to behold   735
Might tempt alone, and in her ears the sound
Yet rung of his persuasive words, impregn'd
With Reason, to her seeming, and with Truth;
Meanwhile the hour of Noon drew on, and wak'd
An eager appetite, rais'd by the smell   740
So savoury of that Fruit, which with desire,

732 **humane** benevolent, with a hint of line 712.

Inclinable now grown to touch or taste,
Solicited her longing eye; yet first
Pausing awhile, thus to herself she mus'd.
     "Great are thy Virtues, doubtless, best of
745   Fruits,
Though kept from Man, and worthy to be admir'd,
Whose taste, too long forborne, at first assay
Gave elocution to the mute, and taught
The Tongue not made for Speech to speak thy praise:
750 Thy praise hee also who forbids thy use,
Conceals not from us, naming thee the Tree
Of Knowledge, knowledge both of good and evil;
Forbids us then to taste, but his forbidding
Commends thee more, while it infers the good
755 By thee communicated, and our want:
For good unknown, sure is not had, or had
And yet unknown, is as not had at all.
In plain then, what forbids he but to know,
Forbids us good, forbids us to be wise?
760 Such prohibitions bind not. But if Death
Bind us with after-bands, what profits then
Our inward freedom? In the day we eat
Of this fair Fruit, our doom is, we shall die.
How dies the Serpent? hee hath eat'n and lives,
765 And knows, and speaks, and reasons, and discerns,
Irrational till then. For us alone
Was death invented? or to us deni'd
This intellectual food, for beasts reserv'd?
For Beasts it seems: yet that one Beast which first
770 Hath tasted, envies not, but brings with joy
The good befall'n him, Author unsuspect,°
Friendly to man, far from deceit or guile.
What fear I then, rather what know to fear
Under this ignorance of Good and Evil,
775 Of God or Death, of Law or Penalty?
Here grows the Cure° of all, this Fruit Divine,
Fair to the Eye, inviting to the Taste,
Of virtue to make wise: what hinders then
To reach, and feed at once both Body and Mind?"

---

771 **Author unsuspect** an authority not to be suspected.   776 **Cure**
with a grim hint of the earlier sense, "care, trouble," Latin *cura.*

      So saying, her rash hand in evil hour   *780*
Forth reaching to the Fruit, she pluck'd, she ate:
Earth felt the wound, and Nature from her seat
Sighing through all her Works gave signs of woe,
That all was lost. Back to the Thicket slunk
The guilty Serpent, and well might, for Eve   *785*
Intent now wholly on her taste, naught else
Regarded, such delight till then, as seem'd,
In Fruit she never tasted, whether true
Or fancied so, through expectation high
Of knowledge, nor was Godhead from her thought.   *790*
Greedily she ingorg'd without restraint,
And knew not eating Death: Satiate at length,
And height'n'd as with Wine, jocund and boon,
Thus to herself she pleasingly began.

      "O Sovran, virtuous, precious of all Trees   *795*
In Paradise, of operation blest
To Sapience,° hitherto obscur'd, infam'd,°
And thy fair Fruit let hang, as to no end
Created; but henceforth my early care,
Not without Song, each Morning, and due praise   *800*
Shall tend thee, and the fertile burden ease
Of thy full branches offer'd free to all;
Till dieted by thee I grow mature
In knowledge, as the Gods who all things know;
Though others envy what they cannot give;   *805*
For had the gift been theirs, it had not here
Thus grown. Experience, next to thee I owe,
Best guide; not following thee, I had remain'd
In ignorance, thou op'n'st Wisdom's way,
And giv'st accéss, though secret she retire.   *810*
And I perhaps am secret; Heav'n is high,
High and remote to see from thence distinct
Each thing on Earth; and other care perhaps
May have diverted from continual watch
Our great Forbidder, safe with all his Spies   *815*
About him. But to Adam in what sort
Shall I appear? shall I to him make known
As yet my change, and give him to partake
Full happiness with mee, or rather not,

797 **Sapience** an important word in the poem, because it combines
"knowledge" and "tasting"; see lines 1017–20. 797 **infam'd** slandered.

820 But keep the odds of Knowledge in my power
     Without Copartner? so to add what wants°
     In Female Sex, the more to draw his Love,
     And render me more equal, and perhaps,
     A thing not undesirable, sometime
825 Superior; for inferior who is free?
     This may be well: but what if God have seen,
     And Death ensue? then I shall be no more,
     And Adam wedded to another Eve,
     Shall live with her enjoying, I extinct;
830 A death to think. Confirm'd then I resolve,
     Adam shall share with me in bliss or woe:
     So dear I love him, that with him all deaths
     I could endure, without him live no life."
             So saying, from the Tree her step she turn'd,
835 But first low Reverence done, as to the power
     That dwelt within, whose presence had infus'd
     Into the plant sciential° sap, deriv'd
     From Nectar, drink of Gods. Adam the while
     Waiting desirous her return, had wove
840 Of choicest Flow'rs a Garland to adorn
     Her Tresses, and her rural labours crown
     As Reapers oft are wont their Harvest Queen.
     Great joy he promis'd to his thoughts, and new
     Solace in her return, so long delay'd;
845 Yet oft his heart, divine of° something ill,
     Misgave him; hee the falt'ring measure° felt;
     And forth to meet her went, the way she took
     That Morn when first they parted; by the Tree
     Of Knowledge he must pass, there he her met,
850 Scarce from the Tree returning; in her hand
     A bough of fairest fruit that downy smil'd,
     New-gather'd, and ambrosial smell diffus'd.
     To him she hasted, in her face excuse
     Came Prologue, and Apology to prompt,
855 Which with bland words at will she thus addrest.
             "Hast thou not wonder'd, Adam, at my stay?
     Thee I have misst, and thought it long, depriv'd

821 **wants** is lacking.   837 **sciential** granting knowledge.   845 **divine of** divining (but "divine" is a pregnant word in the context).   846 **falt'ring measure** his heartbeat (with the hint that Eve's "measure," temperance—as at VII 128—has faltered).

Thy presence, agony of love till now
Not felt, nor shall be twice, for never more
Mean I to try, what rash untri'd I sought,   *860*
The pain of absence from thy sight. But strange
Hath been the cause, and wonderful to hear:
This Tree is not as we are told, a Tree
Of danger tasted, nor to evil unknown
Op'ning the way, but of Divine effect   *865*
To open Eyes, and make them Gods who taste;
And hath been tasted such: the Serpent wise,
Or not restrain'd as wee, or not obeying,
Hath eat'n of the fruit, and is become,
Not dead, as we are threat'n'd, but thenceforth   *870*
Endu'd with human voice and human sense,
Reasoning to admiration, and with mee
Persuasively hath so prevail'd, that I
Have also tasted, and have also found
Th'effects to correspond, opener mine Eyes,   *875*
Dim erst,° dilated Spirits, ampler Heart,
And growing up to Godhead; which for thee
Chiefly I sought, without thee can despise.
For bliss, as thou hast part, to me is bliss,
Tedious, unshar'd with thee, and odious soon.   *880*
Thou therefore also taste, that equal Lot
May join us, equal Joy, as equal Love;
Lest thou not tasting, different degree
Disjoin us, and I then too late renounce
Deity for thee, when Fate will not permit."   *885*
        Thus Eve with Count'nance blithe her story
                told;
But in her Cheek distemper° flushing glow'd.
On th'other side, Adam, soon as he heard
The fatal Trespass done by Eve, amaz'd,
Astonied° stood and Blank, while horror chill   *890*
Ran through his veins, and all his joints relax'd;
From his slack hand the Garland wreath'd for Eve
Down dropp'd, and all the faded Roses shed:
Speechless he stood and pale, till thus at length
First to himself he inward silence broke.   *895*

876 **erst** formerly.   887 **distemper** disorder, disease; also the 17th-
century sense, "intoxication"—see lines 793, 1008, 1050.   890 **Astonied** paralyzed.

"O fairest of Creation, last and best
Of all God's Works, Creature in whom excell'd
Whatever can to sight or thought be form'd,
Holy, divine, good, amiable, or sweet!
900 How art thou lost, how on a sudden lost,
Defac't, deflow'r'd, and now to Death devote?°
Rather how hast thou yielded to transgress
The strict forbiddance, how to violate
The sacred Fruit forbidd'n! some cursed fraud
905 Of enemy hath beguil'd thee, yet unknown,
And mee with thee hath ruin'd, for with thee
Certain my resolution is to Die;
How can I live without thee, how forgo
Thy sweet Converse and Love so dearly join'd,
910 To live again in these wild Woods forlorn?
Should God create another Eve, and I
Another Rib afford, yet loss of thee
Would never from my heart; no no, I feel
The Link of Nature draw me: Flesh of Flesh,
915 Bone of my Bone thou art, and from thy State
Mine never shall be parted, bliss or woe."
        So having said, as one from sad dismay
Recomforted, and after thoughts disturb'd
Submitting to what seem'd remédiless,
920 Thus in calm mood his Words to Eve he turn'd.
        "Bold deed thou hast presum'd, advent'rous
            Eve,
And peril great provok't, who thus hath dar'd
Had it been only coveting to Eye
That sacred Fruit, sacred to abstinence,
925 Much more to taste it under ban to touch.
But past who can recall, or done undo?
Not God Omnipotent, nor Fate, yet so
Perhaps thou shalt not Die, perhaps the Fact°
Is not so heinous now, foretasted Fruit,
930 Profan'd first by the Serpent, by him first
Made common and unhallow'd ere our taste;
Nor yet on him found deadly, he yet lives,
Lives, as thou said'st, and gains to live as Man
Higher degree of Life, inducement strong
935 To us, as likely tasting to attain

901 **devote** doomed.   928 **Fact** deed.

Proportional ascent, which cannot be
But to be Gods, or Angels Demi-gods.
Nor can I think that God, Creator wise,
Though threat'ning, will in earnest so destroy
Us his prime Creatures, dignifi'd so high,   940
Set over all his Works, which in our Fall,
For us created, needs with us must fail,
Dependent made; so God shall uncreate,
Be frustrate, do, undo, and labour lose,
Not well conceiv'd of God, who though his Power   945
Creation could repeat, yet would be loath
Us to abolish, lest the Adversary
Triumph and say; 'Fickle their State whom God
Most Favours, who can please him long? Mee first
He ruin'd, now Mankind; whom will he next?'   950
Matter of scorn, not to be given the Foe.
However I with thee have fixt my Lot,
Certain to undergo like doom, if Death
Consort with thee, Death is to mee as Life;
So forcible within my heart I feel   955
The Bond of Nature draw me to my own,
My own in thee, for what thou art is mine;
Our State cannot be sever'd, we are one,
One Flesh; to lose thee were to lose myself."
        So Adam, and thus Eve to him repli'd.   960
"O glorious trial of exceeding Love,
Illustrious evidence, example high!
Engaging me to emulate, but short
Of thy perfection, how shall I attain,
Adam, from whose dear side I boast me sprung,   965
And gladly of our Union hear thee speak,
One Heart, one Soul in both; whereof good proof
This day affords, declaring thee resolv'd,
Rather than Death or aught than Death more dread
Shall separate us, linkt in Love so dear,   970
To undergo with mee one Guilt, one Crime,
If any be, of tasting this fair Fruit,
Whose virtue, for of good still good proceeds,
Direct, or by occasion hath presented
This happy trial of thy Love, which else   975
So eminently never had been known.
Were it I thought Death menac't would ensue

This my attempt, I would sustain alone
The worst, and not persuade thee, rather die
980 Deserted, than oblige° thee with a fact°
Pernicious to thy Peace, chiefly assur'd
Remarkably so late of thy so true,
So faithful Love unequall'd; but I feel
Far otherwise th'event,° not Death, but Life
985 Augmented, op'n'd Eyes, new Hopes, new Joys,
Taste so Divine, that what of sweet before
Hath toucht my sense, flat seems to this, and harsh.
On my experience, Adam, freely taste,
And fear of Death deliver to the Winds."
990   So saying, she embrac'd him, and for joy
Tenderly wept, much won that he his Love
Had so ennobl'd, as of choice to incur
Divine displeasure for her sake, or Death.
In recompense (for such compliance bad
995 Such recompense best merits) from the bough
She gave him of that fair enticing Fruit
With liberal hand: he scrupl'd not to eat
Against his better knowledge, not deceiv'd,
But fondly overcome with Female charm.
1000 Earth trembl'd from her entrails, as again
In pangs, and Nature gave a second groan,
Sky lour'd and muttering Thunder, some sad drops
Wept at completing of the mortal Sin
Original; while Adam took no thought,
1005 Eating his fill, nor Eve to iterate
Her former trespass fear'd, the more to soothe
Him with her lov'd society, that now
As with new Wine intoxicated both
They swim in mirth, and fancy that they feel
1010 Divinity within them breeding wings
Wherewith to scorn the Earth: but that false Fruit
Far other operation first display'd,
Carnal desire inflaming, hee on Eve
Began to cast lascivious Eyes, she him
1015 As wantonly repaid; in Lust they burn:
Till Adam thus 'gan Eve to dalliance move.
       "Eve, now I see thou art exact of taste,

980 **oblige** make liable to penalty. 980 **fact** deed. 984 **event** outcome.

And elegant, of Sapience no small part,
Since to each meaning° savour we apply,
And Palate call judicious; I the praise   1020
Yield thee, so well this day thou hast purvey'd.°
Much pleasure we have lost, while we abstain'd
From this delightful Fruit, nor known till now
True relish,° tasting; if such pleasure be
In things to us forbidden, it might be wish'd,   1025
For this one Tree had been forbidden ten.
But come, so well refresh't, now let us play,
As meet is, after such delicious Fare;
For never did thy Beauty since the day
I saw thee first and wedded thee, adorn'd   1030
With all perfections, so inflame my sense
With ardor to enjoy thee, fairer now
Than ever, bounty of this virtuous Tree."
          So said he, and forbore not glance or toy°
Of amorous intent, well understood   1035
Of Eve, whose Eye darted contagious Fire.
Her hand he seiz'd, and to a shady bank,
Thick overhead with verdant roof embow'r'd
He led her nothing loath; Flow'rs were the Couch,
Pansies, and Violets, and Asphodel,   1040
And Hyacinth, Earth's freshest softest lap.
There they their fill of Love and Love's disport
Took largely, of their mutual guilt the Seal,°
The solace of their sin, till dewy sleep
Oppress'd them, wearied with their amorous play.   1045
Soon as the force of that fallacious Fruit,
That with exhilarating vapour bland
About their spirits had play'd, and inmost powers
Made err, was now exhal'd, and grosser sleep
Bred of unkindly° fumes, with conscious° dreams   1050
Encumber'd, now had left them, up they rose
As from unrest, and each the other viewing,
Soon found their Eyes how op'n'd, and their minds

1019 **each meaning** "tasting" and "knowledge."   1021 **purvey'd** pro-
vided foodstuffs.   1024 **relish** as with "Sapience," punning on the
etymology, here connected with "release" (no real relish till we re-
leased ourselves from the forbidding).   1034 **toy** caress.   1043 **Seal**
in contrast to true lovemaking, which seals and consummates the
marriage.   1050 **unkindly** unnatural.   1050 **conscious** having guilty
knowledge.

How dark'n'd; innocence, that as a veil
1055 Had shadow'd them from knowing ill, was gone,
Just confidence, and native righteousness,
And honour from about them, naked left
To guilty shame; hee cover'd, but his Robe
Uncover'd more. So rose the Danite strong
1060 Herculean Samson from the Harlot-lap
Of Phílistéan Dálilah, and wak'd
Shorn of his strength, They destitute and bare
Of all their virtue: silent, and in face
Confounded long they sat, as struck'n mute,
1065 Till Adam, though not less than Eve abasht,
At length gave utterance to these words constrain'd.
        "O Eve, in evil hour thou didst give ear
To that false Worm, of whomsoever taught
To counterfeit Man's voice, true in our Fall,
1070 False in our promis'd Rising; since our Eyes
Op'n'd we find indeed, and find we know
Both Good and Evil, Good lost, and Evil got,
Bad Fruit of Knowledge, if this be to know,
Which leaves us naked thus, of Honour void,
1075 Of Innocence, of Faith, of Purity,
Our wonted Ornaments now soil'd and stain'd,
And in our Faces evident the signs
Of foul concupiscence; whence evil store;
Even shame, the last of evils; of the first
1080 Be sure then. How shall I behold the face
Henceforth of God or Angel, erst with joy
And rapture so oft beheld? those heav'nly shapes
Will dazzle now this earthly, with their blaze
Insufferably bright. O might I here
1085 In solitude live savage, in some glade
Obscur'd, where highest Woods impenetrable
To Star or Sun-light, spread their umbrage broad,
And brown as Evening: Cover me ye Pines,
Ye Cedars, with innumerable boughs
1090 Hide me, where I may never see them more.
But let us now, as in bad plight,° devise
What best may for the present serve to hide
The Parts of each from other, that seem most

1091 **plight** with a grimly punning suggestion of the meaning "pleat"
(drapery), the same word as "plight."

To shame obnoxious, and unseemliest seen,
Some Tree whose broad smooth Leaves together
 sew'd,   *1095*
And girded on our loins, may cover round
Those middle parts, that this newcomer, Shame,
There sit not, and reproach us as unclean."
    So counsell'd hee, and both together went
Into the thickest Wood, there soon they chose *1100*
The Figtree, not that kind for Fruit renown'd,
But such as at this day to Indians known
In Malabar or Decan spreads her Arms
Branching so broad and long, that in the ground
The bended Twigs take root, and Daughters grow *1105*
About the Mother Tree, a Pillar'd shade
High overarch't, and echoing Walks between;
There oft the Indian Herdsman shunning heat
Shelters in cool, and tends his pasturing Herds
At Loopholes cut through thickest shade: Those
 Leaves   *1110*
They gather'd, broad as Amazonian Targe,°
And with what skill they had, together sew'd,
To gird their waist, vain Covering if to hide
Their guilt and dreaded shame; O how unlike
To that first naked Glory. Such of late   *1115*
Columbus found th'American so girt
With feather'd Cincture, naked else and wild
Among the Trees on Isles and woody Shores.
Thus fenc't, and as they thought, their shame in part
Cover'd, but not at rest or ease of Mind,   *1120*
They sat them down to weep, nor only Tears
Rain'd at their Eyes, but high Winds worse within
Began to rise, high Passions, Anger, Hate,
Mistrust, Suspicion, Discord, and shook sore
Their inward State of Mind, calm Region once *1125*
And full of Peace, now tost and turbulent:
For Understanding rul'd not, and the Will
Heard not her lore, both in subjection now
To sensual Appetite, who from beneath
Usurping over sovran Reason claim'd   *1130*
Superior sway: From thus distemper'd breast,

1111 **Targe** shield.

Adam, estrang'd in look and alter'd style,
Speech intermitted thus to Eve renew'd.
          "Would thou hadst heark'n'd to my words,
              and stay'd
1135 With me, as I besought thee, when that strange
Desire of wand'ring this unhappy Morn,
I know not whence possess'd thee; we had then
Remain'd still happy, not as now, despoil'd
Of all our good, sham'd, naked, miserable.
1140 Let none henceforth seek needless cause to approve
The Faith they owe;° when earnestly they seek
Such proof, conclude, they then begin to fail."
          To whom soon mov'd with touch of blame
              thus Eve.
"What words have past thy Lips, Adam severe,
1145 Imput'st thou that to my default, or will
Of wandering, as thou call'st it, which who knows
But might as ill have happ'n'd thou being by,
Or to thyself perhaps: hadst thou been there,
Or here th'attempt, thou couldst not have discern'd
1150 Fraud in the Serpent, speaking as he spake;
No ground of enmity between us known,
Why hee should mean me ill, or seek to harm.
Was I to have never parted from thy side?
As good have grown there still a lifeless Rib.
1155 Being as I am, why didst not thou the Head
Command me absolutely not to go,
Going into such danger as thou said'st?
Too facile then thou didst not much gainsay,
Nay, didst permit, approve, and fair dismiss.
1160 Hadst thou been firm and fixt in thy dissent,
Neither had I transgress'd, nor thou with mee."
          To whom then first incenst Adam repli'd.
"Is this the Love, is this the recompense
Of mine to thee, ingrateful Eve, exprest
1165 Immutable° when thou wert lost, not I,
Who might have liv'd and joy'd immortal bliss,
Yet willingly chose rather Death with thee:
And am I now upbraided, as the cause
Of thy transgressing? not enough severe,

1141 owe own.   1164–5 exprest Immutable which was manifested as
unchangeable.

It seems, in thy restraint: what could I more?   1170
I warn'd thee, I admonish'd thee, foretold
The danger, and the lurking Enemy
That lay in wait; beyond this had been force,
And force upon free Will hath here no place.
But confidence then bore thee on, secure   1175
Either to meet no danger, or to find
Matter of glorious trial; and perhaps
I also err'd in overmuch admiring
What seem'd in thee so perfect, that I thought
No evil durst attempt thee, but I rue   1180
That error now, which is become my crime,
And thou th'accuser. Thus it shall befall
Him who to worth in Women overtrusting
Lets her Will rule; restraint she will not brook,
And left to herself, if evil thence ensue,   1185
Shee first his weak indulgence will accuse."
        Thus they in mutual accusation spent
The fruitless hours, but neither self-condemning,
And of their vain contést appear'd no end.

BOOK X

THE ARGUMENT

Man's transgression known, the Guardian Angels forsake
Paradise, and return up to Heaven to approve their vigi-
lance, and are approv'd, God declaring that The entrance
of Satan could not be by them prevented. He sends his
Son to judge the Transgressors, who descends and gives
Sentence accordingly; then in pity clothes them both, and
reascends. Sin and Death sitting till then at the Gates of
Hell, by wondrous sympathy feeling the success of Satan
in this new World, and the sin by Man there committed,
resolve to sit no longer confin'd in Hell, but to follow
Satan their Sire up to the place of Man: To make the

way easier from Hell to this World to and fro, they pav
a broad Highway or Bridge over Chaos, according t
the Track that Satan first made; then preparing for Earth
they meet him proud of his success returning to Hell
their mutual gratulation. Satan arrives at Pandemonium
in full assembly relates with boasting his success agains
Man; instead of applause is entertained with a genera
hiss by all his audience, transform'd with himself als
suddenly into Serpents, according to his doom giv'n i
Paradise; then deluded with a show of the forbidden Tre
springing up before them, they greedily reaching to tak
of the Fruit, chew dust and bitter ashes. The proceeding
of Sin and Death; God foretells the final Victory of hi
Son over them, and the renewing of all things; but fo
the present commands his Angels to make several altera
tions in the Heavens and Elements. Adam more and mor
perceiving his fall'n condition heavily bewails, rejects th
condolement of Eve; she persists and at length appease
him: then to evade the Curse likely to fall on their Off
spring, proposes to Adam violent ways, which he ap
proves not, but conceiving better hope, puts her in min
of the late Promise made them, that her Seed should b
reveng'd on the Serpent, and exhorts her with him t
seek Peace of the offended Deity, by repentance an
supplication.

Meanwhile the heinous and despiteful act
Of Satan done in Paradise, and how
Hee in the Serpent had perverted° Eve,
Her Husband shee, to taste the fatal fruit,
5   Was known in Heav'n; for what can 'scape the Eye
Of God All-seeing, or deceive his Heart
Omniscient, who in all things wise and just,
Hinder'd not Satan to attempt the mind
Of Man, with strength entire, and free Will arm'd,
10   Complete to have discover'd and repulst
Whatever wiles of Foe or seeming Friend.

3 **perverted** including the specific application to turning from a reli-
gious belief.

For still° they knew, and ought to have still re-
    member'd
The high Injunction not to taste that Fruit,
Whoever tempted; which they not obeying,
Incurr'd, what could they less, the penalty,   15
And manifold in sin, deserv'd to fall.
Up into Heav'n from Paradise in haste
Th'Angelic Guards ascended, mute and sad
For Man, for of his state by this they knew,
Much wond'ring how the subtle Fiend had stol'n   20
Entrance unseen. Soon as th'unwelcome news
From Earth arriv'd at Heaven Gate, displeas'd
All were who heard, dim sadness did not spare
That time Celestial visages, yet mixt
With pity, violated not their bliss.   25
About the new-arriv'd, in multitudes
Th'ethereal People ran, to hear and know
How all befell: they towards the Throne Supreme
Accountable made haste to make appear
With righteous plea, their utmost vigilance,   30
And easily approv'd; when the most High
Eternal Father from his secret Cloud,
Amidst in Thunder utter'd thus his voice.

     "Assembl'd Angels, and ye Powers return'd
From unsuccessful charge, be not dismay'd,   35
Nor troubl'd at these tidings from the Earth,
Which your sincerest care could not prevent,
Foretold so lately what would come to pass,
When first this Tempter cross'd the Gulf from Hell.
I told ye then he should prevail and speed   40
On his bad Errand, Man should be seduc't
And flatter'd out of all, believing lies
Against his Maker; no Decree of mine
Concurring to necessitate his Fall,
Or touch with lightest moment of impulse   45
His free Will, to her own inclining left
In ev'n scale. But fall'n he is, and now
What rests,° but that the mortal Sentence pass
On his transgression, Death denounc't° that day,
Which he presumes already vain and void,   50

12 **still** always.   48 **rests** remains.   49 **denounc't** formally threatened.

Because not yet inflicted, as he fear'd,
By some immediate stroke; but soon shall find
Forbearance no acquittance ere day end.
Justice shall not return as bounty scorn'd.
55 But whom send I to judge them? whom but thee
Vicegerent Son, to thee I have transferr'd
All Judgement, whether in Heav'n, or Earth, or Hell.
Easy it might be seen that I intend
Mercy colléague with Justice, sending thee
60 Man's Friend, his Mediator, his design'd
Both Ransom and Redeemer voluntary,
And destin'd Man himself to judge Man fall'n."
            So spake the Father, and unfolding bright
Toward the right hand his Glory, on the Son
65 Blaz'd forth unclouded Deity; he full
Resplendent all his Father manifest
Express'd, and thus divinely answer'd mild.
            "Father Eternal, thine is to decree,
Mine both in Heav'n and Earth to do thy will
70 Supreme, that thou in mee thy Son belov'd
Mayst ever rest well pleas'd. I go to judge
On Earth these thy transgressors, but thou know'st,
Whoever judg'd, the worst on mee must 'light,
When time shall be, for so I undertook
75 Before thee; and not repenting, this obtain
Of right, that I may mitigate their doom
On me deriv'd,° yet I shall temper so
Justice with Mercy, as may illústrate° most
Them° fully satisfied, and thee appease.
80 Attendance none shall need, nor Train, where none
Are to behold the Judgement, but the judg'd,
Those two; the third best absent is condemn'd,
Convict by flight, and Rebel to all Law
Conviction° to the Serpent none belongs."
85   Thus saying, from his radiant Seat he rose
Of high collateral glory: him Thrones and Powers,
Princedoms, and Dominations ministrant
Accompanied to Heaven Gate, from whence
Eden and all the Coast in prospect lay.
90 Down he descended straight; the speed of Gods

77 **deriv'd** brought down, diverted.   78 **illústrate** set in the best light.
79 **Them** justice and mercy.   84 **Conviction** proof of guilt.

Time counts not, though with swiftest minutes wing'd.
Now was the Sun in Western cadence° low
From Noon, and gentle Airs due at their hour
To fan the Earth now wak'd, and usher in
The Ev'ning cool when he from wrath more cool   95
Came the mild Judge and Intercessor both
To sentence Man: the voice of God they heard
Now walking in the Garden, by soft winds
Brought to their Ears, while day declin'd, they heard,
And from his presence hid themselves among   100
The thickest Trees, both Man and Wife, till God
Approaching, thus to Adam call'd aloud.
        "Where art thou Adam, wont with joy to meet
My coming seen far off? I miss thee here,
Not pleas'd, thus entertain'd with solitude,   105
Where obvious° duty erewhile appear'd unsought:
Or come I less conspicuous, or what change
Absents thee, or what chance detains? Come forth."
He came, and with him Eve, more loath, though first
To offend, discount'nanc't both, and discompos'd;   110
Love was not in their looks, either to God
Or to each other, but apparent° guilt,
And shame, and perturbation, and despair,
Anger, and obstinacy, and hate, and guile.
When Adam falt'ring long, thus answer'd brief.   115
        "I heard thee in the Garden, and of thy voice
Afraid, being naked, hid myself." To whom
The gracious Judge without revile repli'd.
        "My voice thou oft hast heard, and hast not
                                        fear'd,
But still rejoic't, how is it now become   120
So dreadful to thee? that thou art naked, who
Hath told thee? hast thou eaten of the Tree
Whereof I gave thee charge thou shouldst not eat?"
        To whom thus Adam sore beset repli'd.
"O Heav'n! in evil strait this day I stand   125
Before my Judge, either to undergo
Myself the total Crime, or to accuse
My other self, the partner of my life;

92 **cadence** falling (and with the musical hint taken up in "Airs due
at their hour" and "usher in"). 106 **obvious** coming forward to
meet. 112 **apparent** manifest.

Whose failing, while her Faith to me remains,
130 I should conceal, and not expose to blame
By my complaint; but strict necessity
Subdues me, and calamitous constraint,
Lest on my head both sin and punishment,
However insupportable, be all
135 Devolv'd; though should I hold my peace, yet thou
Wouldst easily detect what I conceal.
This Woman whom thou mad'st to be my help,
And gav'st me as thy perfect gift, so good,
So fit, so ácceptáble, so Divine,
140 That from her hand I could suspect no ill,
And what she did, whatever in itself,
Her doing seem'd to justify the deed;
Shee gave me of the Tree, and I did eat."
          To whom the sovran Presence thus repli'd.
145 "Was shee thy God, that her thou didst obey
Before his voice, or was shee made thy guide,
Superior, or but equal, that to her
Thou didst resign thy Manhood, and the Place
Wherein God set thee above her made of thee,
150 And for thee, whose perfection far excell'd
Hers in all real dignity: Adorn'd
She was indeed, and lovely to attract
Thy Love, not thy Subjection, and her Gifts
Were such as under Government well seem'd,
155 Unseemly to bear rule, which was thy part
And person, hadst thou known thyself aright."
          So having said, he thus to Eve in few:
"Say Woman, what is this which thou hast done?"
          To whom sad Eve with shame nigh over-
          whelm'd
160 Confessing soon, yet not before her Judge
Bold or loquacious, thus abasht repli'd.
          "The Serpent me beguil'd and I did eat."
          Which when the Lord God heard, without
          delay
To Judgement he proceeded on th'accused
165 Serpent though brute, unable° to transfer
The Guilt on him who made him instrument
Of mischief, and polluted from the end

165 **unable** the serpent being powerless to . . .

Of his Creation; justly then accurst,
As vitiated in Nature: more to know
Concern'd not Man (since he no further knew)   170
Nor alter'd his offence; yet God at last
To Satan first in sin his doom appli'd,
Though in mysterious terms, judg'd as then best:
And on the Serpent thus his curse let fall.
      "Because thou hast done this, thou art accurst   175
Above all Cattle, each Beast of the Field;
Upon thy Belly grovelling thou shalt go,
And dust shalt eat all the days of thy Life.
Between Thee and the Woman I will put
Enmity, and between thine and her Seed;   180
Her Seed shall bruise thy head, thou bruise his heel."
      So spake this Oracle, then verifi'd
When Jesus son of Mary second Eve,
Saw Satan fall like Lightning down from Heav'n,
Prince of the Air; then rising from his Grave   185
Spoil'd Principalities and Powers, triumpht
In open show, and with ascension bright
Captivity led captive through the Air,
The Realm itself of Satan long usurpt,
Whom he shall tread at last under our feet;   190
Ev'n hee who now foretold his fatal bruise,
And to the Woman thus his Sentence turn'd.
      "Thy sorrow I will greatly multiply
By thy Conception; Children thou shalt bring
In sorrow forth, and to thy Husband's will   195
Thine shall submit, hee over thee shall rule."
      On Adam last thus judgement he pronounc'd.
"Because thou hast heark'n'd to the voice of thy
    Wife,
And eaten of the Tree concerning which
I charg'd thee, saying: Thou shalt not eat thereof,   200
Curs'd is the ground for thy sake, thou in sorrow
Shalt eat thereof all the days of thy Life;
Thorns also and Thistles it shall bring thee forth
Unbid, and thou shalt eat th'Herb of the Field,
In the sweat of thy Face shalt thou eat Bread,   205
Till thou return unto the ground, for thou
Out of the ground wast taken, know thy Birth,
For dust thou art, and shalt to dust return."

        So judg'd he Man, both Judge and Saviour sent,
210   And th'instant stroke of Death denounc't that day
      Remov'd far off; then pitying how they stood
      Before him naked to the air, that now
      Must suffer change, disdain'd not to begin
      Thenceforth the form of servant to assume,
215   As when he wash'd his servants' feet, so now
      As Father of his Family he clad
      Their nakedness with Skins of Beasts, or slain,
      Or as the Snake with youthful Coat repaid;°
      And thought not much to clothe his Enemies:
220   Nor hee their outward only with the Skins
      Of Beasts, but inward nakedness, much more
      Opprobrious, with his Robe of righteousness,
      Arraying cover'd from his Father's sight.
      To him with swift ascent he up return'd,
225   Into his blissful bosom reassum'd
      In glory as of old, to him appeas'd
      All, though all-knowing, what had past with Man
      Recounted, mixing intercession sweet.
      Meanwhile ere thus was sinn'd and judg'd on Earth,
230   Within the Gates of Hell sat Sin and Death,
      In counterview within the Gates, that now
      Stood open wide, belching outrageous flame
      Far into Chaos, since the Fiend pass'd through,
      Sin opening, who thus now to Death began.
235   "O Son, why sit we here each other viewing
      Idly, while Satan our great Author thrives
      In other Worlds, and happier Seat provides
      For us his offspring dear? It cannot be
      But that success attends him; if mishap,
240   Ere this he had return'd, with fury driv'n
      By his Avengers,° since no place like this
      Can fit his punishment, or their revenge.
      Methinks I feel new strength within me rise,
      Wings growing, and Dominion giv'n me large
245   Beyond this Deep; whatever draws me on,
      Or sympathy, or some connatural force
      Powerful at greatest distance to unite
      With secret amity things of like kind

218 repaid recompensed.   **241 Avengers** 1674; Avenger 1667.

By secretest conveyance.° Thou my Shade
Inseparable must with mee along: 250
For Death from Sin no power can separate.
But lest the difficulty of passing back
Stay his return perhaps over this Gulf
Impassable, impervious, let us try
Advent'rous work, yet to thy power and mine   255
Not unagreeable, to found a path
Over this Main from Hell to that new World
Where Satan now prevails, a Monument
Of merit high to all th'infernal Host,
Easing their passage hence, for intercourse,   260
Or transmigration, as their lot shall lead.
Nor can I miss the way, so strongly drawn
By this new-felt attraction and instínct."
          Whom thus the meager Shadow answer'd soon.
"Go whither Fate and inclination strong   265
Leads thee, I shall not lag behind, nor err
The way, thou leading, such a scent I draw
Of carnage, prey innumerable, and taste
The savour of Death from all things there that live:
Nor shall I to the work thou enterprisest   270
Be wanting, but afford thee equal aid."
          So saying, with delight he snuff'd the smell
Of mortal change on Earth. As when a flock
Of ravenous Fowl, though many a League remote,
Against the day of Battle, to a Field,   275
Where Armies lie encampt, come flying, lur'd
With scent of living Carcasses design'd
For death, the following day, in bloody fight.
So scented the grim Feature, and upturn'd
His Nostril wide into the murky Air,   280
Sagacious° of his Quarry from so far.
Then Both from out Hell Gates into the waste
Wide Anarchy of Chaos damp and dark
Flew diverse, and with Power (their Power was great)
Hovering upon the Waters; what they met   285
Solid or slimy, as in raging Sea
Tost up and down, together crowded drove
From each side shoaling towards the mouth of Hell.

249 **conveyance** with associations of underhand cunning.   281 **Sagacious** quick of scent.

As when two Polar Winds blowing adverse
290 Upon the Cronian° Sea, together drive
Mountains of Ice, that stop th'imagin'd way
Beyond Petsora° Eastward, to the rich
Cathaian° Coast. The aggregated Soil
Death with his Mace petrific,° cold and dry,
295 As with a Trident smote, and fix't as firm
As Delos° floating once; the rest his look
Bound with Gorgonian° rigor not to move,
And with Asphaltic slime; broad as the Gate,
Deep to the Roots of Hell the gather'd beach
300 They fasten'd, and the Mole° immense wrought on
Over the foaming deep high Archt, a Bridge
Of length prodigious joining to the Wall
Immovable of this now fenceless° world
Forfeit to Death; from hence a passage broad,
305 Smooth, easy, inoffensive° down to Hell.
So, if great things to small may be compar'd,
Xerxes, the Liberty of Greece to yoke,
From Susa° his Memnonian Palace high
Came to the Sea, and over Hellespont
310 Bridging his way, Europe with Asia join'd,
And scourg'd with many a stroke th'indignant waves.°
Now had they brought the work by wondrous Art
Pontifical,° a ridge of pendent Rock
Over the vext Abyss, following the track
315 Of Satan, to the selfsame place where hee
First 'lighted from his Wing, and landed safe
From out of Chaos to the outside bare
Of this round World: with Pins of Adamant
And Chains they made all fast, too fast they made
320 And durable; and now in little space
The Confines met of Empyrean Heav'n
And of this World, and on the left hand Hell
With long reach interpos'd; three sev'ral ways
In sight, to each of these three places led.

290 **Cronian** Arctic. 292 **Petsora** river in Siberia. 293 **Cathaian**
Chinese. 294 **petrific** turning to stone. 296 **Delos** an Aegean is-
land, called up by Neptune's trident and fixed firm by Jove. 297
Gorgonian the Gorgons' gaze turning men to stone. 300 **Mole** mas-
sive bridge or pier. 303 **fenceless** defenseless. 305 **inoffensive**
without obstacle. 308 **Susa** in Persia. 311 **And . . . waves** In his
anger after the waters destroyed a bridge. 313 **Pontifical** bridge-
making.

And now their way to Earth they had descri'd,   325
To Paradise first tending, when behold
Satan in likeness of an Angel bright
Betwixt the Centaur and the Scorpion steering
His Zenith, while the Sun in Aries rose:
Disguis'd he came, but those his Children dear   330
Their Parent soon discern'd, though in disguise.
Hee, after Eve seduc't, unminded slunk
Into the Wood fast by, and changing shape
To observe the sequel, saw his guileful act
By Eve, though all unwitting, seconded   335
Upon her Husband, saw their shame that sought
Vain covertures; but when he saw descend
The Son of God to judge them, terrifi'd
Hee fled, not hoping to escape, but shun
The present, fearing guilty what his wrath   340
Might suddenly inflict; that past, return'd
By Night, and list'ning where the hapless Pair
Sat in their sad discourse, and various plaint,
Thence gather'd his own doom, which understood
Not instant, but of future time. With joy   345
And tidings fraught, to Hell he now return'd,
And at the brink of Chaos, near the foot
Of this new wondrous Pontifice, unhop't
Met who to meet him came, his Offspring dear.
Great joy was at their meeting, and at sight   350
Of that stupendious Bridge his joy increas'd.
Long hee admiring stood, till Sin, his fair
Enchanting Daughter, thus the silence broke.
        "O Parent, these are thy magnific deeds,
Thy Trophies, which thou view'st as not thine own,   355
Thou art their Author and prime Architect:
For I no sooner in my Heart divin'd,
My Heart, which by a secret harmony
Still moves with thine, join'd in connection sweet,
That thou on Earth hadst prosper'd, which thy looks   360
Now also evidence, but straight I felt
Though distant from thee Worlds between, yet felt
That I must after thee with this thy Son;
Such fatal consequence unites us three:
Hell could no longer hold us in her bounds,   365
Nor this unvoyageable Gulf obscure

Detain from following thy illustrious track.
Thou hast achiev'd our liberty, confin'd
Within Hell Gates till now, thou us impow'r'd
370 To fortify thus far, and overlay
With this portentous Bridge the dark Abyss.
Thine now is all this World, thy virtue hath won
What thy hands builded not, thy Wisdom gain'd
With odds what War hath lost, and fully aveng'd
375 Our foil in Heav'n; here thou shalt Monarch reign,
There didst not; there let him still Victor sway,
As Battle hath adjudg'd, from this new World
Retiring, by his own doom alienated,
And henceforth Monarchy with thee divide
380 Of all things, parted by th'Empyreal bounds,
His Quadrature,° from thy Orbicular World,
Or try thee now more dang'rous to his Throne."
        Whom thus the Prince of Darkness answer'd
        glad.
"Fair Daughter, and thou Son and Grandchild both,
385 High proof ye now have giv'n to be the Race
Of Satan (for I glory in the name,
Antagonist of Heav'n's Almighty King)
Amply have merited of me, of all
Th'Infernal Empire, that so near Heav'n's door
390 Triumphal with triumphal act have met,
Mine with this glorious Work, and made one Realm
Hell and this World, one Realm, one Continent
Of easy thoroughfare. Therefore while I
Descend through Darkness, on your Road with ease
395 To my associate Powers, them to acquaint
With these successes, and with them rejoice,
You two this way, among these numerous Orbs
All yours, right down to Paradise descend;
There dwell and Reign in bliss, thence on the Earth
400 Dominion exercise and in the Air,
Chiefly on Man, sole Lord of all declar'd,
Him first make sure your thrall, and lastly kill.
My Substitutes I send ye, and Create
Plenipotent on Earth, of matchless might
405 Issuing from mee: on your joint vigor now
My hold of this new Kingdom all depends,

381 **Quadrature** Heaven as a square.

Through Sin to Death expos'd by my explóit.
If your joint power prevail, th'affairs of Hell
No detriment° need fear, go and be strong."
      So saying he dismiss'd them, they with speed   *410*
Their course through thickest Constellations held
Spreading their bane; the blasted Stars lookt wan,
And Planets, Planet-struck,° real Eclipse
Then suffer'd. Th'other way Satan went down
The Causey° to Hell Gate; on either side   *415*
Disparted Chaos over-built exclaim'd,
And with rebounding surge the bars assail'd,
That scorn'd his indignation: through the Gate,
Wide open and unguarded, Satan pass'd,
And all about found desolate; for those   *420*
Appointed to sit there, had left their charge,
Flown to the upper World; the rest were all
Far to the inland retir'd, about the walls
Of Pandemonium, City and proud seat
Of Lucifer, so by allusion call'd,   *425*
Of that bright Star to Satan paragon'd.
There kept their Watch the Legions, while the Grand
In Council sat, solicitous what chance
Might intercept their Emperor sent, so hee
Departing gave command, and they observ'd.   *430*
As when the Tartar from his Russian Foe
By Astracan over the Snowy Plains
Retires, or Bactrian Sophi° from the horns
Of Turkish Crescent, leaves all waste beyond
The Realm of Aladule, in his retreat   *435*
To Tauris or Casbeen. So these the late
Heav'n-banisht Host, left desert utmost Hell
Many a dark League, reduc't in careful Watch
Round their Metropolis, and now expecting
Each hour their great adventurer from the search   *440*
Of Foreign Worlds: he through the midst unmarkt,
In show plebeian Angel militant
Of lowest order, past; and from the door
Of that Plutonian° Hall, invisible

---

409 **detriment** the word's astrological application (including
"eclipse") leading into the following lines.   413 **Planet-struck**
plagued by an even more evil influence than what they themselves
shed.   415 **Causey** causeway.   433 **Bactrian Sophi** Persian king.
444 **Plutonian** Pluto, god of Hell.

445 Ascended his high Throne, which under state
     Of richest texture spread, at th'upper end
     Was plac't in regal lustre. Down awhile
     He sat, and round about him saw unseen:
     At last as from a Cloud his fulgent head
450 And shape Star-bright appear'd, or brighter, clad
     With what permissive glory since his fall
     Was left him, or false glitter: All amaz'd
     At that so sudden blaze the Stygian throng
     Bent their aspéct, and whom they wish'd beheld,
455 Their mighty Chief return'd: loud was th'acclaim:
     Forth rush'd in haste the great consulting Peers,
     Rais'd from their dark Divan,° and with like joy
     Congratulant approach'd him, who with hand
     Silence, and with these words attention won.
           "Thrones, Dominations, Princedoms, Virtues,
460   Powers,
     For in possession such, not only of right,
     I call ye and declare ye now, return'd
     Successful beyond hope, to lead ye forth
     Triumphant out of this infernal Pit
465 Abominable, accurst, the house of woe,
     And Dungeon of our Tyrant: Now possess,
     As Lords, a spacious World, to our native Heaven
     Little inferior, by my adventure hard
     With peril great achiev'd. Long were to tell
470 What I have done, what suffer'd, with what pain
     Voyag'd th'unreal, vast, unbounded deep
     Of horrible confusion, over which
     By Sin and Death a broad way now is pav'd
     To expedite° your glorious march; but I
475 Toil'd out my uncouth passage, forc't to ride
     Th'untractable Abyss, plung'd in the womb
     Of unoriginal° Night and Chaos wild,
     That jealous of their secrets fiercely oppos'd
     My journey strange, with clamorous uproar
480 Protesting Fate supreme; thence how I found
     The new created World, which fame in Heav'n
     Long had foretold, a Fabric wonderful
     Of absolute perfection, therein Man

457 **Divan** oriental council.   474 **expedite** speed (in origin, "free the feet").   477 **unoriginal** unoriginated.

Plac't in a Paradise, by our exíle
Made happy: Him by fraud I have seduc'd   485
From his Creator, and the more to increase
Your wonder, with an Apple; he threat
Offended, worth your laughter, hath giv'n up
Both his beloved Man and all his World,
To Sin and Death a prey, and so to us,   490
Without our hazard, labour, or alarm,
To range in, and to dwell, and over Man
To rule, as over all he should have rul'd.
True is, mee also he hath judg'd, or rather
Mee not, but the brute Serpent in whose shape   495
Man I deceiv'd: that which to mee belongs,
Is enmity, which he will put between
Mee and Mankind; I am to bruise his heel;
His Seed, when is not set, shall bruise my head:
A World who would not purchase with a bruise,   500
Or much more grievous pain? Ye have th'account
Of my performance: What remains, ye Gods,
But up and enter now into full bliss."
          So having said, awhile he stood, expecting
Their universal shout and high applause   505
To fill his ear, when contrary he hears
On all sides, from innumerable tongues
A dismal universal hiss, the sound
Of public scorn; he wonder'd, but not long
Had leisure, wond'ring at himself now more;   510
His Visage drawn he felt to sharp and spare,
His Arms clung to his Ribs, his Legs entwining
Each other, till supplanted° down he fell
A monstrous Serpent on his Belly prone,
Reluctant,° but in vain, a greater power   515
Now rul'd him, punisht in the shape he sinn'd,
According to his doom: he would have spoke,
But hiss for hiss return'd with forked tongue
To forked tongue, for now were all transform'd
Alike, to Serpents all as áccessóries   520
To his bold Riot: dreadful was the din
Of hissing through the Hall, thick swarming now

___

513 **supplanted** overthrown, Satan himself being traditionally the
"supplanter" of Adam and Eve.   515 **Reluctant** struggling.

With complicated° monsters, head and tail,
Scorpion and Asp, and Amphisboena° dire,
525 Cerastes horn'd, Hydrus,° and Ellops° drear,
And Dipsas° (Not so thick swarm'd once the Soil
Bedropt with blood of Gorgon,° or the Isle
Ophiusa°) but still greatest hee the midst,
Now Dragon grown, larger than whom the Sun
530 Engender'd in the Pythian Vale on slime,
Huge Python,° and his Power no less he seem'd
Above the rest still to retain; they all
Him follow'd issuing forth to th'open Field,
Where all yet left of that revolted Rout
535 Heav'n-fall'n, in station stood or just array,
Sublime with expectation when to see
In Triumph issuing forth their glorious Chief;
They saw, but other sight instead, a crowd
Of ugly Serpents; horror on them fell,
540 And horrid sympathy; for what they saw,
They felt themselves now changing; down their arms,
Down fell both Spear and Shield, down they as fast,
And the dire hiss renew'd, and the dire form
Catcht by Contagion, like in punishment,
545 As in their crime. Thus was th'applause they meant,
Turn'd to exploding° hiss, triumph to shame
Cast on themselves from their own mouths. There
    stood
A Grove hard by, sprung up with this their change,
His will who reigns above, to aggravate
550 Their penance, laden with fair Fruit, like that
Which grew in Paradise, the bait of Eve
Us'd by the Tempter: on that prospect strange
Their earnest eyes they fix'd, imagining
For one forbidden Tree a multitude
555 Now ris'n, to work them further woe or shame;
Yet parcht with scalding thirst and hunger fierce,
Though to delude them sent, could not abstain,

---

523 **complicated** entwined.   524 **Amphisboena** fabled to have a head
at each end.   525 **Hydrus** water snake.   525 **Ellops** a kind of ser-
pent.   526 **Dipsas** whose bite produced raging thirst.   526–27 **Soil ...
Gorgon** The blood of Medusa bred snakes in Libya.   528 **Ophiusa**
named after its "serpents."   531 **Python** serpent slain by Apollo.
546 **exploding** hooting (off the stage, Latin *explaudare*, literally the
opposite of "th'applause").

But on they roll'd in heaps, and up the Trees
Climbing, sat thicker than the snaky locks
That curl'd Megæra:° greedily they pluck'd   560
The Fruitage fair to sight, like that which grew
Near that bituminous Lake where Sodom flam'd;
This more delusive, not the touch, but taste
Deceiv'd; they fondly thinking to allay
Their appetite with gust,° instead of Fruit   565
Chew'd bitter Ashes, which th'offended taste
With spattering noise rejected: oft they assay'd,
Hunger and thirst constraining, drugg'd as oft,
With hatefullest disrelish writh'd their jaws
With soot and cinders fill'd; so oft they fell   570
Into the same illusion, not as Man
Whom they triumph'd once lapst. Thus were they
     plagu'd
And worn with Famine, long and ceaseless hiss,
Till their lost shape, permitted, they resum'd,
Yearly enjoin'd, some say, to undergo   575
This annual humbling certain number'd days,
To dash their pride, and joy for Man seduc't.
However some tradition they dispers'd
Among the Heathen of their purchase° got,
And Fabl'd how the Serpent, whom they call'd   580
Ophion with Eurynome,° the wide-
Encroaching Eve perhaps, had first the rule
Of high Olympus, thence by Saturn driv'n
And Ops,° ere yet Dictæan° Jove was born.
Meanwhile in Paradise the hellish pair   585
Too soon arriv'd, Sin there in power before,
Once actual, now in body, and to dwell
Habitual habitant; behind her Death
Close following pace for pace, not mounted yet
On his pale Horse: to whom Sin thus began.   590
          "Second of Satan sprung, all-conquering
               Death,
What think'st thou of our Empire now, though earn'd
With travail difficult, not better far

560 **Megæra** one of the Furies.   565 **gust** relish.   579 **purchase**
plunder   581 **Ophion . . . Eurynome** the Titan Ophion, "Serpent,"
and his wife Eurynome, "Wide-ruling."   584 **Ops** wife of Saturn.
584 **Dictæan** from Dicte in Crete.

Than still at Hell's dark threshold to have sat watch,
595 Unnam'd, undreaded, and thyself half starv'd?"
                    Whom thus the Sin-born Monster answer'd
                       soon.
"To mee, who with eternal Famine pine,
Alike is Hell, or Paradise, or Heaven,
There best, where most with ravin° I might meet;
600 Which here, though plenteous, all too little seems
To stuff this Maw, this vast unhide-bound° Corpse."
                    To whom th'incestuous Mother thus repli'd.
"Thou therefore on these Herbs, and Fruits, and
    Flow'rs
Feed first, on each Beast next, and Fish, and Fowl,
605 No homely morsels, and whatever thing
The Scyth of Time mows down, devour unspar'd,
Till I in Man residing through the Race,
His thoughts, his looks, words, actions all infect,
And season him thy last and sweetest prey."
610   This said, they both betook them several ways,
Both to destroy, or unimmortal make
All kinds, and for destruction to mature
Sooner or later; which th'Almighty seeing,
From his transcendent Seat the Saints among,
615 To those bright Orders utter'd thus his voice.
                    "See with what heat these Dogs of Hell
                       advance
To waste and havoc yonder World, which I
So fair and good created, and had still
Kept in that state, had not the folly of Man
620 Let in these wasteful Furies, who impute
Folly to mee, so doth the Prince of Hell
And his Adherents, that with so much ease
I suffer them to enter and possess
A place so heav'nly, and conniving° seem
625 To gratify my scornful Enemies,
That laugh, as if transported with some fit
Of Passion, I to them had quitted all,
At random yielded up to their misrule;
And know not that I call'd and drew them thither
630 My Hell-hounds, to lick up the draff and filth

599 **ravin** prey. 601 **unhide-bound** slack-skinned. 624 **conniving** winking at, overlooking.

Which man's polluting Sin with taint hath shed
On what was pure, till cramm'd and gorg'd, nigh burst
With suckt and glutted offal, at one sling
Of thy victorious Arm, well-pleasing Son,
Both Sin, and Death, and yawning Grave at last   635
Through Chaos hurl'd, obstruct the mouth of Hell
For ever, and seal up his ravenous Jaws.
Then Heav'n and Earth renew'd shall be made pure
To sanctity that shall receive no stain:
Till then the Curse pronounc't on both precedes."°   640
          Hee ended, and the heav'nly Audience loud
Sung Halleluia, as the sound of Seas,
Through multitude that sung: "Just are thy ways,
Righteous are thy Decrees on all thy Works;
Who can extenuate° thee? Next, to the Son,   645
Destin'd restorer of Mankind, by whom
New Heav'n and Earth shall to the Ages rise,
Or down from Heav'n descend." Such was their song,
While the Creator calling forth by name
His mighty Angels gave them several charge,   650
As sorted best with present things. The Sun
Had first his precept so to move, so shine,
As might affect the Earth with cold and heat
Scarce tolerable, and from the North to call
Decrepit Winter, from the South to bring   655
Solstitial summer's heat. To the blanc Moon
Her office they prescrib'd, to th'other five
Their planetary motions and aspécts°
In Sextile, Square, and Trine, and Opposite,
Of noxious efficacy, and when to join   660
In Synod° unbenign, and taught the fixt°
Their influence malignant when to show'r,
Which of them rising with the Sun, or falling,
Should prove tempestuous: To the Winds they set
Their corners, when with bluster to confound   665
Sea, Air, and Shore, the Thunder when to roll
With terror through the dark Aereal Hall.
Some say he bid his Angels turn askance
The Poles of Earth twice ten degrees and more

640 **precedes** takes precedence.   645 **extenuate** belittle.   658 **aspécts**
astrological positions.   661 **Synod** astrological conjunction.   661 **fixt**
"sphere" of fixed stars.

670 From the Sun's Axle; they with labour push'd
    Oblique the Centric Globe:° Some say the Sun
    Was bid turn Reins from th'Equinoctial Road
    Like distant breadth to Taurus with the Sev'n
    Atlantic Sisters, and the Spartan Twins
675 Up to the Tropic Crab; thence down amain
    By Leo and the Virgin and the Scales,
    As deep as Capricorn, to bring in change
    Of Seasons to each Clime; else had the Spring
    Perpetual smil'd on Earth with vernant Flow'rs,
680 Equal in Days and Nights, except to those
    Beyond the Polar Circles; to them Day
    Had unbenighted shone, while the low Sun
    To recompense his distance, in their sight
    Had rounded still th'Horizon, and not known
685 Or East or West, which had forbid the Snow
    From cold Estotiland,° and South as far
    Beneath Magellan.° At that tasted Fruit
    The Sun, as from Thyestean° Banquet, turn'd
    His course intended; else how had the World
690 Inhabited, though sinless, more than now,
    Avoided pinching cold and scorching heat?
    These changes in the Heav'ns, though slow, produc'd
    Like change on Sea and Land, sideral blast,°
    Vapour, and Mist, and Exhalation hot,
695 Corrupt and Pestilent: Now from the North
    Of Norumbega,° and the Samoed° shore
    Bursting their brazen Dungeon, arm'd with ice
    And snow and hail and stormy gust and flaw,°
    Boreas and Cæcias and Argestes loud
700 And Thrascias rend the Woods and Seas upturn;
    With adverse blast up-turns them from the South
    Notus and Afer black with thund'rous Clouds
    From Serraliona;° thwart of these as fierce
    Forth rush the Levant and the Ponent Winds
705 Eurus and Zephyr with their lateral noise,

---

671 **Globe** earth.   686 **Estotiland** in North America.   687 **Magellan**
at the extremity of South America.   688 **Thyestean** The flesh of
Thyestes' sons was served to him.   693 **sideral blast** malign influence
from the stars.   696 **Norumbega** in North America.   696 **Samoed**
Siberian.   698 **flaw** squall.   703 **Serraliona** Sierra Leone.

Sirocco, and Libecchio.° Thus began
Outrage from lifeless things; but Discord first
Daughter of Sin, among th'irrational,
Death introduc'd through fierce antipathy:
Beast now with Beast 'gan war, and Fowl with Fowl,   710
And Fish with Fish; to graze the Herb all leaving,
Devour'd each other; nor stood much in awe
Of Man, but fled him, or with count'nance grim
Glar'd on him passing: these were from without
The growing miseries, which Adam saw   715
Already in part, though hid in gloomiest shade,
To sorrow abandon'd, but worse felt within,
And in a troubl'd Sea of passion tost,
Thus to disburd'n sought with sad complaint.

　　"O miserable of happy! is this the end   720
Of this new glorious World, and mee so late
The Glory of that Glory, who now become
Accurst of blessed, hide me from the face
Of God, whom to behold was then my heighth
Of happiness: yet well, if here would end   725
The misery, I deserv'd it, and would bear
My own deservings; but this will not serve;
All that I eat or drink, or shall beget,
Is propagated curse. O voice once heard
Delightfully, *Increase and multiply*,   730
Now death to hear! for what can I increase
Or multiply, but curses on my head?
Who of all Ages to succeed, but feeling
The evil on him brought by me, will curse
My Head, 'Ill fare our Ancestor impure,   735
For this we may thank Adam'; but his thanks
Shall be the execration; so besides
Mine own that bide° upon me, all from mee
Shall with a fierce reflux on mee redound,
On mee as on their natural center 'light   740
Heavy, though in their place.° O fleeting joys
Of Paradise, dear bought with lasting woes!
Did I request thee, Maker, from my Clay

699–706 **Boreas . . . Libecchio** the winds in classical and Italian
terminology.　738 **bide** insistently dwell.　741 **though . . . place** this
being unnatural, since their weight is their tendency to their own
center.

To mould me Man, did I solicit thee
745 From darkness to promote me, or here place
In this delicious Garden? as my Will
Concurr'd not to my being, it were but right
And equal° to reduce me to my dust,
Desirous to resign, and render back
750 All I receiv'd, unable to perform
Thy terms too hard, by which I was to hold
The good I sought not. To the loss of that,
Sufficient penalty, why hast thou added
The sense of endless woes? inexplicable
755 Thy Justice seems; yet to say truth, too late,
I thus contést; then should have been refus'd
Those terms whatever, when they were propos'd:
Thou didst accept them; wilt thou enjoy the good,
Then cavil the conditions? and though God
760 Made thee without thy leave, what if thy Son
Prove disobedient, and reprov'd, retort,
'Wherefore didst thou beget me? I sought it not':
Wouldst thou admit for his contempt of thee
That proud excuse? yet him not thy election,
765 But Natural necessity begot.
God made thee of choice his own, and of his own
To serve him, thy reward was of his grace,
Thy punishment then justly is at his Will.
Be it so, for I submit, his doom is fair,
770 That dust I am, and shall to dust return:
O welcome hour whenever! why delays
His hand to execute what his Decree
Fix'd on this day? why do I overlive,
Why am I mockt with death, and length'n'd out
775 To deathless pain? how gladly would I meet
Mortality my sentence, and be Earth
Insensible, how glad would lay me down
As in my Mother's lap? there I should rest
And sleep secure; his dreadful voice no more
780 Would Thunder in my ears, nor fear of worse
To mee and to my offspring would torment me
With cruel expectation. Yet one doubt
Pursues me still, lest all I cannot die,
Lest that pure breath of Life, the Spirit of Man

748 **equal** equitable.

Which God inspir'd, cannot together perish   785
With this corporeal Clod; then in the Grave,
Or in some other dismal place, who knows
But I shall die a living Death? O thought
Horrid, if true! yet why? it was but breath
Of Life that sinn'd; what dies but what had life   790
And sin? the Body properly hath neither.
All of me then shall die: let this appease
The doubt, since human reach no further knows.
For though the Lord of all be infinite,
Is his wrath also? be it, man is not so,   795
But mortal doom'd. How can he exercise
Wrath without end on Man whom Death must end?
Can he make deathless Death? that were to make
Strange contradiction, which to God himself
Impossible is held, as Argument   800
Of weakness, not of Power. Will he, draw out,
For anger's sake, finite to infinite
In punisht man, to satisfy his rigour
Satisfi'd never; that were to extend
His Sentence beyond dust and Nature's Law,   805
By which all Causes else according still
To the reception of their matter° act,
Not to th'extent of their own Sphere. But say
That Death be not one stroke, as I suppos'd,
Bereaving sense, but endless misery   810
From this day onward, which I feel begun
Both in me, and without me, and so last
To perpetuity; Ay me, that fear
Comes thund'ring back with dreadful revolution
On my defenceless head; both Death and I   815
Am found Eternal, and incorporate° both,
Nor I on my part single, in mee all
Posterity stands curst: Fair Patrimony
That I must leave ye, Sons; O were I able
To waste it all myself, and leave ye none!   820
So disinherited how would ye bless
Me now your Curse! Ah, why should all mankind
For one man's fault thus guiltless be condemn'd,
If guiltless? But from mee what can proceed,

807 **reception . . . matter** receptivity of their materials.   816 **incorporate** united in one body.

825 But all corrupt, both Mind and Will deprav'd,
    Not to do only, but to will the same
    With me? how can they then° acquitted stand
    In sight of God? Him after all Disputes
    Forc't I absolve: all my evasions vain
830 And reasonings, though through Mazes, lead me still
    But to my own conviction: first and last
    On mee, mee only, as the source and spring
    Of all corruption, all the blame 'lights due;
    So might the wrath. Fond wish! couldst thou support
835 That burden heavier than the Earth to bear,
    Than all the World much heavier, though divided
    With that bad Woman? Thus what thou desir'st
    And what thou fear'st, alike destroys all hope
    Of refuge, and concludes° thee miserable
840 Beyond all past example and future,
    To Satan only like both crime and doom.
    O Conscience, into what Abyss of fears
    And horrors hast thou driv'n me; out of which
    I find no way, from deep to deeper plung'd!"
845   Thus Adam to himself lamented loud
    Through the still Night, not now, as ere man fell,
    Wholesome and cool, and mild, but with black Air
    Accompanied, with damps and dreadful gloom,
    Which to his evil Conscience represented
850 All things with double terror: On the ground
    Outstretcht he lay, on the cold ground, and oft
    Curs'd his Creation, Death as oft accus'd
    Of tardy execution, since denounc't°
    The day of his offence. "Why comes not Death,"
855 Said hee, "with one thrice ácceptáble stroke
    To end me? Shall Truth fail to keep her word,
    Justice Divine not hast'n to be just?
    But Death comes not at call, Justice Divine
    Mends not her slowest pace for prayers or cries.
860 O Woods, O Fountains, Hillocks, Dales and Bow'rs,
    With other echo late I taught your Shades
    To answer, and resound far other Song."
    Whom thus afflicted when sad Eve beheld,

827 **they then** *1674*; they *1667*.   839 **concludes** conclusively proves,
and puts an end to, does for ("I will conclude thee, and annihilate
thee," [1612]).   853 **denounc't** threatened.

Desolate where she sat, approaching nigh,
Soft words to his fierce passion she assay'd: 865
But her with stern regard he thus repell'd.

      "Out of my sight, thou Serpent,° that name best
Befits thee with him leagu'd, thyself as false
And hateful; nothing wants, but that thy shape,
Like his, and colour Serpentine may show   870
Thy inward fraud, to warn all Creatures from thee
Henceforth; lest that too heav'nly form, pretended°
To hellish falsehood, snare them. But for thee
I had persisted happy, had not thy pride
And wand'ring vanity, when least was safe,   875
Rejected my forewarning, and disdain'd
Not to be trusted, longing to be seen
Though by the Devil himself, him overweening
To over-reach, but with the Serpent meeting
Fool'd and beguil'd, by him thou, I by thee,   880
To trust thee from my side, imagin'd wise,
Constant, mature, proof against all assaults,
And understood not all was but a show
Rather than solid virtue, all but a Rib
Crooked by nature, bent, as now appears,   885
More to the part siníster° from me drawn,
Well if thrown out, as supernumerary
To my just number found. O why did God,
Creator wise, that peopl'd highest Heav'n
With Spirits Masculine, create at last   890
This novelty on Earth, this fair defect
Of Nature, and not fill the World at once
With Men as Angels without Feminine,
Or find some other way to generate
Mankind? this mischief had not then befall'n,   895
And more that shall befall, innumerable
Disturbances on Earth through Female snares,
And strait conjunction° with this Sex: for either
He never shall find out fit Mate, but such
As some misfortune brings him, or mistake,   900

---

867 **Serpent** The name Eve was thought to be cognate with the Hebrew for serpent. 872 **pretended** extended as a screen. 886 **siníster** left side, with evil associations. 898 **conjunction** including union in marriage, and sexual union.

Or whom he wishes most shall seldom gain
Through her perverseness, but shall see her gain'd
By a far worse, or if she love, withheld
By Parents, or his happiest choice too late
905 Shall meet, already linkt and Wedlock-bound
To a fell Adversary, his hate or shame:
Which infinite calamity shall cause
To Human life, and household peace confound."
      He added not, and from her turn'd, but Eve
910 Not so repulst, with Tears that ceas'd not flowing,
And tresses all disorder'd, at his feet
Fell humble, and embracing them, besought
His peace, and thus proceeded in her plaint.
      "Forsake me not thus, Adam, witness Heav'n
915 What love sincere, and reverence in my heart
I bear thee, and unwitting have offended,
Unhappily deceiv'd; thy suppliant
I beg, and clasp thy knees; bereave me not,
Whereon I live, thy gentle looks, thy aid,
920 Thy counsel in this uttermost distress,
My only strength and stay: forlorn of thee,
Whither shall I betake me, where subsist?
While yet we live, scarce one short hour perhaps,
Between us two let there be peace, both joining,
925 As join'd in injuries, one enmity
Against a Foe by doom express assign'd us,
That cruel Serpent: On me exercise not
Thy hatred for this misery befall'n,
On me already lost, mee than thyself
930 More miserable; both have sinn'd, but thou
Against God only, I against God and thee,
And to the place of judgement will return,
There with my cries importune Heaven, that all
The sentence from thy head remov'd may 'light
935 On me, sole cause to thee of all this woe,
Mee mee only just object of his ire."
      She ended weeping, and her lowly plight,
Immovable till peace obtain'd from fault
Acknowledg'd and deplor'd, in Adam wrought
940 Commiseration; soon his heart relented
Towards her, his life so late and sole delight,
Now at his feet submissive in distress,

Creature so fair his reconcilement seeking,
His counsel whom she had displeas'd, his aid;
As one disarm'd, his anger all he lost,   945
And thus with peaceful words uprais'd her soon.
        "Unwary, and too desirous, as before,
So now of what thou know'st not, who desir'st
The punishment all on thyself; alas,
Bear thine own first, ill able to sustain   950
His full wrath whose thou feel'st as yet least part,
And my displeasure bear'st so ill. If Prayers
Could alter high Decrees, I to that place
Would speed before thee, and be louder heard,
That on my head all might be visited,   955
Thy frailty and infirmer Sex forgiv'n,
To me committed and by me expos'd.
But rise, let us no more contend, nor blame
Each other, blam'd enough elsewhere, but strive
In offices of Love, how we may light'n   960
Each other's burden in our share of woe;
Since this day's Death denounc't, if aught I see,
Will prove no sudden, but a slow-pac't evil,
A long day's dying to augment our pain,
And to our Seed (O hapless Seed!) deriv'd."   965
        To whom thus Eve, recovering heart, repli'd.
"Adam, by sad experiment I know
How little weight my words with thee can find,
Found so erroneous, thence by just event
Found so unfortunate; nevertheless,   970
Restor'd by thee, vile as I am, to place
Of new acceptance, hopeful to regain
Thy Love, the sole contentment of my heart,
Living or dying from thee I will not hide
What thoughts in my unquiet breast are ris'n,   975
Tending to some relief° of our extremes,°
Or end, though sharp and sad, yet tolerable,
As in our evils, and of easier choice.
If care of our descent° perplex us most,
Which must be born to certain woe, devour'd   980
By Death at last, and miserable it is
To be to others cause of misery,

976 **relief** from Latin *relevare*, raise again (following "ris'n"). 976
extremes extreme hardships. 979 **descent** descendants.

Our own begotten, and of our Loins to bring
Into this cursed World a woeful Race,
985 That after wretched Life must be at last
Food for so foul a Monster, in thy power
It lies, yet ere Conception to prevent
The Race unblest, to being yet unbegot.
Childless thou art, Childless remaine: So Death
990 Shall be deceiv'd° his glut, and with us two
Be forc'd° to satisfy his Rav'nous Maw.
But if thou judge it hard and difficult,
Conversing, looking, loving, to abstain
From Love's due Rites, Nuptial embraces sweet,
995 And with desire to languish without hope,
Before the present° object languishing
With like desire, which would be misery
And torment less than none of what we dread,
Then both ourselves and Seed at once to free
1000 From what we fear for both, let us make short,°
Let us seek Death, or hee not found, supply
With our own hands his Office on ourselves;
Why stand we longer shivering under fears,
That show no end but Death, and have the power,
1005 Of many ways to die the shortest choosing,
Destruction with destruction to destroy."
           She ended here, or vehement despair
Broke off the rest; so much of Death her thoughts
Had entertain'd, as dy'd her Cheeks with pale.
1010 But Adam with such counsel nothing sway'd,
To better hopes his more attentive mind
Labouring had rais'd, and thus to Eve repli'd.
           "Eve, thy contempt of life and pleasure seems
To argue in thee something more sublime
1015 And excellent than what thy mind contemns;
But self-destruction therefore sought, refutes
That excellence thought in thee, and implies,
Not thy contempt, but anguish and regret
For loss of life and pleasure overlov'd.
1020 Or if thou covet death, as utmost end

---

990 **deceiv'd** cheated out of.   991 **forc'd** "Glut" and "Maw" suggest
a grim pun in "forc'd," to clash with "stuffed full," as in "forced
meats."   996 **present** in your presence.   1000 **make short** lose no
time.

Of misery, so thinking to evade
The penalty pronounc't, doubt not but God
Hath wiselier arm'd his vengeful ire than so
To be forestall'd; much more I fear lest Death
So snatcht will not exempt us from the pain   1025
We are by doom to pay; rather such acts
Of cóntumácy° will provoke the highest
To make death in us live: Then let us seek
Some safer resolution, which methinks
I have in view, calling to mind with heed   1030
Part of our Sentence, that thy Seed shall bruise
The Serpent's head; piteous amends, unless
Be meant, whom I conjecture, our grand Foe
Satan, who in the Serpent hath contriv'd
Against us this deceit: to crush his head   1035
Would be revenge indeed; which will be lost
By death brought on ourselves, or childless days
Resolv'd, as thou proposest; so our Foe
Shall 'scape his punishment ordain'd, and wee
Instead shall double ours upon our heads.   1040
No more be mention'd then of violence
Against ourselves, and wilful barrenness,
That cuts us off from hope, and savours only
Rancour and pride, impatience and despite,
Reluctance against God and his just yoke   1045
Laid on our Necks. Remember with what mild
And gracious temper he both heard and judg'd
Without wrath or reviling; wee expected
Immediate dissolution, which we thought
Was meant by Death that day, when lo, to thee   1050
Pains only in Child-bearing were foretold,
And bringing forth, soon recompens't with joy,
Fruit of thy Womb: On mee the Curse aslope
Glanc'd on the ground, with labour I must earn
My bread; what harm? Idleness had been worse;   1055
My labour will sustain me; and lest Cold
Or Heat should injure us, his timely care
Hath unbesought provided, and his hands
Cloth'd us unworthy, pitying while he judg'd;
How much more, if we pray him, will his ear   1060

1027 cóntumácy resistance to authority, with a specifically legal application.

Be open, and his heart to pity incline,
And teach us further by what means to shun
Th'inclement Seasons, Rain, Ice, Hail and Snow,
Which now the Sky with various Face begins
1065 To show us in this Mountain, while the Winds
Blow moist and keen, shattering the graceful locks
Of these fair spreading Trees; which bids us seek
Some better shroud,° some better warmth to cherish
Our Limbs benumb'd, ere this diurnal Star
1070 Leave cold the Night, how we his gather'd beams
Reflected, may with matter sere° foment,°
Or by collision of two bodies grind
The Air attrite° to Fire, as late the Clouds
Justling or pusht with Winds rude in their shock
Tine° the slant Lightning, whose thwart flame driv'n
1075   down
Kindles the gummy bark of Fir or Pine,
And sends a comfortable heat from far,
Which might supply the Sun: such Fire to use,
And what may else be remedy or cure
1080 To evils which our own misdeeds have wrought,
Hee will instruct us praying, and of Grace
Beseeching him, so as we need not fear
To pass commodiously this life, sustain'd
By him with many comforts, till we end
1085 In dust, our final rest and native home.
What better can we do, than to the place
Repairing where he judg'd us, prostrate fall
Before him reverent, and there confess
Humbly our faults, and pardon beg, with tears
1090 Watering the ground, and with our sighs the Air
Frequenting,° sent from hearts contrite, in sign
Of sorrow unfeign'd, and humiliation meek.
Undoubtedly he will relent and turn
From his displeasure; in whose look serene,
1095 When angry most he seem'd and most severe,
What else but favour, grace, and mercy shone?"
          So spake our Father penitent, nor Eve
Felt less remorse: they forthwith to the place

1068 **shroud** shelter.   1071 **sere** dry.   **foment** stimulate to heat.
1073 **attrite** by friction.   1075 **Tine** ignite.   1091 **Frequenting**
thronging.

Repairing where he judg'd them prostrate fell
Before him reverent, and both confess'd   *1100*
Humbly their faults, and pardon begg'd, with tears
Watering the ground, and with their sighs the Air
Frequenting, sent from hearts contrite, in sign
Of sorrow unfeign'd, and humiliation meek.

BOOK XI

THE ARGUMENT

The Son of God presents to his Father the Prayers of our
first Parents now repenting, and intercedes for them: God
accepts them, but declares that they must no longer abide
in Paradise; sends Michael with a Band of Cherubim to
dispossess them; but first to reveal to Adam future things:
Michael's coming down. Adam shows to Eve certain signs;
he discerns Michael's approach, goes out to meet him:
the Angel denounces their departure. Eve's Lamentation.
Adam pleads, but submits: The Angel leads him up to
a high Hill, sets before him in vision what shall happen
till the Flood.

Thus they in lowliest plight repentant stood
Praying, for from the Mercy-seat above
Prevenient° Grace descending had remov'd
The stony from their hearts, and made new flesh
5 Regenerate grow instead, that sighs now breath'd
Unutterable, which the Spirit of prayer
Inspir'd, and wing'd for Heav'n with speedier flight
Than loudest Oratory: yet their port
Not of mean suitors, nor important less
10 Seem'd their Petition, than when th'ancient Pair
In Fables old, less ancient yet than these,

3 **Prevenient** a theological term for God's grace, preceding repentance
and predisposing the heart.

Deucalion and chaste Pyrrha° to restore
The Race of Mankind drown'd, before the Shrine
Of Themis° stood devout. To Heav'n their prayers
Flew up, nor miss'd the way, by envious winds   15
Blown vagabond or frustrate: in they pass'd
Dimensionless° through Heav'nly doors; then clad
With incense, where the Golden Altar fum'd,
By their great Intercessor, came in sight
Before the Father's Throne: Them the glad Son   20
Presenting, thus to intercede began.
          "See Father, what first fruits on Earth are
                sprung
From thy implanted Grace in Man, these Sighs
And Prayers, which in this Golden Censer, mixt
With Incense, I thy Priest before thee bring,   25
Fruits of more pleasing savour from thy seed
Sown with contrition in his heart, than those
Which his own hand manuring° all the Trees
Of Paradise could have produc't, ere fall'n
From innocence. Now therefore bend thine ear   30
To supplication, hear his sighs though mute;
Unskilful with what words to pray, let mee
Interpret for him, mee his Advocate
And propitiation, all his works on mee
Good or not good engraft, my Merit those   35
Shall perfect, and for these my Death shall pay.
Accept me, and in mee from these receive
The smell of peace toward Mankind, let him live
Before thee reconcil'd, at least his days
Number'd, though sad, till Death, his doom (which I   40
To mitigate thus plead, not to reverse)
To better life shall yield him, where with mee
All my redeem'd may dwell in joy and bliss,
Made one with me as I with thee am one."
          To whom the Father, without Cloud, serene.   45
"All thy request for Man, accepted Son,
Obtain, all thy request was my Decree:

---

12 **Deucalion . . . Pyrrha** classical counterparts to Noah and his wife.
14 **Themis** goddess of justice. 17 **Dimensionless** immaterial. 28
manuring see IV 628.

But longer in that Paradise to dwell,
The Law I gave to Nature him forbids:
50 Those pure immortal Elements that know
No gross, no unharmonious mixture foul,
Eject him tainted now, and purge him off
As a distemper, gross to air as gross,
And mortal food, as may dispose him best
55 For dissolution° wrought by Sin, that first
Distemper'd all things, and of incorrupt
Corrupted. I at first with two fair gifts
Created him endow'd, with Happiness
And Immortality: that fondly lost,
60 This other serv'd but to eternize woe;
Till I provided Death; so Death becomes
His final remedy, and after Life
Tri'd in sharp tribulation, and refin'd
By Faith and faithful works, to second Life,
65 Wak't in the renovation of the just,
Resigns him up with Heav'n and Earth renew'd.
But let us call to Synod all the Blest
Through Heav'n's wide bounds; from them I will not
    hide
My judgements, how with Mankind I proceed,
70 As how with peccant° Angels late they saw;
And in their state, though firm, stood more confirm'd."
        He ended, and the Son gave signal high
To the bright Minister that watch'd, hee blew
His Trumpet, heard in Oreb since perhaps
75 When God descended, and perhaps once more
To sound at general Doom. Th'Angelic blast
Fill'd all the Regions: from their blissful Bow'rs
Of Amaranthine Shade, Fountain or Spring,
By the waters of Life, where'er they sat
80 In fellowships of joy: the Sons of Light
Hasted, resorting to the Summons high,
And took their Seats; till from his Throne supreme
Th'Almighty thus pronounc'd his sovran Will.
        "O Sons, like one of us Man is become
85 To know both Good and Evil, since his taste

---

55 **dissolution** dissoluteness and eventual death.   70 **peccant** sinning.

Of that defended° Fruit; but let him boast
His knowledge of Good lost, and Evil got,
Happier, had it suffic'd him to have known
Good by itself, and Evil not at all.
He sorrows now, repents, and prays contríte,   90
My motions° in him, longer than they move,
His heart I know, how variable and vain
Self-left. Lest therefore his now bolder hand
Reach also of the Tree of Life, and eat,
And live for ever, dream at least to live   95
For ever, to remove him I decree,
And send him from the Garden forth to Till
The Ground whence he was taken, fitter soil.
          Michael, this my behest have thou in charge,
Take to thee from among the Cherubim   100
Thy choice of flaming Warriors, lest the Fiend
Or in behalf of° Man, or to invade
Vacant possession some new trouble raise:
Haste thee, and from the Paradise of God
Without remorse° drive out the sinful Pair,   105
From hallow'd ground th'unholy, and denounce°
To them and to their Progeny from thence
Perpetual banishment. Yet lest they faint
At the sad Sentence rigorously urg'd,
For I behold them soft'n'd and with tears   110
Bewailing their excess,° all terror hide.
If patiently thy bidding they obey,
Dismiss them not disconsolate; reveal
To Adam what shall come in future days,
As I shall thee enlighten, intermix   115
My Cov'nant in the Woman's seed renew'd;
So send them forth, though sorrowing, yet in peace:
And on the East side of the Garden place,
Where entrance up from Eden easiest climbs,
Cherubic watch, and of a Sword the flame   120
Wide waving, all approach far off to fright,
And guard all passage to the Tree of Life:
Lest Paradise a réceptácle prove

---

86 **defended** forbidden.   91 **motions** workings of God in the soul
(theological).   102 **in behalf of** possibly "with regard to," possibly
"claiming to act in the name of" (see line 125).   105 **remorse** com-
punction.   106 **denounce** formally announce.   111 **excess** violation.

To Spirits foul, and all my Trees their prey,
125 With whose stol'n Fruit Man once more to delude."
          He ceas'd; and th'Archangelic Power prepar'd
For swift descent, with him the Cohort bright
Of watchful Cherubim; four faces each
Had, like a double Janus,° all their shape
130 Spangl'd with eyes more numerous than those
Or Argus,° and more wakeful than to drowze,
Charm'd with Arcadian Pipe, the Pastoral Reed
Of Hermes, or his opiate Rod.° Meanwhile
To resalute the World with sacred Light
135 Leucothea° wak'd, and with fresh dews imbalm'd
The Earth, when Adam and first Matron Eve
Had ended now their Orisons, and found,
Strength added from above, new hope to spring
Out of despair, joy, but with fear yet linkt;
140 Which thus to Eve his welcome words renew'd.
          "Eve, easily may Faith admit, that all
The good which we enjoy, from Heav'n descends
But that from us aught should ascend to Heav'n
So prevalent° as to concern the mind
145 Of God high-blest, or to incline his will,
Hard to belief may seem; yet this will Prayer,
Or one short sigh of human breath, up-borne
Ev'n to the Seat of God. For since I sought
By Prayer th'offended Deity to appease,
150 Kneel'd and before him humbl'd all my heart,
Methought I saw him placable and mild,
Bending his ear; persuasion in me grew
That I was heard with favour; peace return'd
Home to my breast, and to my memory
155 His promise, that thy Seed shall bruise our Foe;
Which then not minded in dismay, yet now
Assures me that the bitterness of death
Is past, and we shall live. Whence Hail to thee,
Eve rightly call'd,° Mother of all Mankind,
160 Mother of all things living, since by thee
Man is to live, and all things live for Man."

129 **Janus** Roman god with two faces.   131 **Argus** with his hundred eyes on guard.   133 **Rod** The wand of Hermes (Mercury) put Argus to sleep.   135 **Leucothea** goddess of dawn.   144 **prevalent** strongly prevailing.   159 **rightly call'd** "Eve" was said to mean "Life."

To whom thus Eve with sad demeanour meek.
"Ill worthy I such title should belong
To me transgressor, who for thee ordain'd
A help, became thy snare; to mee reproach   165
Rather belongs, distrust and all dispraise:
But infinite in pardon was my Judge,
That I who first brought Death on all, am grac't
The source of life; next favourable thou,
Who highly thus to entitle me vouchsaf'st,   170
Far other name deserving. But the Field
To labour calls us now with sweat impos'd,
Though after sleepless Night; for see the Morn,
All unconcern'd with our unrest, begins
Her rosy progress smiling; let us forth,   175
I never from thy side henceforth to stray,
Where'er our day's work lies, though now enjoin'd
Laborious, till day droop; while here we dwell,
What can be toilsome in these pleasant Walks?
Here let us live, though in fall'n state, content."   180
        So spake, so wish'd much-humbl'd Eve, but
                Fate
Subscribed not; Nature first gave Signs, imprest
On Bird, Beast, Air, Air suddenly eclips'd
After short blush of Morn; nigh in her sight
The Bird of Jove,° stoopt° from his airy tow'r,   185
Two Birds of gayest plume before him drove:
Down from a Hill the Beast that reigns° in Woods,
First Hunter then, pursu'd a gentle brace,
Goodliest of all the Forest, Hart and Hind;
Direct to th'Eastern Gate was bent their flight.   190
Adam observ'd, and with his Eye the chase
Pursuing, not unmov'd to Eve thus spake.
        "O Eve, some further change awaits us nigh,
Which Heav'n by these mute signs in Nature shows
Forerunners of his purpose, or to warn   195
Us haply too secure° of our discharge
From penalty, because from death releast
Some days; how long, and what till then our life,
Who knows, or more than this, that we are dust,
And thither must return and be no more.   200

185 **Bird of Jove** eagle.   185 **stoopt** plunged.   187 **Beast that reigns**
lion.   196 **secure** confident.

Why else this double object in our sight
Of flight pursu'd in th'Air and o'er the ground
One way the self-same hour? why in the East
Darkness ere Day's mid-course, and Morning light
205 More orient in yon Western Cloud that draws
O'er the blue Firmament a radiant white,
And slow descends, with something heav'nly fraught."
        He err'd not, for by this the heav'nly Bands
Down from a Sky of Jasper 'lighted now
210 In Paradise, and on a Hill made halt,
A glorious Apparition, had not doubt
And carnal fear that day dimm'd Adam's eye.
Not that more glorious, when the Angels met
Jacob in Mahanaim, where he saw
215 The field Pavilion'd with his Guardians bright;
Nor that which on the flaming Mount appear'd
In Dothan, cover'd with a Camp of Fire,
Against the Syrian King, who to surprise
One man,° Assassin-like had levied War,
220 War unproclaim'd. The Princely Hierarch
In their bright stand,° there left his Powers to seize
Possession of the Garden; hee alone,
To find where Adam shelter'd, took his way,
Not unperceiv'd of Adam, who to Eve,
225 While the great Visitant approach'd, thus spake.
        "Eve, now expect great tidings, which perhaps
Of us will soon determine, or impose
New Laws to be observ'd; for I descry
From yonder blazing Cloud that veils the Hill
230 One of the heav'nly Host, and by his Gait
None of the meanest, some great Potentate
Or of the Thrones above, such Majesty
Invests him coming; yet not terrible,
That I should fear, nor sociably mild,
235 As Raphaël, that I should much confide,
But solemn and sublime, whom not to offend,
With reverence I must meet, and thou retire."
He ended; and th'Arch-Angel soon drew nigh,
Not in his shape Celestial, but as Man
240 Clad to meet Man; over his lucid° Arms

219 **One man** Elisha, protected against the Syrians by a miracle.
221 **stand** station (military).   240 **lucid** bright.

A military Vest of purple flow'd
Livelier than Melibœan,° or the grain°
Of Sarra,° worn by Kings and Heroes old
In time of Truce; Iris° had dipt the woof;
His starry Helm unbuckl'd show'd him prime   245
In Manhood where Youth ended; by his side
As in a glistering Zodiac° hung the Sword,
Satan's dire dread, and in his hand the Spear.
Adam bow'd low, hee Kingly from his State
Inclin'd not, but his coming thus declar'd.   250
    "Adam, Heav'n's high behest no Preface needs:
Sufficient that thy Prayers are heard, and Death,
Then due by sentence when thou didst transgress,
Defeated of his seizure many days
Giv'n thee of Grace, wherein thou may'st repent,   255
And one bad act with many deeds well done
May'st cover: well may then thy Lord appeas'd
Redeem thee quite from Death's rapacious claim;
But longer in this Paradise to dwell
Permits not; to remove thee I am come,   260
And send thee from the Garden forth to till
The ground whence thou wast tak'n, fitter Soil."
    He added not, for Adam at the news
Heart-struck with chilling grip of sorrow stood,
That all his senses bound; Eve, who unseen   265
Yet all had heard, with audible lament
Discover'd soon the place of her retire.
    "O unexpected stroke, worse than of Death!
Must I thus leave thee Paradise? thus leave
Thee Native Soil, these happy Walks and Shades,   270
Fit haunt of Gods? where I had hope to spend,
Quiet though sad, the respite° of that day
That must be mortal to us both. O flow'rs,
That never will in other Climate grow,
My early visitation, and my last   275
At Ev'n, which I bred up with tender hand
From the first op'ning bud, and gave ye Names,
Who now shall rear ye to the Sun, or rank

242 **Melibœan** the purple dye from Thessaly. 242 **grain** dye. 243
Sarra Tyre. 244 **Iris** goddess of the rainbow. 247 **Zodiac** the belt of
the constellations. 272 **respite** time granted till the coming.

Your Tribes, and water from th'ambrosial Fount?
280   Thee lastly nuptial Bow'r, by mee adorn'd
With what to sight or smell was sweet; from thee
How shall I part, and whither wander down
Into a lower World, to° this obscure
And wild, how shall we breathe in other Air
285   Less pure, accustom'd to immortal Fruits?"
            Whom thus the Angel interrupted mild.
"Lament not Eve, but patiently resign
What justly thou hast lost; nor set thy heart,
Thus over-fond, on that which is not thine;
290   Thy going is not lonely, with thee goes
Thy Husband, him to follow thou art bound;
Where he abides, think there thy native soil."
            Adam by this from the cold sudden damp
Recovering, and his scatter'd spirits return'd,
295   To Michael thus his humble words address'd.
                "Celestial, whether among the Thrones, or
                      nam'd
Of them the Highest, for such of shape may seem
Prince above Princes, gently hast thou told
Thy message, which might else in telling wound,
300   And in performing end us; what besides
Of sorrow and dejection and despair
Our frailty can sustain, thy tidings bring,
Departure from this happy place, our sweet
Recess,° and only consolation left
305   Familiar to our eyes, all places else
Inhospitable appear and desolate,
Nor knowing us nor known: and if by prayer
Incessant I could hope to change the will
Of him who all things can, I would not cease
310   To weary him with my assiduous cries:
But prayer against his absolute Decree
No more avails than breath against the wind,
Blown stifling back on him that breathes it forth:
Therefore to his great bidding I submit.
315   This most afflicts me, that departing hence,
As from his face I shall be hid, depriv'd
His blessed count'nance; here I could frequent,
With worship, place by place where he vouchsaf'd

283 to compared to.   304 Recess place of retirement.

Presence Divine, and to my Sons relate;
On this Mount he appear'd, under this Tree   320
Stood visible, among these Pines his voice
I heard, here with him at this Fountain talk'd:
So many grateful° Altars I would rear
Of grassy Turf, and pile up every Stone
Of lustre from the brook, in memory,   325
Or monument to Ages, and thereon
Offer sweet smelling Gums and Fruits and Flow'rs:
In yonder nether World where shall I seek
His bright appearances, or footstep trace?
For though I fled him angry, yet recall'd   330
To life prolong'd and promis'd Race, I now
Gladly behold though but his utmost skirts
Of glory, and far off his steps adore."
          To whom thus Michael with regard benign.
"Adam, though know'st Heav'n his, and all the Earth,   335
Not this Rock only; his Omnipresence fills
Land, Sea, and Air, and every kind that lives,
Fomented by his virtual° power and warm'd:
All th'Earth he gave thee to possess and rule,
No déspicáble gift; surmise not then   340
His presence to these narrow bounds confin'd
Of Paradise or Eden: this had been
Perhaps thy Capital Seat, from whence had spread
All generations, and had hither come
From all the ends of th'Earth, to celebrate   345
And reverence thee their great Progenitor.
But this preeminence thou hast lost, brought down
To dwell on even ground now with thy Sons:
Yet doubt not but in Valley and in Plain
God is as here, and will be found alike   350
Present, and of his presence many a sign
Still following thee, still compassing thee round
With goodness and paternal Love, his Face
Express, and of his steps the track Divine.
Which that thou may'st believe, and be confirm'd, 355
Ere thou from hence depart, know I am sent
To show thee what shall come in future days
To thee and to thy Offspring; good with bad

323 grateful pleasing to God and expressing gratitude.   338 virtual inherently life-giving.

Expect to hear, supernal Grace contending
360 With sinfulness of Men; thereby to learn
True patience, and to temper joy with fear
And pious sorrow, equally inur'd
By moderation either state to bear,
Prosperous or adverse: so shalt thou lead
365 Safest thy life, and best prepar'd endure
Thy mortal passage when it comes. Ascend
This Hill; let Eve (for I have drencht her eyes)
Here sleep below while thou to foresight wak'st,
As once thou slep'st, while Shee to life was form'd."
370   To whom thus Adam gratefully repli'd.
"Ascend, I follow thee, safe Guide, the path
Thou lead'st me, and to the hand of Heav'n submit,
However chast'ning, to the evil turn
My obvious° breast, arming to overcome
375 By suffering, and earn rest from labour won,
If so I may attain." So both ascend
In the Visions of God: It was a Hill
Of Paradise the highest, from whose top
The Hemisphere of Earth in clearest Ken
380 Stretcht out to amplest reach of prospect lay.
Not higher that Hill nor wider looking round,
Whereon for different cause the Tempter set
Our second Adam in the Wilderness,
To show him all Earth's Kingdoms and their Glory.
385 His Eye might there command wherever stood
City of old or modern Fame, the Seat
Of mightiest Empire, from the destin'd Walls
Of Cambalu, seat of Cathaian Khan
And Samarkand by Oxus,° Temir's° Throne,
390 To Paquin° of Sinæan° Kings, and thence
To Agra and Lahor of great Mogúl
Down to the golden Chersonese,° or where
The Persian in Ecbatan sat, or since
In Hispahan, or where the Russian Czar
395 In Moscow, or the Sultan in Bizance,°
Turkéstan-born; nor could his eye not ken

---

374 **obvious** exposed.   389 **Oxus** Asian river.   389 **Temir** the Tartar
ruler Timur.   390 **Paquin** Peking.   390 **Sinæan** Chinese.   392 **Cherso-
nese** East Indies.   395 **Bizance** Byzantium.

Th'Empire of Negus° to his utmost Port
Ercoco and the less Maritine Kings
Mombaza, and Quiloa, and Melind,°
And Sofala thought° Ophir, to the Realm   400
Of Congo, and Angola farthest South;
Or thence from Niger Flood to Atlas Mount
The Kingdoms of Almansor,° Fez and Sus,
Morocco and Algiers, and Tremisen;
On Europe thence, and where Rome was to sway   405
The World: in Spirit perhaps he also saw
Rich Mexico the seat of Motezume,°
And Cusco° in Peru, the richer seat
Of Atabalipa,° and yet unspoil'd°
Guiana, whose great City Geryon's Sons°   410
Call El Dorado: but to nobler sights
Michael from Adam's eyes the Film remov'd
Which that false Fruit that promis'd clearer sight
Had bred; then purg'd with Euphrasy and Rue
The visual Nerve, for he had much to see;   415
And from the Well of Life three drops instill'd.
So deep the power of these Ingredients pierc'd,
Ev'n to the inmost seat of mental sight,
That Adam now enforc't to close his eyes,
Sunk down and all his Spirits became intranst: 420
But him the gentle Angel by the hand
Soon rais'd, and his attention thus recall'd.

　　　"Adam, now ope thine eyes, and first behold
Th'effects which thy original crime hath wrought
In some to spring from thee, who never touch'd   425
Th'excepted Tree,° nor with the Snake conspir'd,
Nor sinn'd thy sin, yet from that sin derive
Corruption to bring forth more violent deeds."

　　　His eyes he op'n'd, and beheld a field,
Part arable and tilth, whereon were Sheaves   430
New reapt, the other part sheep-walks and folds;
I'th' midst an Altar as the Land-mark stood

397 **Negus** title of Abyssinian kings.　399 **Mombaza . . . Melind** in
East Africa.　400 **thought** thought to be the legendary region.　403
Almansor Muslim ruler.　407 **Motezume** Montezuma, Aztec
ruler.　408 **Cusco** Inca capital.　409 **Atabalipa** Inca ruler. **un-
spoil'd** unplundered.　410 **Geryon's Sons** the Spaniards.　426 **Th'ex-
cepted Tree** a traditional phrase for the Tree of Knowledge ("ex-
cluded, forbidden").

Rustic, of grassy sward; thither anon
A sweaty Reaper from his Tillage brought
435 First-Fruits, the green Ear, and the yellow Sheaf,
Uncull'd, as came to hand; a Shepherd next
More meek came with the Firstlings of his Flock
Choicest and best; then sacrificing, laid
The Inwards and their Fat, with Incense strew'd,
440 On the cleft Wood, and all due Rites perform'd.
His Off'ring soon propitious Fire from Heav'n
Consum'd with nimble glance, and grateful steam;
The other's not, for his was not sincere;°
Whereat hee inly rag'd, and as they talk'd,
445 Smote him into the Midriff with a stone
That beat out life; he fell, and deadly pale
Groan'd out his Soul with gushing blood effus'd.
Much at that sight was Adam in his heart
Dismay'd, and thus in haste to th'Angel cri'd.
450   "O Teacher, some great mischief hath befall'n
To that meek man, who well had sacrific'd;
Is Piety thus and pure Devotion paid?"
        T'whom Michael thus, hee also mov'd, repli'd.
"These two are Brethren, Adam, and to come
455 Out of thy loins; th'unjust the just hath slain,
For envy that his Brother's Offering found
From Heav'n acceptance; but the bloody Fact°
Will be aveng'd, and th'other's Faith approv'd
Lose no reward, though here thou see him die,
460 Rolling in dust and gore." To which our Sire.
        "Alas, both for the deed and for the cause!
But have I now seen Death? Is this the way
I must return to native dust? O sight
Of terror, foul and ugly to behold,
465 Horrid to think, how horrible to feel!"
        To whom thus Michaël. "Death thou hast seen
In his first shape on man; but many shapes
Of Death, and many are the ways that lead
To his grim Cave, all dismal; yet to sense
470 More terrible at th'entrance than within.
Some, as thou saw'st, by violent stroke shall die,

443 **sincere** including the literal "pure, uncontaminated."   457 **Fact**
deed.

By Fire, Flood, Famine, by Intemperance more
In Meats and Drinks, which on the Earth shall bring
Diseases dire, of which a monstrous crew
Before thee shall appear; that thou may'st know   475
What misery th'inabstinence of Eve
Shall bring on men." Immediately a place
Before his eyes appear'd, sad, noisome, dark,
A Lazar-house it seem'd, wherein were laid
Numbers of all diseas'd, all maladies   480
Of ghastly Spasm, or racking torture, qualms°
Of heart-sick Agony, all feverous kinds,
Convulsions, Epilepsies, fierce Catarrhs,
Intestine Stone and Ulcer, Colic pangs,
Demoniac Frenzy, moping Melancholy   485
And Moon-struck madness, pining Atrophy,
Marasmus,° and wide-wasting Pestilence,°
Dropsies, and Asthmas, and Joint-racking Rheums.
Dire was the tossing, deep the groans, despair
Tended the sick busiest from Couch to Couch;   490
And over them triumphant Death his Dart
Shook, but delay'd to strike, though oft invok't
With vows, as their chief good, and final hope.
Sight so deform what heart of Rock could long
Dry-ey'd behold? Adam could not, but wept,   495
Though not of Woman born; compassion quell'd
His best of Man, and gave him up to tears
A space, till firmer thoughts restrain'd excess,
And scarce recovering words his plaint renew'd.

         "O miserable Mankind, to what fall   500
Degraded, to what wretched state reserv'd!
Better end here unborn. Why is life giv'n
To be thus wrested from us? rather why
Obtruded on us thus? who if we knew
What we receive, would either not accept   505
Life offer'd, or soon beg to lay it down,
Glad to be so dismisst in peace. Can thus
Th'Image of God in man created once
So goodly and erect, though faulty since,
To such unsightly sufferings be debas't   510

481 qualms plagues. 487 Marasmus consumption. 485–87 Demoniac
. . . Pestilence Lines added 1674.

Under inhuman pains? Why should not Man,
Retaining still Divine similitude
In part, from such deformities be free,
And for his Maker's Image sake exempt?"
         "Their Maker's Image," answer'd Michael,
515   "then
Forsook them, when themselves they vilifi'd
To serve ungovern'd appetite, and took
His Image whom they serv'd, a brutish vice,
Inductive mainly° to the sin of Eve.
520 Therefore so abject is their punishment,
Disfiguring not God's likeness, but their own,
Or if his likeness, by themselves defac't
While they pervert pure Nature's healthful rules
To loathsome sickness, worthily, since they
525 God's Image did not reverence in themselves."
         "I yield it just," said Adam, "and submit.
But is there yet no other way, besides
These painful passages, how we may come
To Death, and mix with our connatural dust?"
530   "There is," said Michael, "if thou well observe
The rule of not too much, by temperance taught
In what thou eat'st and drink'st, seeking from thence
Due nourishment, not gluttonous delight,
Till many years over thy head return:
535 So may'st thou live, till like ripe Fruit thou drop
Into thy Mother's lap, or be with ease
Gather'd, not harshly pluckt, for death mature:
This is old age; but then thou must outlive
Thy youth, thy strength, thy beauty, which will change
540 To wither'd weak and gray; thy Senses then
Obtuse, all taste of pleasure must forgo,
To what thou hast, and for the Air of youth
Hopeful and cheerful, in thy blood will reign
A melancholy damp of cold and dry
545 To weigh thy spirits down, and last consume
The Balm of Life." To whom our Ancestor.
         "Henceforth I fly not Death, nor would pro-
         long
Life much, bent rather how I may be quit
Fairest and easiest of this cumbrous charge,
550 Which I must keep till my appointed day

519 **Inductive mainly** powerful as inducement.

Of rend'ring up, and patiently attend
My dissolution." Michaël repli'd.°
       "Nor love thy Life, nor hate; but what thou
         liv'st
Live well, how long or short permit to Heav'n:
And now prepare thee for another sight."   555
       He look'd and saw a spacious Plain, whereon
Were Tents of various hue; by some were herds
Of Cattle grazing: others, whence the sound
Of Instruments that made melodious chime
Was heard, of Harp and Organ; and who° mov'd   560
Their stops and chords was seen: his volant° touch
Instínct° through all proportions low and high
Fled and pursu'd transverse the resonant fugue.°
In other part stood one° who at the Forge
Labouring, two massy clods of Iron and Brass   565
Had melted (whether found where casual° fire
Had wasted woods on Mountain or in Vale,
Down to the veins of Earth, thence gliding hot
To some Cave's mouth, or whether washt by stream
From underground) the liquid Ore he drain'd   570
Into fit moulds prepar'd; from which he form'd
First his own Tools; then, what might else be wrought
Fusile° or grav'n in metal. After these,
But on the hither side a different sort
From the high neighbouring Hills, which was their
     Seat,   575
Down to the Plain descended: by their guise
Just men they seem'd, and all their study bent
To worship God aright, and know his works
Not hid, nor those things last which might preserve
Freedom and Peace to men: they on the Plain   580
Long had not walkt, when from the Tents behold
A Bevy of fair Women, richly gay
In Gems and wanton dress; to the Harp they sung
Soft amorous Ditties, and in dance came on:
The Men though grave, ey'd them, and let their eyes 585
Rove without rein, till in the amorous Net

551–52 *1674*; Of rend'ring up." Michael to him replied. *1667.* 560
who Jubal (GENESIS 4:21).   561 **volant** flying.   562 **Instínct** skill-
fully impelled.   563 **fugue** from Latin *fuga,* flight.   564 **one** Tubal
Cain.   566 **casual** accidental.   573 **Fusile** by melting or casting.

Fast caught, they lik'd, and each his liking chose;
And now of love they treat till th'Ev'ning Star°
Love's Harbinger appear'd; then all in heat
590 They light the Nuptial Torch, and bid invoke
Hymen, then first to marriage Rites invok't;
With Feast and Music all the Tents resound.
Such happy interview and fair event
Of love and youth not lost, Songs, Garlands, Flow'rs,
595 And charming Symphonies attach'd° the heart
Of Adam, soon inclin'd to admit delight,
The bent of Nature; which he thus express'd.
        "True opener of mine eyes, prime Angel blest,
Much better seems this Vision, and more hope
600 Of peaceful days portends, than those two past;
Those were of hate and death, or pain much worse,
Here Nature seems fulfill'd in all her ends."
        To whom thus Michael. "Judge not what is
            best
By pleasure, though to Nature seeming meet,
605 Created, as thou art, to nobler end
Holy and pure, conformity divine.
Those Tents thou saw'st so pleasant, were the Tents
Of wickedness, wherein shall dwell his Race
Who slew his Brother; studious they appear
610 Of Arts that polish Life, Inventors rare,
Unmindful of their Maker, though his Spirit
Taught them, but they his gifts acknowledg'd none.
Yet they a beauteous offspring shall beget;
For that fair female Troop thou saw'st, that seem'd
615 Of Goddesses, so blithe, so smooth, so gay,
Yet empty of all good wherein consists
Woman's domestic honour and chief praise;
Bred only and completed to the taste
Of lustful appetence, to sing, to dance,
620 To dress, and troll the Tongue, and roll the Eye.
To these that sober Race of Men, whose lives
Religious titl'd them the Sons of God,
Shall yield up all their virtue, all their fame
Ignobly, to the trains and to the smiles
625 Of these fair Atheists, and now swim in joy,

588 **Ev'ning Star** Venus.   595 **attach'd** laid hold of.

(Erelong to swim at large) and laugh; for which
The world erelong a world of tears must weep."
    To whom thus Adam of short joy bereft.
"O pity and shame, that they who to live well
Enter'd so fair, should turn aside to tread   630
Paths indirect, or in the mid-way faint!
But still I see the tenor of Man's woe
Holds on the same, from Woman to begin."
    "From Man's effeminate° slackness it begins,"
Said th'Angel, "who should better hold his place   635
By wisdom, and superior gifts receiv'd.
But now prepare thee for another Scene."
    He look'd and saw wide Territory spread
Before him, Towns, and rural works between,
Cities of Men with lofty Gates and Tow'rs,   640
Concourse in Arms, fierce Faces threat'ning War,
Giants of mighty Bone, and bold emprise;°
Part wield their Arms, part curb the foaming Steed,
Single or in Array of Battle rang'd
Both Horse and Foot, nor idly must'ring stood;   645
One way a Band select from forage drives
A herd of Beeves, fair Oxen and fair Kine
From a fat Meadow ground; or fleecy Flock,
Ewes and their bleating Lambs over the Plain,
Their Booty; scarce with Life the Shepherds fly,   650
But call in aid, which makes° a bloody Fray;
With cruel Tournament the Squadrons join;
Where Cattle pastur'd late, now scatter'd lies
With Carcasses and Arms th'ensanguin'd Field
Deserted: Others to a City strong   655
Lay Siege, encampt; by Battery, Scale, and Mine,
Assaulting; others from the Wall defend
With Dart and Jav'lin, Stones and sulphurous Fire;
On each hand slaughter and gigantic° deeds.
In other part the scepter'd Heralds call   660
To Council in the City Gates: anon
Grey-headed men and grave, with Warriors mixt,
Assemble, and Harangues are heard, but soon
In factious opposition, till at last

634 **effeminate** unmanly, with suggestion of "dominated by women."
642 **emprise** martial enterprise.   651 **makes** *1674*; tacks *1667.*   659
gigantic giant-like.

665 Of middle Age one° rising, eminent
In wise deport, spake much of Right and Wrong,
Of Justice, of Religion, Truth and Peace,
And Judgement from above: him old and young
Exploded,° and had seiz'd with violent hands,

670 Had not a Cloud descending snatch'd him thence
Unseen amid the throng: so violence
Proceeded, and Oppression, and Sword-Law
Through all the Plain, and refuge none was found.
Adam was all in tears, and to his guide

675 Lamenting turn'd full sad; "O what are these,
Death's Ministers, not Men, who thus deal Death
Inhumanly to men, and multiply
Ten-thousand-fold the sin of him who slew
His Brother; for of whom such massacre

680 Make they but of their Brethren, men of men?
But who was that Just Man, whom had not Heav'n
Rescu'd, had in his Righteousness been lost?"
          To whom thus Michael; "These are the
               product
Of those ill-mated Marriages thou saw'st;

685 Where good with bad were matcht, who of themselves
Abhor to join; and by imprudence mixt,
Produce prodigious Births of body or mind.
Such were these Giants, men of high renown;
For in those days Might only shall be admir'd,

690 And Valour and Heroic Virtue call'd;
To overcome in Battle, and subdue
Nations, and bring home spoils with infinite
Man-slaughter, shall be held the highest pitch
Of human Glory, and for Glory done

695 Of triumph, to be styl'd great Conquerors,
Patrons of Mankind, Gods, and Sons of Gods,
Destroyers rightlier call'd and Plagues of men.
Thus Fame shall be achiev'd, renown on Earth,
And what most merits fame in silence hid.

700 But hee the seventh from thee, whom thou beheld'st
The only righteous in a World perverse,
And therefore hated, therefore so beset
With Foes for daring single to be just,

665 **Of ... one** Enoch was very aged, but not for a prophet (GENESIS 5:21–4).   669 **Exploded** hooted at.

And utter odious Truth, that God would come
To judge them with his Saints: Him the most High   705
Rapt in a balmy Cloud with winged Steeds
Did, as thou saw'st, receive, to walk with God
High in Salvation and the Climes of bliss,
Exempt from Death; to show thee what reward
Awaits the good, the rest what punishment;   710
Which now direct thine eyes and soon behold."
      He look'd, and saw the face of things quite
      chang'd;
The brazen Throat of War had ceast to roar,
All now was turn'd to jollity and game,
To luxury° and riot,° feast and dance,   715
Marrying or prostituting, as befell,
Rape or Adultery, where passing fair
Allur'd them; thence from Cups to civil Broils.
At length a Reverend Sire among them came,
And of their doings great dislike declar'd,   720
And testifi'd against their ways; hee oft
Frequented their Assemblies, whereso met,
Triumphs or Festivals, and to them preach'd
Conversion and Repentance, as to Souls
In prison under Judgements imminent;   725
But all in vain: which when he saw, he ceas'd
Contending, and remov'd his Tents far off;
Then from the Mountain hewing Timber tall,
Began to build a Vessel of huge bulk,
Measur'd by Cubit, length, and breadth, and heighth, 730
Smear'd round with Pitch, and in the side a door
Contriv'd, and of provisions laid in large
For Man and Beast: when lo a wonder strange!
Of every Beast, and Bird, and Insect small
Came sevens, and pairs, and enter'd in, as taught   735
Their order: last the Sire, and his three Sons
With their four Wives; and God made fast the door.
Meanwhile the Southwind rose, and with black wings
Wide hovering, all the Clouds together drove
From under Heav'n; the Hills to their supply   740
Vapour, and Exhalation dusk and moist,
Sent up amain; and now the thick'n'd Sky
Like a dark Ceiling stood; down rush'd the Rain

715 luxury lust. riot riotousness.

Impetuous, and continu'd till the Earth
745 No more was seen; the floating Vessel swum
Uplifted; and secure with beaked prow
Rode tilting o'er the Waves, all dwellings else
Flood overwhelm'd, and them with all their pomp
Deep under water roll'd; Sea cover'd Sea,
750 Sea without shore; and in their Palaces
Where luxury late reign'd, Sea-monsters whelp'd
And stabl'd; of Mankind, so numerous late,
All left, in one small bottom swum embark't.
How didst thou grieve then, Adam, to behold
755 The end of all thy Offspring, end so sad,
Depopulation; thee another Flood,
Of tears and sorrow a Flood thee also drown'd,
And sunk thee as thy Sons; till gently rear'd
By th'Angel, on thy feet thou stood'st at last,
760 Though comfortless, as when a Father mourns
His Children, all in view destroy'd at once;
And scarce to th'Angel utter'dst thus thy plaint.
        "O Visions ill foreseen! better had I
Liv'd ignorant of future, so had borne
765 My part of evil only, each day's lot
Enough to bear; those now, that were dispenst
The burd'n of many Ages, on me 'light
At once, by my foreknowledge gaining Birth
Abortive, to torment me ere their being,
770 With thought that they must be. Let no man seek
Henceforth to be foretold what shall befall
Him or his Children, evil he may be sure,
Which neither his foreknowing can prevent,
And hee the future evil shall no less
775 In apprehension than in substance feel
Grievous to bear: but that care now is past,
Man is not whom to warn: those few escap't
Famine and anguish will at last consume
Wand'ring that wat'ry Desert: I had hope
780 When violence was ceas't, and War on Earth,
All would have then gone well, peace would have
    crown'd
With length of happy days the race of man;
But I was far deceiv'd; for now I see
Peace to corrupt no less than War to waste.

How comes it thus? unfold, Celestial Guide,   785
And whether here the Race of man will end."
To whom thus Michael. "Those whom last thou saw'st
In triumph and luxurious wealth, are they
First seen in acts of prowess eminent
And great exploits, but of true virtue void;   790
Who having spilt much blood, and done much waste
Subduing Nations, and achiev'd thereby
Fame in the World, high titles, and rich prey,
Shall change their course to pleasure, ease, and sloth,
Surfeit, and lust, till wantonness and pride   795
Raise out of friendship hostile deeds in Peace.
The conquer'd also, and enslav'd by War
Shall with their freedom lost all virtue lose
And fear of God, from whom their piety feign'd
In sharp contést of Battle found no aid   800
Against invaders; therefore cold in zeal
Thenceforth shall practise how to live secure,
Worldly or dissolute, on what their Lords
Shall leave them to enjoy; for th'Earth shall bear
More than enough, that temperance may be tri'd:°   805
So all shall turn degenerate, all deprav'd,
Justice and Temperance, Truth and Faith forgot;
One Man except, the only Son of light
In a dark Age, against example good,
Against allurement, custom, and a World   810
Offended; fearless of reproach and scorn,
Or violence, hee of their wicked ways
Shall them admonish, and before them set
The paths of righteousness, how much more safe,
And full of peace, denouncing wrath to come   815
On their impenitence; and shall return
Of them derided, but of God observ'd
The one just Man alive; by his command
Shall build a wondrous Ark, as thou beheld'st,
To save himself and household from amidst   820
A World devote° to universal rack.
No sooner hee with them of Man and Beast
Select for life shall in the Ark be lodg'd,
And shelter'd round, but all the Cataracts
Of Heav'n set open on the Earth shall pour   825

805 tri'd tested.   821 devote doomed.

Rain day and night, all fountains of the Deep
Broke up, shall heave the Ocean to usurp
Beyond all bounds, till inundation rise
Above the highest Hills: then shall this Mount
830   Of Paradise by might of waves be mov'd
Out of his place, push'd by the hornèd° flood,
With all his verdure spoil'd, and Trees adrift
Down the great River to the op'ning Gulf,
And there take root an Island salt and bare,
835   The haunt of Seals and Orcs,° and Sea-mews' clang.
To teach thee that God áttribútes to place
No sanctity, if none be thither brought
By Men who there frequent, or therein dwell.
And now what further shall ensue, behold."
840   He look'd, and saw the Ark hull° on the flood,
Which now abated, for the Clouds were fled,
Driv'n by a keen North-wind, that blowing dry
Wrinkl'd the face of Deluge, as decay'd;
And the clear Sun on his wide wat'ry Glass
845   Gaz'd hot, and of the fresh Wave largely drew,
As after thirst, which made their flowing shrink
From standing lake to tripping ebb, that stole
With soft foot towards the deep, who now had stopt
His Sluices, as the Heav'n his windows shut.
850   The Ark no more now floats, but seems on ground
Fast on the top of some high mountain fixt.
And now the tops of Hills as Rocks appear;
With clamour thence the rapid Currents drive
Towards the retreating Sea their furious tide.
855   Forthwith from out the Ark a Raven flies,
And after him, the surer messenger,
A Dove sent forth once and again to spy
Green Tree or ground whereon his foot may 'light;
The second time returning, in his Bill
860   An Olive leaf he brings, pacific sign:
Anon dry ground appears, and from his Ark
The ancient Sire descends with all his Train;
Then with uplifted hands, and eyes devout,
Grateful to Heav'n, over his head beholds
865   A dewy Cloud, and in the Cloud a Bow

831 **horned** branching.   835 **Orcs** whales.   840 **hull** drift.

Conspicuous with three listed° colours gay,
Betok'ning peace from God, and Cov'nant new.
Whereat the heart of Adam erst so sad
Greatly rejoic'd, and thus his joy broke forth.
      "O thou who° future things canst represent   870
As present, Heav'nly instructor, I revive
At this last sight, assur'd that Man shall live
With all the Creatures, and their seed preserve.
Far less I now lament for one whole World
Of wicked Sons destroy'd, than I rejoice   875
For one Man found so perfect and so just,
That God vouchsafes to raise another World
From him, and all his anger to forget.
But say, what mean those colour'd streaks in Heav'n,
Distended° as the Brow of God appeas'd,   880
Or serve they as a flow'ry verge to bind
The fluid skirts of that same wat'ry Cloud,
Lest it again dissolve and show'r the Earth?"
      To whom th'Archangel. "Dextrously thou
        aim'st;
So willingly doth God remit his Ire,   885
Though late repenting him of Man deprav'd,
Griev'd at his heart, when looking down he saw
The whole Earth fill'd with violence, and all flesh
Corrupting each their way; yet those remov'd,
Such grace shall one just Man find in his sight,   880
That he relents, not to blot out mankind,
And makes a Covenant never to destroy
The Earth again by flood, nor let the Sea
Surpass his bounds, nor Rain to drown the World
With Man therein or Beast; but when he brings   895
Over the Earth a Cloud, will therein set
His triple-colour'd Bow, whereon to look
And call to mind his Cov'nant: Day and Night,
Seed time and Harvest, Heat and hoary Frost
Shall hold their course, till fire purge all things new,   900
Both Heav'n and Earth, wherein the just shall dwell."

866 **listed** striped.   870 **who** *1674*; that *1667*.   880 **Distended** ex-
tended.

BOOK XII

THE ARGUMENT

The Angel Michael continues from the Flood to relate
what shall succeed; then, in the mention of Abraham,
comes by degrees to explain, who that Seed of the Woman
shall be, which was promised Adam and Eve in the Fall;
his Incarnation, Death, Resurrection, and Ascension; the
state of the Church till his second Coming. Adam greatly
satisfied and recomforted by these Relations and Prom-
ises descends the Hill with Michael; wakens Eve, who all
this while had slept, but with gentle dreams compos'd to
quietness of mind and submission. Michael in either hand
leads them out of Paradise, the fiery Sword waving be-
hind them, and the Cherubim taking their Situations to
guard the Place.

    As one who in his journey bates° at Noon,
Though bent on speed, so here th'Arch-Angel paus'd
Betwixt the world destroy'd and world restor'd,
If Adam aught perhaps might interpose;
5 Then with transition sweet new Speech resumes.°
"Thus thou hast seen one World begin and end;
And Man as from a second stock proceed.
Much thou hast yet to see, but I perceive
Thy mortal sight to fail; objects divine
10 Must needs impair and weary human sense:
Henceforth what is to come I will relate,
Thou therefore give due audience, and attend.

1 **bates** stops briefly for rest and refreshment. 1–5 Added *1674*,
when the final Book was divided into two Books.

This second source of Men, while yet but few,
And while the dread of judgement past remains
Fresh in their minds, fearing the Deity,   15
With some regard to what is just and right
Shall lead their lives, and multiply apace,
Labouring the soil, and reaping plenteous crop,
Corn, wine and oil; and from the herd or flock,
Oft sacrificing Bullock, Lamb, or Kid,   20
With large Wine-offerings pour'd, and sacred Feast
Shall spend their days in joy unblam'd, and dwell
Long time in peace by Families and Tribes
Under paternal rule; till one° shall rise
Of proud ambitious heart, who not content   25
With fair equality, fraternal state,
Will arrogate Dominion undeserv'd
Over his brethren, and quite dispossess
Concord and law of Nature from the Earth;
Hunting (and Men not Beasts shall be his game)   30
With War and hostile snare such as refuse
Subjection to his Empire tyrannous:
A mighty Hunter thence he shall be styl'd
Before the Lord, as in despite of Heav'n,
Or from Heav'n claiming second Sovranty;   35
And from Rebellion shall derive his name,°
Though of Rebellion others he accuse.
Hee with a crew, whom like Ambition joins
With him or under him to tyrannize,
Marching from Eden towards the West, shall find   40
The Plain, wherein a black bituminous gurge°
Boils out from under ground, the mouth of Hell;
Of Brick, and of that stuff they cast to build
A City and Tow'r, whose top may reach to Heav'n;
And get themselves a name, lest far disperst   45
In foreign Lands their memory be lost,
Regardless whether good or evil fame.
But God who oft descends to visit men
Unseen, and through their habitations walks
To mark their doings, them beholding soon,   50
Comes down to see their City, ere the Tower
Obstruct Heav'n-Tow'rs, and in derision sets

24 one Nimrod (GENESIS 10:8–10).   36 his name "Nimrod" was
thought to be from the Hebrew "to rebel."   41 gurge whirlpool.

Upon their Tongues a various° Spirit to raze
Quite out their Native Language, and instead
55 To sow a jangling noise of words unknown:
Forthwith a hideous gabble rises loud
Among the Builders; each to other calls
Not understood, till hoarse, and all in rage,
As mockt they storm; great laughter was in Heav'n
60 And looking down, to see the hubbub strange
And hear the din; thus was the building left
Ridiculous, and the work Confusion° nam'd."
        Whereto thus Adam fatherly displeas'd.
"O execrable Son so to aspire
65 Above his Brethren, to himself assuming
Authority usurpt, from God not giv'n:
He gave us only over Beast, Fish, Fowl
Dominion absolute; that right we hold
By his donation; but Man over men
70 He made not Lord; such title to himself
Reserving, human left from human free.
But this Usurper his encroachment proud
Stays not on Man; to God his Tower intends
Siege and defiance: Wretched man! what food
75 Will he convey up thither to sustain
Himself and his rash Army, where thin Air
Above the Clouds will pine his entrails gross,
And famish him of Breath, if not of Bread?"
        To whom thus Michael. "Justly thou abhorr'st
80 That Son, who on the quiet state of men
Such trouble brought, affecting° to subdue
Rational Liberty; yet know withal,
Since thy original lapse, true Liberty
Is lost, which always with right Reason dwells
85 Twinn'd, and from her hath no dividual° being:
Reason in man obscur'd, or not obey'd,
Immediately inordinate desires
And upstart Passions catch the Government
From Reason, and to servitude reduce
90 Man till then free. Therefore since hee permits
Within himself unworthy Powers to reign

53 **various** calculated to cause differences.   62 **Confusion** thought to
be the meaning of "Babel."   81 **affecting** aspiring.   85 **dividual**
divisible.

Over free Reason, God in Judgement just
Subjects him from without to violent Lords;
Who oft as undeservedly enthrall
His outward freedom: Tyranny must be,   95
Though to the Tyrant thereby no excuse.
Yet sometimes Nations will decline so low
From virtue, which is reason, that no wrong,
But Justice, and some fatal curse annext
Deprives them of their outward liberty,   100
Their inward lost: Witness th'irreverent Son°
Of him who built the Ark, who for the shame
Done to his Father, heard this heavy curse,
Servant of Servants, on his vicious Race.
Thus will this latter, as the former World,   105
Still tend from bad to worse till God at last
Wearied with their iniquities, withdraw
His presence from among them, and avert
His holy Eyes; resolving from thenceforth
To leave them to their own polluted ways;   110
And one peculiar° Nation to select
From all the rest, of whom to be invok'd,
A Nation from one faithful man to spring:
Him° on this side Euphrates yet residing,
Bred up in Idol-worship; O that men   115
(Canst thou believe?) should be so stupid grown,
While yet the Patriarch liv'd, who 'scap'd the Flood,
As to forsake the living God, and fall
To worship their own work in Wood and Stone
For Gods! yet him God the most High vouchsafes   120
To call by Vision from his Father's house,
His kindred and false Gods, into a Land
Which he will show him, and from him will raise
A mighty Nation, and upon him show'r
His benediction so, that in his Seed   125
All Nations shall be blest; hee straight obeys,
Not knowing to what Land, yet firm believes:
I see him, but thou canst not, with what Faith
He leaves his Gods, his Friends, and native Soil
Ur of Chaldea, passing now the Ford   130
To Haran, after him a cumbrous Train

101 **Son** Ham, son of Noah.   111 **peculiar** traditionally applied to
the Jews as God's own chosen people.   114 **Him** Abraham.

Of Herds and Flocks, and numerous servitude;°
Not wand'ring poor, but trusting all his wealth
With God, who call'd him, in a land unknown.
135 Canaan he now attains, I see his Tents
Pitcht about Sechem, and the neighbouring Plain
Of Moreh; there by promise he receives
Gift to his Progeny of all that Land;
From Hamath Northward to the Desert South
140 (Things by their names I call, though yet unnam'd)
From Hermon East to the great Western Sea,
Mount Hermon, yonder Sea, each place behold
In prospect, as I point them; on the shore
Mount Carmel; here the double-founted stream
145 Jordan, true limit Eastward; but his Sons
Shall dwell to Senir, that long ridge of Hills.
This ponder, that all Nations of the Earth
Shall in his Seed be blessed; by that Seed
Is meant thy great deliverer, who shall bruise
150 The Serpent's head; whereof to thee anon
Plainlier shall be reveal'd. This Patriarch blest,
Whom faithful Abraham due time shall call,
A Son, and of his Son a Grandchild° leaves,
Like him in faith, in wisdom, and renown;
155 The Grandchild with twelve Sons increast, departs
From Canaan, to a Land hereafter call'd
Egypt, divided by the River Nile;
See where it flows, disgorging at seven mouths
Into the Sea: to sojourn in that Land
160 He comes invited by a younger Son°
In time of dearth, a Son whose worthy deeds
Raise him to be the second in that Realm
Of Pharaoh: there he dies, and leaves his Race
Growing into a Nation, and now grown
165 Suspected to a sequent King, who seeks
To stop their overgrowth, as inmate guests
Too numerous; whence of guests he makes them slaves
Inhospitably, and kills their infant Males:
Till by two brethren (those two brethren call
170 Moses and Aaron) sent from God to claim
His people from enthralment, they return

132 **servitude** servants.   153 **Son . . . Grandchild** Isaac and Jacob.
160 **Son** Joseph.

With glory and spoil back to their promis'd Land.
But first the lawless Tyrant, who denies°
To know their God, or message to regard,
Must be compell'd by Signs and Judgements dire;   175
To blood unshed the Rivers must be turn'd,
Frogs, Lice and Flies must all his Palace fill
With loath'd intrusion, and fill all the land;
His Cattle must of Rot and Murrain die,
Botches and blains must all his flesh emboss,°   180
And all his people; Thunder mixt with Hail,
Hail mixt with fire must rend th'Egyptian Sky
And wheel on th'Earth, devouring where it rolls;
What it devours not, Herb, or Fruit, or Grain,
A darksome Cloud of Locusts swarming down   185
Must eat, and on the ground leave nothing green:
Darkness must overshadow all his bounds,
Palpable darkness, and blot out three days;
Last with one midnight stroke all the first-born
Of Egypt must lie dead. Thus with ten wounds   190
The° River-dragon tam'd at length submits
To let his sojourners depart, and oft
Humbles his stubborn heart, but still as Ice
More hard'n'd after thaw, till in his rage
Pursuing whom he late dismiss'd, the Sea   195
Swallows him with his Host, but them lets pass
As on dry land between two crystal walls,
Aw'd by the rod of Moses so to stand
Divided, till his rescu'd gain their shore:
Such wondrous power God to his Saint will lend,   200
Though present in his Angel, who shall go
Before them in a Cloud, and Pillar of Fire,
By day a Cloud, by night a Pillar of Fire,
To guide them in their journey, and remove
Behind them, while th'obdúrate King pursues: 205
All night he will pursue, but his approach
Darkness defends° between till morning Watch;
Then through the Fiery Pillar and the Cloud
God looking forth will trouble all his Host
And craze° their Chariot-wheels: when by command   210
Moses once more his potent Rod extends

---

173 **denies** refuses.   180 **emboss** cover with swellings.   191 **The**
1674; **This** *1667*.   207 **defends** forbids.   210 **craze** crack.

Over the Sea; the Sea his Rod obeys;
On their embattl'd ranks the Waves return,
And overwhelm their War:° the Race elect
215 Safe towards Canaan from the shore advance
Through the wild Desert, not the readiest way,
Lest ent'ring on the Canaanite alarm'd°
War terrify them inexpert, and fear
Return them back to Egypt, choosing rather
220 Inglorious life with servitude; for life
To noble and ignoble is more sweet
Untrain'd in Arms, where rashness leads not on.
This also shall they gain by their delay
In the wide Wilderness, there they shall found
225 Their government, and their great Senate choose
Through the twelve Tribes, to rule by Laws ordain'd:
God from the Mount of Sinai, whose gray top
Shall tremble, he descending, will himself
In Thunder, Lightning and loud Trumpets' sound
230 Ordain them Laws; part such as appertain
To civil Justice, part religious Rites
Of sacrifice, informing them, by types
And shadows, of that destin'd Seed to bruise
The Serpent, by what means he shall achieve
235 Mankind's deliverance. But the voice of God
To mortal ear is dreadful; they beseech
That Moses might report to them his will,
And terror cease; he grants what they besought,°
Instructed that to God is no access
240 Without Mediator, whose high Office now
Moses in figure bears, to introduce
One greater, of whose day he shall foretell,
And all the Prophets in their Age the times
Of great Messiah shall sing. Thus Laws and Rites
245 Establisht, such delight hath God in Men
Obedient to his will, that he vouchsafes
Among them to set up his Tabernacle,
The holy One with mortal Men to dwell:
By his prescript a Sanctuary is fram'd
250 Of Cedar, overlaid with Gold, therein
An Ark, and in the Ark his Testimony,

214 **War** troops.   217 **alarm'd** in arms.   238 **what they besought**
1674; them their desire *1667*.

The Records of his Cov'nant, over these
A Mercy-seat of Gold between the wings
Of two bright Cherubim, before him burn
Seven Lamps as in a Zodiac representing   255
The Heav'nly fires; over the Tent a Cloud
Shall rest by Day, a fiery gleam by Night,
Save when they journey, and at length they come,
Conducted by his Angel to the Land
Promis'd to Abraham and his Seed: the rest   260
Were long to tell, how many Battles fought,
How many Kings destroy'd, and Kingdoms won,
Or how the Sun shall in mid Heav'n stand still
A day entire, and Night's due course adjourn,
Man's voice commanding, Sun in Gibeon stand,   265
And thou Moon in the vale of Aialon,
Till Israel° overcome; so call the third
From Abraham, Son of Isaac, and from him
His whole descent, who thus shall Canaan win."
        Here Adam interpos'd. "O sent from Heav'n,   270
Enlight'ner of my darkness, gracious things
Thou hast reveal'd, those chiefly which concern
Just Abraham and his Seed: now first I find
Mine eyes true op'ning, and my heart much eas'd,
Erewhile perplext with thoughts what would become   275
Of mee and all Mankind; but now I see
His day, in whom all Nations shall be blest,
Favour unmerited by me, who sought
Forbidd'n knowledge by forbidd'n means.
This yet I apprehend not, why to those   280
Among whom God will deign to dwell on Earth
So many and so various Laws are giv'n;
So many Laws argue so many sins
Among them; how can God with such reside?"
        To whom thus Michael. "Doubt not but that
            sin   285
Will reign among them, as of thee begot;
And therefore was Law given them to evince°
Their natural pravity,° by stirring up
Sin against Law to fight; that when they see
Law can discover sin, but not remove,   290

267 **Israel** Jacob.   287 **evince** both indicate and subdue.   288 **natural pravity** Original Sin.

Save by those shadowy expiations weak,
The blood of Bulls and Goats, they may conclude
Some blood more precious must be paid for Man,
Just for unjust, that in such righteousness
295 To them by Faith imputed, they may find
Justification towards God, and peace
Of Conscience, which the Law by Ceremonies
Cannot appease, nor Man the moral part
Perform, and not performing cannot live.
300 So Law appears imperfect, and but giv'n
With purpose to resign them in full time
Up to a better Cov'nant, disciplin'd
From shadowy Types° to Truth, from Flesh to Spirit,
From imposition of strict Laws, to free
305 Acceptance of large Grace, from servile fear
To filial, works of Law to works of Faith.
And therefore shall not Moses, though of God
Highly belov'd, being but the Minister
Of Law, his people into Canaan lead;
310 But Joshua whom the Gentiles Jesus° call,
His Name and Office bearing, who shall quell
The adversary Serpent, and bring back
Through the world's wilderness long-wander'd man
Safe to eternal Paradise of rest.
315 Meanwhile they in their earthly Canaan plac't
Long time shall dwell and prosper, but when sins
National interrupt their public peace,
Provoking God to raise them enemies:
From whom as oft he saves them penitent
320 By Judges first, then under Kings; of whom
The second, both for piety renown'd
And puissant deeds, a promise shall receive
Irrevocable, that his Regal Throne
For ever shall endure; the like shall sing
325 All Prophecy, That of the Royal Stock
Of David (so I name this King) shall rise
A Son, the Woman's Seed to thee foretold,
Foretold to Abraham, as in whom shall trust
All Nations, and to Kings foretold, of Kings

303 **shadowy Types** allegorical anticipations in the Old Testament of
the truths of the New Testament. 310 **Joshua . . . Jesus** the same
name, "Saviour."

The last, for of his Reign shall be no end.   330
But first a long succession must ensue,
And his next Son° for Wealth and Wisdom fam'd,
The clouded Ark of God till then in Tents
Wand'ring, shall in a glorious Temple enshrine.
Such follow him, as shall be register'd   335
Part good, part bad, of bad the longer scroll,
Whose foul Idolatries, and other faults
Heapt to the popular sum,° will so incense
God, as to leave them, and expose their Land,
Their City, his Temple, and his holy Ark   340
With all his sacred things, a scorn and prey
To that proud City, whose high Walls thou saw'st
Left in confusion, Babylon thence call'd.
There in captivity he lets them dwell
The space of seventy years, then brings them back,   345
Rememb'ring mercy, and his Cov'nant sworn
To David, 'stablisht as the days of Heav'n.
Return'd from Babylon by leave of Kings
Their Lords, whom God dispos'd, the house of God
They first re-edify, and for a while   350
In mean estate live moderate, till grown
In wealth and multitude, factious they grow;
But first among the Priests dissension springs,
Men who attend the Altar, and should most
Endeavour Peace; their strife pollution brings   355
Upon the Temple itself: at last they seize
The Scepter, and regard not David's Sons,
Then lose it to a stranger,° that the true
Anointed King Messiah might be born
Barr'd of his right: yet at his Birth a Star   360
Unseen before in Heav'n proclaims him come,
And guides the Eastern Sages, who inquire
His place, to offer Incense, Myrrh, and Gold;
His place of birth a solemn Angel tells
To simple Shepherds, keeping watch by night;   365
They gladly thither haste, and by a Choir
Of squadron'd Angels hear his Carol sung.

332 **his next Son** David's son Solomon.   338 **popular sum** people's total (of sins).   358 **stranger** Antipater (father of Herod), made ruler of Jerusalem by the Romans.

A Virgin is his Mother, but his Sire
The Power of the Most High; he shall ascend
370 The Throne hereditary, and bound his Reign
With earth's wide bounds, his glory with the Heav'ns."
     He ceas'd, discerning Adam with such joy
Surcharg'd, as had like grief been dew'd in tears,
Without the vent of words, which these he breath'd.
375   "O Prophet of glad tidings, finisher
Of utmost hope! now clear I understand
What oft my steadiest thoughts have searcht in vain,
Why our great expectation should be call'd
The seed of Woman: Virgin Mother, Hail,
380 High in the love of Heav'n, yet from my Loins
Thou shalt proceed, and from thy Womb the Son
Of God most High; So God with man unites.
Needs must the Serpent now his capital° bruise
Expect with mortal pain: say where and when
385 Their fight, what stroke shall bruise the Victor's heel."
          To whom thus Michael. "Dream not of their
                    fight,
As of a Duel, or the local wounds
Of head or heel: not therefore joins the Son
Manhood to God-head, with more strength to foil
390 Thy enemy; nor so is overcome
Satan, whose fall from Heav'n, a deadlier bruise,
Disabl'd not to give thee thy death's-wound:
Which hee, who comes thy Saviour, shall recure,
Not by destroying Satan, but his works
395 In thee and in thy Seed: nor can this be,
But by fulfilling that which thou didst want,°
Obedience to the Law of God, impos'd
On penalty of death, and suffering death,
The penalty to thy transgression due,
400 And due to theirs which out of thine will grow:
So only can high Justice rest appaid.°
The Law of God exact he shall fulfill
Both by obedience and by love, though love
Alone fulfill the Law; thy punishment

---

383 **capital** to his head, and deadly.   396 **want** lack.   401 **appaid**
satisfied.

He shall endure by coming in the Flesh   *405*
To a reproachful life and cursed death,
Proclaiming Life to all who shall believe
In his redemption, and that his obedience
Imputed becomes theirs by Faith, his merits
To save them, not their own, though legal works.   *410*
For this he shall live hated, be blasphem'd,
Seiz'd on by force, judg'd, and to death condemn'd
A shameful and accurst, nail'd to the Cross
By his own Nation, slain for bringing Life;
But to the Cross he nails thy Enemies,   *415*
The Law that is against thee, and the sins
Of all mankind, with him there crucifi'd,
Never to hurt them more who rightly trust
In this his satisfaction; so he dies,
But soon revives, Death over him no power   *420*
Shall long usurp; ere the third dawning light
Return, the Stars of Morn shall see him rise
Out of his grave, fresh as the dawning light,
Thy ransom paid, which Man from death redeems,
His death for Man, as many as offer'd Life   *425*
Neglect not, and the benefit embrace
By faith not void of works: this God-like act
Annuls thy doom, the death thou shouldst have di'd,
In sin for ever lost from life; this act
Shall bruise the head of Satan, crush his strength   *430*
Defeating Sin and Death, his two main arms,
And fix far deeper in his head their stings
Than temporal death shall bruise the Victor's heel,
Or theirs whom he redeems, a death like sleep,
A gentle wafting to immortal Life.   *435*
Nor after resurrection shall he stay
Longer on Earth than certain times to appear
To his Disciples, Men who in his Life
Still follow'd him; to them shall leave in charge
To teach all nations what of him they learn'd   *440*
And his Salvation, them who shall believe
Baptizing in the profluent stream, the sign
Of washing them from guilt of sin to Life
Pure, and in mind prepar'd, if so befall,
For death, like that which the redeemer di'd.   *445*

All Nations they shall teach; for from that day
Not only to the Sons of Abraham's Loins
Salvation shall be Preacht, but to the Sons
Of Abraham's Faith wherever through the world;
450 So in his seed all Nations shall be blest.
Then to the Heav'n of Heav'ns he shall ascend
With victory, triúmphing through the air
Over his foes and thine; there shall surprise
The Serpent, Prince of air, and drag in Chains
455 Through all his realm, and there confounded leave;
Then enter into glory, and resume
His Seat at God's right hand, exalted high
Above all names in Heav'n; and thence shall come,
When this world's dissolution shall be ripe,
460 With glory and power to judge both quick and dead,
To judge th'unfaithful dead, but to reward
His faithful, and receive them into bliss,
Whether in Heav'n or Earth, for then the Earth
Shall all be Paradise, far happier place
465 Then this of Eden, and far happier days."
          So spake th'Archangel Michaël, then paus'd,
As at the World's great period;° and our Sire
Replete with joy and wonder thus repli'd.
          "O goodness infinite, goodness immense!°
470 That all this good of evil shall produce,
And evil turn to good; more wonderful
Than that which by creation first brought forth
Light out of darkness! full of doubt I stand,
Whether I should repent me now of sin
475 By mee done and occasion'd, or rejoice
Much more, that much more good thereof shall spring,
To God more glory, more good-will to Men
From God, and over wrath grace shall abound.
But say, if our deliverer up to Heav'n
480 Must reascend, what will betide the few
His faithful, left among th'unfaithful herd,
The enemies of truth; who then shall guide
His people, who defend? will they not deal
Worse with his followers than with him they dealt?"

467 **period** ending.   469 **immense** immeasurable.

"Be sure they will," said th'Angel; "but from
Heav'n   48:
Hee to his own a Comforter will send,
The promise of the Father, who shall dwell
His Spirit within them, and the Law of Faith
Working through love, upon their hearts shall write,
To guide them in all truth, and also arm   490
With spiritual Armour, able to resist
Satan's assaults, and quench his fiery darts,
What Man can do against them, not afraid,
Though to the death, against such cruelties
With inward consolations recompens't,   495
And oft supported so as shall amaze
Their proudest persecutors: for the Spirit
Pour'd first on his Apostles, whom he sends
To evangelize the Nations, then on all
Baptiz'd, shall them with wondrous gifts endue   500
To speak all Tongues, and do all Miracles,
As did their Lord before them. Thus they win
Great numbers of each Nation to receive
With joy the tidings brought from Heav'n: at length
Their Ministry perform'd, and race well run,   505
Their doctrine and their story written left,
They die; but in their room, as they forewarn,
Wolves shall succeed for teachers, grievous Wolves,
Who all the sacred mysteries of Heav'n
To their own vile advantages shall turn   510
Of lucre and ambition, and the truth
With superstitions and traditions taint,
Left only in those written Records pure,
Though not but by the Spirit understood.
Then shall they seek to avail themselves of names, 515
Places and titles, and with these to join
Secular power, though feigning still to act
By spiritual, to themselves appropriating
The Spirit of God, promis'd alike and giv'n
To all Believers; and from that pretense,   520
Spiritual Laws by carnal power shall force
On every conscience; Laws which none shall find
Left them enroll'd, or what the Spirit within
Shall on the heart engrave. What will they then

525 But force the Spirit of Grace itself, and bind
His consort Liberty; what, but unbuild
His living Temples, built by Faith to stand,
Their own Faith not another's: for on Earth
Who against Faith and Conscience can be heard
530 Infallible? yet many will presume:
Whence heavy persecution shall arise
On all who in the worship persevere
Of Spirit and Truth; the rest, far greater part,
Will deem in outward Rites and specious forms
535 Religion satisfi'd; Truth shall retire
Bestuck with sland'rous darts, and works of Faith
Rarely be found: so shall the World go on,
To good malignant, to bad men benign,
Under her own weight groaning, till the day
540 Appear of respiration° to the just,
And vengeance to the wicked, at return
Of him so lately promis'd to thy aid,
The Woman's seed, obscurely then foretold,
Now amplier known the Saviour and thy Lord
545 Last in the Clouds from Heav'n to be reveal'd
In glory of the Father, to dissolve
Satan with his perverted World, then raise
From the conflagrant mass, purg'd and refin'd,
New Heav'ns, new Earth, Ages of endless date
550 Founded in righteousness and peace and love,
To bring forth fruits Joy and eternal Bliss."
          He ended; and thus Adam last repli'd.
"How soon hath thy prediction, Seer blest,
Measur'd this transient World, the Race of time,
555 Till time stand fixt: beyond is all abyss,
Eternity, whose end no eye can reach.
Greatly instructed I shall hence depart,
Greatly in peace of thought, and have my fill
Of knowledge, what this vessel can contain;
560 Beyond which was my folly to aspire.
Henceforth I learn, that to obey is best,
And love with fear the only God, to walk
As in his presence, ever to observe

540 **respiration** freedom, the chance to breathe again.

His Providence, and on him sole depend,
Merciful over all his works, with good   565
Still overcoming evil, and by small
Accomplishing great things, by things deem'd weak
Subverting worldly strong, and worldly wise
By simply meek; that suffering for Truth's sake
Is fortitude to highest victory,   570
And to the faithful Death and Gate of Life;
Taught this by his example whom I now
Acknowledge my Redeemer ever blest."
          To whom thus also th'Angel last repli'd:
"This having learnt, thou has attain'd the sum   575
Of wisdom; hope no higher, though all the Stars
Thou knew'st by name, and all th'Ethereal Powers,
All secrets of the deep, all Nature's works,
Or works of God in Heav'n, Air, Earth, or Sea,
And all the riches of this World enjoy'dst,   580
And all the rule, one Empire; only add
Deeds to thy knowledge answerable, add Faith,
Add Virtue, Patience, Temperance, add Love,
By name to come call'd Charity, the soul
Of all the rest: then wilt thou not be loath   585
To leave this Paradise, but shalt possess
A Paradise within thee, happier far.
Let us descend now therefore from this top
Of Speculation;° for the hour precise
Exacts our parting hence; and see the Guards,   590
By mee encampt on yonder Hill, expect
Their motion, at whose Front a flaming Sword,
In signal of remove, waves fiercely round;
We may no longer stay: go, waken Eve;
Her also I with gentle Dreams have calm'd   595
Portending good, and all her spirits compos'd
To meek submission: thou at season fit
Let her with thee partake what thou hast heard,
Chiefly what may concern her Faith to know,
The great deliverance by her Seed to come   600
(For by the Woman's Seed) on all Mankind.
That ye may live, which will be many days,

_____

588–89 **top Of Speculation** hill of extensive view.

Both in one Faith unanimous though sad,
With cause for evils past, yet much more cheer'd
605   With meditation on the happy end."
          He ended, and they both descend the Hill;
Descended, Adam to the Bow'r where Eve
Lay sleeping ran before, but found her wak't;
And thus with words not sad she him receiv'd.
          "Whence thou return'st, and whither went'st,
610   I know;
For God is also in sleep, and Dreams advise,
Which he hath sent propitious, some great good
Presaging, since with sorrow and heart's distress
Wearied I fell asleep: but now lead on;
615   In mee is no delay; with thee to go,
Is to stay here; without thee here to stay,
Is to go hence unwilling; thou to mee
Art all things under Heav'n, all places thou,
Who for my wilful crime art banisht hence.
620   This further consolation yet secure
I carry hence; though all by mee is lost,
Such favour I unworthy am vouchsaf't,
By mee the Promis'd Seed shall all restore."
          So spake our Mother Eve, and Adam heard
625   Well pleas'd, but answer'd not; for now too nigh
Th'Archangel stood, and from the other Hill
To their fixt Station, all in bright array
The Cherubim descended; on the ground
Gliding Metéorous,° as Ev'ning Mist
630   Ris'n from a River o'er the Marish glides,
And gathers ground fast at the Labourer's heel
Homeward returning. High in Front advanc't,
The brandisht Sword of God before them blaz'd
Fierce as a Comet; which with torrid heat,
635   And vapour as the Libyan Air adust,
Began to parch that temperate Clime; whereat
In either hand the hast'ning Angel caught
Our ling'ring Parents, and to th'Eastern Gate
Led them direct, and down the Cliff as fast
640   To the subjected° Plain; then disappear'd.
They looking back, all th'Eastern side beheld
Of Paradise, so late their happy seat,

629 **Metéorous** aloft like a meteor.   640 **subjected** lying below.

Wav'd over by that flaming Brand, the Gate
With dreadful Faces throng'd and fiery Arms:
Some natural tears they dropp'd, but wip'd them soon;   645
The World was all before them, where to choose
Their place of rest, and Providence their guide:
They hand in hand with wand'ring steps and slow,
Through Eden took their solitary way.

READ MORE IN PENGUIN

READ MORE IN PENGUIN

A CHOICE OF CLASSICS

Armadale Wilkie Collins

Victorian critics were horrified by Lydia Gwilt, the bigamist, husband-poisoner and laudanum addict whose intrigues spur the plot of this most sensational of melodramas.

Aurora Leigh and Other Poems Elizabeth Barrett Browning

Aurora Leigh (1856), Elizabeth Barrett Browning's epic novel in blank verse, tells the story of the making of a woman poet, exploring 'the woman question', art and its relation to politics and social oppression.

Personal Narrative of a Journey to the Equinoctial Regions of the New Continent Alexander von Humboldt

Alexander von Humboldt became a wholly new kind of nineteenth-century hero – the scientist–explorer – and in *Personal Narrative* he invented a new literary genre: the travelogue.

The Pañćatantra Visnu Sarma

The Pañćatantra is one of the earliest books of fables and its influence can be seen in the *Arabian Nights*, the *Decameron*, the *Canterbury Tales* and most notably in the *Fables* of La Fontaine.

A Laodicean Thomas Hardy

The Laodicean of Hardy's title is Paula Power, a thoroughly modern young woman who, despite her wealth and independence, cannot make up her mind.

Brand Henrik Ibsen

The unsparing vision of a priest driven by faith to risk and witness the deaths of his wife and child gives *Brand* its icy ferocity. It was Ibsen's first masterpiece, a poetic drama composed in 1865 and published to tremendous critical and popular acclaim.

READ MORE IN PENGUIN

A CHOICE OF CLASSICS

Sylvia's Lovers   Elizabeth Gaskell

In an atmosphere of unease the rivalries of two men, the sober tradesman Philip Hepburn, who has been devoted to his cousin Sylvia since her childhood, and the gallant, charming whaleship harpooner Charley Kinraid, are played out.

The Republic   Plato

The best-known of Plato's dialogues, *The Republic* is also one of the supreme masterpieces of Western philosophy, whose influence cannot be overestimated.

Ethics   Benedict de Spinoza

'Spinoza (1632–77),' wrote Bertrand Russell, 'is the noblest and most lovable of the great philosophers. Intellectually, some others have surpassed him, but ethically he is supreme.'

Virgil in English

From Chaucer to Auden, Virgil is a defining presence in English poetry. Penguin Classics' new series, Poets in Translation, offers the best translations in English, through the centuries, of the major Classical and European poets.

What is Art?   Leo Tolstoy

Tolstoy wrote prolifically in a series of essays and polemics on issues of morality, social justice and religion. These culminated in *What is Art?*, published in 1898, in which he rejects the idea that art reveals and reinvents through beauty.

An Autobiography   Anthony Trollope

A fascinating insight into a writer's life, in which Trollope also recorded his unhappy youth and his progress to prosperity and social recognition.

READ MORE IN PENGUIN

A CHOICE OF CLASSICS

READ MORE IN PENGUIN

A CHOICE OF CLASSICS

ANTHOLOGIES AND ANONYMOUS WORKS

The Age of Bede
Alfred the Great
Beowulf
A Celtic Miscellany
The Cloud of Unknowing and Other Works
The Death of King Arthur
The Earliest English Poems
Early Irish Myths and Sagas
Egil's Saga
English Mystery Plays
Eyrbyggja Saga
Hrafnkel's Saga and Other Stories
The Letters of Abelard and Heloise
Medieval English Lyrics
Medieval English Verse
Njal's Saga
Roman Poets of the Early Empire
Seven Viking Romances
Sir Gawain and the Green Knight